A PORTRAIT OF
ANDRÉ
MALRAUX

A *Portrait of* ANDRÉ

MALRAUX

ROBERT PAYNE

PRENTICE-HALL, INC.
ENGLEWOOD CLIFFS, NEW JERSEY

A Portrait of André Malraux by Robert Payne
© 1970 by Robert Payne
All rights reserved. No part of this book may be
reproduced in any form or by any means, except for
the inclusion of brief quotations in a review, without
permission in writing from the publisher.
ISBN 0-13-685966-6
Library of Congress Catalog Card Number: 72-118697
Printed in the United States of America T
Prentice-Hall International, Inc., London
Prentice-Hall of Australia, Pty. Ltd., Sydney
Prentice-Hall of Canada, Ltd., Toronto
Prentice-Hall of India Private Ltd., New Delhi
Prentice-Hall of Japan, Inc., Tokyo

for MIREILLE

❧ Introduction ❧

Sometimes a man disappears into his legend and becomes another man altogether. He comes to resemble one of those bronze statues of youthful heroes shipwrecked off the coast of Greece more than two thousand years ago, and when they are found by divers they are encrusted by shellfish and barnacles. The divers imagine they have discovered a statue of Zeus adorned with a white beard, white robe and white scepter. Many months pass, while the archaeologists work on the statue. The beard falls away, the encrustations of centuries vanish, and what appeared to be the Lord of the Universe is revealed as a sixteen-year-old boy holding a javelin.

So it is with André Malraux: the legends have so obscured him that we are in danger of never seeing him plainly. As novelist, soldier, revolutionary, philosopher, orator, archaeologist, adventurer, art critic and minister of culture, he appears to belong to a world remote from ordinary human preoccupations and to be enveloped in legend and mystery. When he speaks, the voice is authoritative and final, and when he is silent, he can still be heard. Of his day-by-day life little is known, and for more than a generation the private man has been concealed in the public figure, and long before he became a minister he belonged to mystery.

The mystery is partly of his own choosing, for he possesses a habitual reticence, stands guard over his private life, rarely believes it worthwhile to discuss his works, and refuses to enter into controversies. He has paid tribute to the goddess Silence with many offerings, and *The Voices of Silence* is not the least of them. There are many other tributes written between the lines of his books, which are always autobiographical even when they describe characters outwardly very different from him. Having revealed so much of himself in his books, he has scrupulously avoided offering hostages to biographers.

A study of Malraux therefore presents unusual difficulties. There are no simple roads through his life, and often the usual signposts are missing. The patient biographer, peering through a silken screen of legends, must inevitably wonder how the legends arose. He must progress from one small ascertainable fact to the next, knowing that in the end there will be enough of them to permit us to see him as he is. Zeus vanishes; the sixteen-year-old boy with the javelin appears, or at least we can make out the shape of the boy. Some mysteries will always remain, but these are the mysteries which are insoluble in every man.

In the following pages I have attempted to unravel some of the mysteries and to present him in perspective and chronological order, seeing him as he is, and was, before the legends accumulated round him. Above all I have been concerned with the springs of his action and his thought, and I have written extensively about his little-known early works, *Paper Moons, The Fireman of the Game of Massacre,* and *The Kingdom of Farfelu,* because they were the seeds from which flowered the works of his maturity. For the same reason I have written at some length about his ancestors, his family, his childhood and youth. He belongs to a generation which has few survivors, and I was lucky enough to discover a few people who knew him when he was young. Nearly all those who knew him in later years remarked that he had few friends and counted themselves among them; they were surprisingly numerous; and though I searched, I found few enemies.

Nearly all the biographical notes and articles written about him were inaccurate. He has been credited with achievements which he had nothing to do with—he did not, for example, play any role in the Canton strike of 1925 or the abortive Shanghai uprising two years later—while his achievements in Spain and as a resistance leader and as commander of the Brigade Alsace-Lorraine during World War II have so far remained unrecorded. T. E. Lawrence omitted from *The Seven Pillars of Wisdom* any account of a secret and desperately dangerous journey behind enemy lines because he thought it was irrelevant to the main purpose of his story. So with Malraux: the real adventures were often more dangerous and spine-chilling than the legendary ones.

For the rest, this is a portrait of a bold and superbly gifted man, who wrote about art and life with feverish intensity and threw himself recklessly into all the important battles of our time, holding nothing back. He said once: "I have a fidelity—and it is dynamite." His fidelity was to France, and to the world's art, and to the oppressed. He was one of those who lived close to the burning heart of things, and was not afraid. He spoke once of "my useless and bloody life," but future historians will see in him a man who illustrated in his own person the violence, the dreams, the torments, and the nobility of our tragic age.

⋖§ *Contents* §⋗

CONTENTS

The occasional drawings at the ends of chapters were made by André Malraux. All except the last, which comes from Professor Walter Langlois' Malraux Miscellany, originally appeared in Malraux par Lui-Même, Gaëton Picon, published by Les Editions du Seuil.

A PORTRAIT OF
ANDRÉ
MALRAUX

THE SORCERER'S APPRENTICE

Who was the sorcerer whose birth turned the waters of the lake into glass?

—PAPER MOONS

৵§ *The Beginnings* §৵

The Malraux family comes originally from Dunkerque, the bustling seaport on the northern edge of France. The people of Dunkerque are more Flemish than French, and their roots go back to the ancient principalities of Flanders with their capitals in Bruges and Antwerp. They are a proud people devoted to their past, to the days when their merchants were the richest in Europe and their artists painted the Virgin enthroned in majesty in their sumptuous homes.

The Flemish have a character of their own: hard-bitten, shy among strangers, deliberate in their speech, not overcautious in their actions. They have a savage gift for caricature and a fierce delight in great colorful processions. They are men of the dunes and the low hills, at home on the sea. Indeed, the sea dominates their lives, and for centuries they have been sailors, fishermen, freebooters, and pirates. The paintings of the Flemish masters are flooded with the cold, clear light of the seacoasts.

André Malraux owes much to his Flemish forefathers. Consciously or unconsciously he has absorbed their characteristics: their peculiar feeling for light, for texture, for caricature, for adventure, for long lonely journeys across the face of the earth. He has the seaman's gait and the seaman's feeling for the lost paradise which always lies over the horizon. In common with the Flemish painter Bruegel, Malraux takes savage delight in the absurdities of life. When he speaks of the dignity of man, he is speaking about man everywhere, but he is also speaking about the dignity that Flanders gave to the world through the gift of art. The cultivated Parisian conceals *un homme flamand*. Even his surname, which French etymologists have derived from *mauvaise charrue,* meaning "an ill-turned plow," is more likely to be derived from a Flemish name like Mellaert. As far back as they can be traced, there were no plowmen among his ancestors: they were always seamen, or they lived close to the sea.

Of Louis Malraux, the great-grandfather of André Malraux, we know only that he married a certain Thérèse Lamy, lived in Dunkerque, commanded a fleet of fishing vessels, and died at sea. *Décédé en mer* is an entry which appears often on the death certificates of the sailors of Dunkerque. His son, Alphonse-Émile, born in 1842, spent most of his life looking after his shop. He was a master cooper, an outfitter, a ship's chandler, a wine merchant, with interests in the Newfoundland fisheries. He was one of those men born to command, who never brooked any interference, proud of his strength and his business successes, and he never learned to speak French, but spoke a Flemish dialect to the end of his life. He had five children by his wife, who was born Mathilde Antoine. There were two daughters and three sons, Maurice, Lucien, and Fernand-Georges, all of whom went into business. His wife died, his children left him, and he grew old, but he still regarded himself as the equal of all the younger men around. Querulous and forgetful, he forgot to insure his ships, and when they were all lost at sea, he was close to ruin. One day he was wealthy, the next day he was doling out most of his remaining wealth to the widows of the drowned fishermen. He cursed the fate which had brought him so high and then so low, and they said he never went into a church again, regarding himself as an outcast. Yet every Sunday he could be seen kneeling outside the church, in summer knee-deep in thistles, in winter knee-deep in mud, railing against the God who had brought him to despair but determined at least to remain in earshot of God's voice.

In *The Royal Way* and *The Walnut Trees of Altenburg*, André Malraux drew a portrait of his grandfather based on family legends. A spirited, bitter, eccentric man with a short white beard, he was proud of his ships and he walked their decks as though they were men-of-war, and he ran his business as though he was the general of an army. His marriage to Mathilde Antoine took place late in life, and he quarreled so bitterly with his wife that she slipped out of the house and threatened never to return. This happened twelve days after the marriage. Her father would have nothing to do with her, her mother counseled obedience to the marriage vows, and she returned at last to confront a husband who loved his business more than his wife. He set her to work on the ledgers, for she had more education and could count better. The time came when she found solace in her work. Then it would happen that the husband would be working by the light of a solitary candle in one wing of the big house, busy with his own affairs, while his wife slaved over the ledgers in another wing; and they would watch each other's candles to see which was the first to go out. It was a large house with an immense courtyard, which was often filled with brown sails drying in the wind. All day long sailors, deckhands, and workmen passed through the courtyard, but at night there was only an immense emptiness and two candles.

As he grew older, his eccentricities became more pronounced: his wife died of consumption, and then there was no one to talk to. One day, according to the legend, the municipality refused to permit a traveling circus to lodge anywhere in Dunkerque, and so the old man ordered the gates of his courtyard to be opened wide, and he watched contentedly while elephants and caravans lumbered across the cobblestones to use his courtyard as their sleeping quarters. Someone wrote that he was once mayor of Dunkerque, but in the records of the mayoralty his name never appears, nor was he the kind of man who would ever run for elective office. He was a law unto himself, and permitted no argument.

Alphonse-Émile Malraux was sixty-seven when he died, and his death was in keeping with his character. One winter day he was exasperated by the sight of a ship's boy clumsily splitting wood. He took the ax in his hand to show him the proper way to do it. Forgetting that it was a double-headed ax, he swung it above his head and split his own skull. He was carried to the local hospital and died a few hours later. According to the death certificate he died at one o'clock on the morning of November 19, 1909, and he was buried three days later in the cemetery of Dunkerque. A heavy granite tombstone, taller than a man, was later placed over the grave. In Dunkerque such huge gravestones are not unusual, and one wanders through that graveyard as through a petrified forest, amid huge tombs built for a race of giants.

André Malraux never knew his grandfather, who therefore assumed the dimensions of a legend, larger than life, all the more impressive because he was invisible. His big house, with its tiled walls, descended to his eldest son, and vanished during the bombardment of Dunkerque in 1940.

Fernand-Georges, the son of Alphonse-Émile Malraux, had few of his father's eccentricities. Tall, handsome, always impeccably dressed, he lived for the moment in a delighted awareness of his own skills. He had clear blue eyes, finely molded features, and bore himself with the studied carelessness of manner of a *boulevardier.* He once spent a year in Spain, but detested the experience so much that he vowed never again to enter a foreign country, and never did. During the First World War he was a second lieutenant in the tank corps, and he always regarded those years in the army as the most rewarding in his life. A photograph of him in military uniform survives. It was taken after the battle of Verdun and shows him standing jauntily against a backcloth of painted vines, a strong-jawed vigorous man who obviously rejoices in being alive, the eyes sparkling and the hand lying lightly on the sword.

After the war he made his living by his wits—as an inventor, as the director of many ephemeral companies, as an investor in the stock exchange, and all these by turns or simultaneously. He was one of those men who are always trying to invent a better mousetrap. He could tell stories well, and he enjoyed improving on them until they were shaped in their most memorable form. He was always gallant with women, and there was some element of frivolity in him, as though he could never take the world quite seriously, and this was perhaps a reaction against his stern, rather puritanical upbringing.

At the turn of the century he married Berthe Lamy, whose family came originally from the region of the Jura mountains. Lamy is a fairly common name, and she was not related to the wife of Louis Malraux. Fernand-Georges was about twenty-five, and Berthe Lamy was about nineteen, a tall, slender, pretty woman who always looked younger than her age. They were well matched in physical appearance, and people seeing them together would have said they were ideally suited to one another. He took her to live in an apartment in the Rue Damrémont in Montmartre, and there on November 3, 1901, their only child, Georges-André Malraux, was born. As a boy and in later years he was always known as André Malraux.

The marriage, which had begun so hopefully, ended in divorce. The parents separated about 1905. Fernand-Georges later remarried and fathered two more sons, Roland and Claude. Berthe Malraux went to live with her mother, the widow of a baker, in a small town, scarcely more than a village, just outside Paris. In those days the town of Bondy, with its few streets huddled around the church and the cemetery, had little to commend it. Drab and ugly, as though no one had ever given any thought to making life tolerable in it, the town lived on its memories of wars and depredations. Since it stood eight miles from Paris on the main road to Lorraine, its fate was to be destroyed by every army that came up to the gates of Paris from the direction of Germany. The Prussians had leveled a large part of the town in 1870, and in the early years of this century it had the look of an overgrown village with a few well-built houses, the rest jerrybuilt and delapidated.

In this town André Malraux spent most of his childhood and youth, living with his mother, his grandmother, and an aunt above a grocer's shop which they owned at 16 Rue de la Gare.

A special sadness hovers over the small towns of France where the exuberance and vitality of the cities are unknown. In those narrow streets life seems to have come to a stop; the people, knowing one another too well, lose interest or turn to gossip and intrigue and malicious rumors in order to amuse themselves. The years pass, and nothing changes. The same priest is always walking down the same street.

So it was in Bondy, a town which seemed to have no reason for its existence, cut off from the mainstream of life. The express trains never stopped there. A few carriages made their way down the Rue de la Gare, the long road that stretches from the railroad station to the Church of St. Pierre, but mostly there were only farmcarts. The small boy stepping out of the grocer's shop on his way to school saw a town that would drive anyone to despair.

Happily, there were compensations. The tightly knit family living above the grocer's shop was dominated by the grandmother, born Adriana Romania. She held the family together with her fierce Italian sense of dignity, and never, even at the worst times, permitted herself to imagine that she could be defeated by life. Tall, straight-backed, wonderfully warm and quick-witted, she was as formidable in her own way as the old grandfather who wasted his fortunes in Dunkerque. While Alphonse-Émile Malraux seemed to act according to the laws of centrifugal force, dissipating his strength, Adriana Romania acted in such a way that no strength was ever dissipated and every reversal was transformed into a victory.

She was an intelligent woman, well read, curious about all things, suspicious of strangers, indeed of everyone outside her immediate family. Within the family no one could do any wrong. As for the rest of the world, every kind of wrong could be expected. André Malraux's first wife Clara remembered her as a woman of grave distinction and quiet fire, like one of the court ladies painted by Franz Hals, and she also remembered that in old age, when exasperated by injustice, Adriana Romania would say: "When I was young, people came out to fight in the streets." If there had been a revolution, she would have stood at the barricades.

From Adriana Romania the small family at Bondy derived more than its strength; she gave them a moral purpose, a sense of their self-sufficiency, and a certain pride. There were hardships, for the grocer's shop produced very little money, and sometimes they wondered whether they could continue to live at Bondy, where they had no deep roots. But the family had invested its capital in the shop, and there was no escape. They were bound to it as though to a treadmill.

The boy, growing up among three women, sometimes felt he was being slowly choked to death by femininity. He would say later that he detested his childhood and there was not a single detail of it that he chose to remember. Nevertheless, he was haunted by the events of his childhood, and in mysterious ways they would break through the veil he had drawn over them. They would come flashing across his memory when he least expected them, insistent and urgent, coloring his novels, his dreams and ambitions. From a very early age he was preoccupied with the theme of escape.

But in Bondy there was nowhere to escape to. There was a time when all this region was covered with thick forests, and to this day a French cutthroat or swindler is sometimes called *une forêt de Bondy.* Brigands had their hideouts in the forests, and travelers could expect to be held up for ransom or worse. Stories were told of the bandits who were captured and then put to the torture.

By the beginning of the century most of the forest had been cut down, and there were only a few small patches of woodland in the neighborhood. The boy liked to wander in the woods, and in his books, insistent as a theme of music, there will be descriptions of immensely tall trees throwing their long shadows in an endless sunset.

The usual punishment for the brigands was the wheel. Roped to the wheel, their legs, arms, buttocks, and loins broken, they would be left to rot on the execution ground near the Church of St. Pierre, a stone's throw away from the little shop on the Rue de la Gare. In the Middle Ages this street had possessed a more resounding name. It was known as the Rue de Martray, the road of torture. Most of Malraux's boyhood was spent within twenty yards of an ancient execution ground.

There was nothing in the Church of St. Pierre to attract his interest. Rebuilt after the bombardment of 1870, it was one of those gray, ugly, undistinguished churches built at a time when architects had forgotten how to design. The one object of interest was the delicately carved tombstone of Clément Raison, *chevalier, seigneur de Bondis et gouverneur pour le roi,* and his wife Honorine de Beauvois, who died in the middle years of the sixteenth century. It was the one work of art in a town which had little use for art, and it is possible that Malraux never set eyes on it.

Since life in Bondy resembled the slow turning of a creaking mill wheel, the boy was thrown on his own resources. He was small, timid, often ill, terrified by the cockroaches and all the other insects that take up their occupation in a grocer's shop and the living rooms upstairs. Thereafter he was to possess an unreasoning fear of insects of all kinds. He had a few close friends, and perhaps the closest was Louis Chevasson who lived round the corner in the Rue de Merlan and whom he first encountered when he was about six years old. Louis Chevasson had a round face and bright eyes, a quick smile and a gentle disposition; he was loyal and trusting, and an admirable listener. André Malraux liked to tell stories and liked reading them.

He was about eight or nine when he read his first full-length novel. This was Alexandre Dumas' *Georges,* a story about a battle to the death between an English colonial governor and a young half-French mulatto named Georges Munier. It was one of the few novels written by Dumas which was based on the experiences of his father, the swash-buckling Thomas-Alexandre Dumas, who was one of Napoleon's most gifted generals.

The novel had a shattering effect on the boy, for it suddenly opened up an entirely new world of color and excitement, and mingled with the story of fantastic adventures there were strange meditations on death. Nothing could be further removed from the dreary, somnolent, ingrown life of Bondy. Hazardous escapades follow one another in quick succession, a man's life hangs on a word, or a gesture, or a sword thrust. Great prizes are offered to him: he accepts or rejects them on a whim. Proud, disdainful, in love with adventure for adventure's sake, Georges Munier was such a character as a boy could grow up with, dreaming of the day when he would perform similar exploits and reap similar rewards.

What chiefly distinguishes the character of Georges Munier are his icy calm, his aristocratic contempt for danger and his phenomenal will power. His mother died when he was very young, and he was brought up on the island of Mauritius by a Formosan nurse who taught him Chinese. At twelve he was sent to school in Paris, and by the time he was eighteen he had become an adventurer, gambling for high stakes. Once he won 25,000 francs and lost it all in a day. On another day he won 230,000 francs, and it was observed that not a muscle of his face moved during the long night of gambling, and he thrust the money nonchalantly into a drawer when he returned home. To test his will power he deliberately picked a quarrel with a famous marksman and they fought a duel at twenty-five paces, Georges taunt-ing his adversary and giving him all the advantages. By sheer force of will he was able to induce the marksman to miss his aim. Georges stands there with his pistol in his hand. "It is now your turn to shoot, Monsieur Munier," the marksman says, knowing that he is as good as dead. Instead of shooting, Georges smiles, picks up his hat, and leaves the dueling ground. He has tested himself, and there is nothing to be

gained by shooting a man. With the same calm determination he se-
duces women. His seductions, too, are exercises in will power.

He travels through Greece, Turkey, Asia Minor, Syria, and Egypt,
and receives a sword of honor for his valor during a campaign in
Nubia. Returning to France in 1823 he joins the Duc d'Angoulême
in his campaign in Spain; from the duke he receives the Legion of
Honor and from King Ferdinand VII of Spain he receives the Cross
of Charles III. The campaign was scarcely a test of his military abili-
ties. "Unhappily the Spaniards could not hold their ground and the
expedition, which should have been so terrible, was merely a military parade."

After twelve years absence he returns to Mauritius to discover that
it no longer belongs to France but is ruled by the British. The governor, Lord Williams Murrey, is the guardian of the beautiful Sara de
Malmédie. Georges is determined to marry her, the governor is determined to prevent the marriage. Wearing a frock coat, a black tie,
immaculate white trousers, the Legion of Honor in his buttonhole,
Georges quietly goes about organizing a slave rebellion against the
British planters. The planters roll barrels full of arrack on the army
of slaves, and the rebellion ends in drunken revelry and massacre.
Georges is sentenced to death by beheading. He is very calm, summons
the executioner to his cell, and quietly discusses his own execution.
Fascinated by death, and by the presence of the huge Negro in a loin-
cloth who will wield the ax, he goes through a mock ceremony of
execution, remembering the many executions he has seen in the past.
Once in Egypt a prisoner knelt down and his head was struck off, and
Georges had been surprised to see the headless man rise to his feet
and stumble a few yards as though in search of his head. At another
execution the head fell near him, he lifted it by the hair, gazed at it,
said: "Are you suffering?" The chapter describing Georges in the death
cell is written with quite extraordinary power.

On his way to his execution Georges escapes, hurries into a church,
marries Sara de Malmédie, and sails away with her. His ship is followed by the flagship of the governor. There is a naval battle, Lord
Murrey's ship is sunk, and Georges has the satisfaction of knowing
that he has no more enemies. Except for the long chapter describing

Georges' life abroad, everything happens as in a dream, with the strange abruptness of dreams. Like cold steel Georges moves through a world of enchantment.

The long meditations on death, the sudden escapes, the hero's travels in the East, the campaign in Spain, and the raising of the slave rebellion left an ineradicable impression on André Malraux, who still remembered the novel vividly fifty years later. Georges Munier, born at the turn of the nineteenth century, was one of the exemplars of André Malraux, born a hundred years later.

Reading became his passion, and he was a good, if erratic student in the small private school which he attended with his friend Louis Chevasson. One of the schoolmasters was a brute who took pleasure in humiliating his pupils. They suffered in silence, but remembered their suffering long afterward. André Malraux became a voracious reader of Dumas and was excited by Shakespeare, which he read in a French translation, especially *Macbeth,* where there were long speeches glorifying revenge. The woods of Bondy were transformed into Birnam wood; Lady Macbeth, the witches, and the apparitions fed his imagination, and he would never forget: "Here's the smell of the blood still: all the perfumes of Arabia will not sweeten this little hand." Dumas and Shakespeare were like chemicals brought together to form an explosive mixture. He was at home with death, blood, and ghosts.

When the Great War broke out, André's father joined up. In September 1914 there came the first decisive engagement. At the battle of the Marne the army of General von Kluck was thrown back near Paris, and soon the schoolchildren from Bondy were being taken to see the battlefield. There had been no time to bury the dead: the bodies were piled up, soaked in gasoline and burned. The children had just arrived on the battlefield when lunch, consisting of bread, was given to them, and at that moment the wind turned and covered the bread with a light sprinkling of ashes from the white funeral pyres. André remembered the children dropping the bread in terror.

When he was fourteen he was admitted as a scholarship student to the École Turgot, a primary school on the Rue de Turbigo in Paris. Every morning he would leave Bondy by an early train for the Gare de l'Est with his friend Louis Chevasson and then hurry to the school.

He did not particularly like the school, but he rejoiced in his escape from Bondy, yet every evening he would find Bondy waiting for him. He worked hard. At the end of his first school year 1915–1916, he was at the head of his class in history and drawing, second in spelling, third in French literature and English, fourth in geography and mathematics, fifth in calligraphy, and sixth in chemistry and the natural sciences. He showed no notable ability in physics, gymnastics, or singing. At this time neither Greek nor Latin were taught in the school, and the emphasis was on modern languages and the sciences. Modeling in clay was also taught, but during the first year he showed little enthusiasm for it, while in the second year he was at the top of his class.

At the end of the first year he could congratulate himself that he had done exceedingly well. When all the marks were added together, he was third in the class.

The École Turgot became a *lycée* many years later, but at this time it was merely a primary school for the lower middle classes, the salaries of the teachers paid for by the city of Paris. Because it was wartime most of the teachers were elderly; and there was about that school, with the drafty corridors and echoing classrooms, a strange air of improvisation, as though it had never settled down on the edge of the *grands boulevards* and did not really believe in its own existence. There were no professors for whom he felt a deep affection; the school was simply a machine for producing a limited and conventional education. What he wanted above all was to escape to one of the prestigious schools like the Lycée Henri IV or the Lycée Condorcet. But these were private institutions, the salaries of the teachers were not paid by the city of Paris, and one could enter them only through a scholarship or by paying high fees.

At the end of the school year 1916–1917 it was clear that he no longer had the same consuming interest in his studies. He came first in spelling and modeling, second in literature, third in diction and drawing, fifth in civics and eighth in natural sciences. He was eighth in his class. This fall from grace was chiefly due to his growing dissatisfaction with the school. He had decided that it was absolutely essential to enter the Lycée Condorcet.

To do this it was necessary to pass a rigorous examination, and he therefore set about finding a tutor. He found what he wanted in a tall, blue-eyed young teacher in Bondy, who had a reputation for conducting cramming courses. Paulette Thouvenin, the daughter of the local policeman, was a woman of character and a determined enemy of ignorance. She spoke rapidly and intensely, and when the student showed the least sign of stupidity, then her enormous blue eyes would open even wider with a look of incomprehension. She was a stern taskmaster, and proved to be the ideal tutor. He passed the examination, and gave her a present in honor of the occasion.

Paulette Thouvenin has long since retired from teaching, but she still remembers the impression the young André Malraux made on her. A brooding, taciturn youth, handsome, always well dressed, he kept a little apart from the other students. Already she thought she detected in him a sense of conscious superiority. She says, "*Il était maître de soi déjà, et avait un peu le sens du chef* [he was already master of himself and had something in him of the commander of men]." And when she was asked whether she could sum up his character in a single word, she remembered the hard indisciplined core in him and said: "*Il était sauvage* [he was savage]."

Even in those days his opinions were vehement and announced with scorn, and he knew where he was going. He read widely, remembered everything he read, and could quote his authorities when any argument arose. He worked ferociously hard. At all costs he was determined to escape the bondage of Bondy.

There exists a photograph of Paulette Thouvenin with her students taken at this time. She sits in the center, maternal amid her brood of four boys and four girls, with André Malraux standing on the right. His hair is slicked neatly down, falling across his forehead, and he wears a high collar with a checkered tie and a pearl stickpin. The widely spaced eyes gaze straight at the photographer, the mouth is firm, the chin pointed, and there is something of the expression of the young Rimbaud, expectant and a little surly, as though he had already tasted the dead sea fruit and wanted no more. He is the only student to carry a watch—the watch chain is dangling majestically between a coat button and an upper pocket. He is in a hurry, though he is not in the least certain what he is in a hurry about.

The Lycée Condorcet has no record of his attendance. He appears to have entered the *lycée*, studied for a few months, and then abruptly left it. At some time in late 1917 or early 1918 he appears to have abandoned formal education finally and irrevocably. He was weary of his teachers and had no interest in acquiring a *baccalauréat*, which is indispensable to any student who wants to go on to a university. There were books all round him, and he would teach himself by a prolonged course of reading. He knew what he wanted to read, and these books were not on the syllabus of any primary school, *lycée*, or university.

He had emerged at last from the long dark tunnel of childhood and youth into an early maturity. Here, in Paris, he would hammer out his own philosophy in his own way and in his own time. Like Georges Munier, he would permit himself the most desirable of all luxuries —the luxury of perfect freedom.

❧ The Young Apprentice ❧

One day in 1919 René-Louis Doyon, a bookseller who had opened a small shop at 9 *bis* Galerie de la Madeleine, just off the Place de la Madeleine, received a strange visitor. The young man who entered the shop was tall, dressed modestly but very correctly in the fashion of the time, and carried himself with an air of distinction. He explained that he was in a position to acquire rare books and first editions, and wondered whether the bookseller would pay for them. What especially attracted Doyon to the young man was his cold reserve, his disinterestedness. It was as though in some mysterious way, simply by appearing in the shop, he was conferring a favor.

René-Louis Doyon was a minor *littérateur,* a bibliophile, a man of sensibility, warm-hearted and impulsive, and he had the habit of taking a man's measure in a few moments. What he saw of the young man he liked, and he agreed to buy whatever books were brought to him. Thereafter, for a period of about a year, André Malraux regularly brought him books, arriving at the shop at eleven o'clock every morning with his bundles. He would establish the price, take his money, and then vanish. He had good taste, knew exactly what books to bring, and seemed to know everything there was to know about rare books and first editions.

The trade he was practicing, well known in Paris, was that of a *chineur,* which means "ragpicker" and by extension "dealer in secondhand goods." He would go to secondhand bookshops in obscure side streets, searching for books that would be important to a bibliophile. Since the secondhand dealers in Paris were rarely knowledgeable about the value of their books, he pitted his knowledge against theirs, bought cheaply, sold dearly. In the process he accumulated an encyclopedic

17

knowledge of seventeenth, eighteenth, and nineteenth century literature and developed a considerable knowledge of printing and typography. He was also accumulating a small personal library of rare books.

His trade was a pleasant one, for it enabled him to spend his days
wandering around Paris at will. The morning might be spent in the
secondhand bookshops on the Rue Soufflot, and in the afternoons he
would be strolling along the banks of the Seine. There were no fixed
hours, and if it rained he could stay at home. The booksellers liked to
gossip, and he would pick up the gossip of the town in his wanderings.

René-Louis Doyon was delighted with the daily offering of his
chineur, all the more because he had a small stock and was hoping
to enlarge his business while at the same time he wanted to devote
more time to publishing and to his own writing. At first their relations were strictly businesslike, but gradually Malraux began to thaw
and he would sometimes relate the gossip he had picked up in his
travels. He had very definite ideas about literature and a happy gift
of sarcasm. The bookseller also observed an element of malice and
even of cruelty which contrasted, he thought, rather oddly with the
young man's air of conscious superiority. No doubt this was the nervous
cruelty of a man not yet sure of himself.

About this time Malraux sought out François Mauriac, the Catholic
novelist, who was then in his middle thirties but already highly regarded for the purity of his style and his profound knowledge of human emotions. He wrote angelically about people possessed by
demons. Malraux, possessed by his own demons, wanted a worthy opponent with whom he could argue the case for atheism; he wanted
definite answers to definite questions. As they sat in Mauriac's study,
the austere novelist and the unknown student of books formed a
strange contrast. Mauriac resembled a prince of the Church, Malraux
a bristling bird of prey. "The Church has everyone in its power, and
what has it done with them?" Malraux asked, and Mauriac explained
patiently that God's justice and mercy were expressed through the
Church, and if there were bad priests that was only to be expected,
since the human soul was not always in a state of grace. So the argument would continue, while the bird of prey—Mauriac called him
ce petit rapace herissé, à l'oeil magnifique, "this little bristling bird

of prey with the magnificent eyes"—advanced his vehement and perhaps unanswerable accusations against Christ and the Church. "There was nothing about him comparable with the old Masonic radicals who were moved to pity by the gentle wanderer of Judea," Mauriac wrote many years later, remembering the ancient arguments under the lamplight. "He knows Christ, and he was the stern adversary of that gentle wanderer."

Mauriac concluded that the young Malraux possessed a profoundly religious temper, and perhaps hated the Church, but did not despise it. On the other hand he despised mankind, and this led him inevitably to belong to Satan's party, to be one of those who deceive and mislead, not because they want to, but because their demons demand it. Malraux, in his eyes, was one of those rebels against Christ who destroy others before they destroy themselves.

There was some truth in Mauriac's summary of Malraux's character, but it was not the whole truth. He was writing his memories of Malraux in February 1937 after seeing him deliver a fighting speech in defence of the Spanish Republic. Mauriac had reason to be angry, for Malraux had suddenly emerged as a potential Gracchus who in some mysterious way might seize power and rule over France. The fear was unjustified—but there were many other Frenchmen who shared it. Malraux was never in a position where he could have seized power, and by this time he was too much the humanist to think power worth having. Mauriac was more accurate when he spoke of his young friend being riddled with the demons of solitude.

Though solitary, Malraux was seeing many people, attending many parties, visiting the studios of many painters. Among his close acquaintances was another Catholic, Max Jacob, poet and visionary, friend of Verlaine, Apollinaire, and Picasso. A Jew, Jacob was baptised a Catholic in the presence of Picasso, who became his godfather. One day in 1909, returning to his sordid little room in Montmartre after a day spent working in the Bibliothèque Nationale, he had seen a vision of Christ in blue and yellow raiment on his wall, and like St. Paul he fell to the ground dazzled by the beauty of the vision. He lived in poverty, helped everyone, and wrote poems which were always rough-edged and gay, even when he was haunted by death, and if his

Max Jacob, a self-portrait.

gaiety was that of a man about to be hanged who sings love songs on the scaffold, it was gaiety nevertheless. He liked to tell ridiculous stories, which could be read on three or four levels of meaning. Here is the beginning of one of his prose poems:

> When the ship arrived among the islands of the Indian Ocean, we realized that no one had any maps. We had to get down. In this way we discovered who was on board: there was that man who in the most bloodthirsty fashion gave tobacco to his wife and then took it back again. Islands were dotted about everywhere. On top of the cliffs we saw little Negroes wearing derby hats. "Well, perhaps they will have maps!" And so we made our way up the cliffs. . . .

In a very real sense Max Jacob spent most of his life searching for maps and climbing up cliffs in the hope of finding them. Malraux adored the man, admired his writings, and dedicated his first published book to him. Here and there in the book, which he called *Paper Moons,* there are echoes of Max Jacob's peculiar prose style, which hops and dances and hiccups and sometimes breaks into a canter for the sheer joy of the race. He had a predilection for "little Negroes wearing derby hats" and liked to invent comic animals, but this was only one aspect of his genius. When the spirit touched him, he could rage like any Hebrew prophet, and the same man who wrote about the mapless Indian Ocean could also write about the earth:

> Send me down beneath the dark candles of the earth,
> Beneath the venomous horns of the earth.
> There is peace only beneath the serpents of the earth.
> The earth is a great dirty mouth. . . .

Violent, comic, always gentle, Max Jacob reigned over a small group of friends at the Café La Savoyarde near the Sacré Coeur one evening a week. At these *soirées* he would dance, mimic the great men of his time, draw sketches, offer his paintings for sale—for he was also a painter—and tell stories which left everyone drunk with laughter.

Another close friend was the painter and engraver Demetrios Em-

Demetrios Galanis, wood engraving by the artist.

manuel Galanis, who was born in Athens in 1882 and came to Paris in 1900. He fought in the war and became a French citizen. Although not a great painter, he possessed a formidable skill in engraving. What especially attracted Malraux to him was his knowledge of the arts and his passionate love of independence, his determination to go his own way without interference and without the aid of the salons; he insisted that his paintings should be exhibited on their own merits. Handsome, sweet-tempered, disciplined, speaking four or five languages, he was in many ways the opposite of Max Jacob. Max Jacob was Dionysus; Galanis was Apollo. With his wife and children he lived in a small house on the Rue Cortot, where Malraux was a frequent visitor. He had a theory that Galanis would one day be recognized as the greatest of modern painters, and that day would be coming very soon.

In this he was wrong, for the talents of Galanis were severely limited. He engraved with a clean line, and his paintings were clean and pure without the least artifice, but they were not great works of art. He is remembered as a magnificent illustrator, whose illustrations were very much better than the books they decorated.

In 1928 Malraux wrote an article on the paintings of Galanis, in which he recorded one of his rare reminiscences of this period. He had accompanied Galanis and some friends on a visit to a painter in Montmartre, who lived in a vast loft. Hearing some disturbing sounds below, they decided to leave, Galanis leading the way.

> And so we climbed down in a long file, one after the other, the painter's flashlight lifted above his head like an aureole, and everyone making his way very slowly and carefully so as not to fall, a little uneasy because the stairway was a ladder. Down below, people were lying on the ground, and they rose when we called out to them and replied to our inquiries by shouting. And then everything was explained: they were the blind men from the Butte Montmartre, who had taken refuge here. I remember the shapes of these men leaning and supporting one another, while our silhouettes scarcely emerged from the shadows, and Galanis with his bushy hair standing there

with an expression of stupefaction, clutching at a sword with which he had armed himself against all perils, and in this light the sword cast a thin yellow streak across the scene.

We left the house, pursued by this vision of Breughel, which was both comic and sad, and Galanis led us to his home. In that apartment Léon Bloy had spent long years of misery and destitution, and there could be heard the echoes of Utrillo's tragic life. Here the shadows of our shapeless hands on the walls reminded us of the gestures of the blind men we saw only a little while before. Here, too, Galanis opened the little harmonium he had built and painted himself, and he sat down and played. We all listened intently, for he was playing Bach.

Galanis, with his kindness and warmth, and his vast knowledge of the arts, proved to be an excellent mentor and a lifelong friend, but while Malraux delighted in his paintings there were other artists who made deeper impressions on him. He was particularly attracted to Odilon Redon, the nineteenth-century painter of dreams and nightmares who filled his canvasses with strange one-eyed giants and sexless girls floating in evanescent landscapes. Redon gave the impression of a man who paints while he sleeps, and his works have a strange authority, as though he copied down exactly what he saw, depicting a coherent world in paroxysms of startling color. Joris Karl Huysmans, the novelist, had described Redon's work in *À Rebours*, and Malraux probably first discovered him in those pages.

Rudolphe Bresdin, the close friend of Redon, was also one of Malraux's favorite artists. Driven half mad by poverty, dreaming endlessly of the untamed forests of America, Bresdin drew imaginary forests of vast intricacy, and almost lost among the shadows there would be a solitary rider or a holy family. He was haunted by death, and his most famous engraving, *The Comedy of Death,* showed an old man, himself, sitting by a stream, while the leaves of all the trees around him turn into skulls.

In art Malraux had developed a taste for the fantastic, the rare, and the little known. Callot, Breughel, Bosch, Piranesi, and Goya were not yet widely known, though they would soon be coming into fashion.

Malraux reveled in them, just as he reveled in everything that was strange and haunted by death. What he asked of an artist was that he should be a revealer of mysteries, a companion in man's dark journeys into the soul: the artist must be a prophet. For the same reason he reveled in Carl Einstein's two books on Negro art, *Negerplastik* and *Afrikanische Plastik,* which appeared in the early nineteen-twenties. Carl Einstein was one of the very first to discuss Negro art rationally and sympathetically.

Adventurous in the arts, Malraux was equally adventurous in literature. He read widely in the Bibliothèque Nationale, where the normal discomforts of scholarship are interminably magnified by custodians who conduct a relentless war with the readers. He would spend long days there, often with his friend Pascal Pia, both of them surrounded by mountains of books. Malraux, with his special predilection for the fantastic, paid a proper tribute to works on satanism and demonology until he wearied of them. He was fascinated, too, by the visionary writings of Catherine Emmerich, who described the Passion of Christ as though she had been present and bore the stigmata on her hands and feet. Her visions, translated from the German, had gone through twenty-six editions in the middle years of the nineteenth century. Malraux suggested to Doyon that a new edition would be timely, and Doyon agreed. It was not one of his most successful publishing ventures, for copies of this edition could still be bought forty years later. Malraux spent about a year with Doyon, and then went to work with the publisher Simon Kra.

Among the books which made the greatest impression on the young Malraux was Paul Claudel's visionary play *Tête d'Or,* written in 1889, when the author was barely twenty-one years old. Tête d'Or (Golden Head) is one of those titanic, visionary characters who dream of nothing less than the conquest of the world. Where he walks, the flames are spewed out of the earth, and the most beautiful princesses kneel before him. After the death of the woman he has loved, he simultaneously rejects the world and solemnly embraces it, goading himself to fierce conquests in the East. An ancient empire is about to fall before the tribes of Asia. Tête d'Or saves the empire, usurps the kingly power, leads his armies against the barbarians, and some-

where among the foothills of the Caucasus he wages war against the
massed armies of all the Asiatic princes. Mortally wounded, he summons into his presence a princess of an earlier dynasty. She has
been found nailed to a tree, and her hands bear the stigmata. Dying,
Tête d'Or offers her his vast empire and laments his fate:

> May the darkness fall on all men!
> O wretched ones, the most wretched of all is the person of your
>   King.
> O earth, receive my body!   O death, receive my mysterious
>   soul!
> Come, my Father, and spread Thy smile over me,
> And may the lion cover me and the eagle enclose me with his
>   wings.
> I have held the Sun like a wheel to my breast!

Claudel's free verse, modeled on Whitman's, possesses an evocative
quality, simple and barbaric, so that he was able to suggest vast spaces
and the flow of history. The outlines were always vague: there is no
center, no hardness anywhere. But Malraux enjoyed his passionate
rhetoric and his barbaric splendor, and sometimes echoes Claudel in
his writings. If Max Jacob, intensely personal and erratic, represented
one extreme of his thought, Claudel, with his flamelike visions, represented the other; and there was perhaps some significance in the fact
that both Jacob and Claudel were deeply religious.

During the twenties French literature was marked by extraordinary
achievement. When Malraux came to live in Paris, Marcel Proust
was still alive, Paul Valéry and André Gide were at the height of
their powers, while Charles Péguy and Guillaume Apollinaire, one
killed in the war, the other dying in the aftermath, were felt as vivid
presences. It was the time of Raymond Radiguet, Roger Martin du
Gard, Georges Duhamel, Jean Cocteau, François Mauriac, Jules Ro-
mains, Jules Supervielle and Georges Bernanos. Even in the age of
Racine and Corneille there had never been such a galaxy of writers.
The jazz age had come, the accepted codes of morality were in dispute, illusions shattered by the war had become the clay out of which

new illusions would be born, but French literature appeared to draw strength from the prevailing *mal de siècle*. It was a time when young writers who had grown to manhood during the war were acutely conscious of disorder and flux and no longer satisfied with the ancient truths. They questioned everything, and most of all they questioned their own purposes. "Let a people fall prey to disorder, and in the works born of that very disorder they will be able to discover their true countenance, their peculiar greatness and beauty and, already, the seeds of their own order." So wrote Marcel Arland, devoted follower of Gide and close friend of Malraux, in February 1924, and the theme was to be repeated throughout the twenties. Out of disorder and flux the young French writers were determined to create their own order and their own monuments. They were superbly sure of themselves, rejoicing in their newfound freedom, for the wars were over and the task of creating a new civilization had begun.

It was a good time for a young writer to settle down in Paris.

⊷§ *The Paper Moons* ᵷ⊷

Malraux's first published story, *Paper Moons,* had a long and respectable ancestry, for it derived from the ancient morality plays, from Charles Perrault's fairy tales, and from Rabelais. He wrote it when he was seventeen, and published it when he was nineteen in a sumptuous edition with illustrations by Fernand Léger. Like nearly all the early works of young and brilliant authors, it was written in a rich and orchestrated language over which he sometimes lost control. Over long passages the language bears the weight of its strange images effortlessly, but sometimes the story seems to lose focus and disintegrate into the purest nonsense, becoming nothing more than a musical *divertissement.* Music, indeed, plays a major role in the story, and nonsense is one of the major themes.

At first sight *Paper Moons* appears to be far removed from the novels of intellectual adventure which Malraux wrote later. The heroes are abstractions who change shape and color, and hop about like luminous dragonflies; the villain is Death wearing a smoking jacket; and the adventures take place against a background of Cubist colors. In this drama, with a prologue and three acts, the essential element of tragedy is missing, for everything happens without cause and without purpose. When Death dies in an acid bath, no one cares, and the Seven Deadly Sins wonder why they were so desperately concerned to bring about the death of Death. When they are last seen, they are sitting disconsolately on the battlements of the highest tower of the castle, each dangling one of Death's bones in his hands, while they gaze down on the city in the evening light and weep over their triumph. At this moment all the images come into focus, for we realize that the Seven Deadly Sins have become transformed into the gar-

goyles of Nôtre-Dame seen on a winter evening, when the trees are
bare and the earth is dead.

It is a strange story. The young Malraux has poured into it all the
accumulated passions of his soul, his nihilism, his distrust of the
world, his belief in the essential absurdity of existence, and his delight in the play of the imagination. There is corrosive bitterness as
well as gaiety, ferocity as well as gentleness, sickness as well as health.
He is giving all of himself, holding nothing back, writing in a prose
that is deliberately sculptured and colored for his purpose. The mood
varies: sometimes deadly serious, at other times gaily ironical, and often
poetic. It is obviously the work of a very young and very talented
writer who knows where he is going.

In *Paper Moons* he introduces one of the themes he will pursue
for the rest of his life: the Kingdom of Farfelu. He found the word
farfelu in Rabelais, but he was to make it peculiarly his own.* It was
not a word that permitted precise definition. It meant the Absurd, the
Incomprehensible, the Other, all that was totally and irremediably
beyond human comprehension and control, and he would use the word
with the utmost seriousness or with a kind of ironical gaiety. *Farfelu*
overflows into life, but has its unchallenged empire within the circumference of death. The *Royaume-Farfelu*, the Kingdom of Farfelu, when
it first appears, is identical with the Kingdom of Death. Later, when
Malraux came to know it better, he would broaden its boundaries to
include such a vast area of life that it threatened life's existence. It
was never the ordinary death of the body; it was Death triumphant,
exultant, aware of its superb comic powers and in full enjoyment of
them.

Once he had discovered the Kingdom of Farfelu, Malraux would
spend a good part of his life closely examining it. It became his familiar,
his private obsession and his public duty, at once a friend to be cherished
and an enemy to be defeated. It appears in all his stories and lies at
the heart of his theories of art, and he could never escape from it.

* French etymologists derive *farfelu* from the Greek $\pi o\mu\phi o\lambda\upsilon\xi$,
a bubble, which became *famfaluca* in late Latin and *fanfelu* in
early French. *Fanfreluche,* meaning a bauble, a gewgaw, tinsel, was
used by Rabelais and survives in current French.

It was as though he had given himself the lifelong task of mapping out the Kingdom in all its immensity: the quiet pastures, the secret pathways, the rushing torrents and the dark forests. There would be no end to the journey, for there was no end to the Kingdom of Farfelu.

At the beginning of *Paper Moons* Malraux offers a note of warning in the shape of an epigraph from one of the fairy tales of E. T. A. Hoffman: "Be on your guard, for you will be dealing with some rather strange people." Here is the young Malraux setting out on his first journey into the Kingdom of Farfelu:

> Like a luminous sign, the yellow moon changed color, becoming first red, then blue, then green, and then, *ding!* it turned yellow again. A shrill musical note dropped from the moon like a tiny frog, and over the lake the pearly fountains played, stretching into the infinite distance.
>
> The floating plug became a box of surprises: a bearded man from Auvergne jumped out and flew off, leaving on the surface of the lake a forked wake like the hands of a clock. Who was the sorcerer, whose birth turned the waters of the lake into glass and put an end to the farandole of the wretched fountains? Even the moon paid no attention to him. Little did the moon care, for it was laughing so much that the notes which were the moon's teeth, disengaged themselves and all fell down together. They hovered in the darkness like stars grown too heavy; and their clear light lingered briefly after they were gone . . .

So he describes the adventures of the moons at a breakneck pace, describing things so light and airy that it is almost beyond the power of words to capture them. Suddenly a cat appears and sentences the bubbles formed by the moon to death. The obstinate bubbles refuse to die, and when we see the cat again, he has hanged himself and his folded paws make the sign of the cross.

So ends the Prologue, and the next scene opens with an army of alligators who become transformed into nine little men, seven of

them white, two of them red. The white ones are the Seven Deadly
Sins, and the red ones are the chemist Hifili and the musician Nosepick. Pride, the leader of the Seven Deadly Sins, asks the chemist and
the musician their opinions about God:

> PRIDE: Gentlemen, I assume you are acquainted with
>   God.
>
> HIFILI: I knew him once—a charming old man.
>
> NOSEPICK: Charming, yes, but a little vulgar.
>
> HIFILI: How could it possibly be otherwise? God came
>   to know a very large number of people, and even
>   today a very large number of people are ac-
>   quainted with him.
>
> PRIDE: He isn't vulgar any more. As a result of old age,
>   he has become completely unconscious. He has
>   already changed his name many times without
>   attaching any importance to it. Well, Satan, who
>   is no fool, has so arranged things as to take his
>   place, and neither God nor anyone else knows
>   anything about it. And since Satan has taken the
>   place of God, then we can take the place of
>   Satan. What do you think about that?
>
> ANGER: I imagine our power to do this is about zero.
>   Death, who is Satan's chief assistant, would sim-
>   ply destroy us.
>
> PRIDE: I have thought about this. It is very easy indeed
>   to refuse to take this argument into considera-
>   tion. All that is necessary is to destroy Death.

With this declaration of war, they go in search of Death. The way
leads through an enchanted forest haunted by the Cable, a strange
snakelike monster who kills by piercing like a needle. Black and terrible, he swings across the forest like a fury. The insane, destructive
powers of the Cable terrify the Seven Deadly Sins, who scurry across

the enchanted forest as quickly as possible. Kangeroos with trape-
zoidal wings appear. "Curiouser and curiouser," says one of the characters, with perhaps a sidelong glance at *Alice in Wonderland*. But
they pay very little attention to the kangeroos; they are much more
frightened by the Cable.

No doubt the Cable derives from the strange and hallucinatory
Rod in the Comte de Lautréamont's *The Songs of Maldoror*. This
Rod was tall as a man, blond-colored, composed of cones thrust into
one another, and it could bend and twist at will, coiling and uncoil-
ing like an eel. Utterly destructive, the Rod went berserk in a brothel,
smashing at the walls in ungovernable fury. We learn that the Rod
is really a hair fallen from God's head. The Comte de Lautréamont
invested the hair with a kind of divine grandeur, but the Cable belongs to nightmare. Finally Hifili attacks the Cable with a pair of
flying glass pincers and it falls to the ground, no more dangerous
than a coil of rope.

With the Cable out of the way, the Seven Deadly Sins escape from
the enchanted forest, only to find themselves in an inn nearly as
terrifying as the forest. They encounter an uproar of gramophone
noises, coral-pink rats, a plague of serpents and some cannibalistic
electric animals, which explode in a flash of blue light, to the intense
pleasure of Pride, who is anxious to continue the journey. "Since we
are concerned with our poor little life of sin," says Pride, "let us
hurry on as soon as possible." They hurry on to the City of Farfelu,
the capital of the kingdom.

When they reach the city, they learn that Death is dying of an
irremediable lassitude. Doctors have been summoned, and to celebrate their presence the city is *en fête*. Orders are given that all the
walls shall be whitewashed. The streets are lit with crystal goblets
with incandescent filaments. Skulls made of congealed champagne
adorn the houses, and the passers-by admire the golden drops of
melted champagne as they fall. Great dignitaries place hollow glass
spheres outside their doors, and from time to time these spheres rise
in the air, singing. This whitewashed city prophetically prefigures
the Paris transformed by Malraux into a white city more than forty
years later.

Death is a female skeleton dressed in a smoking jacket. She lives in her palace in a room hung with mirrors.

A doctor enters and asks her to undress. She consents at once, throws off her smoking jacket and trousers, and reveals her new aluminum ribs, which are, she says, "far more practical than the old bone ones."

"They are always saying: Death! Death!" she complains to the doctor, "but at heart I am just like the telegraph poles which have grown sentimental as a result of listening to so many messages of love. Besides, this new skeleton is much more elegant than the first. Look, when the sun sets—" Saying this, she goes to the window where the dying sun throws a red coppery glow on her shining ribs. "I must march with Progress," she sighs. "Everything now is becoming mechanical, metallic, gleaming."

The time has come to examine the patient with a stethoscope. The diagnosis is grave. The doctor suggests that Death should bathe five times a day in a special liquid he will provide, and she prepares herself for her bath. The doctor, of course, is Pride, and suddenly all the Deadly Sins and Hifili and Nosepick emerge from little red cushions. Pride whispers that he is about to dissolve Death in nitric acid. Death will not suffer, for she is totally insensitive to pain.

Death is just about to step into the bath when her friend Rifloire shouts that she is being poisoned.

"Nonsense, I am being corroded," Death answers.

"Then do something about it!"

"Why should I? I was never able to bring myself to commit suicide, and I owe a debt to those who assist me in avoiding such a troublesome end. The world is tolerable only because we have made a habit of tolerating it. I am ill, people are always quarreling with me, I take my umbrella and go on my way. They call me Death, but they know very well that my real name is Accident, and this slow destruction of my being is only one of my disguises!"

Death lights a cigarette, and the thin column of smoke assumes the shape of a young girl. Until the moment of her death, Death watches the smoke from her cigarette, imagining all kinds of obscene shapes. She dies contentedly.

The Seven Deadly Sins gaze disconsolately over the city from which Death is absent. Pride is the first to awaken from his melancholy dreams.

"Let's get to work," he says.

"Yes, let's all get to work," say the Deadly Sins.

"Where shall we begin?" says Hifili.

There is a long silence, and then Nosepick says: "Why did we kill Death?"

No one knows. Each touches the bone which hangs at his belt like a trophy. "Then they looked at one another. They were exceedingly sad. Soon they buried their heads in their hands and began to weep. Why had they killed Death? They had completely forgotten."

At this point Malraux's first published story comes to an end with an unanswerable question and an ironical flourish. He had said what he had wanted to say, speaking lucidly and sometimes brilliantly, delighting in his improvisations. Except for the Cable, the inventions were his own, although the form was derived from fairy stories and morality plays, and Rabelais was never far away from his thoughts. One of Rabelais's characters goes down to Hell, has a rollicking time with the devils, and speaks familiarly with Lucifer. Pantagruel asks him about the dead heroes of antiquity. "They are doing very well, but their circumstances have changed," he is told. "Alexander is making the barest living darning old hose, Xerxes is a crier of mustard, and Romulus a salt-maker." Malraux regards his heroes, the Seven Deadly Sins, with the same kind of irreverence as they go forth on their adventures. Their transformations are always in character, and they are on familiar terms with Lucifer.

Malraux was saying things that could not be said in any other way. He had found a form which he would use in most of his subsequent writings. Always there would be an enchanted forest, a journey through a landscape of sensations, a final encounter with death. At a very early age he had discovered Death, examining her minutely, and she would remain his companion through all the years of his life. "They call me Death, but they know very well that my real name is Accident." Above all, he has discovered the Kingdom of Farfelu, explored the streets of the city, and attended the obsequies of the reigning Empress. He was not frightened or appalled by her, and he knew that she was more than a little frivolous. On the evidence of this story he had been very close to suicide: deliberately, quietly, over a long period, he had stared into the face of Death, and had then turned away.

Malraux has said often that he detested his childhood, but a great part of it is included in the story, and it was not altogether unhappy. Significantly Pride was given pride of place in his story, and pride sustained him: it was the only sin he took seriously. The boy who had spent his days in an obscure town on the outskirts of Paris had at last found himself.

❦ *The Wandering Years* ❦

When *Paper Moons* was published in April 1921 in an edition limited to a hundred copies, it passed almost completely unobserved. The few people who read it were impressed by the author's command of language and by the savage irony concealed in the strange fairy tale, but it received scarcely any critical attention. Malraux, who appears to have regarded the book as a flag nailed to his pirate ship, took pains that the skull and crossbones should be displayed in the most luxurious manner. Max Jacob had introduced him to Daniel-Henry Kahnweiler, the art dealer and publisher of *éditions de luxe,* who agreed to publish it in association with his partner André Simon. The book appeared in a breathtaking format: *in folio,* with wide margins, a large type admirably designed to reflect the graces of the eighteenth century, the paper wonderfully crisp, the abstract designs by Fernand Léger providing exactly the right kind of decoration. All copies were signed by the author and by the illustrator. To those who are accustomed to reading Malraux's spidery handwriting, his own signature to his first published work comes as something of a surprise, being very bold and Napoleonic, the M resembling a prancing horse. It was not so much an *édition de luxe* as an example of extreme luxury bordering on effrontery. The pirate flag had been embroidered on the most exquisite silk.

When the book was published Malraux was nineteen years old. Already an experienced bibliophile, he showed impeccable taste in choosing Léger to illustrate the work: it was the first time Léger had ever made designs for a book. Altogether there were seven magnificent illustrations. Each finely printed page possessed great beauty, with the result that the story tends to lose itself in the opulence of the décor.

37

There is no reason to believe that Malraux found any fault with the appearance of the book.

The title page was even more opulent than the remaining pages, for it was decorated with two superbly drawn seashells. There was also a formidable subtitle:

PAPER MOONS

*a little book in which the reader may find
an account of little known combats
together with
an account of a voyage
among
certain familiar
but strange
objects,
all being related truthfully,
and ornamented with equally truthful woodcuts
by
Fernand Léger*

Although the subtitle plays a decorative role on the title page, it was an accurate description of the book. Nearly all his novels were to be about little known combats and voyages among strange but familiar objects.

The book was dedicated to Max Jacob, who quickly developed some notable reservations about his protégé. In June, two months after the publication of the book, he wrote about "the erudite Malraux" in a letter to Kahnweiler. Later he expressed the belief that Malraux would become "nothing more than the Gourmont of his time." Remy de Gourmont was a small, beetlelike man who spent his days poring over ancient texts and writing frail romances in an impeccable scholarly style. If Max Jacob feared that Malraux would become a conventional scholar, he was mistaken. Malraux's erudition had little enough to do with scholarship as it is commonly understood. He knew a good deal about the arts and about literature, about printing and typography and publishing, about rare books, about the techniques of painting and sculpture, but this knowledge was never acquired in a scholarly fashion. He made raids on literature and the arts, taking what he wanted and discarding the rest. He regarded any kind of externally imposed discipline with horror, and he resembled a guerrilla leader continually making forays into enemy territory and returning with treasure. He would study these treasures like a palaeontologist who studies a single prehistoric bone and reconstructs the whole animal. Fantasy, ingenuity, wide-ranging knowledge were placed in the service of exotic theories, which changed daily, and he was never happier than when he was elaborating theories that encompassed the histories of nations and the destiny of the human race.

There was also another Malraux, who was already playing the stock exchange—the Bourse in Paris is only a short distance from the Bibliothèque Nationale—and hoping to amass a fortune. He was acting out some of the fantasies of Georges Munier, who made money disinterestedly, casually, almost with distaste, stuffing it in a drawer and then forgetting all about it. There was a period when he dressed like a dandy *à la Lord Seymour* and he frequented the *boîtes* of Montmartre. He was living at high pressure, carried a revolver, and was sometimes in danger. It was a life that suited him perfectly, for he was determined from the beginning to live fully and also to leave a mark on literature.

He was making many friends. Pascal Pia, René Latouche, Georges Gabory, Marcel Arland, and his schoolfriends Louis Chevasson and Marcel Brandin were especially close to him and shared his enthusiasms. The friendship with René Latouche ended abruptly. Not yet twenty, suffering from violent fits of depression and unable to find any reason for living, Latouche killed himself. Eight years later Malraux dedicated his first novel *The Conquerors* "to the memory of my friend René Latouche," thus granting him a small portion of his own mortality.

One day in June 1921, at a dinner given in a restaurant to celebrate the launching of a literary magazine, Malraux encountered for the first time the young woman who would become his wife. Her name was Clara Goldschmidt, the daughter of a rich leather merchant with interests in both France and Germany. She was very small, warm, intelligent, with a smile of great sweetness and a mind filled with the poetry of Novalis and Hölderlin, and there was a forthrightness about her which concealed an almost paralysing shyness. There was only the briefest meeting in the restaurant, but they saw more of one another later the same evening when a small group of dinner guests left the restaurant and made their way to a nearby nightclub called the *Caveau Révolutionnaire,* which was decorated with red, white and blue garlands and hangings to symbolize its dubious revolutionary character. In this revolutionary cave Clara Goldschmidt found herself dancing with a tall, thin youth with jug ears and enormous green eyes, who walked with a curious swinging motion and danced badly. He was pleasant, but made no particular impression on her, and she quickly forgot him. He was just one more of the many young writers who were to be seen whenever a new literary magazine was launched.

On the following Sunday they met again in the apartment of the young poet Yvan Goll, born in Lorraine, and like Clara Goldschmidt equally proficient in French and German. He lived in Auteuil, not five minutes' walk from the Goldschmidt villa, and Clara was a frequent visitor to his Sunday afternoon receptions where one might meet Marc Chagall or Archipenko or any modern sculptor, painter, writer or filmmaker. Yvan Goll kept open house, and was continually on the lookout for new talent, partly because he was a sensitive man with a deep concern for young artists and partly because he represented a German publishing house. On this Sunday Clara Goldschmidt first saw André Malraux in broad daylight. What she saw pleased her, and she was even more pleased by his curiously concentrated conversation, by the play of his ideas, and by the ease with which they were able to communicate. They shared many enthusiasms; they both enjoyed Michelet's *History of the French Revolution* and Paul Claudel's *Tête d'Or;* they had both read widely in Nietzsche and Dostoevsky. Clara knew the German Romantic poets by heart and was especially devoted to Hölderlin. Her companion spoke learnedly about the French eighteenth century satirists and the medieval *Cantilena of St. Eulalia,* which he claimed to have translated. From being absorbed in each other's ideas they were quickly becoming absorbed in each other, and during the following days they were continually seeing each other.

In the large villa at Auteuil Clara lived with her two brothers and her widowed mother, a woman of formidable dignity who was determined that her only daughter should marry into wealth and respectability. Clara had other ideas. What she wanted above all was to travel, to have adventures, to talk about literature, and to read every good book ever written. If necessary, she would do all these things alone; hopefully, there would be a companion to share them with her. She had recently returned from a visit to Italy without benefit of any escort, and was rejoicing in the excitement of freedom.

One Sunday evening Malraux took her to a *bal musette,* a working men's dancehall frequented by workers and their girls, as well as by pimps and gigolos. In such places the bourgeoisie were never welcomed and the women were expected to dance with anyone who claimed the honor. Clara found herself dancing with a pimp. She was enjoying the music of the accordions, the strange *argot* spoken by these Parisians who had nothing whatsoever in common with the people of Auteuil, and their equally strange garments. The pimp soon vanished, and then she was dancing in the arms of her companion, dizzy with excitement, more than ever captivated by the knowledge that it was permissible to go anywhere, even to the lowest dives in Paris.

Finally, in the early hours of the morning, they left the *bal musette* and made their way from the little side street in the direction of the Boulevard des Gobelins. Just as they were leaving, some men jostled them and swept passed them. It was a deliberate affront, but they paid no attention to it until they realized that these men, instead of continuing on their journey, were retracing their steps and coming toward them, obviously intending mischief. Suddenly shots were being fired at them, Malraux whipped out his revolver and fired back, at the same time pushing Clara behind him. He had been wounded in the left hand, the bullet passing between two bones. They washed the blood away at a nearby hydrant, found a taxi, and drove to Clara's house to disinfect the wound with hydrogen peroxide and to bandage it. When Clara's mother appeared, she received a simple explanation: "My friend brought me home, and has come to pick up a book." The answer seemed to satisfy Clara's mother, who quietly returned to her own bedroom.

Life with André was likely to be full of surprises, but Clara was perfectly capable of inventing her own surprises. She decided to take a holiday in Florence. The family encouraged her, hoping that the holiday would put an end to her infatuation for the young man who was clearly a ne'er-do-well, neither wealthy nor respectable. Madame Goldschmidt accompanied her daughter to the Gare de Lyon and saw that she was properly settled in her compartment of the *wagon lit,* and then bade her an affectionate farewell. A moment later André slipped into the compartment.

It was André's first visit to Florence, and he succumbed to its temptations. Every church and museum had to be seen, and he raced through them as though charging into battle on horseback. It was astonishing how quickly he could move through a room and then give a precise account of every sculpture and painting he had seen. Some paintings, of course, would be dismissed out of hand; others would be analysed minutely. Clara observed a certain pattern in his comments. "He always compared the objects in front of him with those he had not yet seen but could imagine," she wrote in her memoirs. He was stretching his mind until it entered the realm of prophecy, where he was at home. The real and the unreal, the present and the future, the known and the unknown were held in an uneasy equilibrium as he strove to broaden the field of inquiry until it reached the frontiers of the possible; then, recklessly, he would advance into the impossible. Sometimes the impossible became true. At nineteen he was already a daring art critic.

From Florence they sent a telegram announcing their engagement, for they had decided to marry with the proviso that they would cheerfully contemplate divorce six months later. There followed a telegram from Madame Goldschmidt: "Return immediately without your friend." This was a tactical error. Clara became even more unyielding in her desire to remain with her lover. They visited San Gimignano, to admire the long lean towers, and Siena, where they admired the solitary horseman who rides in splendor across a landscape so clearcut that it seems to be made of colored crystal. Seeing some lanterns bobbing over the Arno, they were reminded of Venice and immediately left Florence. In Venice they stayed at the Hotel Danieli because it was the only hotel Clara had heard of. Telegrams could wait; they were in love; moody, impulsive, fearless, nearly penniless, they awaited the future with a kind of quiet exasperation because they could already see it unfolding before them. Impatience was their happiness, and merely to be alive among so many artistic treasures was reward enough for their wildest gambles.

When their money ran out they returned to France, both of them hungry, for their sandwiches gave out before they reached the frontier. The Goldschmidt family was up in arms, but the harm had already been done. André and Clara returned to Paris early in September and were married on October 28, 1921. The second story of the Goldschmidt villa was one of their wedding presents. There they lived in close proximity to Clara's two brothers, who resented the presence of a young man whose hair kept falling across his forehead, who spoke with an accent which was not that of Auteuil, and who showed no notable deference to their superior bourgeois culture. In much the same way Malraux's father disapproved of Clara, not so much because she was Jewish as because the Goldschmidt family had its roots in Germany, and he had a robust distrust of foreigners. Clara remembered that whenever he spoke of his own country, he always used the words *la douce France.*

They spent their honeymoon traveling through Germany and Czechoslovakia until they were satiated with the golden lights of Berlin and the shadowy streets of Prague and had met most of Clara's German relatives. They saw Berlin in the exotic aftermath of the war, the blond boys dressed in skirts, the cafés still doing a roaring business, and poverty everywhere. Malraux was struck by the prevailing mood of antimilitarism: there seemed to be no hostility toward the French. Above all, he was immersing himself in the new German paintings and German films; and while his knowledge of German scarcely improved, since his wife spoke the language well enough for both of them, he was coming into close contact with German culture. Nietzsche, Keyserling and Spengler were all to leave a deep impression on him, and for the rest of his life he would be haunted by them.

Back in Paris, in their own sparsely furnished apartment, with its black wooden armchairs, with its painting by Galanis, Derain, and Kisling, they settled down to a gypsylike domesticity. Their visitors were painters and poets, scholars and art critics; they saw much of Kahnweiler, came to know Marc Chagall, and lived as though only art and literature had any significance. About this time Malraux was making his first overtures to Jacques Rivière, the editor of the literary magazine *La Nouvelle Revue Française,* who replied to Malraux in exactly the same way that he replied to Antonin Artaud, saying that he would regret these early *farfelu* works when he had more solid achievement behind him. Rivière, who gave him book reviews to write, possessed examplary literary judgment and rarely made a mistake.

The truth was that Malraux was still attempting to discover himself, still searching among his many selves for the one which would be a springboard to literature. Once he said: "I shall never be a writer. The lover of art is superior to the creator. The Chinese knew this, for they regarded the man capable of appreciating the garden as superior to the gardener." But this was merely a passing tribute to a self-indulgent romanticism; neither he nor his wife had any doubt that they were on the side of the gardeners against the mere contemplators of gardens.

Since *La Nouvelle Revue Française* would not publish his short stories, they appeared in the little magazines. Sometimes he wrote introductions to the books he was editing. These introductions provided him with vehicles for his own tormented attempts to understand the nature of artistic creation. In a short article on Gide, written for *Action,* which was edited by his friend Florent Fels, he discussed the contradictory influences at work on a writer and insisted that an artistic personality has little enough to do with ideas and much more to do with the discipline a writer imposes upon himself. He wrote:

A book is nearly always the consequence of a contradiction. No doubt certain philosophical influences manifest themselves over a long period; they grow weaker, and when they have almost vanished they seem to be very different from what they were, just as a color diluted with water is very different from the color in a pure state. Sometimes it happens that an influence once deeply felt creates a contrary influence at the moment when it is being discarded, and this happened to Remy de Gourmont. But whatever determines that an author is destined to live *as a man creating literature* is scarcely subject to change. The artistic personality of a writer is just as independent of the evolution of his ideas as a painter is independent of the subjects he paints.

The short article on Gide appeared in *Action* in the spring of 1922, when Malraux was twenty-one. The ideas of flux and metamorphosis, which were to dominate so much of his later work, were already present, and already there was the insistence on the *style* of the artist rather than on the content of his work. In the following year, in an introduction written for a new edition of Charles Maurras' *Mademoiselle Monk,* he attempted to show that there was no contradiction between Maurras' early anarchism and his later reactionary tendencies as the editor of *L'Action Française,* the right-wing royalist newspaper:

> In going from intellectual anarchism to *L'Action Française* he was not contradicting himself, but building something. If he had delighted in living in Greece, it was because the philosophers of Greece were accustomed to creating a harmony between their lives and their philosophies; but I see him above all as a man of the Middle Ages, an ardent priest, the father confessor of great men, an architect of cathedrals and an organizer of Crusades.

Though Malraux had little sympathy for *L'Action Française,* he had a good deal of sympathy for a remarkable stylist who lived his ideas, however medieval they were, and attempted to create a system, however mistaken. Above all, Maurras was one of those who possessed a passionate love for France and especially for the landscapes of Provence, which were "as sumptuous and tragic as the corpses of kings." He loved order, because order lay at the heart of the mystery, "for all order," wrote Malraux, "represents beauty and energy." And when Malraux praised Maurras for insisting that ideas should be transformed into acts, he was expressing for the first time one of the central articles of his faith. *"Vivre ses idées"*—"To live one's ideas"—was the banner under which he fought against the Philistines.

But while there was one Malraux who thought in terms of order, discipline, energy, and style, there was another and more human Malraux who was given to fantastic improvisations and ferocious meditations on the subject of death, which was never very far from his thoughts. The Flemish part of him rejoiced in caricature, elaborate jokes, the paintings of Bosch and Breughel, carnival and fairy tales. *Paper Moons* was the work of a man from Flanders; the essays on Gide and Maurras were the work of the Parisian critic and aesthete. One was classical, the other a raging romantic, and the two were always to be in an uneasy alliance. For long periods there would be a truce between them, but sometimes they would break out into open conflict.

The raging romantic had a great affection for the half-English, half-Belgian painter James Ensor, who lived in Ostend and produced during his long life a vast number of paintings of devils and skeletons and insects with human faces. Ensor rejoiced in the absurd: his *Christ Entering Brussels in Triumph,* now in the museum at Antwerp, is a delicate idol in a sea of grimacing clowns. He created the painting of cruelty, as Antonin Artaud created the theater of cruelty. But where Artaud's cruelty came from a desperate desire to inflict pain on himself, Ensor's cruelty arose from a lusty awareness of death's presence, and he ridiculed death as much as he ridiculed men and transformed them into puppets dangling on death's strings. He could paint stingrays and cabbages, and somehow he would suggest that they were the very principles of evil. He was the last of a long line of Flemish painters who delighted in painting their most haunting nightmares.

One day, when visiting Bruges with his wife and Marcel Arland, Malraux slipped off to Ostend to pay his tribute to Ensor. *Christ*

Entering Brussels in Triumph, an enormous canvas painted in raw colors with garish chrome yellow and blood-red predominating, hung above the piano, which supported some mermaids made from monkeys and fish tails. When Malraux returned to Bruges, he reported that he had seen authentic mermaids propped up on Ensor's piano. Clara, who could believe anything, saw no reason to suppose that he was exaggerating. Ensor lived by the sea, and it was perfectly natural to believe that he would occasionally encounter a mermaid during his walks along the shore. Finally Malraux admitted that they were not real mermaids: they were really stuffed monkeys. But no one had any doubt that for a while Malraux had convinced himself that he had seen mermaids on the piano.

Malraux's world—the orderly, precise world of the intellectual steeped in French culture—was continually being invaded by mermaids and stingrays, ghosts and goblins. If he had encountered green elephants with wings, he would have greeted them with his customary politeness, for they were inhabitants of his world, and familiar to him. He had no patience with the Surrealists, who created imaginary nightmares, for his own nightmares were only too vivid. They emerged perhaps out of the darkness of ancestral memory, but they were an essential part of his waking life, never to be exorcised.

In his famous essay on Leonardo da Vinci, Paul Valéry had announced that the watchword was henceforth *Hostinato rigore,* obstinate rigor. Malraux was prepared to accept the watchword on condition that mermaids were permitted to sit on Ensor's piano.

⊸§ *The Fireman of*
Massacre ₴⊷

At various times during the early years of his marriage Malraux returned to the contemplation of a fantastic story, not unlike *Paper Moons,* but written on another plane, more deeply concerned with the death of death and the eternal warfare between the living and the dead. The theme haunted him, and he would return to it again and again, but now he wanted to write about it with a kind of calculated gaiety. He would tell the same story, but this time it would be fully orchestrated, with a richer texture and a deeper passion. The chief characters would no longer be the Seven Deadly Sins. Instead there would be a single protagonist disguised in Rabelaisian colors, recognizably human, by turns heroic and comic, waging war against all the world's absurdities until at last he confronts the ultimate absurdity of death. Quite clearly this Rabelaisian character would be a projection of himself.

This fantastic story was never completed, but fragments of it have survived in obscure literary journals. These fragments, published at long intervals, would throw their long shadows on the works of his maturity.

Altogether he printed four fragments of this work in progress. The first, which appeared in the magazine *Action* in July 1920, serves as a prologue to the drama, and like the opening passages of *Paper Moons* it is designed to set the mood and to paint a landscape where nothing is predictable. There is a sudden splash of light, which is instantly transformed into a silver lake; trees appear, and they are instantly transformed into threatening hands; and then trees and lake vanish to become a spinning top which splits up and forms a mouth that engulfs the sea and the land. Malraux always had a passion for observing the abstract play of light, and in this first fragment he describes a dramatic dance of light with skill and ingenuity:

> A vast pool filled with quicksilver, and all around it a forest like a portcullis.
>
> Every tree is a stalk surmounted by a single lance-shaped leaf coated with an almost luminous amber-colored gum. The leaves break and fall; and all the crystals which went into the composition of the gum slide down the whole length of the tree like little animals, to reunite on the pool in the shape of an enormous Hand; and from each of its fingers a new hand is formed, and so on indefinitely, each hand branching out.
>
> The ground is covered with filaments of amber: the filaments spread out, and the Hand above the pool grows smaller, becomes no more than a dot, then vanishes completely.
>
> The entire network of filaments suddenly bursts into flame. Pearly cinders.
>
> And the great porcelain fish take care not to dash themselves against the blackened trees.
>
> The sun falls into the sea, which immediately becomes a lake covered with scales. Out of it there emerges a white top so vast that it is impossible to see all of it; and the top is spinning.
>
> One of the tawny speckles of the scales leaps, then bursts into flame, climbs higher, falls, and then ascends the whole length of the spinning top, tracing three black lines.
>
> The top comes to a stop: one of the three segments of the surface falls away. Through this opening the top swallows the sea, grows still larger, and suddenly hurtling downward, engulfs the earth. Like a mouth the opening closes.
>
> The top begins to spin again.

So ends the first section of the story, which is oddly convincing, though it has little reference to anything we know in the real world. He is clearly influenced by Cubist painting. He is establishing clearcut scenes in spherical geometry. Only the porcelain fishes, suddenly emerging from nowhere and vanishing just as mysteriously, relate to the world we know.

In the magazine *Signaux de France et de Belgique* there appeared in August 1921 Malraux's story *The Tamed Hedgehogs*. It has nothing to do with hedgehogs. From the subtitle we learn that it is a diary written by the Fireman of Massacre, published after the death of the Author, with Notes, by the Sieur des Étourneaux. The grandiloquent name of the editor should not mislead us. Étourneaux means "scatterbrained."

The Fireman's diary relates to some fantastic events taking place in Bhouzylle, which is presumably Bondy. A mysterious stranger has appeared in the town, calling himself "The Charlatan," but it is not at all certain that this is his real name. The Fireman and his friends, the Policeman, Tremble-in-the-wind, and Pickled Pork, have received word from the Charlatan that he would be delighted to welcome them in his château if any disaster should befall the town.

As the Fireman notes in his diary, disasters are happening all the time. One day the red feathers of his helmet flew away and curled up to sleep on the sofa. An even more shocking event occurred on another day. "All the gold buttons of my coat fell down on the ground and became the eyes of cats, and as soon as the lamp went out, they climbed up the wall like luminous butterflies." Worse still, little people emerged from the ham on the table, shouted with laughter, and vanished up the chimney. The Fireman observed that even when his companions said that nothing untoward was happening, they stammered with fear.

The long-promised disaster fell at 8:30 P.M. on January 18, when the Fireman's house was invaded by an army of horned ducks, which committed mass suicide, thus filling the door and the windows up to the third story with their bodies. The problem was to find a way out. There were two possibilities—the chimney or the back door. The Fireman escaped through the chimney and was exceedingly annoyed because the red feather of his helmet had become black with soot. He was in no mood to watch the kitchen minions dancing round the flaming house with well-cooked chickens under their aprons.

So ends the second fragment of the improbable story. There are no footnotes. The Fireman is no fireman: he is a watcher of flames, a diarist of conflagrations. In later novels Malraux will continue to use the diary form, delighting in its freedom and sudden alterations of tempo. In the second fragment the cubist stage setting is abandoned, but it reappears in the third fragment published during the same month in the magazine *Accords* under the title *The Diary of a Fireman of the Game of Massacre.*

We are introduced to a strange arctic landscape of glittering stone and black fountains. The Fireman and his companions emerge from a château and make their way across a white esplanade as smooth as ice. A forest lies nearby, and there is a canal cutting through it. They look for some chairs, but find only a table. Under the tablecloth they discover "four wooden personages lying in a drunken stupor." Out of these wooden personages they make a bench and sit down to watch the searchlights playing on the forest and the canal, and to their intense pleasure they see an army of animal skeletons riding the searchlights. The skeletons of the cats move voluptuously, rubbing themselves deliciously against one another, while the skeletons of the dogs leap and wag their tails. The Fireman's enjoyment in the searchlight display is interrupted by a voice coming from one of those wooden personages he is sitting on. The Fireman can make out only a white shirt front.

"Do you know," the voice asks, "why everything passes away?"

"I haven't the faintest idea," the Fireman replies.

"Then I will tell you. Monsieur, everything passes away, because there is no longer any moral order."

Surprised, the Fireman demands to know the identity of this personage with the white shirt front.

"Monsieur, I am the Devil," the voice replies. "The title gives me no pride, for I have a sweet and retiring disposition. Do not look at me so closely or your sensitive eyes will grow tired."

The dialogue between the Devil and the Fireman will be repeated many times in Malraux's works. The Devil's assertion that there is no longer any moral order will be examined elsewhere at greater length, especially in *The Walnut Trees of Altenburg.* The discussion between the Devil and the Fireman continues:

Then the Devil lit a small cigarette lighter.

"Can you see me?" he asked. "Very well. Everything is all right. As you see, I am exactly as you imagined me. Although I have been condemned to wear for eternity the vermillion skin invented for me by poor Adonai—a person of limited intelligence—I have done everything in my power to avoid the ridiculous silhouette fastened on me by the good people of the world. My checkered costume is vulgar; only my tie, which my relatives regard as being altogether too small, may be worth noting. It is enough that you should pay attention to my eyes, dark and rapacious as the night, to recognize my demoniacal nature.

"I was saying that the moral order has ceased to exist. I do not take into consideration the fact that it never played a very prominent role. I tempted men, but they tempted me still more. Intelligent people are permitted to believe that I created evil; nevertheless, it is possible that evil created me. The various legends constituting what I may call my civil status are obscure and contradictory, and we often create without being aware of it."

"Monsieur the Devil, your uncertainty astounds me."

"Monsieur Fireman, if you want to laugh—"

"I don't want to laugh. It is not a matter of any great importance that I should be astounded by your uncertainty, but it is regrettable that you should be disturbed by my astonishment."

"I am not in the least disturbed. Forgive an old, ill-tempered Devil for having annoyed you a little. This was far from my intention. I rarely have the opportunity of engaging in conversation with someone capable of understanding me. Perhaps I would have been less loquacious if drunkenness had not contributed to my loquacity. Thank you, Monsieur Fireman, for the kindness and patience you have shown me, and I would be pleased if you would accept this little whistle as a gift. The assistance of certain personages endowed with more senses than you possess may prove on occasion to be useful. You have only to blow on this whistle, and two kindly demons will at once appear and obey your orders. You will find them excellent servants, and from time to time you should give them tips. In this age without slaves, it is often the mark of a clever man to cling fast to good servants."

The Devil stretched out on the ground and immediately fell asleep. And I thought: "What can he want of me? This unexpected gift troubles me." I gazed at him: he was lying on his side, snoring gently, and the unseen crickets nearby seemed to be answering the call of the innumerable crickets chirping on the banks of the grand canal, the distant music of banjos adding to the music of the alarming skeletons.

With the gift of the whistle, the Fireman was in the position to call upon the Devil's aid in time of need. Whether he ever used the whistle is uncertain, but it is known that he developed a talent for music. Henceforth he would be known as the Fireman-Musician, and he was evidently more skilled in music than in putting out fires.

The Devil's point of view, as described in *The Diary of a Fireman of the Game of Massacre,* is a familiar one. He is the affable nineteenth-century Devil, resembling an elegant *maître d'hôtel* or a contented bourgeois, who has long ago forgotten his journeys through interstellar space and wishes to pass for a well-bred man with a penchant for self-mockery. "I dream of becoming incarnate once and for all and irrevocably in the form of a merchant's wife weighing eighteen stone, and believing all she believes," the Devil tells Ivan Karamazov, and indeed the Devil who appears in *The Brothers Karamazov* has contributed some minor sartorial elements to Malraux's Devil. Dostoevsky's Devil also wears a checkered costume and is proud of his necktie, "such as is worn by people who aim to be fashionable."

The further adventures of the Fireman were published in the literary magazine *900* in the summer of 1927 under the title *Written for a Teddybear.* Like the tamed hedgehog of an earlier fragment, the teddybear is remarkably absent, and it may be assumed that he is merely an agreeable spectator.

With this fragment Malraux concludes his account of the Fireman on a note of triumph. The fantasies are more abundant than ever, but now more than ever they appear to be gathering around some psychological wound, like hummingbirds around a honey-pot. He seems to be attempting to say things about himself which could only be told in this way. Concerning these fragments Malraux's friend Marcel Arland wrote: "Let no one make a mistake about the apparent fantasy in these pages by Malraux; this fantasy is a mask thrust upon him as a consequence of his great modesty; he juggles with ideas, but each one wounds him; with words, and there is not one he despises."

Once more Bhouzylle is threatened with disaster, this time from a serpent known as *Clef de Sol* from his resemblance to a treble clef. The serpent has been annually deflowering two hundred women from the poorer quarters of the town. A competition is therefore organized to discover a musician who will have the power to charm the serpent. The Fireman enters the competition, which is held in the local theater before judges who are all professors of mathematics. The Fireman is fitted with a three-cornered hat with golden spiders hanging from the corners, mounts the stage, and plays the saxophone so well that he is unanimously proclaimed the winner. In the serpent's castle, which glows with fantastic colors, he is perfectly at ease. Predictably, the serpent is female, and when the Fireman plays on his saxophone, she is enchanted by him, coils round him, kisses him on the mouth, offers herself to him, and becomes his willing prisoner.

Four days later the Fireman leads the monster in triumph to Bhouzylle. Malraux describes the triumphal procession in a bravura passage written with a certain ironical detachment, but there can be no doubting the sense of exaltation of the great conquistador as he returns to his native town. The irony is intermittent; the achievement is absurd; the triumph is real. The Fireman writes in his diary:

> I desire to record everything that happened when, as a conqueror, I made my triumphal entry into Bhouzylle, omitting nothing. One day my triumph will receive official tribute in the form of a bronze plaque inserted in the wall of the town hall. I shall also record all the circumstances that preceded my triumph, for I made it my business to seek out this infor-

mation from authoritative sources lest this record remain incomplete for lack of their testimony.

From nine o'clock boats laden with flowers made their way along the principal canal through the town, to be joined by small craft coming from a great distance along the smaller canals. To avoid collisions, the sailors shouted in rather singsong voices, and all these voices blended together, ringing clearly across the water. When collisions occurred, great heaps of flowers tumbled into the canal, and there for a while they would remain until they were gradually scattered, moving away from one another with a gentle swaying motion.

An arch of triumph was set up at the East Gate. It was not decorated with leaves but with flowers, strewn with white grapes made transparent by the sun. The moment after I passed underneath the arch, it disintegrated, for fireworks had been attached to the flowers. This luminous unfolding of petals in broad daylight, their exquisite tints, and the unexpectedness of their blossoming somewhat perturbed me. Some of these flowers were Japanese, and when they exploded they released grotesque little people who remained afloat in the air above the town until the evening.

Twenty-four comic figures went before me, each sailing in his own little ebony boat delicately drawn by a dolphin striped like a zebra, and these dolphins held reins in their mouths. Some days previously a blue dye from Mytilene had been poured into the Pool of the Dolphins, and accordingly the plumes of water that adorned their heads like aigrettes were deep blue. They were followed by twenty little monkeys in swimsuits half green and half red, with bells suspended from their long tails, which they raised to demonstrate their joy. They sailed in motor-driven vessels shaped like snail shells, turning round and round, with the result that their tails described immense circles and the little bells tinkled. There followed sixteen bespectacled sturgeon, their noses peering up from the water, and behind them came six beautiful young girls naked in their seashells. At last came my ship, preceded by dazzling reflections that turned the water into liquid gold. And I, the Fireman-Musician, the same who is now addressing you, stood there beside the *Clef de Sol,* whom I had unwound and made prisoner and now held at the end of a leash. Her eyes were closed and she appeared to be sleeping.

This great tribute, paid by the Fireman to himself, derives from the triumphs of ancient Rome: the *triumphator* appearing in all his glory as he leads the captured kings to the foot of the Capitoline Hill, where they will be executed. The same fate awaits the monster.

So solemn is the occasion that the people of Bhouzylle watch the coming of the Fireman in total silence. They are a people, he notes, who hate violence. Nevertheless, violence has been decreed by the municipal councillors, who have chosen this day for a mass execution of all the condemned prisoners in the town. Gallows have been erected on small boats moored along the banks of the canal, and on these gallows the prisoners are hanged upside down, each prisoner wearing a bronze helmet adorned with a lacy halo which gleams like the sun. The *Clef de Sol* still sleeps, unaware of the arrival of the official executioner, who swiftly inserts a long needle into her head. She dies immediately, and at that moment the hanged men stop singing, the sun sets, and night falls on the town. From the towers and the surrounding heights a blue glimmering light appears, and in this strange light the Fireman observes that the people of Bhouzylle have the color of the dead.

In this way the triumphal procession comes to an end in delirium and death, and the Fireman is cheated of his victory. There is no applause: only a dreadful silence and a ghastly light. In much the same way Malraux will write the concluding chapters of his novels, for all ends in the Game of Massacre, the Fireman defeated, the chessmen swept off the board.

A recent critic, André Vandegans, has sought to show that *The Diary of a Fireman of the Game of Massacre* is largely derivative. Obscure contemporary works and less obscure nineteenth-century works are introduced to show that Malraux had unconsciously borrowed from them. He is said to have borrowed from the marionette plays of Maeterlinck, the fairy tales of E. T. A. Hoffmann, Pierre Mac Orlan's *Le Nègre Léonard et Maître Jean Moulin,* Joseph von Görres' *Christliche Mystik,* and Père Jean Baptiste Labat's *Voyages aux Isles de l'Amérique,* and many more. André Vandegans identifies Bhouzylle with Tenochtitlán, the Aztec capital of Mexico, where there were also canals, pyramids, offerings of flowers, and a snake goddess who presided over death. "The refined, bloody, mysterious, and civilized city of Bhouzylle," he writes "is Tenochtitlán as described in the letters of Hernán Cortés to the Emperor Charles V, the writings of Bernardino de Sahagún and Bernal Díaz del Castillo and many others which Malraux read in order to satisfy his obsession with remote civilizations." But this is to grant more historical weight to the diary than it deserves. Bhouzylle was Bondy, the small town dying from the accumulated lethargy of centuries, and the Fireman of Massacre was Malraux himself.

In this story Malraux bade farewell to his childhood and exorcised the demons of the past. *The Diary of a Fireman of the Game of Massacre* represented an attempt to come to terms with the childhood he detested and therefore transformed into miraculous adventures and desperate triumphs. Thereafter the way was open to write about the world as it is, without recourse to dreams. Yet the Fireman of Massacre and the *Clef de Sol* continued to haunt him throughout his life. To the very end the little Fireman with the bulbous nose and the red plume in his helmet would go in search of the serpent Death.

The Devil taking flight.

ADVENTURE IN INDOCHINA

Adventure is not so much a way of exalting or amusing oneself; rather, it is crushing ants beneath the palms of one's hands; it is insects, reptiles, repulsive dangers confronted at every step by someone making his way through the brush.

MALRAUX IN AN INTERVIEW
WITH *Candide*

&s *The Temple of*
Banteay Srei &>

Neither André Malraux nor his wife Clara was capable of living the conventional life. They had no gift for keeping regular hours, or for maintaining themselves in bourgeois dignity and respectability. Although they lived in an apartment in a fashionable town house off the Avenue Mozart, this was only because the house belonged to Clara's mother and was freely available. As often as they could, they escaped from the house and went traveling. Restless, without any real roots in Paris, eager for adventure, they were as footloose as gypsies.

In the twenties the word "adventure" possessed a special meaning among the literary coteries of Paris. It meant an escape from the bourgeoisie performed dramatically and with style and bravado. Gauguin's escape to Tahiti was an "adventure" of the first order, and so too was Rimbaud's escape to Abyssinia. An "adventure" was a slap in the face of existing values, a vindication of a man's right to achieve his own personal freedom. Once Diaghilev said to Jean Cocteau: "Astonish me," and it was necessary that the "adventurer" should astonish himself by the sheer enormity of his act.

Malraux was caught up in this tradition, together with most of his friends. Nearly all of them were bohemians who flaunted their detestation of the bourgeoisie and dreamed of astounding the world. A close friend, Georges Gabory, wrote an article in *Action* entitled "Homage to Landru," in which he extolled the virtues of a casual murderer. "For superior men, for artists, for emperors, for madmen and lovers, for all those who are above the level of mediocrity, there is only one way to 'perform one's duty,' and that is by the complete fulfilment of one's desires," he declared. "The end sanctifies the means." Georges Gabory was not writing entirely with his tongue in his cheek, and these specious and dangerous arguments were taken quite seriously, even though they merely reflected the romantic fallacy current in the nineteenth century. In much the same way Baudelaire had extolled the great criminals.

Malraux was half inclined to agree with Gabory's thesis, though he felt it necessary to indicate certain refinements. Many years later, in notes written to accompany an extended commentary on his work by Gaëtan Picon, he wrote concerning "adventure": "Around 1920 the word had great prestige among literary circles. . . . The adventurer is outside the law, and the mistake is to believe he is merely outside the written law, outside the conventions. He is opposed to society insofar as society is a *form* of life: he is not so much concerned to combat reasonable conventions as to combat the nature of society. Triumph kills him."

Malraux went on to explain that in this sense neither Napoleon nor Lenin could be regarded as adventurers, while Rimbaud and Lawrence of Arabia could be regarded as true adventurers. By definition, the adventurer must wear the badge of failure. If Lawrence had become Governor of Egypt, a post that was offered to him by Winston Churchill, he would have shown that he did not possess the fiber of the true adventurer. Adventure has little to do with risking one's life, otherwise the Foreign Legion would be full of adventurers. "Adventure begins with being uprooted, and at the end the adventurer becomes a madman, a king or a solitary; it is the realism of magic—*le réalisme de la féerie.*"

For Malraux, adventure was an attitude of mind and a magic destiny.

The trouble, of course, was to find the right adventure. Ideally, it would take place in a little-known, legendary, and untraveled country, where the landscape was not totally dissimilar to the one described by Rimbaud in *The Drunken Boat,* and where the natives were hospitable only to adventurers. Some gunrunning was perhaps called for. Rimbaud had made gunrunning respectable. Cities and temples never seen before by Western eyes would be explored and looted, and all these extravagant adventures would take place somewhere in the Far East, which had haunted him since his childhood. The dreams began to take shape when it occurred to him that just as all the pilgrim roads leading to Santiago de Compostella were studded with cathedrals and chapels, so along the Royal Road of Cambodia there must be great temples and chapels and rest houses all the way from the Dangrek mountains to Angkor. This road had never been fully explored, and there was therefore a possibility of coming upon great treasure. Khmer art was coming into fashion, and American museums were vying with one another for possession of Khmer sculptures, which were then being exported through Saigon with the connivance of customs officials.

About this time, in early 1923, the great scholar and art critic Alfred Salmony came to visit them. A heavily built man, with a heavy face and heavily lidded eyes, he was one of those men who lost all their heaviness in the presence of a work of art. What especially interested him was the art of protohistoric Asia, the strange forms produced by the tribes on the shores of Lake Baikal and the frontiers of China. He had a vast knowledge of all the other arts, and had recently become interested in comparative art. There must be some reason why a Wei dynasty *bodhisattva,* with bent knees and bowed head, carved in northern China in the early sixth century, so closely resembles a Romanesque statue carved in the early twelfth century in Spain or France. Why does a Gandhara sculpture sometimes look as though it comes from a workshop in Athens? A Chinese urn of the Shang dynasty may resemble an African mask. Why? There were no simple answers, but at least one could set the photographs together and study them.

Alfred Salmony came armed with photographs, for he was preparing an exhibition of comparative art. As he spread them out on a table, Malraux and his wife were both excited by the spectacle of so many complicities and alliances in the history of art. The photographs demonstrated better than anything else the ultimate unity of art, the strange companionship of artists in all ages and all countries, all working, so it seemed, in very much the same way to obtain the same ends. The Wei and Romanesque sculptors worshipped different gods, but these gods wore the same disguise. A new and powerful element entered the lives of Malraux and his wife. Henceforth both of them were to be consumed with a passion for comparative art, seeking out those profound resemblances and making their own discoveries. "We were overwhelmed," Clara Malraux wrote in her memoirs. "When Salmony went away, he left some of his precious photographs with us, and he also left with us—within us—the intuition of a new way of grasping the world."

For the rest of his life Malraux found one of his greatest pleasures in doing exactly what Alfred Salmony had done. He would gather photographs of paintings and sculptures, and put them together according to subtle arrangements of his own, until the problems raised by one would be answered by another. He would marry them or set them in violent conflict, turn them upside down, erase some details in order to emphasize something that seemed more important, playing with them like a man shuffling cards. But the purpose was a serious one: close study of photographs of works of art was to give him a vast knowledge of art *as a simultaneous experience.* Dates, derivations, influences, even the names of the artists meant very little to him. What concerned him was the work of art stripped of all its scholarly adornments. He was an explorer of art, not a scholar.

The plan to mount an expedition to Cambodia in search of treasure was at first very tentative, with no clear outlines, as tempting and illusory as the smile carved on the face of a Cambodian goddess. Malraux and his wife visited the Musée Guimet, which possessed a small but important collection of Khmer art, studied Lunet de la Jonquière's three-volume *Inventaire descriptif des monuments du Cambodge,* which described the temples and ruins of Cambodia as they were known in 1911, attended the Opera to see the Royal Cambodian dancers whose hieratic gestures were so strange to the Parisians that they burst into laughter, and peered over maps and traced out a provisional route. They read deeply in the works of Pierre Loti, and formed some surprising conclusions about life in Indochina. Even then it was still a dream or a childhood game played with no hope of realization.

The final decision to undertake the expedition was precipitated by the knowledge that the paper fortune Malraux had amassed by manipulations on the stock exchange had suddenly vanished. Unwise speculations in Mexican mining properties led to financial disaster. For two years they had been living in a dream world, serenely observing the increase in their fortunes on ticker-tape machines, but now they were ruined. The journey to Indochina was no longer a game; it had become a necessity.

On October 12, 1923, they sailed for Indochina from Marseilles. In their possession they had first-class tickets, enough money to tide them over for two or three months, an official document proclaiming that they had received permission to embark on an archaeological mission which was never clearly defined, a small portable electric flashlight, and a dozen saws to be used to cut statues away from the temple walls. The letter announcing that they were *chargés de mission* gave them authority to requisition bullocks and carts, but this was the extent of the authority granted to them. Malraux had already settled on the temple which would be the scene of his operations. It was the small ruined temple of Banteay Srei, built in reddish sandstone, about twenty miles east of Angkor, and reached by a winding path through the jungle. It had been discovered by a certain Lieutenant Marek in 1914, and therefore did not appear in Lunet de la Jonquière's inventory. Mentioned only briefly in the available literature, this small temple subsequently proved to be one of the supreme jewels of Khmer art. With unerring instinct which derived from long study, Malraux had found a fabulous treasure.

It was the usual long and uneventful journey to the Far East, with all the disadvantages of traveling first-class. The *S.S. Angkor* of the Messageries Maritimes Line was one of those ships in which the first-class passengers traveled like kings and all the rest like coolies. Luc Durtain, who wrote magnificently about Indochina, described these first-class passengers as a strange assortment of "the elegant, the obtuse, and the cunning." For André and Clara Malraux, who were elegant and perhaps cunning, the journey was a succession of enchanting explosions. They had dreamed interminably about the Orient, and the reality was even more violent and more beautiful than their dreams.

Djibuti delighted them because it was associated with the poet Arthur Rimbaud and because at nightfall naked girls danced before them in the shadow of beehive huts; then came Colombo and the honey-scented island of Penang, where Clara Malraux was nearly drowned in a flash flood, and Singapore with its Victorian monuments, the cathedral set on a green lawn on the foreshore, and the tables at the Raffles Hotel weighed down with *rijstafel*. Saigon was a steaming checkerboard of green, and Hanoi, the administrative capital of French Indochina, was equally delectable and equally improbable. At Hanoi was to be found the headquarters of the École Française d'Extrême Orient, the agency supervising all archaeological explorations. Here Malraux gave the official letter he had received from the Colonial Office to Léonard Aurousseau, the acting director of the school. Malraux described him in a vivid scene in his novel *The Royal Way,* where he appears under the name of Albert Ramèges. The young archaeologist Claude Vannec confronts the old scholar Ramèges as though they were residents of different planets, at once hostile and determined to make friendly gestures to each other, each lost in his own world. Vannec explains his theory of the metamorphosis of works of art. "For me," he says, "museums are places where the works of the past lie sleeping, living out their historical lives, waiting for the day when the artist will summon them into real existence." The artist has the power to resurrect these ancient works of art by pouring his own breath on them. When the myths of the present coincide with the myths of the past, then the act of resurrection takes place.

The old scholar can make nothing of these theories, for he has almost no interest in the processes by which a work of art is reborn in our own time, and so he comes to the conclusion that Vannec is unlearned and inexperienced. Though he validates the letter from the Colonial Office, he does so with reluctance, insisting that no stones must be removed; and when Vannec hints that he has come precisely in order to remove the stones, the acting director shows no disposition to argue with him. He has his own ways of ensuring that the stones will be left unharmed.

Ramèges is portrayed with some heart. Vannec clearly dislikes him, but both men retain a kind of grudging admiration for each other. There is little doubt that the scene faithfully conveys Malraux's meeting with Léonard Aurousseau.

There were congenial meetings with a French scholar in the following week when Henri Parmentier accompanied them during their journey from Saigon to Pnom Penh along the Mekong River. He was by far the greatest authority on Khmer art, the author of many special studies, and one of the few people who had examined the temple at Banteay Srei. His drawings and photographs of the temple had appeared in a lengthy monograph called *The Art of Indravarman,* which Malraux had carefully read and pondered in Paris. Parmentier was one of those vivid, ebullient men who are always amused by life even when they are most serious. He wore a white goatee, and talked enchantingly about all the misinformation related by French novelists about Indochina. He had no high opinion of Pierre Loti, who spoke of vultures crowding together on the branches of a banana tree. "If he had looked at a banana tree, he would know that their branches bend too much to support the weight of a single vulture." André and Clara got on well with Parmentier, who was kindly and humorous, and disposed to regard Malraux with affection and even a little envy, for Clara remembers him saying about her husband: "So young and so wealthy, and he makes such good use of his time. And what disinterestedness!" Her husband was not, of course, so very disinterested.

At Pnom Penh the old scholar helped them to choose their equipment for the journey through the jungle, approved of Clara's tropical uniform designed in Paris, and was responsible for giving them the boy Xa as guide and general factotum. Xa was an excellent cook, he could bake bread, sew and iron, and he was also an inveterate gambler. He had in fact been sent to prison for gambling, and when Malraux was warned against him by a meddlesome sergeant of gendarmerie, he told the boy: "I don't give a damn about what the sergeant has just told me. Do well by us—that is all we ask of you. And here is an advance on your wages!"

They decided they would not sleep out in tents: instead, they would simply erect four poles and spread canvas over them. They bought mosquito netting and rubber buckets, stoves, saucepans, axes, hammers, lamps and rope, and they were so busy buying things that they saw very little of Pnom Penh, though they had time enough to visit the museum, which was small and beautiful. The official who accompanied them on their tour gazed indifferently at the sculptures, and they wondered why he was not moved by them, for nowhere on earth was there a greater collection of Khmer art. By this time Louis Chevasson, Malraux's friend from his school days, had arrived to join them, and since he had a practical turn of mind, and was by nature deliberate and cautious, he was to prove a useful ally. Clara disliked him, but her dislike was probably no more than a reflection of her refusal to share her husband with anyone.

From Pnom Penh they took the riverboat to Siem Reap, the pleasant, sleepy, sun-baked village which serves as the port of call for the great complex of temples and lotus-shaped towers of Angkor Wat. They spent a day visiting Angkor Wat, and the next morning set out for Banteay Srei on horseback, with four buffalo carts to carry the statues they intended to pry loose from the small ruined temple lost in the jungle. Clara, who was accustomed to horses, was amused by the sight of her husband's long legs trailing along the ground, for the Cambodian horses were very small. She suspected rightly that he had never ridden on horseback before.

Soon they were in the forest, following a slender trail which was so narrow that they had to follow one another in a single column. Xa rode ahead, then came Clara, Malraux, and Chevasson, and the four bullock carts, each with two drivers wearing only loincloths, made up the rear. They were an army of twelve people in the half-darkness of a Cambodian forest, which was rarely traveled except by the local villagers. The two-wheeled bullock carts creaked, and sometimes the lianas hanging from the trees brushed against their faces; mosquitoes gathered around them in clouds, and the monkeys screamed on the high branches; and there were places where the forest seemed to be impassable, a vast encircling screen cutting them off from any hope of seeing civilization again. Sometimes, too, they wondered whether they would ever see daylight again, so dark was the canopy of leaves above their heads.

It was not, of course, a particularly arduous journey; if they had come during the monsoon season, they would have found no trail at all, but now it was winter, the best time for traveling in Indochina. Here and there the forest opened out to reveal grass huts raised on stilts set amid small untidy orchards and rice fields. At the village of Rohal, knowing that they were close to the ruined temple, they made inquiries and learned to their horror that none of the villagers knew anything about Banteay Srei. For a few moments they felt they had

come on one of those expeditions which are doomed to failure from
the beginning, and it was some time before Xa was able to convince
the villagers that a temple did in fact exist. An old man offered to
lead the way to some nearby ruins. By this time it was growing late, and
they went to sleep. They were up at the first dawn, very eager, for the
prize was now within reach.

Banteay Srei was only about a mile away, but it was one of the
longest miles they had ever traveled, for the forest was now very dense,
the trail had vanished, and the heat was suffocating. The old man from
the village went on ahead, cutting through the undergrowth with a
machete, his gray body silver with sweat. Then, late in the morning,
when they had almost given up hope of seeing the temple, they came
to a small clearing with the strangest ruins they had ever seen—nothing
more than a heap of red sandstone overgrown with thick moss and
sprawling trees growing out of it. There were three broken towers, two
or three times the height of a man. There were crumbling walls. There
were statues with their faces buried in the soft clay. There were serpents
guarding the treasure, and Clara saw a magnificent emerald-green
serpent coiled at her feet. The path through the forest led straight to a
delicately carved ornamental gateway so beautiful that it took their
breath away.

They set to work to disengage some of the statues still standing, con-
centrating on the bas-reliefs of two *devas,* guardian goddesses of great
beauty and elegance. They were full-bosomed, crowned with jewels,
and their long skirts hung from heavily ornamented girdles. Half-
dreaming, their heads inclined a little, one hand raised in blessing,
aware of their beauty, these *devas* could only have been carved in an
age of great artistic achievement. Banteay Srei, which means "the
citadel of the maiden," was constructed in 967 A.D. in the last year of
the reign of King Rajendravarman, at the very highest period of Khmer
art.

While he was clambering over the ruins, Malraux was not in the
least interested in artistic periods. He was oppressed by the dangers
and difficulties of the enterprise. The cross-saws broke one after another, for the *devas* were firmly embedded in the walls. He hated the
slimy moss, the innumerable insects, the snakes crawling under the

stones. "Adventure," he said later, "is not so much a way to exalt or amuse oneself; instead, it is crushing ants beneath the palms of one's hands; it is insects, reptiles, repulsive dangers confronted at every step by someone making his way through the brush."

He overcame his repulsion sufficiently to organize a well-conducted series of stratagems with the help of chisels and ropes. It was slow work, and took the better part of two sweltering days. On the third day two *devas* and five smaller fragments were placed in camphorwood chests on the buffalo carts. The smaller fragments, representing men sitting cross-legged in meditation, lacked the beauty of the *devas*. Their fortunes depended upon the sale of the *devas,* for the smaller fragments were comparatively unimportant.

With the camphorwood chests securely locked, they returned without further incident to Siem Reap. It was only a nine hour journey, for they had no difficulty following a familiar trail. The buffalo drivers were paid off, the chests were loaded into the hold of the riverboat, and they set off for Pnom Penh, which they reached late in the evening of December 24. It was Christmas Eve and the churchbells were ringing.

About midnight, while they were still sleeping, three plain-clothes officers of the Sûreté boarded the riverboat and demanded to see the captain. They explained that they had received information from Siem Reap concerning certain sculptures stolen from a temple and it would be necessary to confront Malraux and Chevasson, who were accordingly awakened, taken down to the hold, and ordered to open the camphorwood chests. Since they were in no position to disobey, they did what they were told. They went down into the dark hold where the chests were opened by the flickering light of flashlights. There was no doubt that they contained the statues. Clara was amused because the opening of the chests was accompanied by little tinkling sounds, the locks being provided, as so often in Indochina, with musical boxes. There followed a short, sharp interrogation, and then the plain-clothes officers of the Sûreté announced that Malraux and Chevasson must remain in Pnom Penh and hold themselves at the disposition of the authorities.

The following months were among the longest they ever lived

through. Clara came down with dengue fever, and Malraux too suffered from intermittent fevers, which made him look drawn and emaciated. They stayed in the Manolis Hotel which, while being the best in Pnom Penh at that time, was seedy and down-at-heel. Happily, Xa remained in their service, and through him they were able to meet many Cambodians and to remain in touch with the silent world around them, for the French in Pnom Penh carefully avoided them. It was agreed that Chevasson should take the blame, since he was not married. If Malraux could return to France, he would be in a position to find lawyers and exert sufficient influence to bring about Chevasson's release. They all knew that the case would proceed in typical Indochinese fashion: it would be slow, difficult and confused, with the main issues unsettled even when the judgment was handed down. But none guessed how slow and difficult it would be.

Months passed, while the police and the prosecution made their laborious inquiries. The Paris police conducted a detailed search into the backgrounds of Malraux and Chevasson. They learned little about Chevasson, for he lived quietly and soberly and earned his living as a clerk in a bookstore. The dossier on Malraux was voluminous and included a documented survey of his family, his friends and acquaintances, his books and his work for various publishers, his marriage to Clara Goldschmidt, and his sources of income. There was even a description of his apartment with its cubist paintings. There was nothing particularly damaging in the dossier, although it was evident that Malraux had been living a bohemian life and associating with other bohemians. This dossier was sent to Pnom Penh and the relevant portions were produced at the trial for the use of the defense and the prosecution, who could make what use of it they pleased. Since the police were inclined to regard all bohemians as potential criminals, they also sent a secret dossier for the use of the prosecution alone. In the secret dossier Malraux was described as a dangerous revolutionary.

Malraux learned of the existence of the second dossier much later. "It is the classic procedure," he wrote. "They made two investigations, one administrative, the other judicial. In case of need—that is to say, in a case in which I am involved—the administrative investigation is also a political one. The administrative dossier, or the impression conveyed by it, or the impression 'that it should convey,' is communicated to the judges, but remains carefully concealed from the defense." This secret document was to have an extraordinary effect on his fortunes, for when at last the case came up for trial, the judge who read it handed down a savage sentence against the weight of the evidence.

From the beginning Malraux and Chevasson realized that they had little to hope for. The colonial administration was determined to make an example of them. They had almost no money, very little influence, and no illusions about their fate at the hands of a corrupt colonial administration. In their enforced leisure they were to learn a good deal about this corrupt administration, which was universally detested by the Indochinese. At the end of March Clara took an overdose of sleeping tablets and was taken to the hospital, and although she had hoped in this way to bring their affairs to a crisis and to ensure that she would be set free and return to France, the cure was worse than the disease. For several weeks she was seriously ill, and her weight dropped to eighty pounds. The government decided to release her, and an official accordingly came to the hospital and read out a long statement, drawn up in the appropriate legal form, stating that there was no case for prosecution. Early in July 1924, shortly before the trial opened, she was driven in an ambulance to Saigon. From there she sailed for France in one of the ships of the Messageries Maritimes.

The trial opened at eight o'clock in the morning on July 16, in the court at Pnom Penh, nearly seven months after Malraux and Chevasson were placed under the disposition of the court. Judge Jodin had recently arrived from Pondicherry in the company of a mulatto mistress. An abrupt, harsh man, his principal aim in life was his advancement in the judicial profession. Maître Giordani, the public prosecutor, was one of those quiet, outwardly gentle men whose indolent manner conceals a savage verdict on humanity: he would always ask for the heaviest sentences in a soft voice. Malraux was defended by Maître De Parceveaux, and Chevasson by Maître Lortat-Jacob. There were three sessions: the morning was occupied by the interrogation, the afternoon by a parade of witnesses, and on the following morning there would be the closing pleas of the prosecution and the defense.

From the beginning Malraux went over to the attack. In answering the questions of Judge Jodin he made no effort to conceal his contempt for the court. The judge seemed to be paying more attention to the young women in the gallery than to the matter at hand. The evidence, as presented by the public prosecutor, was damaging. The camphor-wood chests, found in the hold of the riverboat, were labeled "chemical products" and addressed to Berthet and Charrière, general importers and exporters in Saigon. They were certainly not chemical products: they were in fact objects of art, belonging to the patrimony of Indo-china. In his quiet voice Maître Giordani demanded a penalty so severe that any future depredators would think twice before embarking on a similar adventure.

A correspondent of the principal Saigon newspaper, *L'Impartial*, described the impression created by the accused in an article that appeared on July 22. He wrote:

> Malraux is a tall, thin, clean-shaven young man whose features are illuminated by two extremely penetrating eyes. He is very facile in his speech and defends himself with a sharpness that reveals in him unquestionable qualities of energy and tenacity. In addition he appears to possess considerable culture.
>
> Chevasson, the second accused, is much more self-effacing. A humble employee of a bookstore, he seems to have very little to do with the affair, while continually insisting that he alone was responsible, admitting all the evidence, and ascribing to himself the sole authorship of the crime, while Malraux denies that he had any part in it, saying that he never knew Chevasson in France and met him for the first time at Banteay Srei.

Unhappily for Malraux the judge was aware that Chevasson had gone to the same school as Malraux and that they had known each other for a long time. The small, sturdy, self-controlled Chevasson, sitting quietly in the dock and admitting everything; the fiery, electric Malraux, who denied everything—they were a study in contrasts, and it did not need a judicial intelligence to recognize that the defense had committed a tactical error of the first magnitude.

During the afternoon came the cross-examination of the witnesses.

The manager of the bungalow at Siem Reap described their brief appearance at the bungalow. He was followed by a certain Crémazy, the administrative officer at Siem Reap, who said he had received a coded telegram from the Colonial Office ordering him to keep a close watch on Malraux's party. The telegram arrived only a few hours before Malraux reached Siem Reap, and he had immediately summoned the local police, ordering them to report on every movement made by the party. The exact terms of the coded telegram could not be divulged; it belonged to the "administrative dossier" and was not to be communicated to the defense "because of its confidential political character."

The third witness was Henri Parmentier, who had been sent to Banteay Srei in January to report on the ruined temple and especially on the damage caused by the removal of the statues. Genuinely fond of Malraux, he was inclined to minimize the affair, and went out of his way to praise him for his skill and intelligence as an "amateur archaeologist." Parmentier was a renowned authority on Khmer art and spoke with an authority possessed by no one else in the courtroom.

In its closing arguments the defense raised one issue that was never satisfactorily solved. Since Banteay Srei had never been officially classified as an historic monument, and was perhaps not within the jurisdiction of the French government in Indochina, how could anyone be prosecuted for entering an abandoned site and making off with a few blocks of stone? Does a man commit a crime when he picks up an object abandoned by everyone? The prosecution glided gently over these questions, and the defense merely mentioned them in passing, as though there was nothing to be gained by an inquiry which must in the nature of things be long and exhausting.

The judge was satisfied that a crime had been committed. He sentenced Malraux to three years imprisonment. Chevasson, because he was evidently less culpable, was sentenced to eighteen months imprisonment. As for the sculptures, the judge ruled that they belonged to the government.

❧ *The Trial* ❧

When Clara Malraux arrived in Paris, she was still weak and exhausted from her experiences in Indochina. She knew what had to be done—she must organize all available forces to bring about the release of her husband and Chevasson—but she had no idea how to go about it. Penniless, ill, so thin that she could scarcely recognize herself in a mirror, she confronted her family, begged for their help, and was shown the door. They would do nothing for her. Her brothers were up in arms, her mother was suffering from nervous prostration, the family doctor was of the opinion that Clara was mentally ill and should be removed to the same rest home where her mother was staying. Scarcely knowing what she was doing, Clara went to the rest home and found herself caught in a trap.

It was like a scene from *The Cabinet of Dr. Caligari,* a film she knew well. Three doctors faced her across a table, urging her to submit to a long period of enforced rest and treatment, while every fiber of her being told her she was sane and had urgent business to attend to. The doctors were hinting that they had the power to certify her insane; they would prefer her to submit voluntarily to their orders. She suddenly flung herself from the room and raced across the garden. One of her brothers had stationed himself at the gate and brought her back to the doctors in triumph, assuring her that she was mad. The doctors whispered among themselves: she was proving her own insanity by her abrupt departure. She said: "Have you the right to keep me here?" They answered that they had no right, but proposed to force her to surrender to them. Then she stood against the wall with her arms spread out, not in the gesture of a crucifixion, but like an owl nailed to the wall, saying over and over again: "You have no right to keep

75

me here." Finally they let her out into a Paris which had become even more menacing.

She was in despair, for she knew no judges or high officials who might intercede for her husband. For weeks the newspapers had been amusing themselves at the expense of "the robber of Angkor," who was usually described as a young bohemian who wore strange clothes and manifested a contempt for society which had led him to robbery as a way of life. His character was despicable, his writings were worthless, and society was well rid of him. Clara had been shown the clippings in her mother's house, and she knew the power of newspapers to destroy people's lives.

Help was much closer than she could possibly have dreamed. She had arrived in Marseilles on August 7, 1924. Two days later there appeared in the newspaper *L'Éclair* an open letter signed by René-Louis Doyon. Exasperated by the sniping attacks against Malraux with their malicious inaccuracies, he praised the newspaper for at least keeping to the facts and went on to deliver a reasoned plea for quashing the conviction. Doyon's letter and an introductory note covered two columns of the newspaper:

A PLEA FOR ANDRE MALRAUX

Our readers have not forgotten a recent item about a young man of letters, poet, essayist and critic, who robbed the temples of Angkor and was arrested while crossing the Siamese frontier in possession of over a thousand kilograms of statues and bas-reliefs, etc. worth over a million francs. André Malraux was brought before the court at Pnom Penh and sentenced to three years imprisonment.

Monsieur R.-L. Doyon, the publisher of *Connaissance,* where Malraux had his literary beginnings, has sent us a moving plea for his former collaborator. We willingly publish his letter, even though we have opposing views on most of the points raised by him. . . .

Dear Sir,

The press has been particularly aggressive, gratuitously ironical, not to say evilly disposed toward a young writer who has recently made an unexpected appearance in the public domain, one which no doubt he did not desire and was certainly not in conformity with the judgments passed on him in the public press. I am referring to André Malraux, about whom only *L'Éclair* published an accurate and discreet account without any acrimony. For this reason I would express the wish that your influence and widespread circulation might serve to modify opinions and judgments made on him before they become final.

As you correctly stated, André Malraux had his literary beginnings at *La Connaissance,* being at first concerned with bibliographical research; in all this he showed an astonishing self-assurance and an amazing erudition. Correct, reserved, without the least emotion, he showed himself to be a man possessed of considerable intellectual energy and an over-whelming affection, more for Lautréamont than for Rimbaud, more for Max Jacob than for Tristan Tzara. He read me his first poems long before they received the honor of being printed in a rare and luxurious edition. As he read the poems with a certain emotion, he emphasized the intellectuality of their lyricism. He was learned in financial affairs, and it is certain that he dreamed of conquests and treasures and impor-tant affairs. He began with taste, culture and art; and perhaps he was dedicated to making money: the one excuses the other. I am deeply afraid that his judges, like his contemners, knowing nothing about his intellectualism and passionate aestheticism, have judged this young man to be a thief falling within the jurisdiction of the law; and this is regrettable. Malraux had studied Angkor, its design, its treasures. From this there was only a step to dreaming of an adventure unfortunately involv-ing theft and pillage, the daring step of a man who is *the enemy of all actions which are not the sisters of dreams.* . . .

May one thus without blushing present a reasoned defense of one of our colleagues, an artist of taste, an author after all, and a young, *very young,* man, now threatened with the prospect of wasting his life away in a country and in a prison with dubious hygiene? May one pardon a daring that has

a certain elegance, an audacity that wears the badge of courage
and lightheartedness? I go further: I am even afraid that
a severe and highly publicized verdict may lead him to become
the victim of religious persecution. I would be very happy
if *L'Éclair* would demand a full review of his case. It may
be that the after effects of this dangerous adventure will be
the gravest punishment inflicted on an ambition now
deprived of splendid aims. I am not a friend of Malraux,
who has none. But I condemn the injustice of the comments
that the press has abundantly bestowed on him, thus
aggravating a sentence rare in this country. I hope you will
support this appeal for justice on behalf of a poet and a man
of true distinction. After all, we have so few of them! . . .

Doyon's letter has been quoted at considerable length because it
shows him struggling with his ideas about Malraux, forcing himself to
examine his former *chineur* and collaborator with fresh eyes. He was
writing with elegance and skill, in the somewhat strained manner associated with the Boulevard Saint-Germain. He did not especially like
Malraux, and had been hurt when Malraux left him to work with
Simon Kra. Inevitably, his repetitions betray him, for he finds himself
constantly reverting to the portrait of a cold, impassive intelligence
given to vast ambitions. "I am not a friend of Malraux, who has none."
What especially disconcerted him was the thought that a man of great
promise might die in a jail cell in Indochina.

If Clara Malraux had read this letter the day it appeared, she would
have been less disturbed. She went to live in a run-down hotel kept by
a former Goldschmidt servant on the Place Clichy, where the hotels
had the reputation of being flophouses, and worse. From here she set
out to arouse everyone with the story of her husband's plight. She sent
off letters and telegrams, and was continually on the telephone. One
telegram went to Malraux's father, who was then living at Orleans;
another to Marcel Arland at Varennes; a letter went to Max Jacob and
found him in Brittany. She telephoned Paul Monin, a young lawyer
she had met on the ship, a man with powerful connections in Indochina. On the third or fourth day after her arrival, she went to call on

André Breton, the surrealist poet. Early in the morning, with Paris still dark, she took a taxi half way across the city, determined to see this man whom she scarcely knew, grateful to him because he was one of the very few who had written to her offering his help. At first the concierge would not let her into the house, but somehow she succeeded in climbing up to his apartment. Once awake, he immediately plunged into the conspiracy, comforted her, surrounded her with exactly the right kind of atmosphere, helped her to raise money, introduced her to his friends, and saw that she never gave way to despair. Soon from being a waif in danger of being shut up in a rest home, she became a center of attention.

Malraux's father hurried to Paris, deeply puzzled; he had known nothing about the affair until the telegram arrived from Clara. "He arrived in the early afternoon," Clara reported, "with the grave and afflicted air suitable to the father of a man who has been condemned— a condemnation of which he had heard only two days before." He rallied quickly, made sensible suggestions, took a deeper interest in his daughter-in-law than ever before, and escorted her around Paris. Paul Monin came to see her. He had a chiseled, cleancut face, a long mouth, penetrating blue eyes, and one of those remarkably low foreheads sometimes found among the French aristocracy, although he came from a bourgeois family in Lyons. He had long ago reached the conclusion that the French government of Indochina was rotten with corruption and decay, and he pleased Clara when he remarked that she and Malraux were "spotless souls" compared with all the other Frenchmen busily exploiting the Indochinese. Monin was on a very brief visit to France. Soon he would return to Saigon, meet Malraux, and together they would plan an attack in depth against the colonial government.

The first fruits of the meeting with Breton and Monin was a brief manifesto, drawn up by Clara, to be signed by as many well-known writers as possible. The manifesto read:

> The undersigned, deeply concerned by the sentence passed on André Malraux, have confidence in the consideration with which justice commonly regards all those who help to increase the intellectual heritage of the nation. They are eager to attest

to the intelligence and genuine literary value of this writer whose youth and work already accomplished give rise to the highest expectations. They would profoundly deplore the loss resulting from a punishment that would prevent André Malraux from accomplishing what we can all rightfully expect from him.

With the help of Marcel Arland an astonishing number of eminent signatories was found. When the manifesto appeared in *Les Nouvelles Littéraires* on September 6, 1924, there were twenty-three signatures, among them the most famous names in French literature. They were Edmond Jaloux, Jacques Rivière, Raymond Gallimard, Pascal Pia, André Gide, Max Jacob, Philippe Soupault, André Houlaire, François Mauriac, François Le Grix, Florent Fels, André Desson, Pierre Mac Orlan, Maurice Martin du Gard, Louis Aragon, André Breton, Jean Paulhan, Charles du Bos, Pierre de Lanux, Marcel Arland, André Maurois, Gaston Gallimard, and Guy de Pourtalès.

Of these perhaps half had met Malraux, and no more than four or five could be said to have known him well. At this time he had written one small book published in an edition of a hundred copies.

Although this was the most widely known manifesto, there were many others. Following the long letter from René-Louis Doyon, *L'Éclair* published another signed by Marcel Arland, André Breton, François Mauriac and Jean Paulhan, and on August 16 André Breton took up the cudgels alone in a long and moving letter printed in *Les Nouvelles Littéraires*. Later the testimonials came in showers, more signatures were added, and Clara could congratulate herself that she had opened up an unsuspected reservoir of sympathy for her husband. She did not forget Doyon, the first to proclaim his belief that Malraux was innocent or at least undeserving of punishment. As soon as she read his letter, she ran to his small shop and flung her arms around him. "I do not blush often," he wrote later, "but this time I blushed."

Breton's wife Simone and Doyon's wife Marcelle became her fellow conspirators. Because it was necessary to raise money to keep Malraux alive in Indochina—hotel bills were mounting and legal costs were skyrocketting—Clara arranged to sell all the possessions left in her mother's house, all that remained of their paintings, sculptures, and

African masks, and most of their books. Malraux and Chevasson had moved to Saigon, where the appeal against Judge Jodin's sentence would be heard later in the year. They were in good spirits, for the shock of the sentence had worn off and they had hopes of being acquitted in the court of appeal, or at least of having to endure a much lighter sentence. Meanwhile what Doyon called "a veritable conflagration of protest" was continuing from Paris. Unknown to Malraux, the Paris police under instructions from the French Colonial Office were deliberately planting stories about him in the foreign press to counteract these protests.

On September 21, 1924, the readers of *The New York Times* read a completely apocryphal version of the events leading up to Malraux's arrest:

FRENCH SLEUTH TRAILS MAN TO ANNAM JUNGLE, DROPS HIS DISGUISE AND ARRESTS ROBBER OF PARIS MUSEUMS AND NATIVE TEMPLES

PARIS, August 25 (Associated Press Correspondence).

This is the story of a Paris detective who traveled half way round the world for his quarry, and finally, in the dense jungle of Annam, threw aside his disguise and arrested his man, who is now doing three years in jail.

An antiquary named Malraux was under the observance of the Paris police, suspected of being responsible for thefts from French museums. It was thought he had designs on collections of antiques in one of the French provinces, and as a matter of routine a detective was assigned to trail Malraux and a companion, wherever he might go.

The pair went to a seaport and there took passage on a steamer for Saigon, French Indo-China, and the detective went along in the same vessel. He did not even have time to buy a change of clothing, but made friends among the crew and borrowed what he needed.

At Saigon Malraux and his friend posed as rich travelers,

anxious to see the country, while the detective kept in the background. He had, however, made known his mission to the local French authorities, and when Malraux asked for guides to the remote districts of Annam, the detective was among the natives assigned, but cleverly disguised.

The party scoured the region of Angkor, rich in holy relics and fine specimens of old Chinese art, and Malraux and his companion bought freely. Also they did not hesitate, conditions being favorable, to rob Annamite temples of particularly fine specimens.

The border of Siam was not far away, and the collectors, having decided to leave the country by that route, called up the native guides and dismissed them.

Then the Paris detective had his day. The humble disguise was cast aside, the French policeman stepped out, and Malraux and his friend were placed under arrest.

In this lengthy report to *The New York Times* not a single sentence was true, while most of the statements were ludicrous. There could be no doubt about the origin of the report, for only one person emerged with credit—a detective from Paris.

Newspapers all over the world were reporting the strange affair of the purloined statues with varying degrees of misinformation. Even in Saigon, where the facts were readily available, misinformation was widespread. *L'Impartial,* edited by Henry Chavigny de la Chevrotière, was far from being impartial. This newspaper led the attack against Malraux in a series of front-page editorials designed to show him in the worst possible light. Financed through an illegal arrangement with the government, the newspaper represented official opinion and always defended official interests. Malraux was described as a thief, a liar, and a dangerous source of corruption, who had grown rich trading in Khmer works of art. In fact he was desperately poor, had sold no works of art, and his enemies were more corrupt than he could ever have dreamed.

Henry Chavigny de la Chevrotière was the assumed name of an adventurer who had acquired considerable wealth and power in Cochinchina. A quarter French, a quarter Senegalese and half Annamite, he

had risen from obscurity to become one of the chief advisers and bene-
ficiaries of the government. He was mercenary and unscrupulous, an
accomplished philanderer who had long ago abandoned his wife and
six children for a succession of mistresses. Blackmailer, *agent provocateur*, stool pigeon, he represented almost to perfection the type of the
corrupt official. In 1917, when he was called up for service in the
French Army, he employed every available ruse to avoid being in-
ducted, and since exemption was usually given for fathers of large
families he signed an affidavit claiming he was the sole support of his
six children. Since the claim was patently untrue, he was brought before a court-martial but was released through the influence of powerful
friends. In 1924 he was forty-one years old, a veteran of innumerable
intrigues, and a past master in the art of defamation. The full extent of
Chavigny's corruption was still unknown to Malraux, who was so perplexed by the vehemence of the attacks against him that he gave an
interview to one of the correspondents of *L'Impartial* in the hope of
bringing the attacks to an end.

The interview, which appeared in the issue of September 16, is a
somewhat puzzling document which shows signs of having been
severely edited by someone who had never met Malraux. It appeared
under the deliberately misleading heading "The Affair of the Angkor
Statues—The Declarations of M. André Malraux," and began promis-
ingly:

> He has blond hair swept back, a pale complexion, eyes which
> are now blazing with fire, now veiled with melancholy—per-
> haps also with regret. Such is the appearance of André Malraux,
> man of letters and lover of art.

Since the blond hair was a product of the interviewer's imagination,
it may be assumed that there were other fictions embedded in the interview. According to the reporter, Malraux claimed that he would soon
receive a petition signed by forty-eight leading French authors, including Anatole France and Claude Farrère. He spoke of his book *Paper
Moons*, which had appeared in a limited edition of a hundred copies
with illustrations by Picasso, and since then he had written and pub-

lished a rather specialized book on a metaphysical subject. "I am rich," he is reported to have said, "and I can permit myself the luxury of these literary essays. I also write for the *Revue Archéologique,* the *Mercure de France* and the *Nouvelle Revue Française.*" When the reporter asked why he had come to Indochina, he explained that he was sent by the Colonial Office and was under the high patronage of the École Française d'Extrême Orient. He had been commanded to write a study of Siamese and Khmer art and to conduct delicate negotiations over the sale of the art collection of the Siamese Prince D——, the entire collection being worth fifty thousand dollars, a considerable sum for art works in those days. Asked about Chevasson, he said: "I have known him for a long time, and it is untrue that I ever said I did not know him. He was sent by a commercial house to buy art objects here, and we met at Saigon after my return from Tonkin." Since he claimed to be innocent, the reporter asked him whether he thought there was any reason why he should be under arrest. Malraux answered that he thought it might have something to do with the fact that his father was "the director of one of the largest petroleum companies in the world bearing a name famous on the stock exchange." Finally he said he was incensed when Judge Jodin asked him to recite the first two verses of the *Aeneid* to prove that he knew Latin.

By granting the interview Malraux had offered hostages to fortune, and was in serious danger of being compromised. Chavigny added some biting editorial comments, and Malraux replied to them with a still more biting request for an explanation of why he had printed the heading "The Affair of the Angkor Statues," since Banteay Srei was a long way from Angkor. Under French law Chavigny was obliged to print Malraux's reply on the front page. The dispute continued, becoming increasingly bitter, for Malraux reminded Chavigny of his court martial and Chavigny countered with another long article under the heading "The Malraux-Chevasson Affair—The Theft of the Bas-Reliefs from Angkor." When the appeal was heard at the high court in Saigon on October 8, *L'Impartial* was more circumspect, perhaps because it was becoming too obvious that the newspaper was attempting to influence the judge. On that day there was merely a brief article announcing that the appeal had been held that day.

During the morning the judge outlined the known facts of the case

at considerable length; during the afternoon the advocate general
Moreau spoke for three hours for the prosecution. Malraux was described as *un vaniteux et un menteur*—a vainglorious man and a liar.
Had not Malraux said he was a *licensié ès lettres* and the son of a
director of the Royal Dutch Oil Company? Both statements were false.
The crime had been premeditated to the last detail; there was not the
least doubt that they had acted in collusion and that Malraux was
"the prime instigator." He went on to pass in review all the steps
Malraux had taken to conceal his traces, and he followed the prisoner's
movements from Paris to Hanoi and so to Saigon and Pnom Penh and
Siem Reap, until the moment when the statues were discovered in the
hold of the riverboat. As for the legal point raised by the defense,
Banteay Srei was in territory ceded by Siam to France in 1907 and by
a decree of the French President the district had been ceded to the King
of Cambodia, a French protectorate. He demanded that the sentence
of three years imprisonment be confirmed, and in addition Malraux
should be deprived of all civil rights. "When he leaves this country,"
the advocate general thundered, "let him bear the double stigma of liar
and thief!"

On the following afternoon the defense lawyers presented their
arguments. Maître Béziat, representing Malraux, examined minute
points of law. There was the question of whether the French President
had the right to cede the territory, since only the French legislature was
empowered to dispose of French territory, and he brought forward a
number of precedents to confirm this view. Then there was the question
of whether or not Banteay Srei was *res delicta,* for it certainly did not
appear in the list of classical monuments and no one had ever claimed
possession of it. It did not fall within the provisions of the law, and he
pointed out that it would have been very easy for Henri Parmentier,
who had briefly examined the ruins, to place it on the list of protected
monuments. To the argument that Malraux was nothing more than a
rapacious adventurer, he opposed the judgment of the leading French
writers, who praised his literary and intellectual gifts. Finally, he put
in evidence the manifesto signed by the most eminent writers in France,
which had appeared in the *Nouvelles Littéraires* during the previous
month.

Maître Gallois-Montbrun, who defended Chevasson, was less disposed to argue points of law and appealed to the court's humanity and mercy. Here were two young men of talent, and should their lives be blighted for doing what all the governors and all the high officials in Indochina had been doing for years? They had all carried statues away; they were all guilty; and none of them was punished. He referred to Chevasson as a *brave petit garçon,* a description which was not likely to please his client. The lawyer's appeal did not fall on deaf ears, for the judge handed down a reduced sentence three weeks later. Malraux would have to endure only a single year of imprisonment, and Chevasson was sentenced to eight months imprisonment. Both prisoners were granted the right to petition for a suspended sentence.

Malraux immediately announced that he would appeal to the Court of Cassation in Paris, the highest appellate court in France. The prisoners were therefore allowed to leave Indochina in order to prepare their pleas. When the *Chantilly* left Saigon at six o'clock in the morning of November 1, 1924, the names of Malraux and Chevasson appeared on the passenger list.

Clara came to meet them at Marseilles, so happy that the long agony had finally come to an end that she was nearly incoherent. They traveled to Paris, visited friends, went to stay with Malraux's father at Orleans, and settled in a small unfurnished apartment near the Gare Montparnasse just above the apartment where Malraux's mother, grandmother, and aunt were staying, for they had finally sold the grocery store at Bondy and were now free to live where they pleased.

There were duties to be performed, and Malraux dutifully performed them. He visited most of the signatories of the manifesto and made a special journey to Saint-Benoît-sur-Loire, where Max Jacob had retired to the seclusion of a monastery, spending his days in prayer. In Saigon Malraux had met Paul Monin, and they had decided upon an adventure even more hazardous than the one that led to Banteay Srei. Together, in Saigon, they would edit a French language newspaper which would speak against the colonial government on behalf of the people of Indochina. Money must be raised, arrangements must be made with French publishers to permit the newspaper to print articles and *feuilletons,* news items, short stories and special supplements. It was hoped that the newspaper would be at least as well produced as *L'Impartial,* and more appealing to the general reader.

In the middle of January, 1925, after barely seven weeks in France, Malraux and his wife set out for Indochina again, traveling third class. To avoid being followed, they slipped off the steamer at Singapore and took the train to Bangkok, suffocating in the heat, at home once more in the Asia they loved and half-feared, while the train chugged through primitive forests and the Chinese passengers spat sunflower seeds. A few days in Bangkok, and then they were off again in a leaking boat to Saigon. Malraux's purposes were very simple: he had come to wage war against the colonial administration and all its corruptions.

≈§ *The Printing Press* ξ≈

When Malraux returned to Indochina early in 1925 in the hope of publishing a newspaper with Paul Monin, he had very little knowledge of the problems confronting him. He knew a good deal about publishing books, but nothing about newspapers. He was familiar with printing, but not with deadlines; he could write a trenchant editorial, but did not know how to manage a business. Nor was Monin, a lawyer with a brilliant analytical mind and a passionate sympathy for the oppressed, any more capable of managing so complex a business as a newspaper. They were like children entering a forest inhabited by hangmen and thieves.

In fact, they succeeded in publishing an excellent newspaper on good paper with fine type and with all the usual features of newspapers: editorials, photographs, news bulletins, wire-service dispatches, articles from "our special correspondent," *feuilletons,* advertisements, and fashion notes. There were even crossword puzzles. Some of the news items were lifted bodily from the *Straits Times* of Singapore or from radio broadcasts, and were not always accurate: straight news was not its forte. Where the paper excelled was in the communication of ideas, particularly ideas about the French colonial government. From the beginning the French authorities in Saigon did everything possible to destroy it, while Henry Chavigny de la Chevrotière, the editor-in-chief and owner of *L'Impartial,* waged unremitting war against it.

The newspaper, which was called *Indochine,* survived by a series of miracles. Some of these miracles were performed by a remarkable journalist called Dejean de la Batie, the son of a French father and an Annamite mother. He was the managing editor, chief make-up man, and the author of many of the articles in the newspaper. He was

previously one of the chief contributors to *L'Echo Annamite,* but at
Monin's urging he gave up an easy job for a much more demanding
one, saying that he could not refuse to work with Frenchmen "who
came rushing to meet the Annamites with open hearts and outstretched
arms, resolved to make themselves the champions of the legitimate demands of the natives."

After many delays, the first issue of *Indochine* appeared on June 17,
1925. The masthead announced that it was a "newspaper for Franco-
Annamite reconciliation." There was a printing of five thousand copies,
and for the first day and the two following days they were distributed
free. Outwardly the eight-page newspaper resembled any other newspaper in Saigon, but it concealed dynamite. The first explosion occurred
in the second issue, in a blistering attack on Maurice Cognacq, the
venal Governor of Cochinchina, who used his high office to acquire a
vast fortune. Malraux's article, which appeared on the front page, skil-
fully parodied Anatole France's *Les Opinions de M. Jérôme Coignard,*
and was entitled "First Letter from Jacques Tournebroche to Jérôme
Coignard," Jacques being Malraux and Coignard being only too evidently Cognacq. Jacques begins mildly with an evocation of happier
days:

> What has happened to those happy days when you softly
> caressed your Catherine, the lace-maker, in shady places, while
> slowly drinking a choice wine? You listened to my father, the
> owner of a cookshop, and there was only a hint of irony in your
> features, and you found much to enjoy. Ancient wisdom, which
> had fled to the mutilated marbles of the Acropolis, came to you
> and proferred an infinite indulgence toward the errors of man-
> kind.

The infinite indulgence, we learn later, extends far beyond the simple errors of mankind: it extends to theft, not small thefts, but thefts
amounting to expropriation of whole districts, whole communities, an
entire culture. Instead of gently leading the people, Coignard was
busily twisting its neck. Elections were rigged, a small coterie of loyal
Indochinese was bribed into acquiescence, and anyone who disputed

his authority was granted "the right to remain silent" in prison or in the graveyard. Only a monster, of course, could produce such a perverted governorship, and Jacques Tournebroche proclaimed his surprise that the Governor did not in the least resemble a monster. "You are no more ugly than anyone else who is not handsome," he wrote. "The reputation for violence, which you have made for yourself, is not at all reflected in your face and in your little turned up nose." In a later issue Malraux published a caricature of the Governor, emphasizing his low forehead, long ears, protruding eyes, and piglike nose. In conclusion Jacques Tournebroche gave his ironic benediction to the unhappy Governor, promising him eternal felicity. "My dearest child," he wrote, "you will be blessed through all the years, and your soul, filled with music, will eternally rejoice: for in the celestial hierarchy, among the Angels, Archangels, Thrones, Virtues and Dominations, God will certainly not grant you Virtues, but He will grant you Domination."

The editorials continued to attack the Governor and his acolytes, employing the weapons of scorn. On July 8 there appeared Malraux's "First Letter to Monsieur Henry Forward-to-the-Rear, stern moralist

and healthy journalist." The attack on Henry Chavigny de la Chevrotière was signed: *André Malraux, audacious adventurer and unhealthy
journalist.* "You are perfectly right, Mr. Henry Forward-to-the-Rear.
I am an audacious adventurer. That is the difference between you, the
stern moralist, and me." He praised the virtues of Chavigny, as he
had praised the virtues of Cognacq. "On seeing you, everyone asked:
'Who is that virtuous virgin?' And in your wake, the perfume of
orange blossoms long floated." Then Malraux, having performed the
preliminary greetings demanded by courtesy, aimed at his heart, telling
the full story of Chavigny's court-matial, his escape to Colombo to
avoid arrest, and his subsequent career as a time-serving stool pigeon
and *agent provocateur* continually currying favor with the authorities.
The editorial, covering three columns of the front page, was deliberately
intended to draw Chavigny's fire, going so far as to accuse him of
"grotesque cowardice." According to the code of the colony, the insult
could only be wiped out by a duel. There were two more ferocious
attacks on Chavigny, who failed to send his seconds, and thus Malraux
was deprived of the opportunity of meeting his adversary face to face.
Meanwhile *L'Impartial* continued to attack Malraux as a thief and
Monin as a Communist.

Sometimes, too, there would appear in *Indochine* stories written by
Malraux under a variety of pseudonyms. The most impressive and the
most memorable appeared on the last page of the issue of August 6
under the title *Expedition to Isfahan.* It was signed Maurice Sainte-
Rose. Once more Malraux was wrestling with his demons: death and
devastation sweeping over Asia, and himself in the midst of them.
He imagines himself as a young Russian student from Ekaterinburg
who has joined the Red Army in its march across Persia, a purely
imaginary Persia, for he had never been there and had only a vague
idea what the country looked like. Teheran was quiet and peaceful,
still ruled in theory by the Shah, but in fact already in the hands of its
Bolshevik conquerors, strange men in buttoned blouses, with shining
eyes, who ruled the country from their penthouses overlooking the city.
The Shah still gave audiences in palaces filled with Venetian glass, the
tramways were running, the confectioners' shops were open, and the
women were astonishingly beautiful. But this glimpse of Teheran is
merely a curtain-raiser. After Teheran comes the long march across

the desert, the horror of a great emptiness where the wells have long
since dried up and sometimes they come upon the ghostly figures of
ancient kings carved out of granite, their hands pointing toward long-
forgotten cities. For eleven days the young Russian student leads his
band of Cossacks across the desert, and then at last they come in sight
of Isfahan. In the distance they see the mosques gleaming like blue
flames, and they gallop toward it.

What they saw was a ruined city which had never recovered from
the Afghan invasions; once two million people lived there, and now
there were perhaps sixty thousand men, women and children, silent and
invisible, hidden within the walled labyrinthine streets stretching over
an area twice as large as Moscow. Isfahan is a real city, but Malraux
was inventing a new and stranger city. Here he describes the plight of
the small Cossack army:

> Night came down. By dawn nearly all our horses were dead.
> The following day was passed in useless reconnaissances, for
> Isfahan retained the secret of its existence and left us solitary
> among the murderous ruins. And then the night came, and fifty
> of us died.
>
> Truly, the city was defending itself. You could not see a living
> soul. The whole day was spent in useless reconnaissances. Every
> little street led to another, and from the flat roofs there was
> nothing to help us find our way.
>
> Night came down quickly; and nothing disturbed the icy
> silence, not even a gunshot or the cry of the muezzin. And as the
> great hands of the shadows stretched across the city, from every
> nook and cranny, and from every hole, there emerged a scorpion.
> As though the demons of the desert or the antique statues
> wanted the city defended, and recruited them to be its defenders.
> There was no way of understanding the inconceivable flood tide
> of events which touched neither our eyes nor our ears, and we
> realized what was happening when one of us would give a
> sudden wild shout or when our horses suddenly fell on one
> another with the sound of clashing accoutrements which rever-
> berated for a long time amid the sleeping echoes.
>
> One day by chance during a reconnaissance we reached the

Chahar Bagh, that extraordinary avenue which the builder of
Isfahan built for his pleasure, thus producing some of the finest
works of Persian art. Few people have set eyes on the Chahar
Bagh, and those who have seen it have a disquieting memory of
it, as they remember the reflections of stars at the bottom of
deep wells.

Three hundred years of disaster weigh down those delicate
palaces; the pieces of mosaic fall with a curiously uneven sound,
and no longer disturb the melancholy solemnity of the place.
An incomparable purity roams among the slender columns and
the mingling of melancholy, ruin and beauty appears to find its
symbol in the mutilated statues and the frescoes which have
grown pale. In the middle of the immense faïence pool the
angelfish, brought centuries ago by the Mongols, form gentle
waves as they glide in the water.

Like all Russians, we were seized with a sense of profound
veneration at the sight of the white angelfish which had seen
the passing of five empires. When night fell at last, there rose
the first reflections of the stars, the white angelfish whose gentle
stirring scarcely caused any ripples, and as they came to the
surface they were one with the reflections of ancient palaces and
the eternal stars.

For two days we ate nothing. The gods carved on the capitals
of the columns watched us as we bent over these blue pools
trying to catch the centuries-old angelfish. And we roasted them
on little fires, while the clear flames rose straight to the sky and
our nervous silhouettes reached as far as the ancient palaces.

As I told you, we had absolutely no idea of time. Every day
this terror-stricken city defended itself and grew larger; and
every day we became more lost and solitary amid the illustrious
dead and the invisible insects.

How did we make our way back to Teheran? I do not know.
Mad. Overwhelmed with fear, not knowing whether the city
was real or whether some demon had not created it out of the
sands, we fled across the desert. And then the Red Army found
us, and there were only eleven soldiers and myself.

In this way, with passionate intensity, Malraux describes the imaginary devastation of Isfahan, a city he would come to know well in later years. Significantly, we never see the city in daylight: ruin is associated with darkness, stars, the gleam of water, the sense of unknown terrors springing from the shadows. No people walk through the ruins; they are lost in the shadows. Only the scorpions and the angelfish come to life in this night scene, the first of many night scenes to appear in his novels, and perhaps the most brilliant.

Maurice Sainte-Rose vanished, never to write again. But *Expedition to Isfahan* showed that Malraux had at last acquired the supple, resonant style, closer to Flaubert than to Stendhal, which he had been striving for. For the first time the authentic Malrauvian music, with its plaintive violins and deep organ notes, could be heard, and there was some irony in the fact that it should have appeared on the last page of a dying newspaper.

For *Indochine* was in deep trouble, with the government determined to put an end to it. Louis Minh, the owner of the printing press, was threatened by the police. Malraux was warned that he would be beaten with a cane weighted with lead, and Monin woke up one night to find one of the plain-clothes police who kept watch over his house standing by his bed. The man had ripped through the mosquito curtain with a razor and was about to cut his throat. Monin had wakened just in time. This incident was to be used by Malraux in the opening pages of *Man's Fate*. Meanwhile, in spite of threats on their lives, the editors pressed on with their attacks. On August 11 there appeared Malraux's open letter to the *très pur, très noble, très loyal gentilhomme Henry Chavigny d'en avant pour l'arrière,* demonstrating that he was neither pure nor noble nor loyal nor a gentleman, and proving his case by printing at considerable length the record of his trial before a military court. In the same issue were revelations of Cognacq's fraudulent political maneuvers, a report on the trial of a policeman who had massacred some natives, and a lengthy survey of the land frauds perpetrated by the government. The newspaper showed no mercy to the government, which now decided to act vigorously. Threats had produced no result, but other methods were available.

On August 14, 1925, the eve of the Feast of the Assumption,

Indochine came out for the last time. No one in the editorial office knew that this was the last issue. For some time Malraux had been working on a series of articles on the nature of colonization with special reference to the Annamites, and this series was heralded on the front page with the announcement: "We request our Annamite readers to note the leading article on this page, the first of a long series, in which we shall examine our colonization, its virtues and defects, and the hopes it has brought to birth. These articles will also suggest certain methods of conciliation."

The article was entitled *Selection of Energies* and dealt with problems much greater than those which usually occupied the front pages of *Indochine*. Malraux was concerned with nothing less than the future of the French colonies in the East and whether they could withstand the pressure of inevitable reforms and the explosive energy of the Annamites breaking through the crust of French colonial bureaucracy. The young Annamites, deprived of any possibility of education in France, would inevitably rise in revolt unless their just demands were answered. In the past the French had always allied themselves with the strongest forces in the colonies: then how had it come about that they had completely failed to observe that the strongest force, the greatest energy, lay with the students who were so determined to acquire an education that they took ships secretly to China, England and America, preparing themselves for the time when Indochina would be free? The crime was not that the French were colonizers, but that they had failed to recognize their logical allies. Malraux wrote with fervor and without bitterness, concerned to heal wounds, not to inflame them. At the age of twenty-four he was writing with prophetic fury, as though from a mountaintop, with the histories of all the empires unrolling below him. He wrote:

> Every power that is conscious of a will to expand beyond its frontiers and possesses the controlled violence necessary for transforming people into colonizers gives itself as its first task the search for strength. Those who were sent by Rome to the frontiers of the empire, those whom T'ai Tsung sent into the depths of the Gobi, those whom our kings sent to Louisiana,

sought above all to seek out among the scattered forces opposing them those possessing a hidden vigor, energy and capacity
for resistance, and thus binding them to their own cause by
granting them, without dispute, the unmistakable prerogatives
of masters. Never did a great king, never did a great statesman
forget to seek out these characteristics of independence and
quickly stimulated honor, by which we recognize the strong.

Our policy in Annam and Cochinchina is very simple: it
affirms that no Annamite whatever has any reason for coming
to France, and thus there is created *against us* an immediate
coalition of the noblest characters and the most tenacious energies of Annam. It appears that politically motivated and
avaricious fools are applying themselves with rare perserverance
to destroying everything we have succeeded in creating, with
the result that this ancient land, imbued with vast memories, is
awakening to the sleeping echoes of more than six hundred
revolutions.

Whatever educated Annamites here may say, the history of
the Chinese domination of Annam, in spite of all the reservations that must be made, took place under the sign of blood.
I remember the old streets of Florence, near the Arno: on every
tawny or golden palace an inscription commemorated a murder
to acquire domination over the city. The Hell of the *Divine
Comedy* is inscribed in its entirety over the walls of the old
princely houses, while today the glory of the city towers above
the tumult of these stilled battles. Annam, when you travel
across it from the mouths of the Red River to the Mekong
Delta, leaves a single impression: the name of every illustrious
city commemorates a revolution, and the most famous of the
plains bear the names of battles. The tomb of Le-Loi * is in
ruins, but the songs which exalted the somber grandeur of his
life of courage and adventure can still be heard from the lips
of women and of fishermen. In Quang-Ngai, in Than-Hoa, in

* Le-Loi was the Annamite general who, in 1428, threw off the
yoke of Chinese domination and founded a dynasty which survived until the end of the eighteenth century.

Vinh, the accumulated energies which are so necessary to us in the Far East await the realization of the collaboration we have promised them. . . .

Government officials are the sole judges whether an Annamite can come to Paris, but before giving his permission he demands a proof of loyalty, which is in effect a proof of treachery. A Cochinchinese will borrow the papers of a cabinboy or a ship's engineer and make his way by ship to China, England or America, and an Annamite will acquire papers from a Protestant American missionary, and within fourteen days he will be in San Francisco. Since January 1, 1924, more than four hundred Annamites have left for England and America, knowing that they would be refused entry in France.

Is France so ugly or so shameful that it must be hidden from them?

Malraux went on to demand that the colonial government should appoint a special commission in Hanoi to "select the energies" of the youthful Indochinese, permitting them to study in France without hindrance. The selection should be made on the basis of intelligence, not on the basis of wealth or loyalty, and he poured vials of wrath on the colonials who assumed that the students would automatically become agitators when they returned from France. What was needed above all was a colonial administration which understood that the energy of youth was precious and deserving of the utmost respect. Unless the colonists understood this, they would lose their colonies.

There was nothing particularly novel in the plan outlined by Malraux: what was new was the passionate insistence that Indochina deserved better from the French. He was an essayist taking his place in the long tradition of French essayists, writing with somber irony and deliberate cadence. Here and there one could detect faint echoes of Michelet and Baudelaire, but the music was essentially his own. In *Expedition to Isfahan* he found the music which would later flow through his novels, and in *Selection of Energies* he found the music which would flow through his political speeches and sermons.

At this precise moment, August 14, 1925, there were few signs that he would ever become a novelist or ever again deliver himself

of political pronouncements. His career was in ruins. Louis Minh
announced that he could no longer print *Indochine,* because he was
being harassed by the government and his typesetters were being
threatened with imprisonment. No other printing press was available, because the government saw to it that any printer who worked
for Monin and Malraux would immediately be put out of business.
The two editors were in despair. They had built up a newspaper
which had survived for forty-nine issues, and they were in no mood
to surrender, but there seemed to be absolutely nothing they could
do. Eleven days later, on August 25, Chavigny celebrated the demise
of the adversary with an article in *L'Impartial* filled with abuse and
feverish polemics, accusing Monin and Malraux of every kind of
malfeasance. Had they not collected subscriptions a year in advance,
knowing very well that their pathetic newspaper was not likely to
survive for more than a few weeks? They had promised decorations
and honorific titles to their credulous subscribers; they were swindlers
and pickpockets, and far from being responsible journalists, they had
merely entered journalism in order to make quick profits and then
abscond. The front page article was headed "Absconding Birds."
Nothing was said about the revolutionary character of the newspaper. Chavigny was content to paint them as thieves and black-
guards whose presence polluted the air of Indochina. In its own
way it was a formidable attack, and nothing in the pages of *L'Impartial*
so much resembled a cock crowing on a dunghill.

    Both Monin and Malraux were determined to resurrect the news-
paper, whatever the cost. Somehow or other it should be possible
to acquire a font of type and a printing press. A smaller, less pro-
fessional-looking newspaper could be produced with the help of
Annamite friends. The first task therefore was to buy some odd sets
of type from the established printing houses. A few weeks later Malraux described their lack of success in a hilarious parody:

> *The scene is a large French printing house in Saigon. Enter
> a young Annamite, seventeen years old.*

> Monsieur, I would like to buy some type?
> Is it for *Indochine?*

No, for a newspaper I am going to publish.

What is its name?

The Bomb!

But . . . but . . . that's a revolutionary newspaper!

Certainly.

Wait a moment.

Whereupon the worthy director mobilizes three of his employees, who seize the young Annamite—At all costs don't let him escape!—and carry him off to the police station, which is perfectly illegal.

The superintendent of police twists himself in spirals as he listens to the head of the printing house and orders the release of the dangerous revolutionary, who is beginning to fear that he hasn't come up to scratch.

Soon I shall be sending the printer another Annamite friend, also a prospective publisher of a Bolshevik newspaper. He is two and a half years old, and the wind plays pleasantly through his downy hair.

Logic demanded that if type could not be found in Saigon, then it should be found elsewhere. Toward the end of August Malraux slipped out of Saigon with his wife and sailed for Hong Kong, where by good fortune he learned through a newspaper advertisement that the Jesuit mission was offering a whole case of type for sale. The mission was halfway up the Peak, and they immediately went there. They were well received, no questions were asked, the type was sold to them. Only half of it, for some reason, could be delivered immediately; the rest would be sent on later to Saigon. They spent a few days wandering around Hong Kong, with a police spy always in attendance, and paid a brief visit to Macao, where they watched the croupiers and saw prostitutes more brazen than they had seen anywhere. Then, happy in their new acquisition, they sailed back to Saigon.

The finding of the type had proved unexpectedly easy; to bring it safely to Saigon was far more difficult. The government was following their movements closely, and the police were well aware of the purpose of their visit to Hong Kong. Orders were given that the type should be impounded, and when Malraux and his wife returned to Saigon the type was seized. Normally impounded goods were put up for sale, and for a brief while Malraux hoped to buy back what he had already bought. All his efforts to recover the type failed.

Malraux had reached Hong Kong at a time when the Chinese mainland was convulsed by the assassination of Liao Chung-k'ai, a pro-Communist Kuomintang leader who, if he had lived a little longer, might have inherited the mantle of Dr. Sun Yat-sen, who had died in Peking in the spring. The Kuomintang in Canton was now largely under the control of Mikhail Borodin, who had been dispatched by the Kremlin to bring about a Communist revolution in China. His legend had been growing, while his influence declined, for he knew little about China, could not speak or read Chinese, and was surprisingly ill-informed on many Chinese matters. Yet to a very large extent he still controlled the left wing of the party, while the right wing and the center were implacably opposed to him.

In his novel *The Conquerors* Malraux described some of the bloody events that occurred in Canton earlier in the year; he had not participated in them and derived much of his knowledge from newspaper reports. He was a sick man when he arrived back in Saigon. Paul Morand, the novelist and essayist, was on his way to Siam to become French ambassador to Bangkok, but fell ill before he could take up his duties and was hospitalized in Saigon. Malraux visited him in hospital. "He was like a ghost," Paul Morand wrote of his visitor. "Pale, thin, looking like a hunted man, he was infinitely more sick than the patients in the hospital."

Although obviously ill and in need of a prolonged rest, Malraux was still making plans to publish *Indochine.* Although half a case of type had been lost, there still remained the remaining half, which the Jesuits had promised to deliver when they had no further need for it. The case arrived finally on October 26, with Malraux and Monin waiting at the dockside to receive it. Once more the government sent orders that it should be impounded. The commissioner in charge of the dock police, telephoned the customs authorities and ordered them to confiscate the type "at all costs," but the customs au-

thorities refused, apparently because they were weary of receiving
illegal orders. Malraux wrote later that Maurice Cognacq fell into
"a black fury" when he heard his orders had been disobeyed, and
there was no doubt that he was disturbed by this new turn of events,
for he had spent a good deal of time and energy in attempting to
suppress the newspaper which would soon reappear. At the docks
the crate containing the type was solemnly handed over to Monin
and Malraux, who bore it away in triumph.

With this new type they would publish a newspaper even more
trenchant and corrosive than the first. They would hammer away at
Cognacq and Chavigny with all the old fire, but with an added
ferocity. They had already decided to change the name of the newspaper. It would be called *Indochine Enchaînée* (Indochina in Chains).
For a few weeks it would enjoy a brief and feverish life, and then
die out like a gutting candle.

∽§ *Indochina in Chains* ह∾

The privileged reader in the Bibliothèque Nationale may occasionally examine what may be the last surviving set of the issues of *Indochine Enchaînée*. The pages are flaking away, and many of them are discolored by age. Some of the pages are torn and some words and sentences have vanished beyond recovery. Atrociously printed on a defective press, but written with extraordinary vitality, it conveys the excitement of those times. The new newspaper amply fulfilled the promise of its editors to attack the government until it drew blood.

In the strict sense *Indochine Enchaînée* was not so much a newspaper as a fly sheet which appeared twice a week, on Wednesdays and Saturdays. It did not have the appearance of a newspaper, being half the size of *Indochine* and resembling in format a slender literary magazine. There was precious little news, and a good deal of commentary and opinion. According to the rubric on the first page of the first issue, it was a *provisional* newspaper, "awaiting the day, certainly far distant, when the government will agree to return the type that belongs to us, although at present the government deems it necessary to keep the type in its own custody." The rubric appeared over a list of contents which included an interview with Lloyd George and the opening chapter of a novel by Claude Farrère. Above the list of contents there was a woodblock caricature of Maurice Cognacq looking like a stuck pig.

There was something strangely anonymous and ephemeral about this newspaper, which was not a newspaper. It looked as though it had been put together with enormous difficulty, and at the same time with gaiety and nonchalance. Nothing was quite right: neither the size of the page, nor the type, nor the woodblocks. The first issue bore no date, no publisher was mentioned, and there was no pagination. Words were misspelled, accents were omitted, and there was more than the permissible number of upside down letters. Quite obviously the printing press lacked the metal frames which hold the blocks of type firmly in place, with the result that the paragraphs tended to wave across the page. But all these defects somehow gave it vitality. As Malraux pointed out in an editorial note printed in capital letters to save the expense of inserting accents: "Our readers should not forget that this issue of *Indochine* is provisional—we shall soon be appearing daily. Meanwhile *Indochine* must be considered as a bibliographical rarity. In order to appear at all, we have sometimes replaced the characters we lack by characters made of wood, as in the sixteenth century."

Malraux, the bibliophile, with his vast knowledge of printing types and his love of rare books, delighted in the ragged, homemade appearance of *Indochine Enchaînée.* Unlike *Paper Moons,* which had been printed almost too perfectly, the newspaper had a character of its own, rough-hewn, determined, wayward. The publication of the newspaper was an education in the uses and misuses of typography, a subject of consuming interest to him.

Part of the trouble lay with the type imported from Hong Kong, which was lacking in French accents, cedillas, and circumflexes. There was a surprising lack of colons, and far too few *l*'s, with the inevitable result that capital I was often substituted for *l.* By improvising, by borrowing, and by making wooden letters, they were able to produce a page which was always legible and comprehensible, though sometimes startling. When Malraux printed his story of the young Annamite who invaded a publishing home to purchase type for a newspaper to be called *La Bombe,* the two words appeared as: "Lal bm o be." But such alarming experiments were rare, and there are few examples of words violently scrambled.

By good luck they were able to acquire accented letters from young Annamite typesetters working in the established printing presses, but there were never enough of them. Ten years later, when writing an introduction to Andrée Viollis's book *S.O.S. Indochine,* Malraux vividly remembered his excitement when a friendly Annamite came

L Indochine enchainee

Sommaire

EDITION PROVISOIRE DE L'INDOCHINE PARAISSANT DEUX FOIS PAR SEMAINE, LE MERCREDI ET LE SEMEDI, EN ATTENDANT QUE L'ADMINISTRATION NOUS RENDE OU SE DECIDE A METTRE EN VENTE, LES CARACTERES E'IMPRIMERIE QUI NOUS APPARTIENNENT ET QU'ELLE A CONFISQUES AU MEPRIS DE TOUTE LOI ET DE TOUT USAGE.

DIRECTEURS :

ANDRE MALRAUX ET PAUL MONIN

DIRECTION : 12, RUE TABERD
LE NUMERO ; 20 CENTS.

Editorial

LETTRE OUVERTE A MONSIEUR ALEXANDRE VARENNE GOUVERNEUR GENERAL.

Monsieur le Gouverneur Général,

La dé è he annonçant votre nomination au poste que vous allez occuper était à peine parvenue en Cochinchine, que le Gouverneur se mettait à l'œuvre pour vous donner en spectacle, lors de votre arri é , la Comédie qu'on appelle votre Réception

Vous n'ê es pas sans avoir entendu parler du mécontentement qui, de jour en jour, grandit en Cochinchine. Vous l'avez marqué dans vos discours, où vous avez parlé, à plusieurs reprises, de réformes nécessaires. Or, il va de soi que lorsque les institutions sont bonnes, il n'est point nécessaire de les réformer ; lorsque les hommes qui les appliquent sont justes, il n'est point nécessaire de les mettre à la retraite.

Donc, vous ne croyiez point que tout allât pour le mieux en Cochinchine. Cette pensée qui annonçait des demandes d'explications, voire même des enquêtes, ne pouvait être admise. Il convenait de vous préparer une Cochinchine toute en or, avec de beaux discours dans lesquels l'émotion voilât l'indigence de la lan ue fran aise ; de vous faire savoir que le Gouverneur Cognacq était aimé de ses administrés ; de former un bloc impressionnant et de vous amener, enfin, à vous pénétrer de cette idée que la politique antillaise des pourboires ingénieusement distribués est la plus précieuse acquisition de l'esprit français et la base de toute action coloniale.

Maintenant, Monsieur le Gouverneur général, que les diverses fanfares vous laissent en paix, nous voudrions vous demander un effort : celui de lire cette lettre, dans laquelle nous avons l'intention d'établir ceci :

Front page of L'Indochine Enchaînée, *November 18, 1925.*

to his office and presented him with a priceless gift of accented type wrapped in a pocket handkerchief. It was a spontaneous act of generosity, and he was deeply moved by it. He wrote affectionately about the unknown Annamite workman, addressing him by the familiar *tu* and celebrating his revolutionary courage.

I well remember you. When you sought me out, the government had finally put an end to the only revolutionary journal in Indochina, and the peasants of Baclieu had been plundered in a great tranquil silence.

For some weeks the police had been sabotaging the distribution of our newspaper, but even so the Annamite workers in the post office had ensured its safe delivery; at last there came a day when our printer was paralysed by threats.

Nevertheless our workmen once more set up our old presses. The characters we had bought in China were seized on our return by orders of the customs authorities. And these characters made in China were English type without accents. And while the plundering of the farmers in the South went on as before, we gazed at our old presses with their useless characters.

Then you drew from your pocket a handkerchief knotted into a bundle with the corners erect like the ears of a rabbit. "There are only acute *e*'s, and some acute, grave, and circumflex accents. As for the twice-dotted *i*'s, that will be more difficult, but perhaps you can get along without them. Tomorrow many workers will do as I have done, and we will bring you all the accents we can." You opened the handkerchief and emptied the letters, all tangled like jackstraws, onto the printing block and aligned them with the tip of your printer's finger, saying nothing. You had removed them from the presses of the government newspapers and you knew that if you were caught you would be condemned, not as a revolutionary, but as a thief. And when they were all lined up flat, like pawns in a game of chess, you merely said: "If we are punished, tell them in Europe that we did this, so that they will know what is happening here."

In Malraux's eyes this was a moment of grandeur, to be remembered and savored during the agonizing weeks that followed, when the fight against Maurice Cognacq and his cohorts assumed the dimensions of a rearguard campaign against overwhelming forces. The government was autocratic, corrupt, and vengeful. It could do whatever it pleased, and regarded the least criticism as a sign of revolutionary activity.

The weapons used by Malraux and Monin in *Indochine Enchaînée* were the same they had used in *Indochine,* but they were now sharper, more concentrated, deadlier in their aim. Now the entire newspaper, except for the serials and some articles imported from the French magazine *Candide,* was devoted to the single cause of ousting Cognacq from his position of power and influence, or at least of making his position untenable. They were like mosquitoes hovering around the puffed-up figure of the Governor, hoping to sting him to death. They were aware of the disparity of their forces, but they had one advantage denied to the bureaucracy: they were writing exceedingly well in the classic tradition of French invective, with an anguished sense of urgency, with the knowledge that they had nothing to lose and a world to gain. They had already been tempered in battle and they had taken the full measure of the adversary.

The first issue of the newspaper came out on November 4 with a leading article by Malraux celebrating the Governor's love of truth. He loved it so much that he resembled a jealous husband who locks up his wife. Truth had become his private prisoner, his own monopoly. In the name of truth he enlarged or compressed the ballot boxes as though they were concertinas, gave out honorific titles, terrorized typesetters, stole the lands worked by the Annamites, and gave vast subsidies to his friends and followers, listing them in the annual budget under the heading "Charity: Deaf mutes." Malraux was in no mood to pull his punches, and the long catalogue of errors committed by the government under the repressive rule of Maurice Cognacq would be continued in further installments "like a serial novel." For full measure he added in the same issue a long article spread over two columns with the simple heading "Government by Traitors." Here he pointed out that the Annamites, who suffered so

terribly from the exactions of the government, were becoming increasingly hostile to France, hating her with a pure and unalloyed
hatred, which would become "the song of a terrible harvest." The
French administration consisted largely of traitors, people who had
not the slightest interest in the well-being of the Annamites, with no
sense of an enlarging mission, and chief among them was the man
"who wore the double mask of the buffoon and the valet, the spy and
the traitor."

Toward Cognacq Malraux was absolutely unrelenting, and he had
good reason to be. The administration was a farce, like so many
colonial administrations, and the best that could be said about it was
that it was just as farcical in its public acts as in its public pronouncements; it never succeeded in concealing its real nature. The annual
report, called the *Livre Vert,* or the Green Book, had just appeared,
a huge compendium of official documents, statistics, and self-
congratulatory comments. Malraux was particularly struck by a statement in the introduction to the effect that the government had faithfully
pursued during the past year the same policy it had pursued in
previous years, a policy characterized by benevolence, the mainte-
nance of order, and good relations between the rulers and the ruled.
These phrases stuck in his throat, and he wrote a commentary on
them in the spirit of a theologian commenting on a secret text:

> Yes, indeed, all these statements are perfectly true. I affirm
> and certify them, and my testimony will no doubt please Mon-
> sieur Cognacq, who has spent liberally of his resources in the
> hope of suppressing my testimony. He has benevolently re-
> warded his good Annamite brothers, who have benevolently
> committed acts of treason against their own people; he has
> given them decorations and medals—as it happens, they took
> the forms of coins of the realm. He has benevolently
> threatened those who consorted with his political enemies with
> imprisonment at Hatien and Poulo-Condore. He has benevo-
> lently sent the poor agents of the Sûreté on our trails: they
> were given delicate missions and they need to eat. As for the
> peasants of Camau, they were the recipients of his special

solicitude, for he went among them in person to examine their rice fields so that in case of need he could benevolently steal them.

Benevolence, according to Malraux, was the watchword of the regime, but to understand this benevolence properly it was necessary to rephrase the Governor's statements: "We have condemned them to death and benevolently executed them. After their deaths they repented and now possess an immeasurable love for us."

This editorial, "Reflections on the Green Book," appeared on November 11 in the third issue of *Indochine Enchaînée*. In the previous issue Malraux wrote another editorial called "In Praise of Torture," in which he described the fate of an Annamite in Baclieu who was viciously tortured by the police in order, according to the police, to extract a confession, though others believed that it was done to extort money. "Of course," Malraux noted, "there is no question here concerning the validity of torture in order to extract confessions." The government must be given its due. A friendly doctor who examined the patient pronounced that no torture had been inflicted. Other doctors pronounced otherwise. The matter reached the attention of Maurice Cognacq who ordered still another doctor to examine the patient. Unhappily, the government doctor could not bring himself to pronounce that no torture had taken place. The policeman who was the cause of all the trouble was rewarded with a high position in the Saigon constabulary.

Such stories were legion, and the government had excellent reasons for covering them up, since a new Governor General of Indochina was due to arrive soon. *Indochine* had announced his imminent departure from Paris at the end of July, but he did not reach Saigon until the middle of November. The new Governor General was Alexandre Varenne, lawyer, journalist, socialist, and vice president of the French Chamber of Deputies. He was a man of pronounced liberal sympathies, well known as an eloquent defender of human rights and as a man who took his socialist beliefs seriously. Born in 1870, he was first elected to the Chamber of Deputies at the age of twenty-six. He had been a member of the parliamentary committee for universal suffrage and on the budget committee for education. He was not a man to be trifled with, and he could be expected to make sweeping changes in the administration. As a practicing journalist and the founder of the socialist newspaper *La Montagne,* he could also be expected to have some sympathy for journalists in Indochina. In July Malraux and Monin had welcomed his appointment, saying that for twenty years Monsieur Varenne had been "a friend of liberty." This was an underestimate, for he had been devoted to liberty through all his working life.

For Maurice Cognacq, the Governor of Cochinchina, the coming of a socialist deputy as Governor General of all the kingdoms and provinces of French Indochina could only be a disaster. Officially he was compelled to welcome the appointment, while unofficially he would have to do everything in his power to undermine the influence of an unwelcome visitor. When Alexandre Varenne arrived in Saigon on November 18, he made an excellent impression on the Annamites, for he appeared in a plain dark suit, not in the elaborate gold-braided white uniform usually worn by colonial potentates. When asked why he did not wear the uniform to which he was entitled, he answered: "It is the Annamites who have to pay for that gold embroidery." He was the first socialist ever to become Governor General of a European colony, and his coming augured well for the future of Indochina.

Monin and Malraux celebrated the event in *Indochine Enchaînée* with an open letter addressed to the new Governor General. They pleaded with him not to be blinded by the brilliance of his reception: tragedy lurked in that comedy of errors, and it was especially present in the speech by Maurice Cognacq, who enlarged on the benefits he had conferred on his people. On the contrary, the Annamites were desperately unhappy with his administration which continually concealed its crimes. They wrote:

> When the celebrations finally come to an end, Monsieur le Gouverneur General, we would request you to make the effort of reading this letter, wherein it is our intention to establish the following:
> The elected bodies, as offered to us, have been formed under

conditions of flagrant illegality. The leaders, whom the Governor holds by the hand as though they were children, are without authority.

And the press is dominated by the same Governor.

They were fighting a deadly and dangerous war against Cognacq, hoping that Alexandre Varenne would become an ally. Whenever they attacked the administration, they offered to provide the new Governor General with documentary evidence, but there is no evidence that he read their editorials. They believed that Indochina had reached a turning point. It was not yet too late to transform the colonial government, but time was running out. In a few months or a few years they expected the Indochinese to rise in fury against the French. If that happened, Malraux was certain that he would find himself on the side of the Indochinese.

In their attacks on Cognacq, Malraux and Monin both wrote with controlled violence. But *Indochine Enchaînée* was not essentially an inflammatory newssheet. There were the usual articles and serials, and in every issue there was a chronicle of the days' events under the heading "Chronicles of Saigon." This was written by Monin and Malraux jointly, and signed with their joint initials A.P.M. Social questions were discussed. Malraux wrote a long article on infant mortality, pointing out that the government could easily reduce the high mortality rate by a concerted propaganda effort among the Annamite women. He begged them to broadcast leaflets demonstrating how they should look after their newborn babies, and if the leaflets were provided with pictures so much the better. In the article he told how he had once asked for official permission to bring out a magazine in the Annamite language which would deal exclusively with scientific problems. Permission was refused. This was one more tragedy to be laid at the door of the administration. "The Annamites like to share their knowledge," he commented, "and they are very good at propagating information. If four or five newspapers were given the order to supply useful information, they would surely be performing a greater service than they are performing with their daily attacks on Monsieurs Monin and Malraux."

The longer he stayed in Indochina the more certain Malraux became that the Indochinese would rise and throw out the French, and he half suspected that Cognacq would like nothing better than a few small revolts. One of the imaginary interviews published in *Indochine Enchaînée* was entitled "Interview with the Governor of Chynoiserie." The Governor proves to be very affable. He reminds his interviewer that the big stick is quite useless unless legal documents are wrapped around it. On the subject of revolts the Governor is equally affable. "Nothing would please me more than a little revolt," he says. "Ten or twelve revolters, half of them of course from the police. I could then call up the troops, speak of the necessity of Force and Order and of the ingratitude of the natives, and when the revolters have been duly executed, I could adjourn indefinitely all questions about those demands which are so annoying to my good friends." The interviewer reminds the Governor that it might not be so easy to put down the revolt. Many hundreds of French soldiers may be killed. What then?

> Thereupon the Governor gazed at us for a long while, an expression of friendly disdain animating his charming features; then a burst of hearty laughter revealed his white teeth.
> "What in hell has that got to do with me?" he said, and with the utmost cordiality he gave me a little pat on the stomach.

The danger of a revolt was a very real one, and the French colonial government had already had a taste of it. In April 1925 a district commissioner marched with two native guards into the little village of Krang Leou to collect an additional special tax on the summer rice crop. The natives refused to pay, and the commissioner ordered his guards to arrest some of the villagers and keep them under arrest until the money was paid. A woman dashed among them and pulled her husband away, a guard cocked a rifle, and suddenly the infuriated villagers hurled themselves on the hated commissioner and the guards, who were beaten to death. Eighteen villagers were later arrested and placed on trial at Pnom Penh. In an editorial which appeared in December, while the trial was still going on, Malraux wrote: "Perhaps you believe this affair is somehow related to a deplorable tax levy on the rice fields? How wrong you are! The murder was purely accidental. Some pirates were passing by . . ."

The trial was a nightmare. The prime witness for the defense was the commissioner's driver; he was killed shortly before the trial opened while "resisting arrest." Maître Gallet, the lawyer for the defense, was served herb tea one morning; it tasted remarkably bitter, and he sent away for another cup which proved to be equally bitter. Nevertheless he drank the tea and soon collapsed. An attempt had been made to poison him. He recovered sufficiently to appear in court and lodge a complaint. The judge was unsympathetic. Malraux observed caustically: "In order that the complaint should be followed up, there was need for evidence which Maître Gallet did not possess. Since he was not even dead, an autopsy could not be performed. The motion was turned down."

The defense motions were constantly denied; the defense was scarcely allowed to speak; the judge was obviously acting under orders to punish the villagers. Malraux concluded that the laws promulgated in the colonies were in need of revision. He wrote:

> I would rather like to see a code of laws based on the following principles:
> 1. Every defendant shall have his head cut off.
> 2. Later he will be defended by a lawyer.
> 3. The lawyer shall have his head cut off.
> 4. And so on.
> In this way everything would be simpler, and the judges would have nothing to do.

Judge Mottais, who presided over the case of the Krang Leou villagers, sentenced one of the defendants to death, four to life imprisonment, and seven to many years of hard labor. Five, who obviously had nothing to do with the affair, were acquitted.

By this time *Indochine Enchaînée* was coming to the end of its resources. Both Monin and Malraux realized that a small badly printed newssheet was not an effective weapon against a powerfully entrenched government. If they had been able to continue *Indochine* without interference, there would have been a different story to tell, for this newspaper with its large format and spacious columns spoke with an air of authority. The Indochinese recognized power, and there was no power behind the poor newssheet, however brilliantly it was written.

Power, real power, the power to change the country, was to be found perhaps in the revolutionary organization of the Kuomintang, which already had its agents in Cholon, the Chinese section of Saigon. Monin had long been a secret member of the party, and about this time Malraux and his wife both became members. For a while Malraux had hoped to organize his own revolutionary party, which he called "Young Annam." Some of the Annamites working for *Indochine Enchaînée* joined it during its brief and ephemeral existence during the later part of 1925, but it left no trace on the revolutionary movement of Indochina. Like the newssheet, "Young Annam" was a product and a victim of the repressive measures of the government.

Although "Young Annam" left no trace on history, it left profound traces on Malraux's two novels about revolution in China, *The Conquerors* and *Man's Fate,* where the leaders of small revolutionary groups are seen engaged in struggle with ruthless and powerful enemies. From the beginning these leaders are doomed, and they die in the knowledge that their deaths are necessary even though meaningless.

There remained one potentially powerful weapon still unused—a direct appeal to the French people. Malraux hoped and believed it would be possible to go over the heads of the colonial officials to the people in whose name they acted. He had a profound belief in the power of one man to alter the course of history. He would return to Paris, address meetings, stir up enthusiasm for the cause of the Indochinese, publish a newspaper, tracts and leaflets, and thus bring about the downfall of the colonial government and avert the bloody revolution which was now inevitable. On December 26, 1925, there appeared his last editorial in *Indochine Enchaînée.* It was written as vehemently as all the other editorials, but this time there was a practical plan for bringing about the reconciliation between France and Indochina which was so desirable and so difficult to accomplish. He wrote:

> We can have no confidence in the men the French government sends us, for those men, whether they speak to us about

machine guns or liberties, know only one thing when they come among us: they know the liberty of taking our money.

We cannot appeal to violence, because we have no weapons.

Then to whom can we appeal for allies, when the government gives us only the choice between lies and servility?

I answer:

We shall appeal to all those who, like yourselves, are suffering. The people, in France, will not permit the sufferings whose scars you bear to be inflicted in their name. . . . We must appeal to them by speeches, by meetings, by newspapers, by pamphlets. We must have the working masses sign petitions on behalf of the Annamites. Those of our writers—and they are still numerous—who have some generosity must appeal to those who admire them.

The great voice of the people must be raised to ask their leaders for an explanation of all this heavy affliction, of this devastating anguish that hangs oppressively over the plains of Indochina.

Shall we obtain freedom? We cannot know yet. At least we shall obtain some freedoms.

That is why I am leaving for France.

A few days later he left for France, ill and worn out by the long struggle which had very nearly broken him. *Indochine* and *Indochine Enchaînée* were abandoned, never to be revived again: they were the bruised fruit of a bruised tree. Those who saw him when he returned to France were surprised by the change in his appearance. "He could not look you in the eye," wrote Jean Prévost. "His shoulders squeezed together as though there was a dagger in his back, and his hands burned, shuddered, and attempted to extricate themselves from their knots. When anyone drew near, his emaciated features grew disturbed. He looked like a whipped boy, a youthful revolutionary who has embraced only death."

Tragically, he was unable to fulfill his promise to his friends in Saigon. There were no speeches, no meetings, no newspapers, no pamphlets. At long intervals he wrote articles on the colonial question: one appeared in October 1933 in *Marianne* and another in January 1936 in *Crapouillot*. The opening statement of his article in *Marianne* explained his long silence. "To avoid any misunderstanding, let this be clearly understood," he wrote. "Personally, having lived in Indochina, I cannot conceive that a courageous Annamite could be anything other than a revolutionary." As he saw it, the task of throwing the French out of Indochina would have to be assumed by the Indochinese, and the time for half-measures had passed.

The trial against Malraux for the "theft" of the Banteay Srei statues was abandoned, apparently because the court at Saigon did not relish any further encounters with him. Forty years later, when Malraux was a minister of state, he received a communication from a certain Raymond Roche, a former magistrate at Saigon, who had known what was happening behind the scenes. According to the magistrate, the judiciary in Saigon wanted to avoid any more trouble and conveniently dropped the affair.

When Malraux returned to Paris, he brought with him the manuscript of a short book, long ago promised to the publisher Grasset and now almost completed. It was called *The Temptation of the West,* and it was full of his knowledge and feeling for the temptations of the East.

⊷ The Temptations
of the East ⊱

I n the summer of 1895 the young poet Paul Valéry, then twenty-four years old, took up a post in the Ministry of War. His task was to edit reports coming in from abroad, among them the telegrams concerning the Sino-Japanese War which was then in progress. The war terrified him, for he saw its shadow falling on Europe. Never before had Europe been threatened so menacingly by a power emerging from the East, all the more menacing because it adopted Western ideas and Western machines. One day in September he imagined himself transported to the banks of the Yalu river in the company of a Chinese sage. He had never been to the East, but he possessed an instinctive understanding of Eastern ways of thought, and his Chinese sage, raging against the pride and violence of Europe, is a perfectly credible character. "You encourage the violence of the imagination," says the Chinese sage. "Your ideas are terrible and your hearts are weak. You are terrified by blood and by Time."

What chiefly appalls the Chinese sage is the European intelligence in its ungoverned pursuit of domination over everything that comes within the sphere of its influence: its unbridled determination to solve all problems, even the problems that cannot be solved, and its complete contempt for humanity and the orderly processes of nature. Hungry, anarchic, intolerant, the Western intelligence consumes everything that exists and appears to act as though it wanted to recreate society every day. The Chinese sage contrasts the wilfullness of the West with the calm of the East:

> Our empire is a tapestry of the living and of the dead and of
> Nature. It exists because it sets all things in order, and here

117

everything is a part of history. . . . Thus, we seem to be sleeping and so we are despised. Yet all things dissolve in our magnificent multitude. Conquerors lose their way in our yellow waters. Foreign armies are drowned in the flood of our descendants or crushed under the weight of our ancestors. The majestic cascades of our rivers of human existence and the ever increasing succession from our fathers carry them away.

We must therefore provide ourselves with an infinite politics, reaching out to both ends of time, commanding a thousand million men, in such a way that the ties of kinship are never broken or confounded. Here lies prodigious mastery without desire. You regard us as being indolent. Instead, we preserve a sufficient wisdom to grow immeasurably, beyond all human power, and we gaze upon you as you dissolve in spite of your raging science into the deep and perfect waters of Tsin. You who know so many things do not know the most ancient and the most powerful, and you rage with desire for what is immediate, and at the same time you destroy your fathers and your sons.

Paul Valéry was not, of course, the first Frenchman to discover that East and West were, in terms of sensibility and intelligence, poles apart. The East tends toward pure sensibility, the West toward pure intelligence with all its terrible yearning for the Absolute. All this was known to the early Jesuit fathers who established themselves in the courts of the Chinese emperors. But Valéry appears to have been the first to point out that once the East acquired the intelligence of the West, then monsters would be born. Henceforth the bird of paradise would wear the head of a vulture.

When Malraux made his first serious attempt to wrestle with the two cultures, he had acquired a considerable knowledge of the East. His dialogue between an Eastern and a Western scholar, which he called *The Temptation of the West,* was first published in 1926, but the problem had been occupying his thoughts since 1921, the year when he first became interested in oriental art. The book therefore was the fruit of long pondering, of many earnest debates, and of many anxieties and subterfuges, for it is not easy—it is virtually impossible—for the Western mind to understand the Eastern mind, and the bridge can be crossed only by a profound knowledge of the arts, the literature and the people. By the time he came to write the *Temptation of the West* he had acquired a vast knowledge of the arts, he knew many Indochinese intimately, and on the evidence of his writings he had only a cursory knowledge of oriental literature. Nevertheless, the attempt had to be made. The book, when it finally appeared, showed evidence of containing many strata, many different ideas, and many unsolved problems.

Although the work consisted ostensibly of a series of letters exchanged between a cultivated Frenchman and a young Chinese scholar, it was really a series of expanded notes written at different times and under different circumstances. The ideas of the Chinese scholar are not notably at variance with those of the Frenchman, for they speak in the same tone, employ similar locutions and attack the problems in very much the same way. Valéry had spoken of "the senseless disorder" of European civilization, and on this subject Malraux's two spokesmen are in full agreement. The letters are almost interchangeable.

The Frenchman is called A.D., presumably an abbreviation for André, and he is twenty-five years old, the exact age of Malraux when the book was published. The Chinese, Ling, is twenty-three, and we are warned in a prefatory note that he must not be taken as a symbol of oriental culture, for such a symbol could not possibly exist. Malraux had appended a similar warning to *Paper Moons*. It is not a warning to be taken seriously, for though Ling does in fact symbolize Chinese culture, he is also to a much larger extent a reflection of one side of Malraux's character. Most of the letters, some twelve altogether, are written by Ling, and only six are written by A.D., who writes the first letter while on his way to China. Ling writes his first letter from Marseilles and all the remaining letters from Paris.

A.D.'s first letter, written on board the *Chambord,* recreates the mythical Asia of his dreams—palaces and temples, pagodas flashing in the sun, camels laden with bales which burst open like pomegranates, strange women peering from behind curtains. "All the enchantments of the snowy kingdom, stones the color of clear sky or frostbound rivers, stones that flash like ice, and pale feathers of grey birds, frost-silvery furs and turquoises veined with silver, pour over their nimble

fingers." Snow falls over China and the islands, and the vision of the
falling snow is suddenly transformed into the white funeral gown of
a princess with a red jewel between her lips. Then, as in a film, the
scene changes abruptly to some old men in a sunlit courtyard making
magical gestures as they describe the buildings they have known in distant Turkestan and Tibet. These, in turn, give place to the European
adventurers who have married Manchurian women and become generals in the Manchurian armies, fierce and despotic men who have cut
themselves off from the West. These adventurers then fade into the
portrait of a cunning and all-powerful Emperor stretching his thin,
transparent hand over the whole of China as he huddles in the most
solemn palace in the Forbidden City, a blind man crowned with black
poppies. Then, as though in procession, we see a ghostly Empress trans-
fixed to the wall by barbarian arrows, warriors waving weapons adorned
with horse tails, soldiers guarding tombs in a vast wilderness, night falling on ancient triumphs. What, A.D. asks, can be recaptured from the
silent past?

What he recaptures is an elegiac vision of China as seen by someone
immersed in the arts of the East. Critics who argue that the opening
letter merely reflects an earlier style which is then abruptly abandoned
fail to recognize that the elegiac theme is present throughout the book.
Ling will ask unanswerable questions in the same style. "A great empire is beautiful," he says, "and so is its fall." But he is not referring to
the fall of the Chinese empire: he is thinking of the fall of the Roman
empire and all the empires of the West. China, too, is doomed. It is not
perhaps a matter of much consequence. It is important only that men
should live in harmony with nature, without striving, without grief,
perfecting their works of art, enjoying the calm of their dreams, scarcely
conscious of themselves as individuals, knowing themselves to be whole
in the wholeness of the universe. Ling surveys the West dispassionately,
and he is saddened by the knowledge that it has not begun to understand serenity.

His verdict on Europe is a disquieting one, for he comes to the same
conclusion as Spengler although for entirely different reasons. He finds
the Europeans a prey to their delusions of power, incapable of contemplation, immersed in traditional ceremonies which have lost all
meaning, ceaselessly striving to destroy nature. The inevitable result

is that they are confused and riddled with fears. Having dethroned God, they have nowhere to turn. The very intensity of their ideas is destructive. He says:

> The intensity which ideas create in you today seems to me to explain your life better than the ideas themselves. For you, absolute reality was first God, then Man; but *Man is dead*, following God, and you are searching with anguish for something to which you can entrust his strange heritage. Your petty attempts to construct a moderate nihilism do not seem to me destined to have a long life.

A.D. has even less hope for Europe, though he will sometimes soften the blow with an appeal to reason, knowing that reason is wholly absent among the Chinese. What Ling calls a "moderate nihilism," A.D. calls "a negative classicism, almost entirely dependent upon a transparent horror of being seduced." But there is considerable evidence that the European mind is constantly seduced by the latest novelties, cheerfully abandoning itself to every new twist and turn of reason. With the help of reason Western culture has succeeded in creating an impressive structure of negations. A.D.'s conclusions are expressed even more sombrely than Ling's, for he knows Europe better:

> The Europeans are weary of themselves, weary of their individualism which is crumbling away, weary of their exaltation. What sustains them is less an idea than a fine structure of negations. Capable of acting to the limits of self-sacrifice, but full of disgust when confronted by the will to act, which today torments the race, they want to find deeper reasons for men's actions. Their defenses are disappearing one by one. They are unwilling to oppose the claims on their sensibility; they can no longer do without understanding. . . . Sick kings, who receive each morning the most beautiful gifts of the kingdom, and each evening brings with it a familiar, desperate desire.

The desperate desire to which he refers is, of course, the Faustian quest to receive more presents, learn of more discoveries, avidly embrace more experiences. Europe was dedicated to the new, the exotic, the foreign, everything that had the power to create new sensations, even though they were painful. There was no purpose in this methodical and protracted act of suicide, not even the purpose of accomplishing its own destruction. Europe was like an abandoned palace attacked by the winter winds, the intellect falling into ruins, and the cracks, once thought to possess a charming decorative effect, continually widening. What breath or spirit can make the palace whole again?

According to A.D., nothing, nothing at all, can make the palace whole again, and he half suggests that the time of great wanderings has come again. Somewhere, on some unknown shore, a new palace will be built, containing none of the treasures of the old palace; in fact, it is not even certain what constitutes treasure in the eyes of the founders of the new kingdom. From Tientsin, on his way to Peking, he bids his last farewell to Europe, taking with him only an *avide lucidité*, an eager clarity of mind, as an offering to the new dispensation that will one day arise. On the last page of the book A.D. wrote a threnody over Europe as vivid and densely contrived as one of the odes of Paul Claudel:

> Europe, great cemetery where only the dead conquerors sleep and whose melancholy deepens as it wraps itself around their illustrious names, you leave me with only a naked horizon and the mirror held by despair, the old master of solitude. Perhaps he, too, will die of his own existence. Far away, in the port, a whistle howls like an abandoned dog. The sound of conquered shames. . . . I contemplate my own image. I shall never forget it.
>
> Shifting image of myself, I have no love for you. Like a wide and unhealed wound, you are my dead glory and my living suffering. I gave you everything; and yet I know I shall never love you. Every day I will bring you my tribute of peace, but I will never bow down. Avid lucidity, I still burn before you, a solitary and upright flame, in this heavy night where the yellow wind cries, as in all those foreign nights reiterated around me the proud clamor of the sterile sea.

Although Malraux owed much to Claudel's rhythms and imagery—
"the yellow wind," for example, is a direct borrowing from the *Five
Great Odes*—his own music predominates, and that particular way of
breaking up the rhythm of sentences becomes quickly recognizable.
Malraux liked his words to ring on the page like metal. The danger,
of course, is that the reader may find himself deafened by the clanging
of the anvil. Adjectives fascinated him. *Avid, solitary, upright, heavy,
yellow, foreign, proud, sterile* are almost too great a burden for a single
sentence to bear. In time he would learn to winnow the adjectives and
let the nouns and verbs speak for themselves. But he would never,
throughout his life, depart from his faith in avid lucidity.

This lucidity derives its strength from despair, from the certain
knowledge of failure. "Man," says A.D., "has been seeking for many
thousands of years to find his limitation and his image within himself,
and he is never satisfied until his research falls in ruins around him."
Every victory brings its inevitable defeat; the Emperor has only to
pause in a moment of boredom to realize that his battles have been in
vain. Nevertheless, the young Frenchman who dreams he is Napoleon
is sometimes galvanized into action, and at such moments "a perfect
lucidity lends a hand to madness, and the imaginary general prepares
logical plans and disposes of imagined difficulties with methodical precision." Malraux was to play the part of the "imaginary general" many
times. He saw the proof of the power of dreams in the Western novel,
which makes madness credible, for Western man is never more at home
than in the world of fantasy.

Against these fantasies Ling opposes "the calm of dreams," tranquil
meditations. He has no use for "imaginary generals": he wants "lucidity," not "avid lucidity." For him it is enough that the mind should
come to some harmony with the universe without destroying itself in
the process, for the world is there to be enjoyed, not to be reconstructed
or taken to pieces with the help of scientific instruments, or dreams, or
nightmares. For him a general has no more value than a blade of grass,
perhaps less. He wants peace; the Western world wants turmoil.

Ling finds the same lack of harmony in the Louvre, where the paintings appear to be eternally debating with one another. They are arranged awkwardly, with a kind of deliberate impropriety. Death haunts

them, for the artists, in order to render the human body, have patiently
dissected corpses. Much better to gaze out of the windows of the Louvre
at the Seine glowing in the enchanting springtime! To be in the open,
with nature, is to acquire wisdom, and a man wandering through the
Louvre learns only how to sharpen his critical faculties, comparing one
master with another.

When Ling returns to his apartment in Paris, he spends hours turning over the pages of books which are almost totally incomprehensible
to him. What can he make of Western history, even more bloodthirsty
than the history of China? And those books on Western art—Ling is
evidently staying in A.D.'s apartment and has come upon a whole shelf
of books dealing with *l'art fantastique*—what can one make of those
horned demons, each one asserting the inalienable right to possess an
individuality of his own? When he visited Rome, Ling was more atten-
tive to the fountains than to the voluptuous statues. Not surprisingly,
he was more at ease in Athens, where the Acropolis Museum with its
archaic marble torsos reminded him of the great Buddhist statues
carved on the rock cliffs of China.

As Ling quietly searches for the reasons which have brought so much
power and vitality to the West, he is haunted by the thought that the
answer lies in conquest—conquest that feeds on conquest. In a single
century Rome conquered the Western world. For what purpose? "The
only grandeur I can see in this adventure is due to sacrifice. There was
no intelligence behind it. These men were dedicated to death, whether
they receive it or give it. Is barbarism, by being powerful, any less
barbaric?" He had hoped to find in the West the vitality needed by the
East: he found a vitality corrupted by death. At the heart of the mystery
there was the death wish, a primitive nihilism. There was nothing to be
gained from the West, for of what use were power and death to the
East, which knew them only too well?

A.D. offers no reasoned defense of the West; he is altogether inclined to agree with the summary judgments of his Chinese friend.
Significantly, it is Ling who provides the clue to the real achievements
of the West, which have little enough to do with power or death. He
says:

A single human life. For me, an Asian, all of the Greek genius lies in this idea and in the sensibility derived from it. The Greeks saw Man set apart from the world, as the Christians saw Man bound to God, and as we see him bound to the world. For the Greeks all things were ordered in relationship to Man. . . . The Greeks conceived of Man as *a* man, a being who is born and dies. The span of life, which our oriental thinking and sensibility regards as being of no more importance than a simple division—youth, maturity, old age—this span of life the Western mind regards as the most important element in the universe. For the awareness, or what I would call the sensation, of being a particle of the universe, which necessarily precedes the totally abstract notion of Man, they substituted the awareness of being a living entity, complete, separate, on a kindly earth where the only impassioned images were those of men and of the sea. Thus it was a peculiar sensibility, rather than an idea, which rose from those nearly naked landscapes to influence your progenitors. The West was born there, under the austere face of Minerva, with its armor and also with the stigmata of its future madness.

The argument has shifted ground. Instead of power and death, we see the individual born in a barren land, concerned to relate all things to himself and the weapons he will use to dominate his adversaries. The individual armed with the naked strength of the will—therein, ultimately, lies the passion of the West. Minerva, goddess of science, of intelligence, is also the goddess of war. Once she had acquired the veneration of men, the West was doomed to its endless advancement in the sciences and its endless wars.

In an article called "Concerning a European Youth," which he contributed to *Les Cahiers Verts* in 1927, Malraux examined the further consequences of Ling's strictures on the West. Was there any hope anywhere in a culture which was "nihilist, destructive, fundamentally negative"? What were men's spiritual aims? He answered: "Our civilization was deprived of every spiritual aim when it lost all hope of discovering an intelligible concept of the universe through the sciences." As for individualism, it had "annihilated everything except itself." Minerva and the individual were both bankrupt. It remained for man to start again from the beginning, seeking out a new, a hitherto undreamed of promised land. He goes forth "like the knights whose victories give them the right to penetrate into the palace in search of the objects of their dreams, and where they find only the darkest shadows."

Malraux offers no hope, no certainties; at the best, men may be able to erect some provisional shelters from which they can watch the approaching storm. Everything was provisional, and perhaps there was beauty in this impermanence. "Youth would like to see in every man an interpreter of a provisional reality." Without doctrines, without weapons, youth would go in search of provisional answers to its hard questions.

"Concerning a European Youth" is tightly written, and like *The Temptations of the West* it gives the appearance of having been written over a long period of time. Again and again the argument returns to the hopeless quest of the Western mind in search of its peace, for almost by definition the West was incapable of peace. The fatherland, justice, grandeur, truth—they were no more than the ironic, accusing statues built by human hands. Then where can one turn? To the Cross, which stands in all the villages and crowns the graves of the dead? But the Cross was another ironic statue, and raised more questions than it answered.

Nevertheless an answer, perhaps *the* answer, was provided by Ling's letters, with their celebration of the ancient culture of the East, of a way of life which is more instinctive and gracious, and more impersonal, than anything known in the West. The cry of Ling—"We are men, but you are geometers"— echoes throughout the book; and perhaps, after all, it was enough to be a man, trying to live in harmony with the universe, living for the seasons, no longer dreaming of conquest or immortality. *The Temptations of the West* was an ironic title. More and more, as we reread the book, we become aware that Malraux is talking about the more subtle temptations of the East .

André Malraux (right), aged sixteen. Mlle. Paulette Thouvenin at center. (MLLE. THOUVENIN)

Claude Malraux.   (ANDRÉ MALRAUX)

Roland Malraux.   (ANDRÉ MALRAUX)

Facing: Fernand-Georges Malraux, in
1918.   (ANDRÉ MALRAUX)

Malraux in his study in the late twenties. (ROGER VIOLLET)

Facing: *Malraux in the early twenties.* (ROGER VIOLLET)

Clara Malraux and daughter Florence, 1933. (CLARA MALRAUX)

Facing: Clara Malraux at the time of her marriage. (CLARA MALRAUX)

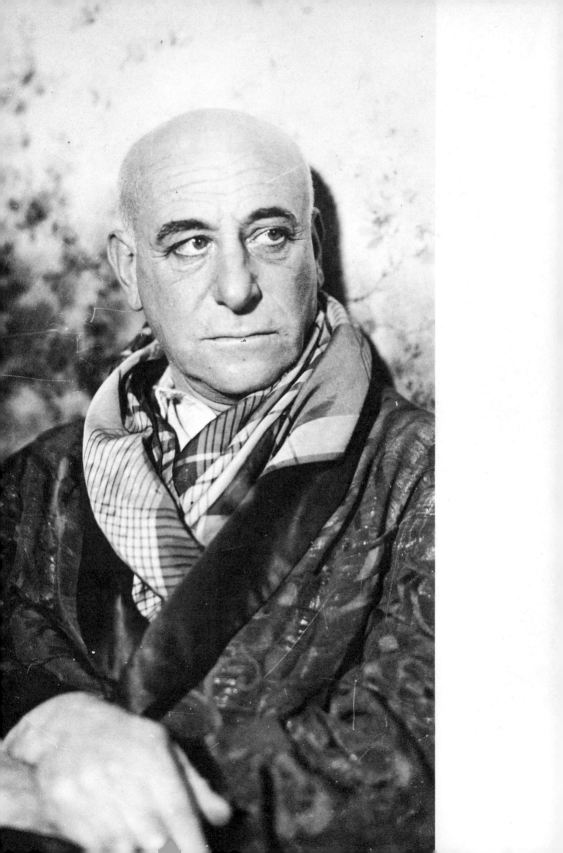

André Gide.   (FRENCH EMBASSY PRESS AND INFORMATION DIVISION, NEW YORK)

Facing: Max Jacob.   (FRENCH EMBASSY PRESS AND INFORMATION DIVISION, NEW YORK)

The Temple at Banteay Srei: the gateway. (FRENCH EMBASSY PRESS AND INFORMATION DIVISION, NEW YORK)

Facing: Sandstone deva from Banteay Srei. (ROGER VIOLLET)

André Malraux and Edward Corniglion-Molinier, and the airplane in which they flew over South Arabia. (ROGER VIOLLET)

Facing: *Malraux with a Gandhara statue brought back from Afghanistan.* (ROGER VIOLLET)

Malraux and Sergey Eisenstein, 1934. (GAETAN PICON, *Malraux par Lui-Même,* LES ÉDITIONS DU SEUIL)

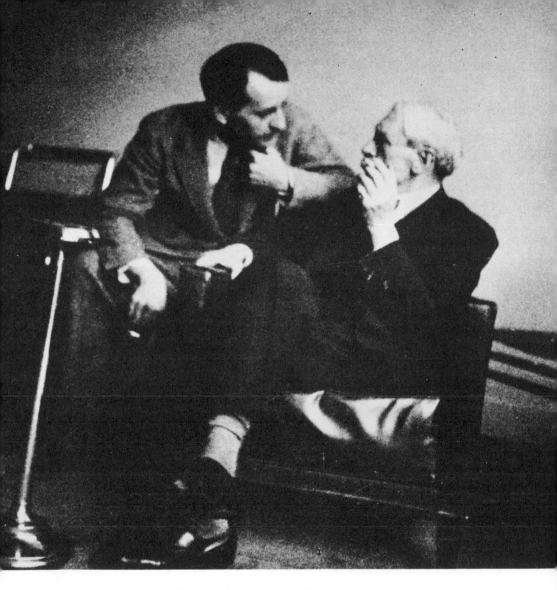

Malraux and Paul Valéry, about 1935.   (ANDRÉ MALRAUX)

Malraux and Gorky, 1934. (GAETAN PICON, *Malraux par Lui-Même*, LES ÉDITIONS DU SEUIL)

FOUR NOVELS

A great conflagration—why, that is one of the most perfect works of God. To everything it touches, fire gives a precious substance.
　　　　　　—THE KINGDOM OF FARFELU

⊸§ *The Conquerors* ৡৢ

Between 1928 and 1932 Malraux completed four novels, all of them set against oriental backgrounds, all of them concerned, though in different ways, to present a portrait of the intellectual anarchist at odds with the world and in defiance of his own destiny. There is a sense in which all the characters are self-portraits: peel off the thin chamois leather mask, and there is always the pale, unsmiling face of Malraux beneath. Sometimes the characters adorn themselves with beards, like Pharaohs, and sometimes it will amuse them to add many years to their age. Whether young or old, they are merely the disguises of a singularly gifted young Frenchman in his twenties. They all talk in the same way, discuss the same things, pursue their destinies with the same disturbing excitement. They know where they are going. They are going to their deaths.

Death, indeed, is the companion of all their journeys, never out of sight. She parades herself before them, and even when they pretend to be indifferent to her, they are secretly in love with her. At all the crossroads she is waiting for them, and they discuss her at interminable length. All have known her and enjoyed her; they are not especially afraid of her, because they have known her too well; and they are familiar with all her games. Death is like a bird whose plumes have molted, and each of them wears one of her dark feathers as a badge of honor.

Yet, strangely, the novels are far from being morbid. On the contrary, they are exhilarating and exciting. The novelist is describing life and death at their sharpest points, passionately and intellectually, showing no mercy to his characters. Because he identifies with them so closely, there is no need for subterfuges. Each novel is an auto-

biography. It is as though a man were playing Russian roulette, and
in the instant before he pulls the trigger he imagines an entire adventure which will lead inevitably to his death, thus providing him
with the appropriate reason for dying. Only a dull click comes from
the revolver. With a sense of relief he grants himself still another vision
of high adventure, and once again he pulls the trigger. In this interval
the imagination is stretched to the utmost, the colors are invariably
blinding, the arguments are pursued with undiminished zest, and the
mind reels with the excitement of knowing that it is on the edge of
extinction. The explosion may come, or it may not come. The man
playing at Russian roulette is totally indifferent to its coming. He is
determined to extract from that last blinding second all the adventures
of which the mind is capable, life flowing before him in its ultimate
intensity.

Not that Malraux in his novels continually achieves this high pitch
of excitment—that excitement which is composed in equal measure of
wild daring and extreme nervous exhaustion—but he achieves it surprisingly often. Like Lautréamont, who also wrote as though he were
on the verge of extinction at every moment, he looks death straight in
the face, has no illusions about her power, and regrets nothing. His
heroes belong among the damned and are content to remain among
them.

La hantise de la mort, the haunting awareness of death's presence,
is not necessarily morbid. The greatest artists have been those who were
acutely aware of death, and their works were created in defiance of
death. Scarcely a day passed without Mozart meditating on death, and
the gaiety of his music reflects his defiance of it. When Malraux writes
about death, there is always a heightening of the prose, the pulse is
quicker, the light is fiercer, and he gives the impression of a hunter
coming in for the kill.

The characters in his novels lend themselves to these preoccupations.
With rare exceptions they have no living fathers or mothers or brothers
or sisters or wives or children. They have cut themselves off from
their roots, if ever they had any roots. Having no responsibilities, they
are free to dispose of their lives as they please. Many of them are
gamblers, all of them are well educated or at least widely read. Their
aim is to dominate events and to acquire the utmost power over them-

selves and all those who are brought within the sphere of their influence. They suffer from the sin of pride, and are thus led to their destruction.

Pierre Garin, the hero of *The Conquerors,* was born in Geneva on November 5, 1894, the son of Maurice Garin, a Swiss citizen, and Sophia Alexandrovna Mirsky his Russian wife. Sophia Mirsky was Jewish, and the boy was brought up in the no man's land between three cultures. His mother died and left him a fortune, and we hear nothing more about the father. At twenty Pierre Garin was studying literature in Paris, engaging in anarchist conspiracies and immersing himself in the works of Saint-Just, the most violent and ruthless of revolutionary dictators. Quite suddenly he was arrested—not for his anarchist exploits, but for something very different. He was placed on trial for complicity in procuring an abortion, and since his motive for procuring the abortion was a reasonable and humanitarian one—he had established a fund for helping young women who found themselves in difficulties—he regarded the trial as a farce and his sentence of six months imprisonment as an act of lunatic absurdity. Although the sentence was quashed, he was so outraged by the absurd behavior of the judges and lawyers that he declared war on society. In August 1914, shortly after his trial, he enlisted in the Foreign Legion, deserted a year later, lost most of his remaining money in gambling, and then went to work in a Zurich publishing house, where he encountered the revolutionaries who would later seize power in Russia. After the October Revolution he wrote to his Russian friends that he wanted nothing better than a revolutionary career, but his letters went unanswered. In June 1918 a friend he had known in his *lycée,* the son of a merchant in Haiphong, wrote to him from China, saying that there were opportunities open to him in the revolutionary movement led by Dr. Sun Yat-sen. He sailed for China, was appointed one of Dr. Sun Yat-sen's advisers, and later became head of the propaganda bureau of the Canton government, a founder of the Whampoa Military Academy, and together with Borodin the organizer of the Canton general strike in 1925. Although there are many characters, the novel is essentially a study of one man, Pierre Garin, and of his rise to power and his death at the height of the revolutionary movement in Canton.

In the first draft of the manuscript Garin had another name. He was

Starin, a name evidently derived from Stavrogin, the wilful revolutionary who lost his faith in revolution and finally hanged himself with a rope smeared with soap in the last pages of Dostoevsky's novel *The Possessed*. "I wanted to try my strength everywhere," Stavrogin wrote in his farewell letter, "but my desire was never strong enough." Brilliant, wayward, cruel, aristocratic in temperament and by birth, capable of great feats of endurance, he was offered the post of revolutionary dictator by the conspirators at a time when they must have known that their revolution was doomed to failure.

Malraux had carefully studied *The Possessed,* with the result that Pierre Garin sometimes speaks with the voice of Stavrogin and performs the characteristic gestures of that youthful and princely revolutionary. They share a certain aristocratic contempt for the masses, the consciousness that they are "above the crowd." They are heroic, but without any enjoyment of heroism, and almost from the beginning they know they are doomed. "The possibility of reforming society is a question that does not interest me," Garin says. "I do not love mankind. I do not even love the poor, the people, those for whom I am going to fight." Why then does he fight? Because he is intoxicated with the prospect of performing great deeds and regards a revolution as among the greatest of deeds. This is part of the answer, but it is only a small part. As Malraux describes him, Garin is a complex, impatient, brooding, brusque and commanding man, the slave of his phenomenal will power, determined to leave a scar on history, and at the same time intelligent enough to know that so many scars have been inflicted on the body of history that his own clawings may pass unnoticed. Behind all his actions there is the shadow of futility.

In terms of history *The Conquerors* is an oddly disappointing work. The strike did not take place in the way Malraux describes it, the protagonists were not the protagonists drawn by him, and the descriptions of Canton are unconvincing. Chen-Dai, the Gandhi-like Kuomintang leader who sacrifices himself for the revolution, is a wholly impossible Chinese character, because a Chinese Gandhi is wholly impossible. The Committee of Seven, described as the ruling junta of revolutionary Canton, never had any existence. A long list of factual errors could be compiled, and no doubt a similar list could be compiled for Tolstoy's *War and Peace*. Malraux was not present during the Canton strike, and he had no very clear idea how a Chinese revolutionary situation is created. The Chinese revolutionaries are vastly outnumbered by the Russian, French, German and Italian adventurers who flock to Canton and take charge of the revolution. Garin, Borodin, Klein, Nikolaieff, Rebecci, Myroff, are not Chinese names. The revolution might be taking place in Hamburg or Sebastopol, and the Chinese setting is little more than a painted backcloth. Significantly, Malraux provides abundant descriptions of Hong Kong, but there are only cursory descriptions of Canton.

Nevertheless the novel succeeds brilliantly in conveying the intellectual excitement, the progress and the horror, of a revolution, and this was far more important than any factual accuracy. Malraux was twenty-five, and his sole knowledge of revolution came from a more or less prolonged immersion in the revolutionary politics of Indochina and the short-lived "Young Annam" movement which he helped to found. He had no more knowledge of how a revolution is organized than any intelligent reader of the newspapers; what he did have was an imaginative grasp of revolutionary processes and a style admirably equipped to show their spasmodic character:

> We leave our revolvers on the seat, close to our hands. The city seems very quiet. As we drive, we can scarcely distinguish the electric lamps, which resemble streaks of light, and the shops constructed out of badly joined planks give off only a faint light. Life is glued to the earth: no moon, no clearcut buildings. Lanterns, hawkers, cheap eating houses, lamps with flames which go straight up in the hot airless night, quick-moving shadows, motionless silhouettes, phonographs, phonographs. . . . And far away there are rifle shots.

First the revolvers; then the city; then the panorama of lights and hazy darkness seen in medium and long shots in rapid cinematographic technique. It is a satisfying method, but it has its limitations. Irrelevance creeps in; the picture becomes blurred; the characters tend to lose themselves in the streaming lights, becoming no more than

Original manuscript page of The Conquerors. *With very slight changes, this corresponds to the text on pages 85–86 of the Pléiade edition of Malraux's collected novels.*

shadowy presences. What, we ask ourselves, is the significance of "lamps with flames which go straight up in the hot airless night"? They were traveling too fast to linger over these lamps. Sometimes irrelevance becomes part of the prevailing pattern of a civil war, and at such moments the method acquires validity. Absurdity, the grossest absurdities, become commonplace when men wage war against one another without knowing exactly why they are fighting.

Garin himself scarcely knows why he is fighting, though he knows how to deal with the men he is fighting and he is especially adept at the arts of the torture chamber. "It is terribly easy to deal with a man who is about to die," he says. In *Man's Fate* Malraux will come to a contrary opinion. Indeed, it is essential to an understanding of Garin that his ideas and opinions are provisional. He has the romantic hero's habit of delivering *obiter dicta* which sometimes reflect Malraux's preoccupations, but more often come from the general stock of romantic illusions. "What books," he asks, "are worth anything except memoirs?" Or again: "I have learned that though a life is worth nothing, there is nothing that is worth so much as a life." Or again: "I don't think of society as evil—and thus capable of improvement—but as absurd." As one gathers together these utterances by Garin, there emerges the pattern of the intellectual anarchist, in love with power and experience for their own sake, hating all discipline except the discipline he imposes on himself. He is a man riddled with the seeds of self-destruction.

Yet he sees himself as the man of action, while Borodin is no more than the abject disciplinarian who wants everyone to conform to a rigid plan manufactured in Moscow. Borodin is a Jewish prophet who has seen visions and works to ensure that everyone obeys the commands written on the tablets. He is the ultimate policeman, Garin the ultimate criminal. In a chapter omitted from the novel but later published in the literary magazine *Bifur,* Malraux lets Garin discuss the character of Borodin at some length:

> Borodin is not a man of genius, not a romantic hero. He is a businessman, hard-working, brave, audacious on occasion, but very simple, his chief characteristic being the intensity with which he is obsessed by action. . . . He lives in his own par-

ticular universe, where the idea of pleasure never penetrates.
This is roughly my idea, but at least I know that it is not universal, while he thinks it is true of everyone. In short, he is the
kind of man who regards an artist, someone who creates for
enjoyment, as a barbarian. . . . Nearly all the Bolsheviks have
the cult of the technician, but if they are Jews they usually feel
that this is not everything: they have an intense curiosity about
moral forces. . . . Once he said about me, "What is annoying
about Garin is that you never know when you wake up whether
he has committed suicide during the night." He was making a
terrible mistake, but it was clear what he meant.

There is no very clear reason why Malraux should have abandoned
the short chapter devoted to Borodin, for it brought into focus the two
contrasting types of the revolutionary leader.

There is a third type, the pure terrorist. In Borodin's eyes the terrorists are expendable, they are used, and then thrown away. Sometimes,
of course, the terrorists get their blows in first, and the revolutionary
leaders are in mortal fear of them. Sometimes, too, the terrorists
quarrel murderously among themselves.

There is no other novel by Malraux so full of murder. The corpses
litter the pages; the executioners are on the rampage, and though we
rarely see the killings, we are aware of an atmosphere of sullen, erratic
violence. Klein, a Bolshevik with a long experience of executions, tells
the story of a fat man who was arrested during the Commune. "But,
sir, I have nothing to do with politics," the fat man complains. "Exactly," replies an intellectual, and breaks the poor man's head. In Malraux's works the act of killing is rare, but the dead are everywhere.
When Klein is murdered together with three Chinese, the narrator accompanies Garin to see the bodies:

> We enter. A bare workshop, with a well-trodden earth floor,
> with heaps of dust in the corners. Although the light filtered
> down through blue skylights, it shone with a dazzling brilliance,
> and as soon as I raised my eyes, I saw the four corpses, *all of
> them standing*. I had been looking for them on the floor. They

are already stiff, and they have been placed against the wall, like posts. At first sight I was amazed and almost stupefied; for, in the silence and the light, these straight bodies were not in the least fantastic, but excessively real. Now I breathe again, and as I inhale there comes to me an odor unlike any I have known before, an animal smell, strong and at the same time stale: the smell of corpses. . . .

As I turn round, I see the body of Klein—I recognized it immediately, because of its height—a large stain in the middle of his face, the mouth made larger by a razor blade. At this moment my muscles contract again, so much so that I hold my arms tightly against my body, and I too have to lean against the wall. I look away from the open wounds, the great black splashes of clotted blood, the eyes turned inward. All the bodies are alike. They have been tortured. One of the flies buzzing around alights on my forehead, and I cannot, simply cannot, lift my arms.

"Still we must close his eyes," Garin says almost in a whisper as he moves toward Klein's body.

His voice rouses me, and with a quick, violent, and awkward movement I brush away the fly. With two fingers stretched apart like scissors Garin makes a movement to touch Klein's eyeballs, which are completely white.

The hand falls away.

"They must have cut off the eyelids," he says.

This passage comes toward the end of the novel, when Garin is already disillusioned with the revolution and no longer possesses the strength to guide it effectively. He has seen too much horror and committed too many crimes to feel any emotion. There remains only a kind of hard desperation, the knowledge that he will continue his revolutionary work, but without enjoyment, without hope. Like Hong, who once tattooed on his arm words reputedly said by Lenin, "Shall we ever take possession of a world that has not bled to death?" he finds himself wondering whether there is any merit in a revolutionary blood-bath that threatens to engulf the whole world.

Malraux's macabre description of the four dead men standing in the bare workshop has a hallucinatory quality, as though he were recounting a nightmare rather than something seen or imagined. Later, he introduces Klein's mistress and describes how she clung to the body and rubbed her face in the wounds; but these Gothic horrors added little to the original picture. Malraux needed the scene of the four dead men to underscore the terror of terrorism. In the workshop we are confronted with the revolution as it is, when all the pronunciamentos and interrogations are over.

When Trotsky read *The Conquerors* two years after its publication, he praised its style and its daring, while observing that it suffered from grave defects. "The author's truly profound sympathy for insurrectionist China is unquestionable," he wrote. "But it is corrupted by excesses of individualism and of aesthetic caprice." He noted, too, that "the book lacks a natural affinity between the author, in spite of all he knows and understands, and his heroine, the Revolution." Something was missing, and what was missing, according to Trotsky, was precisely the knowledge of how to fight a revolution. On this subject Trotsky could speak with more authority than most. Malraux had painted Borodin as an experienced revolutionary. In fact Borodin's experience was severely limited, since he left Russia before the 1905 revolution and did not return until after the 1917 revolution. Trotsky showed a greater liking for Garin, who was closer to the type of a true revolutionary.

Trotsky's strictures were not altogether justified. Malraux's Borodin rings true, even though he has been given a more impressive biography than he deserved; and when Trotsky went on to say that "a solid inoculation of Marxism might have protected the author from his fatal mistakes," he was asking for the impossible. Malraux answered that it was not his business to write a Marxist tract; he was writing a novel, with all the limitations of a novel. Trotsky was furious because Malraux had shown Garin and Borodin exterminating the terrorists, not for revolutionary reasons, but in order to save their own necks. Malraux answered that this was precisely what Lenin and Trotsky had done during the revolution: they had not, of course, killed their enemies with their own hands, but they had employed the resources of the Cheka to do their killing for them. Trotsky described Malraux's heroes as sym-

bols of revolution. Malraux replied, "In bestowing on my characters
the honor of considering them symbols, Trotsky takes them out of
time. My defense is to put them back in."

It was not a complete defense, and Trotsky was not wholly wrong
when he spoke about symbols. Twenty years later, pondering the continued success of his novel, Malraux found himself half agreeing with
Trotsky. "If this novel has survived," he wrote, "it is not because it
depicted this or that episode of the Chinese revolution, but because
it presented a type of hero who combined natural talent with action,
intelligence, and lucidity." There were better reasons for the novel's
survival, in spite of its failings. It was violent, gripping, fast-paced,
totally credible. Garin came alive off the page. Out of fantasies of
revolutionary violence Malraux had constructed a mythological hero,
who haunted men's minds. In the nineteenth century Chernyshevsky
had invented the character of Rakhmetev, the harsh intellectual revolutionary, and Lenin had learned at the feet of this imaginary revolutionary. It remained to be seen whether another Lenin would model
himself on Garin.

ᴁ *The Kingdom of* *Farfelu* ᴂ

In Jean Cocteau's film *Blood of a Poet* there is a strange interlude showing the poet wandering down a long lonely corridor where the doors are numbered and the wallpaper is falling away and there is a general air of impending ruin. He has come to an abandoned hotel, which is also the world, for each of those numbered rooms contains a civilization. The poet pauses, peers through a keyhole, sees the shadows of hands playing on the ceiling and someone filling an opium pipe with infinite delicacy. Then, before he can explore the room further, a huge eye appears at the keyhole. All these, says the poet, represent "the mysteries of China."

Again and again Malraux would find himself contemplating these mysteries without ever coming to terms with them. Of all the civilizations of the Far East, China attracted him most, yet remained the most obstinately intractable, so that he was forever returning to contemplate it if only from a distance. For him there were two Chinas: the China of legend, compounded of all the travelers' tales he had read—he had read so many that he could almost walk about in that legendary landscape—and the China of revolution. One was calm, gentle, sensuous. The other consisted largely of the treaty ports with their foreign enclaves served by teeming coolies and ricksha pullers, violent, sensual, ugly, proliferating with small revolutionary committees under the control of foreign communists. The China of legend was seen in a continual noonday, while revolutionary China belonged to the night, the mists, the rain gleaming on the cobblestones. If the legendary China was more real to him, the China of revolution also possessed its own legends, and phantoms lurked in the shadows of Canton and Shanghai.

Shortly after *The Conquerors* was published, Malraux appears to

141

have felt the need to reassert the dominion of the legendary Orient. In
November 1928 Gallimard published *The Kingdom of Farfelu* in a
sumptuous edition limited to five hundred copies with the text in bold
italics printed only on the right hand pages. Malraux evidently went
to great pains to produce a book to please even the most exacting
bibliophile, and the choice of type, the dimensions of the page and
margins, and the gray-blue cover are all admirably balanced. Altogether there are only thirty-five printed pages. Like *Paper Moons* and
the fragments of *The Fireman of Massacre,* the new story is a kind of
fairy tale, but this time the fairy tale is told against a background of
oriental splendor. *Paper Moons* takes place in Paris, *The Fireman
of Massacre* in Bondy, *The Kingdom of Farfelu* in Asia, or perhaps on
a stage filled with Frenchmen in oriental costume.

   The Kingdom of Farfelu, which has never been translated into
English, is one of Malraux's most satisfying works. The mood is that
of *The Tempest:* all is magic, luxury, quietness. Strange and wonderful
things are always happening, but they have the appearance of inevitability and we do not question them any more than we question
Prospero's cell or Ariel's flights around the earth. The sea is a painted
backcloth and all the wonders of the Orient are displayed in the
magical marketplace. Here the nameless hero, arriving on a strange
shore, discovers a city where the architecture somehow resembles mushrooms and shellfish, and the men wear immense embroidered turbans
and sport long black beards like Charlemagne:

> As soon as we stepped ashore, the merchants threw them-
> selves upon us. One of them, a seller of phoenixes, set a phoenix
> aflame before our eyes. A moment later it was reborn from the
> ashes, but taking advantage of the foolhardy joy of the mer-
> chant, it flew away, flying in a heavy and ungainly manner.
> Everyone looked up, everyone followed the flight of the phoenix.
> In the silence there could be heard only the voice crying in the
> distance: "O city born of the sea, one day your palaces shaped
> like animals will be invaded by the fish of darkness. . . ."
>   "Myself, I am a merchant of dragons. They are immortal, and
> so beautiful that merely to contemplate them overcomes the
> greatest suffering and the keenest sorrows. They may also be

used as barometers, for when the crests along their backs are vertical, then rain is not far away. In emergencies, they may be consulted for good advice. I purchase them in the country of their origin."

In this enchanting marketplace the hero discovers all the familiar objects of his childhood dreams. There are cloth merchants whose shops glow with all the colors of the rainbow, antique dealers selling magic caskets from Siam, vendors of orange-colored eggs and tattooed ducks and horses made of paper—no doubt these are the paper horses which the Chinese Immortals rode on every day, carefully folding them up at night. In addition there were dervishes selling books, priests stirring cauldrons where the little copper gods were being brewed, and everywhere there were flower sellers, so that the whole marketplace was drenched with the perfume of flowers.

The hero, however, does not spend much time in the marketplace. Since he is a stranger, he meets the fate reserved for all strangers— he is arrested and thrown into prison, where he bemoans the fate that led him from his Mediterranean island to this inhospitable land. He dreams of his own city with its port filled with ships, "where the squirrels and the shrew mice played in the rigging," an old city, fast falling into ruins. In the subterranean galleries, he remembers, there were the mummies of sacred alligators and sometimes he saw the phosphorescent gleam in the eyes of the sacred cats. From these dreams he is awakened by a guard, who orders him to appear before the ruling prince, who is granting an audience to his ministers. One minister reports that Babylon is no more, and that in the farthest forests of his kingdom there are only the white bones of dragons gleaming with black insects. Another reports that he has successfully concluded the mission entrusted to him: he has given the young princess into the hands of the Fish-eating Tsar, who held the tail of a fish in his fist and the head of a fish in his mouth and there was even a tiny fish clinging to his beard. He ruled over a land covered with perpetual ice and was accustomed to receive from the tributary chieftains offerings of bleeding flesh. The Fish-eating Tsar did not rule for long. The princess set fire to his temple and succeeded him on the throne.

This was satisfying news, and the prince thereupon motioned to another minister to deliver his report. This time the news was less welcome, for it appeared that one of the prince's cities had been invaded by butterfly-colored birds of vast size, the people had fled, and now these terrible birds perched fast asleep on the blackened walls of the city. The people were clamoring for help against the aggressors, but the prince had no thought of aiding them. He closed his eyes wearily and began to dictate in Persian to a white-bearded secretary a letter to the Chinese princess, who was the object of his most passionate desire. Then, turning to the visitor who has just been released from prison, he says: "Have you ever set eyes on the Chinese princess?"

"No," replies the former prisoner.

"Oh, weariness, weariness! Neither have I," says the prince.

Thereupon the former prisoner is ordered into the army, where he will serve his time as historian of the prince's wars. Idekel, an old man who has suffered many adventures in the prince's service, is given to him as an assistant.

Idekel knows the appropriate spells. He has tossed the dust-laden roses of Tartary into the blood of mermaids; he has seen the Magi in their lion-embroidered costumes hanging from the branches of the trees of Irkenise; he has cut the throats of the Persian guards defending the royal palace of Isfahan, which went up in flames.

"You are an old man," Idekel says, turning to the historian of the wars, "but I doubt whether you have ever seen a great conflagration. A great conflagration—why, that is one of the most perfect works of God. To everything it touches fire gives a precious substance!"

Idekel is half-brother to the Fireman of Massacre, the well-known incendiary who has no talent for putting out fires. He rejoices in flames far more than he rejoices in cutting throats. Now the army has received orders to mount a second campaign against Isfahan, and Idekel becomes the historian's companion in arms.

We never learn why a second campaign has become necessary: presumably the prince wants confirmation of his former triumph. During the journey Idekel entertains his friend with accounts of the Byzantine Emperor Basil II, "whom we historians call Bulgaroctonus," a singularly unpleasant monarch who blinded his Bulgarian prisoners and sent them marching back to Bulgaria. Ten blinded men, holding hands, are led by an eleventh, who has only had one eye torn out. Thousands of these small columns of blind men make their way to Bulgaria in the depth of winter, across the stark mountains and the barren plains. Centuries later men could still trace the route they had followed by observing the tombs of the blinded men; on every tomb there was painted an eye.

As he tells these stories, we are obscurely aware that Idekel, a Magus since the age of thirty, is prophesying disaster. The army invading Isfahan is doomed to failure. This is the same expedition described by Maurice Sainte-Rose in the pages of *Indochine,* with the hero transformed from a student of Ekaterinburg into a medieval historiographer and with some important variations in the text. This time Isfahan is presented as even more menacing. The people who fled into the interior of the walled city have blocked up the gates and covered them with dirt so that the gates are indistinguishable from the walls, and in addition they have built thousands of low walls within the city, forming a maze in which the invaders will lose themselves. The invaders tear down a part of the wall, observe the labyrinth within, and turn back. They camp on the outskirts of the city, where they are plagued by scorpions. The narrator describes the irresolution and mounting terror of the invaders:

> Several hours passed while I remained asleep on my rooftop, dreaming of conquests. When I came down I learned that some of my companions had just died. They had been bitten by scorpions. And they said that some of the horses had also perished.
>
> Already the animals which had been put to flight by our arrival no longer feared us; they returned. The dogs hurled themselves across the road, got between the legs of the soldiers, and threw them to the ground, as though they were dolls. Cats came, and skilfully stole our food, and sometimes at the corner of a road we would see the melancholy silhouette of a camel without a master. We killed the dogs and the cats, and the other animals vanished.
>
> Our provisions moreover were running out. The soldiers tore

down the walls after attempting to determine from the rooftops
the general direction leading to the center of the city: but since
they lacked the necessary implements, they had to strike at the
walls with their weapons, and progress was slow. Then the night
came down with its cortege of constellations and black scorpions; and again the soldiers died.

Many days passed in this way, while our triumph drew nearer,
but we were starving. . . . Thus there were born the demons
of the ruins, who are faceless and live within our own bodies.
(No doubt one of these demons was born in every one of us.)

These are the demons that drive men mad with visions and exalta-
tions. The narrator has visions of bronze peacocks, many-armed gods,
masks of silver, cities where the walls are fashioned of laced horns and
where the singing tree lies concealed, and there are other cities built
of enormous blocks of crystal where the colors of the rainbow glide
like birds in flight: the mysteries of Asia. Idekel, too, has his nightmares. He believes that a vast army is being formed in the south to
defend Isfahan and nothing will be gained by going to India to conquer this army, for between Isfahan and Golconda there are immense
deserts of salt shining like hoarfrost, an excellent setting for skeletons.
When evening comes down in Isfahan, there can be heard only the
whispering of the demons, like a rustling rising from the depths of
every soldier. Half the soldiers are dead from scorpion bites, or have
fled into the desert. The rest are numbed, as though gripped by winter.

Fear has taken possession of the army, which knows it is trapped,
incapable of advancing or retreating. They have entered the Kingdom
of Farfelu, once the city of Isfahan, now a nightmare of formidable
proportions. The mercenaries of the army of the Ganges have entered
the city. It is no longer possible to hope for victory; the invaders are
merely waiting for the day of their defeat.

One evening, unable to sleep, the narrator decides to walk through
the labyrinthine city. In the shadows he sees an officer whose aigrette
gleams in the light of the stars, and decides to follow him, scarcely
caring where the journey will lead him.

We walked for a long time, making our way down narrow lanes between walls whose dark and serpentine ridges appeared to have been gnawed by some animal living at the time of the ancient people who worshipped Fire, and we crossed deserted squares whose geometric outlines dissolved in the dust. In this way we reached the great avenue of the Emperor Abbas with its willows and mosaic palaces.

Silence! Silence! A warm and gentle wind was breaking off small fragments of mosaic; the dog roses and pomegranate trees were in flower; and there were other flowers, still invisible, filling the air with perfume. In the long pools beside the avenue the marvelous fish brought in by Timur surrounded the reflected stars with wavy designs. It seemed as though mankind had vanished from the earth, as though plants and stones and silent animals lived in that perfect liberty which is the gift of irremediable ruin. The officer I was following approached one of those statues beside the pools; the statue rose and followed him. Stupefied, I looked more closely and saw that those gray shapes which could be seen stretching into the distance were not statues but men. I walked beside the pools, hidden by the bushes; and in the soft mist I watched our officers, clothed in silk, starving like us, fishing for the centuries-old fish.

We are now close to the end, for the terror of the dark and shadowy avenue gives place to a darker and even more shadowy terror. Out of the mist and the darkness there comes something like a dark cloth or a growing stain—an army of scorpions. Against this enemy the invaders have no weapons, and like madmen they flee across the desert to become the prey of vultures.

The narrator survives, making his way to Trebizond where he is received by the prince, who shows no particular interest in his plight. All the world knows about the army lost in the sands of Isfahan: it is one of those defeats which do not bear talking about. There, on the shores of the Black Sea, the narrator makes a living as a seller of seashells. He has bought two mermaids and hopes to sell them to the prince: they were fashioned in Korea from the head and arms of small monkeys and the tails of fishes. With the money from the prince, he will sail away to the Fortunate Isles.

In his study of the early writings of Malraux, André Vandegans has devoted a hundred and fifty pages to an analysis of *The Kingdom of Farfelu,* seeking to discover every reference and every source. Thus we learn that Idekel is perhaps derived from Hiddekel, a river flowing out of Eden, and that various significant details in the story have their origin in the works of Pierre Loti, the Comte de Gobineau, Marco Polo, *The Thousand and One Nights,* Sir John Malcolm's *History of Persia,* René Grousset's *History of Asia,* the works of Friar Johannes de Carpini, and perhaps fifty others. He finds similarities between the attack on Isfahan and the attack on the Summer Palace in Peking in 1860. He gives a detailed summary of the Soviet plans to annex Persia shortly after World War I, and concludes that these events provided the stimulus for the strange story about the Cossack invasion of Isfahan led by a young student from Ekaterinburg. Perhaps; but it is just as likely that the events in Persia had nothing whatsoever to do with the story, which was not in the least concerned with historical events.

The Kingdom of Farfelu is a work of the imagination comparable with Coleridge's *Kubla Khan,* which has also been provided with an impressive commentary illustrating the origin of every image and every adjective. Malraux's Isfahan is as imaginary as Xanadu, and where Coleridge describes a fleeting glimpse of Paradise, Malraux, haunted by death, describes a fleeting glimpse of death's kingdom with all its defenses, its panoply, and its monuments. We never see its inhabitants, nor are we ever permitted to enter its palaces. We see the city only in the evening or late at night, full of menace, and very quiet. The shadows are haunted with the invisible creatures of death, while the invaders grope among the ruins like blind men groping among tomb- stones. Long before the scorpions come rushing out of the darkness, the invaders have succumbed to the demons of ruin and death has claimed them.

Altogether there were three versions of *The Kingdom of Farfelu,* and a fourth manuscript version is known to exist. In the first version, *Expedition to Isfahan,* we are offered the spectacle of a city in ruins, strangely beautiful, defending itself in silence against the invaders, who never set eyes on the defenders. The most memorable passage concerns the centuries old angelfish in the sacred pools, which the invaders catch and cook because they are starving. Scorpions emerge from the crannies in the walls, but they are not the worst enemy. The Cossacks abandon the city quietly, because "every day we became more lost and solitary amid the illustrious dead and the invisible insects." Isfahan is a city of terror, but it is not yet the city of death.

The second version, which appeared in the literary magazine *Commerce* in the summer of 1927, was called *The Voyage to the Fortunate Islands*. The text of the *Expedition to Isfahan* has been reworked and combined with an earlier fragment, dating from 1920 and describing the narrator's arrival on a strange eastern shore. From this version comes the charming story about the seller of phoenixes who burned a phoenix to ashes.

In the final version Malraux was more concerned with allegory and mystery than with fairy tales. So he cut away all that was decorative and anecdotal, until the whole story was bathed in a supernatural light. In the second version he sees chocolate-colored children bathing in the sea, the boys naked, the girls "wearing a little cache-sexe of metal in the shape of a heart engraved with moral maxims." This, too, is a charming invention, but adds nothing to the development of a story concerned with death and damnation. The grotesqueries which delighted him in *Paper Moons* and *The Fireman of Massacre* were similarly abandoned, and the long catalogue of benign sea monsters, "some shaped like dragons, others like mandolins and umbrellas and sausages and the heads of ducks," which the narrator remembered in prison, has no place in the final version. The dead wood is cut away. For the first time we are able to watch the succeeding stages of a manuscript. Through page after page we see him at work, transforming one story into another, changing an adjective here, canceling a whole paragraph there, until he has knitted it together in a single whole dominated by the cry of the phoenix: "O city born of the sea, one day your palaces shaped like animals will be invaded by the fish of darkness!"

In Malraux's works *The Kingdom of Farfelu* holds a special place. In the past he played with death, though it was serious play. Hence-

forth there will be no question of playing with death. He will wrestle
with it with all his strength, like Jacob wrestling with the angel, never
letting it alone for long, never giving it time to hide. In Isfahan he
had seen it racing out of the darkness, and he had gazed at it long
enough to know that it resembled an immense black cloth with a fringe
formed of the pincers of scorpions. Henceforth he will be haunted by
"that perfect liberty which is the gift of irremediable ruin." The scorpions of the Apocalypse have come to haunt him, for ultimately there
is no escape from them. He had read Revelation: "Unto them was
given power, as the scorpions of the earth have power. . . . And in
those days shall men seek death, and shall not find it, and shall desire
to die, and death shall flee from them. . . ."

❦ *The Royal Way* ❧

One day in 1928, while pacing the deck of a cargo ship in the Straits of Messina, the idea came to Malraux that David de Mayrena, the legendary king of the Sedangs, might serve as the hero of his next novel. Little was known about Mayrena, who belonged to the folklore of the East. A Dutchman, he had abandoned his estates in Sumatra for the highlands of Indochina, where he had carved out a small kingdom for himself, demanding implicit obedience to his slightest commands; like Rajah Brooke of Sarawak he made himself an absolute ruler over savages. This much was central to the legend, but beyond this lay an ever-widening circumference of speculations, inventions and traditions, all mingled with a few crumbs of local history. His ferocious will, his innumerable concubines, his duels with the local chieftains, his audacious encounters with French government officials, his army of elephants, his praetorian guard, all these were discussed in the bars of Indochina by people who swore that they had known Mayrena at the height of his glory, which was perhaps at the turn of the century. Stories were told about how he had suffered torture calmly, with a quiet and terrifying joy, and there were still other stories about how he had once built a ship and manned it with pirates and cutthroats for a raid on Mecca. There was also a legend that he had died miserably in a grotesque little hut, having been reduced to extreme poverty and perhaps to slavery. All this was apocrypha. But what if one could invent a real Mayrena, a perfectly convincing white conquistador, brutal, intelligent, given to fierce rages yet dominated by a superb will power, rich and powerful, dying at last in misery and squalor?

While the cargo ship was taking him to Batum, Malraux's mind was far away in the Orient as he paced the deck, working out the general shape of the novel that had begun to haunt him and would continue to haunt him for more than a year. What interested him most of all was Mayrena confronted with death, not death in the abstract, but the death that grips a man by the throat and shakes him out of the lethargy of living. He was more and more haunted by death. Like a Jesuit novice who throws himself on the floor of his cell, imagining himself suffering the agonies of Christ, his body and soul surrendering to mortality until he can feel the claws of death on his flesh, Malraux had submitted himself to the regimen of death in long meditations that left him drained of all energy, but strangely quiet and with no desire to die. These meditations acted upon him like a drug, one that enlivened the senses rather than deadened them. He had become obsessed with death to the point of exhilaration.

The novel therefore would be the fruit of these long meditations and of his journeys in Indochina, with the mysterious Mayrena appearing at the end of the trail. There is some evidence to show that the novel was originally begun in the familiar diary form, but the diary idea was quickly abandoned.

Malraux has always shown a deep interest in the way novelists create their characters, continually changing them, substituting the traits of one for the traits of another, altering their features as though they were made of wax, discarding one after another the architectural plans on which the novel is based. In Dostoevsky's notebooks for *The Idiot* the Idiot appears first as a powerful, proud, and Byronic figure, sensual and extravagant, a demon of pride. Then, from notebook to notebook, we watch him divesting himself of all his disguises until he appears as a monument of humility. There were seven notebooks, and in each there are abrupt changes, false starts, sudden illuminations. Fascinated by the Idiot, Dostoevsky cannot make up his mind whether he is a fearful scoundrel or a model of perfection. At last he wrote the cryptic note: "He is a Prince. An idiot Prince (he is with the children)?!" Question and exclamation mark: uncertainty and discovery. Thereafter there were no more problems, and Dostoevsky went on to write the novel as though he had known Prince Myshkin intimately over many years, although he had come to birth only at the moment when he was seen with the children. Malraux, who drew attention to the difficult birth

of Prince Myshkin in the comments he wrote for Gaëton Picon's brief
study, was well aware of the difficult births of his own characters.

Unlike *The Conquerors,* which was concerned with a revolutionary
uprising and therefore with a score of characters, *The Royal Way* is
concerned with only two characters, Perken and Vannec, both adventurers. Vannec is largely a self-portrait, Perken is Mayrena without his
empire and without any real hope of building one, though he talks of
conquering a vast area of Indochina once he has succeeded in buying
machine guns. The young Vannec meets Perken on board a ship sailing
to the Far East, and immediately they form a bond of friendship.
Thereafter, until the very end of the novel, we shall hear them talking.
It is spirited talk, crisp and allusive, sometimes jerky, like a gramophone
record when the needle jumps over the grooves, and nearly always it is
a talk about death, a subject which obsesses them. The middle-aged
Perken marches toward his death, and the young Vannec is the
neophyte who eagerly permits himself to be introduced into death's
rituals.

Vannec is a trained archaeologist, knows Sanskrit, and has a deep
respect for scholarship and the arts. Bookish, sensitive—he can still
remember the agonizing sensation of being pricked by the doctor with
a hypodermic needle in his childhood—and with considerable intellectual daring, he has long ago come to regard himself as a misfit in
the modern world. He refuses to choose "between eating in bargain
restaurants and selling automobiles." His aim is to make a fortune and
thus ensure his independence. He is one of those who are so determined to escape from bourgeois civilization that they find themselves unwittingly embracing bourgeois values; and he can think of
only one way of making a fortune. He will uncover Khmer statues,
transport them out of Cambodia, and sell them to the highest bidder.

He is not a pleasant character, nor are we expected to have very
much sympathy for him. Unlike Garin, who possesses a certain tenuous
nobility, Vannec is almost entirely lacking in noble qualities. He becomes hysterical at the slightest provocation, and the screaming of his
nerves can be heard as a musical accompaniment throughout the novel.
(Perken is slower, more cautions, more inclined to believe that power
and money are illusions.) Only when Vannec speaks about art does he

measure his words quietly. On an early page of the novel he announces a theme which was to preoccupy Malraux for at least a quarter of a century. He is talking to the director of the French Institute in Saigon, and with the assertiveness that arises from timidity and insecurity, he announces his views on art:

> My view is that the essential value we set on the artist may conceal one of the main features in the life of a work of art: the state of the civilization appraising it. It looks as though in art time has no existence. You understand, what interests me is the decomposition and transformation of these works of art, their most secret life, which is fashioned out of the deaths of men. Briefly, every work of art tends to become myth.
>
> For me, museums are places where the works of the past have become myth and lie sleeping—though they continue to possess a historical life—waiting for the day when the artists will recall them into a real existence. If they have a definite appeal to me, it is because the artist has the power to resurrect them. In the last analysis, no civilization can be understood by another. But the works of art remain, and we remain blind to them until the time comes when our myths are in agreement with theirs.

These ideas are not examined in any detail, and we learn nothing more about the secret life of works of art, that life "which is fashioned out of the deaths of men." Vannec has merely thrown out his ideas, and the director of the Institute listens to them. The resurrection of works of art will have its ironic commentary when Vannec and Perken find an abandoned temple in a forest and resurrect the sculptures.

The account of the discovery of the temple in *The Royal Way* follows closely on Malraux's experiences at Banteay Srei with one important difference: the experiences are heightened and transformed by a totally different excitement. Fear dominates. The rather casual expedition which set out light-heartedly to discover the ruins of Banteay Srei is transformed into a desperate venture through tropical forests, with savage tribesmen always threatening to destroy them. Terrified by the

leeches, the half-glimpsed spears of the tribesmen, the darkness of the
forest, and the sense of danger which seems to come from all directions,
Vannec surrenders to a delirium of fear. Perken, with his greater
knowledge of the East, remains calm. If danger comes, he will give
a good account of himself. "Keep under cover," he tells Vannec, who
scarcely needs to be told to hide.

It is not that Vannec is without courage: it is simply that courage
has no meaning in the enchanted forest. He remembers that in his
childhood he was terrified by live crabs, lobsters and snakes, but these
were small terrors. The forest is terror writ large, an unending nightmare, where the swinging Cable of *Paper Moons* has been let loose,
invisible and implacable. As they make their way through the forest in
a strange quietness, we become aware that Malraux is no longer simply
reporting his experiences in Indochina but adding to them and summoning up the ghosts of his childhood dreams and fantasies. Suddenly
they arrive at the edge of a clearing, where armed warriors can be dimly
seen. They have thick lips and they carry spears glittering in the sun.
In the middle of the clearing there stands a wattle tower surmounted
by four buffalo heads with enormous horns. On top of the tower some
meat is being cooked, and thick white smoke curls up from the fire.
Vannec, crouching on the edge of the clearing, observes a naked warrior near the fire leaning on his spear, while in a state of sexual excita-
tion. From somewhere nearby there comes the sound of muffled
chanting.

The tower surmounted by a naked warrior leaning on his spear has
the force of a hallucination. We hear no more about the armed warrior,
and the two adventurers continue their journey through the forest, as
though nothing had happened. But in fact, during that strange interlude, something of very great importance has happened. For a brief
moment Vannec has had a vision of the life he would like to lead, of
perfect freedom and perfect indolence, without fear and without any
sexual inhibitions. The mirage vanishes, but he will never forget the
vision of paradise.

A few days later they come to a ruined temple buried in the forest,
hidden among leaves and plants. At first they cannot make out its
shape, and there is no sign of any sculptures. Then they see a sandstone

figure wearing an intricately carved crown, and a moment later they see a stone bird with outspread wings and a parrot's beak. They have found what they were looking for: the temple is a repository of statues of the very best period of Khmer art, and they are elated at the prospects before them.

Malraux's description of the ruined temple appears to be based on notes written shortly after the discovery of the temple of Banteay Srei:

> Stones, stones, a few lying flat, most of them upended; a stonemason's yard invaded by the jungle. There were large stretches of purple sandstone wall, some sculptured, others un-adorned, with ferns hanging from them; and there were some bearing the red patina of fire. Facing him were bas-reliefs of the best period, with a pronounced Indian influence—Claude [Vannec] was standing very close to them—and very beautiful under the ancient decorative archways half hidden beneath a breastwork of fallen stones. With an effort he was able to look beyond them. Above them were three ruined towers razed to within six feet of the ground, the three mutilated stumps stick-ing out of such an overwhelming mass of rubble that all the vegetation around them was stunted, as though stuck into the debris; and the yellow frogs wandered sluggishly over them.

As they set to work to remove the most attractive sculptures, they were plagued by frogs, monkeys and insects of all kinds. The sculptured blocks were so large that they had to be cut with a handsaw, but the teeth broke off and the saw proved to be useless on the hard sandstone. They thought of lifting up the sculptured blocks which had fallen face downward on the ground, but gave up in despair when, having lifted one block, they saw that it was painfully discolored. Two enchanting stone dancing girls formed a corner-stone. Vannec thought they might fetch a fortune, perhaps as much as half a million francs, if they could be brought out intact. This sculpture was carved out of three closely fitting blocks. With immense difficulty they were able to remove the heads and the feet of the dancing girls, while the bodies remained on the middle block, impervious to their hammers and chisels. Finally, with the help of a sledge-hammer Perken was able to dislodge the middle block, and the three blocks of stone are laid in the covered buffalo carts.

The account of the ruined temple and the excavation of the statues is rather perfunctory; it is merely a short interlude in the story, which is concerned with the landscape of fear, the journey into the heart of darkness. Deliberately the travelers strike out into unknown territory, as though they were determined to confront every possible danger. Perken wants power, machine guns, a people who will obey him and follow him, all the attributes of earthly kingship. Vannec wants to sell the sculptures, make a fortune, and retire from the battle of life. He is half in love with Perken, who respects only one man on this earth. The man he respects is called Grabot, a strange Faustian character with one eye—he had infected the other eye with gonorrheal pus in a private battle with an army doctor, who suspected him of malingering or of cowardice. Grabot, too, had dreamed of being a chieftain ruling over barbaric tribes. He was one of those who wring destiny's neck and are never content unless they are attempting the impossible. Perken calls him a man of "malignant grandeur" and never tires of extolling his barbaric pride. Somewhere in this region he expects to find Grabot and perhaps join forces with him. Together they will carve out an empire of their own, for they are both determined on conquest.

Meanwhile everything is going wrong with the expedition. They are deserted by their guides, and have only a handful of servants. Sometimes they catch glimpses of the half-savage tribesmen; a new guide in a sarong clotted with blood leads them along the forest trails; he is the messenger of evil tidings, leading them to the long-lost Grabot as the witch in the fairy tale leads the innocent children to the small house in the forest where the ultimate horrors are revealed to them. But neither Vannec nor Perken are innocent; all their lives they have been marked by corruption.

In all Malraux's novels there are passages of quite extraordinary intensity where the veils fall away and the lightning strikes. These passages are usually short, covering no more than a page or two, and they are curiously self-contained, as though they were independent of the rest of the novel. So it is when Vannec and Perken enter a Moi village and come upon an isolated hut beside a clump of banana trees, and they know or half guess, in their misery and hopefulness, that they will find Grabot there. What they find is a kind of animal, a man so mutilated that he appears to have no human qualities. His other eye has been put out, his matted hair falls round his face, he has been harnessed by leather thongs to a treadmill and spends his day crawling around the airless hut in interminable circles. Half-crazed, living only for the day when an impossible revenge will be granted to him, he lives in eternal torment. The brief passages describing the discovery of Grabot have the hallucinatory quality of a nightmare remembered to the last terrifying detail. Grabot has died many times, yet he still lives.

They free Grabot from the leather thongs, but make no attempt to escape from the village. Instead they seize the hut belonging to the chieftain, finding it empty; the tribesmen are invisible, but their presence can be felt. The chieftain's hut is on stilts, and Grabot warns them that it will be a simple matter for the Mois to set fire to it during the night. At dusk comes the confrontation, as Perken marches out of the hut to face the Moi warriors and their aged chieftain to parley for his life. The march is described minutely at length, with an overwhelming sense of suspense. There had been a hint of that power to evoke suspense in *Expedition to Isfahan,* and now once again the hero is marching along the avenue of death toward an unpredictable enemy. Perken marches toward them very stiffly, almost doll-like. Fear and ferocious excitement grip him. He can see the heads of the tribesmen, but their bodies are hidden in the thick mists rising from the ground, and he knows that their spears are leveled at him. The only hope lies in his relentless will, but when he steps on a war-spike his will falters. When he falls, he half expects the Mois to hurl their spears at him. Bleeding and in pain, he rises and continues the march. He succeeds in parleying with the chieftain.

All this is told with great skill, for Malraux is always at his best when describing an encounter with darkness and death. The closer Perken comes to the enemy, the more intense the excitement, the more hopeless his chances of survival. Some Mois slip behind him, cutting him off from Vannec, who remains in the chieftain's hut, and Perken continues to march straight up to the chieftain, his perceptions quickened by the pain in his wounded leg. The march toward the armed Mois is brilliantly sustained. Perken is not killed, but he has already suffered a mortal wound from the spike. Many years later, in *Man's Hope,* Malraux described prisoners marching out of Toledo to be shot down by a Fascist firing squad, and once again there is the sense of abstract terror conveyed with astonishing power.

On the morning after that fantastic march across the Moi village, Perken displays his magic powers to the chieftain by shooting at a wild ox's skull, which bleeds copiously. "The spreading blood, carving out shapes like claws, resembled a large insect and left on the sunlit blue skull the sign of possession." Perken explains later that he had fired a hollow bullet filled with his own blood. The chieftain is properly impressed, but the reader who has followed Perken's march up to the spears of the tribal warriors finds himself wondering why conjuring tricks are necessary: the magic was in the march, not in the hollow bullet. Malraux had found the incident in the memoirs of the great French conjuror Robert-Houdin, who fired blood-filled bullets at skulls to inspire terror among the marabouts of Algeria. Malraux's borrowings are usually unhappy, and they are immediately noticeable because they break the rhythm of the novel.

For Perken, with his wounded and infected knee, there can be no issue except in death. Opium will keep the pain away; amputation of the leg might save his life, but in this wild region on the Siamese border there are no medical facilities. He has escaped from the tribesmen, but he is doomed, and knows it, and in his own way takes pleasure in it. For the last time he takes a native woman to his bed.

> He gazed at her face with the bluish eyelids from the distance of a few inches, and it seemed to be a mask almost wholly removed from the savage sensations gluing him to this body, which he possessed as though he had struck it down. The whole of her face, the whole woman, was concentrated in her uplifted mouth. Suddenly the swollen lips parted, quivering over the teeth, and as though beginning from her lips a long tremor convulsed the whole of her outstretched body, until then motionless and inhuman, like trees transfixed by the heat of sum-

mer. The face had no life except for the mouth, although in response to each of Perken's movements her fingernail gritted on the sheet. But as the tremors grew in intensity, her finger no longer touched the sheet and pointed in mid-air. And then her lips closed, and her eyelids fell over her eyes.

The mask with the blue eyelids is summoning him to his death, and Perken finds himself fighting against the desire to crush her, to obliterate her. Yet Malraux is not completely convincing when he describes the sex act: it seems oddly contrived. Like the hollow bullet it gives the impression of having strayed from another novel. But at the very end, when Perken is dying in agony, Malraux is in his element. Perken lies in a crowded hut, the natives watching him silently, without expression, while the dying man watches himself, fascinated by his own disintegration, the pain and the horror of knowing that all those around him will see another sunrise, continuing their lives as though nothing had happened. The mosquitoes torment him, but he has no strength to brush them away. His teeth are covered with blood, because he has bitten his lips to ease the pain. Finally he whispers: "There is . . . no death . . . There is only . . . *I* . . . *I, who am going to die. . . .*"

At that moment all the dreams of power and all the abstract arguments on the subject of death and fame and man's place in the universe fall away. Like Corneille's Medea, who stripped herself of her ornaments of pride to achieve a greater pride, and cried: *"Moi, dis-je, et c'est assez!"* Perken achieves his death by stripping it of all that is inessential and inconsequential. There are no heroics. There is only a man who is going to die, and that is enough.

Though Vannec provides a necessary commentary and has a claim on the development of the plot, there is really only one character in the novel. There is a sense in which the whole novel can be read as a monologue by Perken, the disenchanted hero marching to his inevitable death through the enchanted forest. He wears the cloak of doom, and his ancestors are to be found in the Gothic tales of the early nineteenth century. Malraux has given him a modern face, a modern sensibility, and a modern death.

Published by Bernard Grasset, *The Royal Way* appeared in October 1930, after being serialized in *La Revue de Paris* from August 15 to October 1. A note at the end of the original edition reads, *"The Royal Way* constitutes the first volume of *The Powers of the Desert,* and this tragic beginning is merely the prologue." No doubt the second volume, if it had ever been written, would have described Vannec's arrest and trial for stealing the statues, and the third volume might have dealt with the formation of the "Young Annam" movement and the revolutionary ferment in Indochina. The project was abandoned, perhaps because Vannec was too implausible a character to sustain the weight of a trilogy. *The Powers of the Desert* was one of many projects left uncompleted.

More and more Malraux was turning to the study of art as a means of solving those problems that Perken had left unsolved. Since art was the most triumphant form of human expression, man's only worthy weapon against destiny, Malraux felt the need to immerse himself in the greatest periods of art. Persian art, with its three great waves culminating in Achaemenian, Sassanian, and Islamic times, especially attracted him, and his first visit to Persia in the summer of 1928 was followed by another in the summer of 1929, and still a third visit the following year. He lived quietly in Isfahan and Shiraz, made friends with the Bakhtiari tribesmen, visited Persepolis, and attempted without much success to learn Persian. Isfahan, with its blue mosques and ornate palaces, must be counted among the three or four most beautiful cities in the world, and he was perfectly content to wander along the shaded streets, pay ceremonious visits to the tribal chieftains and haunt the antique shops with his wife, who was equally enchanted by the prospects of Persia. Rumor proclaimed that he took part in battles between the tribes and the armies of Riza Shah Pahlavi, but the rumor was unfounded.

The real Isfahan had no relation at all to the city described in *Expedition to Isfahan.* There were no enemies, no scorpions. The palaces of Shah Abbas were still immaculately beautiful, and the *maidan,* the great dusty square surrounded by glowing mosques and a solitary palace, was scarcely changed since the city was the capital of a great empire.

In 1929 Malraux set out for Afghanistan, visited Kabul, which was so full of Indians that he described it later as "a corrugated iron suburb of Lahore or Peshawar," and he wondered whether Lhasa might not be equally horrible. Recent excavations at Hadda near Kabul had uncovered a vast hoard of Greco-Buddhist sculptures in white stucco, and the grave beauty of these sculptures, so often resembling the work of Gothic artists, came to him as a revelation. The marriage of Hellenistic art and Buddhism brought into existence a vast progeny, for all the carved Buddhas of the east ultimately derive from these superb sculptures made in Bactria at the order of kings and abbots who spoke Greek and worshipped Buddha. Today we know a good deal more about Greco-Buddhist art, but in 1929 it was still little known, and Malraux was deeply puzzled by it. What particularly puzzled him was that these sculptures spoke of a delighted awareness of the world while the religion of Buddha was dedicated to a withdrawal from the world.

During the following year Malraux wrote an introduction for an exhibition of Greco-Buddhist art which was being shown in Paris. This small pamphlet, now among the rarest of Malraux's writings, had the rather odd title *Exposition Gothico-Bouddhique, Oeuvres Gothico-Bouddhiques du Pamir.* The intention was clear: he wanted to emphasize the extraordinary similarity between these sculptures and Gothic sculptures. "Here and at Rheims," he wrote, "we see the same feeling of tenderness before humanity conceived as living people rejoicing in the world, not as people suffering in the world," and he went on to claim that throughout the history of Asia there had been only one brief moment when Buddhist art was concerned to portray the living flesh:

> They kneel with their hands joined in prayer, and these living bodies demonstrate a grave tenderness. We shall not find this again in Buddhism in its progress toward China, Japan and Cambodia. After this secret flowering in Central Asia, the human body would become formless and abstract, and the lizards of Yunkang would glide over them and in the Cambodian temples the frogs would take possession of them. They would become merely architecture or effeminate torsos with ele-

phant feet, supporting marvelous heads and conveying serenity in stone. For Buddhism rejects the world. . . .

Twenty years later, in *The Psychology of Art,* Malraux would come to realize that Buddhist art as it traveled across Asia involved considerably more than marvelous heads on effeminate torsos with elephant feet, yet he continued to believe that the stucco sculptures of Hadda had little to do with Greece and could quite properly be called "Gothic-Buddhist." He spoke with authority, for he owned a number of these sculptures and was able to study them minutely. One could place a princely *bodhisattva* carved in the fourth century in Afghanistan beside a Gothic angel from twelfth-century France, and almost they seemed to be by the same hand. Both Gothic and Bactrian art derived from Hellenistic Greece, but this did not explain the astonishing similarity between the *bodhisattva* and the angel.

In those days Malraux was still working as an editor at Gallimard, where he was given one of those small cubicles which are rather smaller than a prison cell. Gaston Gallimard, the founder of the publishing house, was fond of him and gave him considerably more freedom than he gave to other editors: hence the long holidays, and the annual pilgrimages to Persia. But it was the time of the depression, the market for art books was limited, and editors sometimes had to perform unpleasant chores. For a while Malraux was placed in charge of a series of documentary lives of great men. In 1930, the same year in which he published *The Royal Way,* there appeared his *Life of Napoleon, based upon the original documents, letters, proclamations and writings.* The book appeared anonymously and was soon forgotten. Compiled with the aid of scissors and paste, without scholarly notes or sources, printed on cheap paper, the book was aimed at the popular market. Although it was a substantial work consisting almost entirely of documents with short bridge passages, it added very little to the common stock of knowledge about Napoleon, and the series of documentary lives was soon abandoned.

For Malraux the year 1930, which had seen so many pleasant journeys and so many quiet discoveries, ended in disaster. On December 20 Fernand-Georges Malraux committed suicide in his apartment

in the Rue de Lubeck in Paris. He was only fifty-four. A few days
before his death he had spoken of his intense curiosity about the world
beyond the grave, but he had never previously shown any tendency
toward suicide. His second marriage had been reasonably happy, he
was on affectionate terms with his three sons, and there seemed to be
no reason why he should kill himself.

Because it was the Christmas season, the burial at Dunkerque was
inevitably delayed, and two weeks passed before the sealed coffin
was taken to the cemetery beside the sea. There, among the tall gravestones, he was laid beside his father on January 3, 1931. André and
Clara Malraux, and a large contingent of the Malraux clan, attended
the ceremonies on a cold, windy day. Some months later the name of
Fernand-Georges Malraux was carved lightly on the stone, so lightly
that today it can scarcely be seen.

For the rest of his life Malraux was to be haunted by the death
of his father.

‧§ *Man's Fate* ‧‧

I f Malraux had written only *Paper Moons, The Conquerors, The Royal Way,* and *The Kingdom of Farfelu,* he would not have achieved any lasting fame. They were good, indeed excellent novels, brilliantly constructed, filled with poetry, and bearing the indelible marks of great promise. But the promise had not yet been fulfilled, and these novels would have been remembered, if at all, by specialists in the literature of the nineteen-twenties, while the author himself would have been gradually forgotten. Occasionally these books would continue to turn up in the boxes along the banks of the Seine, and on rare occasions people would be heard saying: "Whatever happened to André Malraux? Didn't he die during one of those wars in China?"

With *Man's Fate,* which was published early in 1933, Malraux emerged for the first time as a writer of extraordinary powers. The book won the Prix Goncourt and was generally regarded as a literary event of the first magnitude. Something new and strange had entered French literature: a new music, a new *frisson,* a new attitude to life. Where *The Conquerors* had failed to present a convincing portrait of a contemporary revolutionary terrorist, *Man's Fate* succeeded triumphantly in presenting a whole gallery of such portraits. The simple themes of the earlier novel were now fully orchestrated, and the novelist showed himself in full command of his craft. If the events described were not always credible, and if the characters talked endlessly about their revolutionary duty and inevitable destiny, they nevertheless glowed with an inner fire. We do not expect a Dostoevsky or a Gogol to record credible events: what we expect from them is the breath of life, the sense of high drama, man in his mortal anguish, the spirit flowing in and out of him. In *Man's Fate* the characters live *in extremis,* on the tormented edge of their being. They are not so much living people as ideas cloaked with flesh and living with nightmarish intensity. Almost they are caricatures, and sometimes they seem to move with the spasmodic jerky motion of puppets, so that it is quite possible to imagine them on a small, crowded stage with strings attached to their hands, legs and heads. But the puppet-master has been pouring his own life into them, to the last drop.

The English title fails to evoke the cruel implications of the French title, *La Condition Humaine,* which refers to Pascal's apothegm: "Let us imagine a number of men in chains, and all condemned to death, while every day some of them had their throats cut in the sight of the others: those who remain see their true condition in that of their fellows, and look at one another in sorrow and without hope, awaiting their turn. This is the image of the condition of men."

Since man's fate is to have his throat cut, and there is no reprieve from the sentence of death, the only weapon remaining to him is a heroic self-affirmation in the face of inevitable defeat. In this way his death becomes a justification for his life, an act of homage to the vastly superior forces that have him in their grasp. Those who choose their own death are blessed; and if, in dying, they can serve their fellow men, they are all the more blessed. Malraux's achievement was to be able to draw convincing portraits of men who were aware of death at every moment of their lives, and defied it.

The novel begins with murder and ends with murder, and nearly all the characters die horrible deaths. The most horrible death of all is reserved for Katov, the former medical student and veteran of the Russian revolution, who gives the pellets of cyanide hidden in the flat buckle of his belt to two friends lying wounded in Chiang Kai-shek's prison; it is an act of heroic renunciation, for he will die by fire, thrown alive into the boiler of a locomotive at Chapei station. The gift of cyanide was the gift of love, of perfect friendship. Katov knew exactly what he was doing: he was affirming human dignity in the only way left to him, in the darkness of a vast prison, the prisoners no more than cattle waiting to be butchered. Katov, flung into the fire, dies like a king.

At the beginning of *Man's Fate* the young terrorist Ch'en finds himself standing in the near darkness of a bedroom close to the bed of the man he will kill. We are not told why the man must be killed, or who sent the terrorist on this mission. Suddenly, abruptly, we are in the bedroom, seeing the world through the terrorist's eyes, listening to the beating of his heart and the anguished thoughts passing through his mind as he debates with himself whether to tear away the mosquito curtain and stab the man to death, or whether to stab through the curtain. Everything rests on this decision. If he stabs through the curtain, then he is obviously running the risk of merely wounding the man; if he rips the curtain away, he may awake him. There can be no second thoughts, no repetition of this instant of time, the instant of murder. There is a sense in which the whole novel is concerned with this instant: the knife still hanging in the air, the dead man still sleeping.

There is Ch'en, seen dimly, and the setting, which is simple to the point of nonexistence. A barred window, a faint light falling on the mosquito curtain in a room of unknown size and shape in a city which we assume to be Chinese only because Ch'en has a Chinese name. Because we are permitted to see so little, we are compelled to fasten our attention on the terrorist. There is no escape from him, because his thoughts and actions are described in a haunting, incantatory prose that brings the reader immediately into his presence. Ch'en knows very well that to assassinate is not only to kill. He is at the end of all his resources, and he is about to assume the heaviest burden of all—the knowledge that he has killed a defenseless man. There passes through his mind, like a prayer, the thought that it would be far better to combat enemies who defend themselves, enemies who are awake. *Combattre, combattre des ennemis qui se défendent, des ennemis éveillés!* But throughout the novel there are no enemies who are awake. All are dead, or sleeping, or have become monsters, mechanically operating their machines. Ch'en is aware of the doom that awaits him after the murder. He, too, will become a monster.

As Malraux describes the long instant in which Ch'en approaches the bed, we are made aware that something very much more than a simple assassination is taking place. Almost it is ritual murder, a story out of ancient mythologies. The murder is taking place on a stage with the white mosquito curtain forming a kind of altar, and Ch'en reciting his agonies might be a character out of Aeschylus or Shakespeare. Destiny is implicated, perhaps the destiny of a whole race. Once Ch'en has killed the man and stolen the documents—those terribly important documents which will give him the authority to take possession of the guns and rifles now lying in a ship anchored in the river—then the Communists in Shanghai will have sufficient arms to conquer the city. Everything depends on the documents: the man in the bed, faceless and nameless, is merely "the owner of the documents." We are not told that he was ever aware of Ch'en's presence: he dies, becomes a shadow, and nothing more is ever heard about him.

In later chapters we learn a good deal about Ch'en, who has entered the world of murder "as if it were a warm place." We learn that his parents were killed during the sack of Kalgan, that he went to school at a Lutheran college and fell under the influence of an elderly Lutheran pastor, a consumptive with a vivid awareness of the body's shame and degradation. In the pastor's view, the body was so irremediably shameful that it would be sacrilegious for any man to speak to God: hence Christ, the mediator, who eternally suffers on the Cross, shares with man the sense of degradation. The boy had been sent to the mission school to learn French and English, but instead learns about damnation, about sin, about the terrible penalties reserved for sinners. Just in time an uncle removed him from the pastor's influence and sent him to the University of Peking, where he earned diplomas which proved to be totally useless, for later he made a living as a truck driver and as an assistant to a chemist. He no longer believed in Christ, but he still believed in damnation.

Ch'en's biography, as it emerges during a long discussion with the Frenchman Gisors, is not completely satisfying: one feels that too much responsibility is being placed on the Lutheran pastor. We learn more about Ch'en by watching him murder than by reading those brief biographical fragments of a man who is essentially rootless, and therefore a revolutionary. Yet he was more than a revolutionary: by the act of murder he had become a terrorist fascinated by terrorism, knowing that he would die soon, that terror breeds terror, that there is a "fatality"

in all activity, that death is present whenever a terrorist so much as
opens his mouth. Gisors, gazing at his former student, finds himself
caught up in a wave of admiration for the young man who is prepared
to confront the absolute with another absolute—his own will.

Gisors, the professor of sociology, with his cloud of white hair and
long slender nose, vaguely aristocratic in manner, having acquired all
the tastes of the Chinese scholar without any scholarly devotion to the
past, is scarcely a foil for Ch'en. The old professor has organized Communist cadres, but has never been active in them. Just as he has turned
away from the past, so he has turned away from the present, drowning
his fears and sorrows in opium, occasionally emerging from his pipe
dreams to announce a sardonic verdict on mankind or to express astonishment that he should have fathered a son who is a revolutionary
determined like Ch'en to sacrifice his life for the revolution.

Though he plays a passive role throughout the novel, Gisors is an
authentic tragic figure. He represents the Old King, who watches the
kingdom tottering to its downfall even though the young princes wage
war against his enemies with ferocious boldness. Malraux watches lovingly as he prepares the pellets for his opium pipe, and he has more
than a little sympathy for the old professor lost in dreams of a world
where all the suffering is extinguished within the arms of two waves
silently flowing over the waters of a lake:

> He remembered an afternoon in September when the perfect
> gray of the sky turned the waters of a lake milky white, amid
> the patches formed by vast fields of water lilies; from the curv-
> ing, worm-eaten gables of an abandoned pavilion to the mag-
> nificent and desolate horizon he saw only a world suffused with
> solemn melancholy. A Buddhist priest leaned on the balustrade
> of the pavilion, making no sound with his bell, abandoning his
> sanctuary to the dust, to the fragrance of sweet-smelling wood,
> which was burning; peasants gathering the seeds of water lilies
> passed by in a boat, making not the slightest sound; and when
> they came to the last flowers, two long folds of water emerged
> from the rudder and lost themselves listlessly in the gray waters.
> And now these waves were losing themselves within himself,

the fan enclosing all the world's oppressions, a suffering without
bitterness, transformed by opium to a perfect purity. His eyes
closed, uplifted on immense motionless wings, Gisors contem-
plated his solitude: a desolation reunited with divinity, while at
the same time the wave of serenity, which lay over the abysses
of death, widened to infinity.

In this way, Gisors holds the ghosts at bay, remote from life, immune from the temptations of violence. His opium pipe in his hiding
place; under the tray which holds the opium pipe there is a photograph
of his only son Kyo, the child of his marriage with a Japanese wife;
and Kyo, too, is a kind of hiding place, a refuge from disaster, a justification for his own existence.

In Malraux's earlier novels the heroes stand alone; they have no
families, no husbands, wives, or children. It is unthinkable, for example, that Perken ever married or that Garin ever had children. Now
for the first time Malraux invents a family: Gisors, Kyo, Kyo's wife.
Significantly Gisors' wife never appears on the scene and we assume she
is dead. Equally significantly Kyo, half-French, half-Japanese, is married to a young German woman, a doctor in a local hospital, who has
turned to communism out of an intense hatred of suffering and op-
pression. Kyo's wife is never fully realized: she stands in the wings,
waiting for her cue, which comes only when Kyo is dead. Then she
carries his body to the house, combs his hair, prepares him for burial,
and watches silently while Gisors silently throws away the opium pipe
which has shielded him so long from the world. At that moment—but
only for a moment—the woman comes to life, all the more alive because she is in the presence of death.

Indeed, throughout the novel, the characters are most alive when
they are close to death. Whenever they are in mortal danger, they see
more clearly, their blood flows more quickly, they are aware of themselves as members of a heroic fraternity doomed to extinction but in
some mysterious way exalted among the elect. They throw bombs, capture a police station, fight against Chiang Kai-shek's armored train, at
hopeless odds with the world around them, and we are made aware
of their human dignity as lonely fighters for an unobtainable freedom.

Although they are described as Communists, they behave like anarchists, and we shall see them again in the opening pages of *Man's Hope*. It is not in them to obey: they strike out against the darkness, as though by their very energy they could strike a match on the walls of the night and see themselves in the sudden flare.

When Malraux describes them at their murderous tasks, he seems to see them from inside, as though he was one of them. When Ch'en hurls his bomb at the automobile in which Chiang Kai-shek is a passenger, or so he believes, the narrative takes on an extraordinary immediacy. The revolutionary runs into the road, hurls himself at the automobile, and is half blown to pieces by his own bomb. "He remembered that he had to take out his revolver. He tried to reach into his trouser pocket. No pocket, no trouser, no leg: only the mangled flesh. The other revolver, in his shirt pocket. The button had broken off. He grasped the weapon by the barrel, turned it round without knowing how, instinctively pulled the safety catch with his thumb." He fires wildly, is suddenly kicked by a policeman, and succeeds finally in getting the barrel of the revolver into his mouth. Then he fires for the second time, and for the second time the policeman kicks him. This time he is dead. These scenes of terror are conveyed with a kind of dreamlike precision, in a prose that exactly mirrors the shapes of horror.

Kyo dominates the novel: he is the young prince who incarnates the nobility of the revolution, virile and sweet-tempered, without pride and incapable of malice. Almost alone, he represents the generosity of the true revolutionary, and almost alone he is never plagued by doubts. "A man resembles his suffering," he says, but his own sufferings are of the mind, in remorse for all the evils inflicted on a helpless people. Yet to the end he remains a stranger to the people, remote from them, if only because he is doubly a foreigner. Of the important characters only Ch'en is Chinese. Just as in *The Conquerors* Malraux crowded the stage with foreigners, so once again in *Man's Fate* we find ourselves in a world where the Chinese seem to be deliberately excluded, though the battle is being fought in China. Later, in *Man's Hope*, Malraux paints scene after scene of the Spanish Civil War in which no Spaniards appear.

Quite early in the novel there enters a character who at first sight would seem to have no proper place in it. This is the Baron de Clappique, a former dealer in antiquities in Peking, now a rootless, debonair, rather infantile gentleman with no visible means of support. He talks charming nonsense, runs errands for the revolutionaries who trust him sufficiently to tell him their secrets, and from time to time he will amuse himself by inventing new and always more improbable biographies of himself. He possesses an acute sense of his own nothingness, even of his own improbability. He is a very strange creature indeed.

We meet him first at two o'clock in the morning of March 22, 1927, talking to two sing-song girls in the Black Cat Café in Shanghai. His voice is nasal, bitter, curiously appropriate to the background noises provided by the tinkling glasses, and there is something about it that suggests the voice of Punchinello in the *commedia dell'arte*. He wears a black patch over one eye, the conventional adornment of a pirate. He wears an evening jacket, but whatever he wears he always seems to be in disguise. He knows a good deal about the forthcoming attack on Shanghai by Chiang Kai-shek's forces, and it pleases him to reduce everything to comedy. He is saying:

> "Absolutely, my dear girl, absolutely! Chiang Kai-shek will come here with his revolutionaries and shout—in the classic manner, I tell you, clas-sic! just like when he takes cities. 'Let the merchants be dressed up like monkeys, and the soldiers like leopards (as when they sit down on freshly painted benches)! Like the last prince of the Liang dynasty, absolutely, my dear, let us climb on board the imperial junks, let us contemplate our people all dressed for our amusement in the colors of their professions, blue, red, green, with pigtails and topknots; not a word, my dear girl, not a word I tell you!'"
>
> And then confidentially:
> "The only music we shall permit will be Chinese bells."
> "What will you do in all this?"
> His voice grew plaintive, sobbing.
> "Haven't you guessed, my dear girl? I shall be the court

astrologer, I shall die trying to pluck the moon from a pond one
evening when I am drunk—perhaps tonight?"
    Scientifically:
    ". . . like the poet Tu Fu, whose poems assuredly cast a
spell—not a word more!—on the days when you have nothing
to do! Moreover . . ."

The conversation comes to an end on this "moreover," because a
ship's siren and a deafening clash of cymbals together put an end to
all conversation. The Baron de Clappique resumes his seat. He is obviously a little drunk, for he has confused the poets Li Po and Tu Fu,
but he has succeeded in revealing his essential nihilism, his total surrender to fantasy. Kyo, who has overheard the speech, is not in the
least dismayed by it, for he had heard similar conversations many times
before, and he will continue to trust the Baron even though all the
evidence points to the fact that he is untrustworthy, as all drunkards
are untrustworthy. The strange confrontation between the mythomaniac
and the determined revolutionary will never be resolved, but they will
continue to confront one another. Gisors has a high regard for the
Baron's detachment. "The Baron was made for opium; instead he
drinks," Gisors explains. "It is also possible that he chose the wrong
vice." Kyo remains unconvinced. It seems to him that something has
gone terribly wrong, that no man can continue to live while constantly
denying life, and that every man resembles his own suffering. What is
he suffering from?
    No precise answer to the question is ever offered. Having entered
the novel like a clown bursting through a paper hoop, the Baron continues to display his prowess at intervals throughout the novel. Because
he has nothing to live for, he will try on all the available disguises,
even the disguise of a revolutionary, or at least of someone who
sympathises with the revolution. When Shanghai falls to the enemy
he disguises himself as a sailor and flees for his life: it is the most successful of all his disguises.
    Gradually, as the novel unfolds, the significance, if not the explana-
tion, of the Baron becomes clear. In every high tragedy there is need for
a clown. Like the Fool in *King Lear,* he has the task of uttering

imbecilities which are closer to the truth than the statements of the high officials. Living outside the drama, is an enclosed world of his own, he offers his comments in a spirit of detachment and disinterestedness, carries messages, rebukes the haughty, and generally makes his appearance at moments of intense crisis. White-faced and ceremonious, he represents a mode of being removed from the ordinary world. When Gisors compares the Baron to the black carp with their filmy fins gliding silently and secretly through the blue waters of his aquarium, he shows that he recognizes the source of the Baron's strength, and when the Baron announces, pointing a finger to his lips, that he is Fantomas, he is also offering information about himself. Fantomas was the black-hooded "emperor of crime" whose adventures, recounted by the novelists Pierre Souvestre and Marcel Alain, filled a thousand *feuilletons* eagerly read by French schoolchildren.

The Baron de Clappique is an astonishingly complex figure, and Malraux developed a great fondness for him, as though determined to come to grips with him by the power of his affection. It was dangerous ground, for the Baron could easily slip through his fingers. His nonsense could disintegrate into mawkishness, and his self-imitations ran the risk of boring the reader. Nevertheless, he has a proper place in the novel and he is one of Malraux's most successful inventions.

His genealogy can be traced without much difficulty, for while he clearly derives from Fantomas he also descends from "the wooden personage" in the white shirt front, who appears in *The Diary of a Fireman of the Game of Massacre,* announcing with impeccable logic, "Monsieur, everything passes away, because there is no longer any moral order." The Baron de Clappique is in fact the Devil in his modern sophisticated disguise, and he has a proper place in any story concerned with revolutionary terrorism.

As for his more immediate origins, we learn that his father was French and his mother Hungarian, apparently of noble stock, for her father possessed a castle somewhere in northern Hungary. The Baron has a profound admiration for his grandfather, who had many traits in common with Alphonse-Émile Malraux, the shipowner of Dunkerque. The Baron is relating his family history to two dancing girls:

> "Well, then, my dear little grandfather lived in this castle with those enormous rooms—they were immense—and there

was the confraternity of the dead below, and the fir trees all round, so many fir trees. A widower, living alone with a gi-gan-tic hunting horn hanging over the fireplace. A circus passes through. With a female equestrienne performer. Pretty, too . . ."

Magisterially:

"I say: pretty."

Winking again:

"He takes her—not at all difficult. Carries her into one of the great rooms."

Commanding attention, his hand raised:

"Not a word! . . . She lives there. Stays on. Gets bored. You would, too, little one,"—he caressed the Filipino girl—"but patience . . . He didn't have such a good time, for that matter: he spent half the afternoon having his fingernails and toe-nails worked on by his barber (there was still a barber attached to the castle), while his secretary, the son of a filthy serf, read to him—read over and over again—the history of the family in a loud voice."

That is the trouble with the Baron de Clappique: he is always dream-ing about his family history, revising it, re-editing it, never convincing anyone that there was any family history at all. Like Baron Samedi, who presides over the Voodoo ceremonies in Haiti as god of cemeteries and chief of the legions of the dead, he has escaped out of history al-together.

Ferral, the head of the Franco-Asiatic Consortium, a financial ad-venturer, could almost be taken as the Baron's half-brother, for he, too, is evil personified. Rapacious, sensual, tyrannical, larger than life be-cause he suffers from an inordinate desire to dominate, he represents the international money market and is wholly lost in his dreams of loans, bank rates, concessions and ministries of finance. Compared with the vivid young terrorists, he resembles a stuffed goose. There is no humanity in him. When his mistress Valerie abandons him for another man, he goes to the nearest pet shop, buys every bird in the place to-gether with a kangaroo, takes them to her hotel, and in her absence releases them in her room. At that moment he is almost human, for at least he has permitted himself an act of unalloyed revenge. Having disposed of Valerie, he picks up a Chinese prostitute for the pleasure of humiliating her.

Ferral is almost a caricature, lifeless except in the sudden spasmodic exercise of his will. The stuffed goose occasionally jerks into frenetic action, then subsides again into the sleep reserved for the damned. Shortly before the end of the novel, he has a long conversation with Gisors. "Can one know—really know—a human being?" he asks pathetically. From the heights of his opium dream Gisors answers: "Knowing someone is a purely negative sentiment: the positive sentiment, the reality, is the agony of being always a stranger to what one loves. Time sometimes puts an end to this agony, time alone. One never knows a human being, but one occasionally ceases to feel that one does not know him."

It is not an entirely satisfactory answer, and Gisors has wiser things to say when he discusses power with special reference to Ferral's adoration of financial power. He says:

> "Men are perhaps indifferent to power. What fascinates them in this idea, you understand, is not so much real power as the illusion of having their own sweet will. The king's power is the power to govern, isn't it? But man has no desire to govern: he wants to force others to obey him, as you said. To be more than a man in a world of men. As I was saying, he wants to escape from the human condition. Not powerful: all-powerful. Man has the fantastic disease of desiring divinity, and the will to power is merely the intellectual justification for it. Every man dreams of being God.

Gisors' verdict on mankind derives from his own prolonged self-examination, but it embraces many of the characters in the novel. He finds divine peace in opium, while Ferral will only find his peace when he owns all the money in the world. Kyo, Ch'en and Katov find their peace in sacrifice. The Baron de Clappique finds peace nowhere, not even in the brothel.

In a chapter of *Man's Fate* which was not included in the published version, but printed in December 1933 in *Marianne,* the Baron de Clappique, having twenty-four hours to squander, enters an American hotel in Shanghai and goes to bed with a woman, only to realize that he is being watched closely by *voyeurs* who have taken up their positions in another room. The incident is recounted graphically; except for a brief scene in *The Royal Way* it is the only erotic scene in the entire corpus of Malraux's works. The Baron finally leaps from the bed, staggers to the door, opens it with enormous difficulty, only to confront a passing servant who laughs at him because his trousers are "open like a strip of torn canvas." Malraux properly deleted the chapter on the grounds that it was aesthetically unnecessary. One could wish that he had deleted a little more of the Baron, who is continually talking out of turn. In *Antimémoires* he is permitted to talk for a hundred pages and very nearly wrecks the entire book.

The formidable achievement of *Man's Fate* has very little to do with the Baron. What makes the novel memorable is the recital of the adventures of the doomed terrorists, the agonized search through the territory of terror. "There is always terror in oneself," says Ch'en. "You have only to look deep in yourself to find it. Happily one may act." Happily, art and music may sometimes remove the pain and suffering from life. When his son is dead and he has little left to live for, Gisors contemplates the clouds and music, finding an inexplicable happiness in their beauty.

> Very high up, the soft clouds passed over the dark pines and little by little were absorbed again into the sky; and it seemed to him that one among them, precisely the one he was looking at, expressed the men he had known and loved, and who were dead. Humanity was dense and heavy, heavy with flesh, with blood, with suffering, eternally clinging to itself like all that dies; but even blood, even flesh, even suffering, even death, were being absorbed up there in the light like music in the silent night: he thought of Kama's music, and human sorrow seemed to rise and lose itself in the very song of earth; over his trembling sense of deliverance, concealed within him like his heart, sorrow once more enclosed him within her inhuman arms.

In such passages, written with his nerve-ends, Malraux found his own music. In *Man's Fate* he conducted a full orchestra, and it is perhaps a part of his triumph that he was able to command the piccolo as well as the organ and the violins. Henceforth there was no turning back: he would be wedded to art and nature and music to the end.

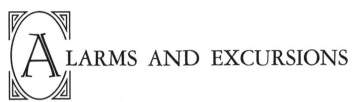

ALARMS AND EXCURSIONS

Our task is to restore the sight to the blind statues.

THE WORK OF ART

≈ *A Journey to Russia* ≈

W hen Hitler came to power, Malraux had no difficulty in realizing that Europe was in danger. Strange and terrible forces were at work in Germany, threatening to destroy the entire fabric of European civilization. "We know now that our civilization is mortal," Paul Valéry had written at the end of the First World War. Now in the person of Hitler, with his white clown's face, wild eyes, unruly hair and fierce smudge of mustache, there had appeared the destroyer, the judge with the power to sentence an entire civilization to death.

In January 1933, when Hitler became Reich Chancellor, the first chapters of *Man's Fate* were beginning to appear in the *Nouvelle Revue Française.* For the next six months, while Europe looked fearfully toward Berlin and listened to the raucous voice of the Chancellor over the radio, the chapters followed one another at monthly intervals. The accident of timing did not go unremarked, for in the novel Malraux had described a revolutionary situation not unlike the one in Germany, where the Communists were desperately attempting to snatch victory from overwhelming defeat. It was not difficult to imagine Ch'en, Kyo and Gisors as German Communists plotting to destroy Hitler, and indeed Malraux had borrowed some characteristics of German Communists to describe them. Chiang Kai-shek could just as easily have been Hitler, and Shanghai could just as easily have been Hamburg. The Communists regarded Malraux as a potential ally, a potential convert, although they were perfectly aware that the fiery conversations in *Man's Fate* demonstrated an astonishing lack of interest in Communist theory and were devoted to aspects of philosophical anarchism.

German Communists escaping from the Reich sometimes called at Malraux's apartment on the Rue de Bac with its sparse furniture and

whitewashed walls decorated with a few modern paintings. Gustav
Regler, Manes Sperber, and many others came to dinner and stayed half
the night, and those who stayed longest were usually Communists who
rejoiced in the arts and were therefore unlikely to submit to rigid
discipline. Regler was a novelist and poet with a deep affection for the
arts, a wry humor, and an absolute determination to pour out his life
in the fight against fascism. Manes Sperber was a Marxist who had
fallen under the influence of Alfred Adler. He was a small, precise
man with an intricate mind and a grave devotion to the arts, to books,
and to humanitarian principles. Regler was pure flame and Sperber was
dry tinder, and both in their different ways were close to Malraux,
worshiped him, and absorbed something of his philosophy. They could
be relied upon to think clearly and dispassionately without parading
their egos, and Malraux was fond of them.

It was also growing closer to André Gide, who was then at
the height of his power and influence. They had of course known each
other for many years, but they were now meeting more frequently and
often appeared on the same platforms, for their political views were
almost identical. Both regarded the Soviet Union with favor, as a
bastion against the spread of fascism, but neither would ever become
Communist. At first Gide had disliked *Man's Fate,* saying that it was
too episodic, too intellectualized, but rereading it later he realized that
it was episodic by deliberate design and that the sheer weight of its
intellectual content gave it distinction. He had also developed the habit
of dropping in for afternoon tea with Clara Malraux.

It was a year of many changes, many chance encounters, and many
desperate stratagems. As an editor at Gallimard, Malraux earned only
a small salary, but it was becoming necessary to raise large sums for the
refugees pouring into France. He spent prodigally from his own resources, and established *ad hoc* committees in aid of the causes he believed in. In this way there came into existence the World League
against Anti-Semitism and the International Committee to Aid Victims
of the Nazis. He made speeches to small private groups and at mass
meetings, and developed a style of oratory at once passionate and intellectual. In the following years he would acquire a dangerous ability
to play on the minds of the masses, his speeches having the effect of

incantations, the voice rising and falling according to the mood he intended to convey, so that he held the audience at his mercy, and yet always there was the knowledge that the abstract intelligence was in command. White-faced in the arc lights, his black hair falling across his forehead, his clenched fist shaking violently, he would begin his addresses with a shrill *"Camarades!"* and then launch immediately into a logical argument on the necessity of safeguarding the values of Western civilization by paying honor to the survivors of Nazi persecutions and by opposing fascism wherever it appeared. He attended Communist party rallies, but the Communists themselves had no illusions about his dependability. Would he accept party discipline? Would he do what the party ordered? The answer was always very clear. He would do what he wanted to do, and he would accept no discipline whatsoever. He would make common cause with the Communists only so long as he felt that they were following the right path and he would abandon them the moment they left it.

The more intelligent Communists like Regler and Ilya Ehrenburg recognized that he was a valuable ally; the party hacks wondered aloud whether he was not an enemy in disguise. One day in Leningrad the Soviet poet Vasily Lebedev-Kumach put the question to Regler: Will Malraux remain loyal to the revolution? Regler answered that to talk of loyalty and disloyalty was nonsense. The party should be thankful for sympathizers of his stature, who were worth a dozen Aragons. Does the lion in the zoo worry about the wild cats in the next cage? The Soviet poet said: "What happens if they are in the same cage?" "Malraux will never go into the same cage," Regler answered. Although Malraux did not enter the cage, he sometimes gazed into it with admiring glances. He especially admired the German Communists who fought desperately against Hitler's Stormtroopers.

During that year Malraux lived at an extraordinary pitch of intensity. He read, wrote, edited, made speeches, presided over conferences, raised money, and conducted a vast correspondence on a regimen which consisted of working for eighteen or nineteen hours a day without rest. By the end of the year he was drained of energy. Happily, in December, he was awarded the Prix Goncourt for *Man's Fate,* and with this award there came a sudden alteration in his fortunes. The prize itself was not particularly valuable, for it was only five thousand francs, worth perhaps two hundred dollars in the devalued currency of the time. But any book chosen for the Goncourt award sold well throughout France and within a few weeks after the prize was announced he had acquired a small fortune.

He needed the money, for he had always possessed extravagant tastes. Also, his housekeeping expenses had gone up. On March 28, 1933, Clara Malraux had given birth to a daughter, Florence. His delight in the birth of a daughter was mingled with the realization that he was ill-equipped for the tasks of paternity, and he could no more imagine himself wheeling a perambulator through the Luxembourg Gardens than he could imagine himself opening a small shop. Florence grew up to become a beautiful and intelligent woman with a consuming passion for the arts and especially for the cinema. One day, when she was quite small, Clara Malraux took her to a museum and was surprised to see her racing through the galleries exactly like her father. She remembered everything and could describe in great detail all the paintings that pleased her, and yet she had scarcely paused for a moment as she ran through the museum. And Clara Malraux, who liked to look at paintings slowly, was puzzled by the thought that her daughter had inherited from her father a faculty which was essentially aesthetic.

If at the end of the year Malraux had drawn up a balance sheet of his affairs, he would have found much to please him. For the first time he was financially independent; he could go wherever he pleased, do whatever he pleased, throw all his strength into the fight against fascism. He had become a power to be reckoned with and could no longer complain, like Dante, that he was fated to climb the stairways of his patrons. The world was opening up to him, and wherever he walked a passage was made for him.

François Mauriac, who had known him in his youth and ever since kept a wary eye open for him, wondered what it would all come to. What he feared above all was the spectacle of the youthful tribune, the Gracchus determined to wrest power from the elected officials. At the end of the year he drew up a half-fearful, half-admiring balance sheet. He wrote:

We live in a strange society, old, bored, that pardons anyone who entertains it, even with fear. Imagine a man who since his adolescence has set himself up against the laws and derives his strength by opposing them. Imagine such a man throwing himself into the revolutionary struggle from his twentieth year—not that he hopes for anything, for he is a man doomed to despair—but he becomes conscious of himself only in the struggle. To act dangerously, to act for the sake of action: these, in his eyes, among all the methods of escape, are the ones most tempting to him. Against despair a man never has enough weapons. . . .

The more characters appear in his novels, the more we become aware that each one is a portrait of himself, lucid and despairing. They do not differ among themselves except through the means they choose in order to escape from reality: terrorism, love, eroticism, drugs, adventures. And always we recognize the same convulsed features—those features which I first saw when he was eighteen years old, full of fire, magnificently intelligent, but already marked by a mysterious reproach.

Now, this Malraux, long before the Prix Goncourt had brought him to the attention of the crowd, had already reached first place, and this without any effort. But one should look at the facts. He has talent; he has more talent than any youth of his age, and whether one is indignant or whether one approves, it is a fact that in the year of grace 1933 a fine book excuses everything.

François Mauriac never quite lost his fear of Malraux the potential tribune, just as he never lost his admiration for Malraux's writings. The fear, however, was misplaced. There was a hard core of good sense in the revolutionary, which saved him from excesses. Above all, he remained the humanist, with a total aversion for inhumanity, political and otherwise.

The test came the following year when Malraux accompanied André Gide to Berlin to intercede for the life of Giorgy Dimitrov, the Bulgarian Communist who had been arrested at the time of the Reichstag fire, acquitted after a long trial, but kept in prison. Dimitrov had defied the Nazi court and brilliantly defended himself against Goering, who appeared in the courtroom and threatened to have his head. Since Malraux had helped to organize Dimitrov's defense, a fact well known to the German authorities, he was *persona non grata* in Berlin and could scarcely expect to be regarded favorably by Goebbels, to whom the appeal was delivered. It was January 1934; the Nazis were riding high; Dimitrov was doomed. Though neither Malraux nor Gide was able to speak to a single member of the Nazi government, they had the satisfaction of knowing that they had dramatized the plight of Dimitrov and they were not particularly surprised when he was released some months later on the direct orders of Hitler. Thereafter Malraux would regard that bleak winter journey to Berlin with considerable satisfaction.

A further test came in August, this time in the Soviet Union, where the first All-Union Congress of Soviet Writers was being held. The reasons for holding the Congress were well known: Stalin had decided that the Soviet writers were insufficiently enthusiastic in defending and proclaiming the Communist cause, and it had become necessary to bring them to heel. New directives were issued; socialist realism would be the watchword; the Central Committee had debated earnestly on the exact phrasing of the laws which writers were expected to obey, and Stalin himself had devised a slogan in keeping with the new dispensation. "Writers," he declared, "are the engineers of the human soul." From all over Europe poets and novelists sympathetic to Communism gathered in the Bolshoy Theater in Moscow to listen to the new Moses announcing the tablets of the law. It was generally believed that Stalin would deliver the main speech.

Malraux attended the Congress together with about thirty left-wing writers from western Europe. Ernst Toller, Klaus Mann, Gustav Regler, Louis Aragon, Oskar Maria Graf were among those who were invited. The Bolshoy Theater was draped with immense banners with pictures of Lenin, Stalin and Maxim Gorky, once an impenitent opponent of the Bolsheviks, now in old age the pampered darling of the Central Committee, close friend of Stalin and Yagoda, the head of the secret police. On the banner Gorky was represented as a youthful peasant, his features unmarked by any wrinkles, his hair cut short, gentle and affectionate. In fact, he was old and withered, with a harsh edge to his mind, though he could be kindly on occasion. The keynote speech was delivered by Andrey Zhdanov, the secretary of the Central Committee. "Our literature is permeated with enthusiasm and heroism," he declared. "It is optimistic because it is the literature of the class which is rising, the proletariat, the most advanced and the most prospering class." Literature which did not praise Stalin enthusiastically for his heroic achievements was no longer to be regarded as literature. The age of Stalinist literature was announced with formulas and fanfares.

Such things could be expected from Zhdanov, but it was much harder to accept them from the lips of Gorky, who read a forty-page address of incredible dullness and prolixity. He presented himself as a social philosopher and materialistic atheist, contemptuous of the Church and of all philosophies except Marxism-Leninism. Plato, Kant and Bergson were consigned to the dustbin of history; there was nothing to be said for Dostoevsky, the product of a capitalistic environment, the renegade who never understood the workings of the human mind and contented himself with describing the adventures of "superfluous men." No, comrades, the real literature, the real truth lay among the folk heroes, those ancient and ever-present heroes of the laboring classes—Prometheus, Svyatagor, Ivan the Simple, Petrushka, and finally Lenin. They had all risen out of the people and were not imposed on the people, and therefore they possessed a validity denied to the heroes and heroines of romantic novels.

Gorky came to some surprising conclusions. He believed the detective novel had been deliberately invented by the capitalists to prevent the growth of class-consciousness. He was oppressed by the thought that bourgeois literature was full of murderers, swindlers, and thieves, forgetting that his own novels were also full of them. He believed that in the Soviet state there were no leaders and no underlings, for all were bound together in comradely affection to spread the boundaries of socialism. Henceforth literature must concern itself only with socialist progress, for no other theme was worth contemplating. He proclaimed: "We must make labor the principal hero of our books, i.e. man as organized by labor processes, one who, in our country, is equipped with the might of modern techniques, and is, in his turn, making labor easier and more productive, and raising it to the level of an art."

Malraux endured all this, and much more, with angelic patience, sitting there with his friend Gustav Regler and a full-bosomed, perfumed interpreter from the offices of *Pravda*. She was an intelligent woman, and she did the best she could with the intractable material uttered in a hoarse, reedy voice by a white-haired old man who seemed to regard himself as the standard-bearer of the laboring classes against all the entrenched forces of Western civilization—Plato, Sophocles, Dante went down like ninepins. Regler was muttering to himself in agony, while the crowd cheered. "What is Regler saying?" Malraux asked the interpreter. "I think he is groaning," the interpreter said with a professional smile. "He has good reason to," Malraux commented.

When at last the interminable speech came to an end, Regler told Malraux about the Indian custom of putting a stone on the back of a donkey when it is relieved of a heavy burden; in this way it does not suffer so much. He suggested that Gorky had very little feeling for the sensitivity of the Russian back. "Perhaps," Malraux replied, "he does not think it will be so easy to remove the burden."

When the time came for Malraux to deliver his own speech at the Congress, there was some apprehension that he would take issue with the official doctrine by appending some discreet reservations expressed in good taste. Instead, he went over to the offensive, attacked socialist realism with fury, and demanded that Soviet writers be given more freedom to express themselves. Art had little enough to do with labor; it was concerned with the contradictions, the hesitancies, the triumphs of the human soul, and its chief instrument was the psychological understanding of man and his behavior on earth. He said:

> In one of the factories in Moscow I asked a workman: "Why do you read?" He answered: "To learn how to live." Culture then is always: to learn. But, comrades, when we go to our teachers, we must ask where they found their learning. We read Tolstoy, but for Tolstoy there was no Tolstoy to fall back on. What he gave us he had to invent for himself. When we hear

that writers are "the engineers of the human soul," do not forget that the chief function of the engineer is to invent.

Art is not an act of submission, but a conquest.

The conquest of what?

The feelings, and the way to express them.

Over what?

Over the unconscious, nearly always, and over logic, very often.

Whatever socialist realism was, it had nothing to do with the conquest of the unconscious and of logic: for the Marxists such a concept could have no meaning. Malraux was insisting that art was not an act of submission just at the moment when Stalin, Zhdanov and Gorky were demanding absolute submission to the party line.

Worse still, Malraux pointed out that the great nineteenth-century novelists were more contemporary than the Soviet novelists, for they spoke more urgently and had more to say about the human soul. They were not bound to doctrines: their aim was to discover and to understand. What they discovered was sometimes very strange, but psychologically true and therefore valuable. One of Tolstoy's heroes goes out into a dark winter night, shivers with cold, and discovers that all his love for a woman has withered in the icy wind. Raskolnikov murders an old woman in the belief that the murder will bring him immense power; instead he discovers that the murder brings him only loneliness. There was no logic in these insights, and no one could say that in themselves they were important discoveries; yet out of them came the stuff of great drama.

The Russians were passionately fond of their great prerevolutionary novelists. Why? Because they were admirable in their own right, but there were also other reasons.

Your classic writers give a richer and more complex picture of the inner life than the Soviet novelists, and so it sometimes happens that a reader will feel that Tolstoy is more real to them than many of the novelists attending this Congress. If you reject psychology, then you arrive at the most absurd kind of individualism. Every man endeavours to think out his own personal life, whether he wishes to do so or not. If you eliminate psychology it simply means that men who have seen most deeply keep their discoveries to themselves instead of handing them down to others.

Of these poetic discoveries Malraux gave as the supreme example the clouds seen by Prince Andrey Bolkonsky as he lies wounded on the battlefield at Austerlitz, those serene and effortless clouds riding high above the agonies and perturbations of men.

He would return again and again to those clouds, but for the moment his task was to attempt to convince the Soviet writers that art was autonomous, not to be ruled by official commands. They had described the outward appearance of the Soviet Union in their novels, but what about its inner appearance? About morality and psychology they had remained silent. Why? Because the writers were not sufficiently trusted? Perhaps. And yet the revolution, the civil war, the years of famine, all these had prepared the way for a literature of giants, for out of all that suffering there had come about a new society in which men could have full confidence in one another. In this way, alternately praising and goading the Soviet writers, he suggested that it was not enough to depict the surface appearance of noble or desirable qualities: sacrifice, heroism, fortitude; it was necessary to go deeper, to seek out the causes of things, and to probe into the morality and psychology of communism. He seemed to be saying that socialist realism was irrelevant. What was necessary was an art equal to the tragic grandeur of the times.

The doctrinaire Communists were incensed by Malraux's speech, for its implications went far beyond the permissible limits of criticism. Malraux however was not alone in attacking the new code of socialist realism. The veteran Bolshevik Nikolay Bukharin, once the close friend of Lenin and soon to fall before Stalin's firing squad, delivered an earnest defense of the poet Boris Pasternak, thus demonstrating his inability to understand the purpose of the Congress. Even more daringly the novelist and short story writer Yuri Olyesha defended his right to speak about human emotions divorced from any political context, with the result that his works were quietly consigned to oblivion. Many others made speeches adroitly praising socialist realism while simultaneously reserving for themselves small portions of individual freedom. The Soviet government knew how to deal with them, but Malraux, as the most distinguished foreign guest of the Congress, could not be dealt with so easily. He insisted on being heard, and he was invulnerable.

Inevitably the first Congress of Soviet Writers offered a banquet to the hundreds of delegates. The banquet was attended by all the high dignitaries of the government with one notable exception. It was rumored that Stalin failed to attend because he was not absolutely convinced of the devotion of the Soviet writers and he had long ago promised himself that he would never enter a room where there was the least possibility of danger. But Molotov, Voroshilov, Bukharin, Radek, Zhdanov, Surkov, and many others attended, drank toasts, gave speeches, and wandered amiably among the guests. There were toasts for Stalin, for Gorky, for the foreign guests, and soon nearly everyone was in a state of mild drunkenness. Voroshilov, who had little interest in literature, drank himself into a state of stupor, but Molotov, as always, remained sober. Radek, already in disfavor in the Kremlin, and already drunk, marched among the guests in a strange penitential mood, denouncing all those who rejected socialist realism, confessing his own errors, and beating his breast. It was a frightening spectacle, for he had once been close to Lenin and during Lenin's lifetime he had exercised vast although ill-defined powers. He tore open his shirt to demonstrate that he still possessed a heart, and he began to talk about the failure of the Revolution.

"We are still far from our objective," he said in his high-pitched voice. "We thought the child had come of age, and we have invited the whole world to admire it. But it is self-knowledge, not admiration, that we need. The Revolution is no safari, a source of agreeable thrills. Heroism has no worth in itself. Executions must be evaluated, not made mysteries of. We are all still petit bourgeois!"

Radek was a small ugly man with blazing eyes and a reddish fringe of beard, learned in seven languages, intelligent and savage. He walked among the guests like a ghost from the past, and at last he stood before

Malraux and began to upbraid him. "Art is not an act of submission but a conquest," Malraux had said in a city where all the newspapers and books were censored, and Radek took issue with him.

Standing there, rubbing his grotesque fringe of beard, he shouted that Malraux was perhaps the greatest sinner of them all.

"Why does Malraux ask the young Communists what they think about death? Why does he adopt this unfruitful attitude in a century in which the individual has at last been given the chance to fulfill himself in community with others?" Radek asked, then concluded, "Comrade Malraux, too, is a *petit bourgeois!*"

He was drunk and disheveled, and scarcely knew what he was saying. Malraux, with his innate sense of good manners, could not be expected to reply to a drunken man who had once hoped to be Lenin's successor. Radek continued to attack Malraux, misquoting him, taunting him, hoping to draw blood, spitting out the words "petit bourgeois" with drunken venom, as though he hoped in some obscure way to bring the adversary to justice and so to destroy him. Death and executions were on his mind. At last, wearying of the unequal combat, he drifted away among the clouds of tobacco smoke past the glittering tables heaped with caviare and half-eaten chicken, until he vanished in the distance. He was like one of those ghosts who return to haunt the merrymakers, prophesying doom.

Doom was in the air, and no one yet knew what shape it would take. Stalin had not attended the feast, but he would have agreed with Radek: "Executions must be evaluated, not made mysteries of."

The absence of Stalin was discussed at length: up to the last moment it was hoped that he would appear. Louis Aragon, the French novelist, had announced very early during the Congress that Stalin would offer directives for centuries to come. He was one of those who felt that writers were in need of directives from above. Malraux was one of those who knew that the directives must come from the writer himself.

Meanwhile he was enjoying his days in Moscow. In 1934 there was still a vast excitement in the air and it was still possible to hope that the Communists would somehow succeed in producing an egalitarian society. He came to admire Gorky, in spite of his elephantine speech at the Congress. He visited Gorky's *datcha* in the country, stayed overnight, and discussed the publication of a vast encyclopedia to be edited by a galaxy of scholars. This encyclopedia would include the sum total of all the experience and knowledge men had accumulated up to this time; it would be the supreme intellectual achievement of the century, comparable to the encyclopedia produced by Voltaire, Diderot, Helvétius and many others on the eve of the French Revolution. It would be published in four languages: Russian, English, French and Spanish. Gorky was enthusiastic and offered his assistance, but nothing came of the idea. Malraux met Sergey Eisenstein, the film director, and they discussed making a film of *Man's Fate* with music by Shostakovich. An incurable filmgoer, possessing a scholarly knowledge of films, Malraux sometimes wondered whether he had not missed his vocation. Visiting Eisenstein in his studio, he said in a burst of enthusiasm: "If I were working here, I would be ashamed to write books." Eisenstein, who sometimes talked like a pedagogue, reminded him that books were as important as films or factories, and it was therefore improper to be ashamed of writing them.

Nothing came of the film, and discussions with Meyerhold, the director of Moscow's Revolutionary Theater, about transforming the novel into a play with music by Prokofiev were equally fruitless. Meyerhold, affable, eager, superbly intelligent concerning the theater and literature but entirely childlike when it came to living, proved to be an ideal companion in Malraux's wanderings round Moscow. Meyerhold took him to see the house where Dostoevsky was born. It had been converted into a museum: the Sistine Madonna hung over the desk, and a life-size faded daguerreotype of Dostoevsky gazed down from the wall. Malraux was haunted by this photograph, which seemed to derive a terrible authenticity from the discolorations of age, so that it resembled another Lazarus emerging from the tomb. Years later he could still remember the vivid impression it made on him: the skull-like accusing face, the ragged beard, the grayness of the skin which might have been the color of an insect. Manifestly the face belonged to death. He wrote that it was the face of a man who had come on earth "not to console the assassins and the prostitutes, but to shake the pillars on which repose the mystery of the world: beyond even the preachings of love, beyond the clouds of the irremediable and of human suffering, the supreme mystery of 'What art thou doing on this earth where sorrow reigns?' "

There was no one for whom Malraux had greater reverence than for Dostoevsky, and he stood there like someone rooted to the ground, in awe of a photograph. The guardian of the museum showed him the Bible Dostoevsky brought back from prison, and as he turned the pages he observed that the margins were often scribbled with the word *Nyet*. Russians consulted their Bibles in the same way that scholars in the middle ages consulted Virgil, opening the book at random and hoping to discover the appropriate auguries for the day. Too often the Bible had told him nothing.

During his stay in Moscow Malraux met most of the Soviet writers of importance. His speech was remembered and eagerly discussed. He also met Borodin, the *éminence grise* of the Chinese revolution, whose whispers once produced panic among the representatives of the colonial powers. He was one of the characters in *The Conquerors,* and Malraux had shown a certain uneasy admiration for the dedicated Communist who had once wielded so much power. Now he was reduced to editing an English language newspaper in Moscow; he had shrunk and wore clothes too large for him. Malraux was struck by the way history destroyed its own idols. In a wheedling voice Borodin said: "Since you are on such good terms with the authorities, perhaps you will be able to find me an apartment with a fireplace."

In the year after the Moscow Congress, Malraux helped to organize another Congress in Paris. This was held in the old Mutualité Theater, and was known officially as the International Congress in the Defense of Culture. Henri Barbusse, Malraux and André Gide presided, and it was at this congress that Gide proclaimed his allegiance to Communism, or at least to an imaginary Communism which simultaneously preserved freedom, democracy and the right of a critic to criticize to his heart's content. Gide said many things about Stalin's Russia which he later preferred to forget. There was no possibility of submitting him to strict party discipline. Louis Aragon had emerged as the intellectual dictator of the French Communists, and it was unlikely that Gide would ever take orders from him.

Alain, Romain Rolland, Élie Faure, Victor Margueritte, Jean-

Richard Bloch, Heinrich Mann, Gustav Regler, Ilya Ehrenburg, Mikhail Koltsov, and a host of minor Soviet writers attended. The level of the Soviet representation was so low that Ilya Ehrenburg, then the Paris correspondent for the newspaper *Izvestia,* wondered aloud whether it might not be possible to summon even at this last moment some more impressive figures from Moscow. Gustav Regler suggested Isaac Babel, Malraux suggested Boris Pasternak. A telegram went off to Bukharin, who was still editor-in-chief of *Izvestia,* with the result that Babel and Pasternak arrived in Paris by airplane within twenty-four hours.

Babel gave a humorous address, shuffling onto the platform like an elderly professor about to address a handful of students. He seemed unable to take the conference seriously, told Jewish stories, laughed at his own jokes, captivated everyone by his modesty and gentleness, and was wildly applauded. Pasternak followed him, gaunt and hollow-eyed, ill at ease on the platform. He spoke haltingly, stumbling over his words. "There will always be poetry in the grass, and it will always be necessary to bend down and receive," he said, and those words, hinting at so many humble tragedies, were in fact a despairing plea for poetic freedom. He was on the verge of a nervous breakdown and kept himself apart from most of the delegates to the Congress.

The audience expected Malraux to follow Gide with another ringing assertion of the triumph of socialism over fascist barbarism. Instead, as in Moscow, he was more preoccupied with the nature of art than with the nature of socialism. The title of his speech was "The Work of Art" and only indirectly was it concerned with the problem of the artist in the modern world. What is a work of art? What changes does it undergo during its progress through the centuries? What is meant by our artistic heritage? What is man's responsibility to a work of art? He was going back to fundamentals, to the very core of the artistic experience, and he was reaching out toward conclusions that would be formulated more precisely many years later in *The Voices of Silence* and *The Metamorphosis of the Gods.*

During a visit to Cairo in his search for the city of Sheba early in 1934, shortly after his journey to Berlin, Malraux had looked spellbound at the funeral masks of the Pharaohs. The makers of these masks could never in their wildest dreams have imagined that these masks would one day be excavated and presented to the people as works of art; the sculptors would have shaken their heads in bewilderment at such an idea. They would not have understood what was meant by a work of art; in their eyes the masks had a purpose, being acts of homage to the divine Pharaoh and to the gods.

In the course of centuries these works had suffered many transformations. Many times they had died and been reborn; time flowed into them, and subtly changed them. From being objects of worship they became the shapes of men, their significance changing according to human needs and desires. At the heart of the mystery of art there was this continual process of transformation. At the Congress Malraux said:

> Every work of art is created to satisfy a need, a need that is passionate enough to give it birth. Then the need withdraws from the work of art as blood from a body, and a mysterious transfiguration begins. It enters into the shades, and only our own need, our own passion, can summon it forth again. Until such time as we bring our own passion to it, it remains like a great statue with sightless eyes confronted with a long procession of blind men. And the same necessity which draws one of these blind men to the statue will open the eyes of the statue and of the blind man simultaneously.

> If we go back a hundred years, we shall find that works of art we regard as indispensable were completely ignored. Go back two hundred years, and we learn that the nervous, radiant smile of Gothic is synonymous with a grimace. A work of art is an object, but it is also an encounter with time. I am aware that we have made the discovery of history. Works that went unloved to the attic may find themselves unloved in a museum, which is scarcely a happier fate. Every work is dead when love recedes from it.

> Nevertheless, there is a meaning in this movement. Arts, thoughts, poems, all the old dreams of mankind—if we have need of them in order to live, they have need of us in order to live again. Need of our passion, need of our desires—*need of*

our will. They are not there like the furniture listed in an inventory after someone has died; rather, they are like the shades who, in the ancient Infernos, eagerly await the coming of the living. Whether we desire it or not, we create them at the same time that we ourselves create ourselves. This very impulse to create leads Ronsard to resurrect Greece; Racine, Rome; Hugo, Rabelais; Corot, Vermeer, and there does not exist a single great work of art that is not enmeshed in the centuries and does not trail behind it the slumbering grandeurs of the past. Our inheritance is not handed down; it must be conquered. . . .

Every work of art becomes a symbol and a sign, but not always of the same thing. A work of art implies the possibility of reincarnation. And the secular world can only lose significance in the contemporary will of men. It is for each of us, in his own field and through his own efforts, and for the sake of all those who are engaged in a quest of themselves, to recreate the ghostly heritage that lies all round us—to restore the sight to the blind statues—to transform hopes into wills and bloody uprisings into revolutions, and thereby to shape the consciousness of mankind out of the age-old sorrows of man.

Malraux spoke so rapidly that he was always in danger of outrunning the stenographic reports of his speeches, and the reports, which were later published in *Commune,* are not always completely trustworthy. Nevertheless the sense was clear: great works of art must be conquered afresh by each succeeding generation as it pours its own life into them, and this outpouring belongs to a continuing revolutionary process. In this way a bridge is thrown across the wasteland between aesthetics and revolution. But though Malraux appealed to the Soviet writers to wrest a new artistic significance from their revolutionary experiences, "having safeguarded their masterpieces through blood and famine and typhus," he was clearly less interested in Soviet literature than in works of art handed down through the ages. The Soviet writers had not breathed new life into their ancient masterpieces, and they cared very little for the past.

In later years it would be said that Malraux's interest in the arts began about the time of this speech, but this was to misunderstand

him completely. He could scarcely remember a time when he was not
devoted to the arts. Although he had written nothing about art except
his brief "Gothic-Buddhist Works of Art from the Pamirs," which was
published in 1930, he was already training himself for the three-volume
work on the psychology of art which would not appear for another
fifteen years.

Nevertheless the speech on "The Work of Art" marked a turning
point. He had come to certain conclusions which were not likely to
change. A work of art satisfied a human need at the time of its creation, but thereafter it acquired a life of its own and suffered strange
transformations according to the welcome it received. It was never an
object fixed in time, but continually changing with the flow of time.
Originally it satisfied a need; thereafter it needed to be seen, to be
studied, to be warmed into new life by human eyes. Again and again
Malraux would say: "Our inheritance is not handed down; it must be
conquered" and "Our task is to restore the sight to the blind statues."
The ideas of conquest and resurrection would be examined at length in
his later writings on art.

He realized that the Communists were unaware of the relevance of
art. They paid it lip service, sometimes took the trouble to preserve
ancient monuments, and could not understand that a painting of the
Virgin answered a human need. Gorky had poured scorn on the
mythologies of men, reserving for himself the right to approve of a
few selected myths that could be reconciled with Communist principles. Malraux regarded mythologies with the same reverence with
which he regarded art; they could not be argued away; and they were
necessary to man's spiritual health. In a speech delivered in November
1935 he said:

> No civilization—and certainly no barbarism—is strong
> enough to tear away from men the myths that are their most
> ancient strength. Barbarism sacrifices men to the myths, while
> we desire a civilization that places myths in the service of men.

But the mythologies were now on the march. Hitler was summoning
the ancient Germanic heroes, Mussolini was conjuring up the glories

of ancient Rome by waging war against Abyssinia. Malraux's attitude toward the rise of fascism was one of helpless sorrow before all the suffering it would inflict. Fascism was merely colonialism armed with the authority of myths. What did the Italians hope to gain by establishing an African empire? In the same speech he said:

> Just at the moment when Abyssinia is in need of European specialists, they send guns against her. If she wins the war, she will be no more nor less westernized than if she is beaten.
>
> Killing these multitudes of people is one way of establishing hospitals in the country, but it is not certain that it is the better way. What paradise these colonies would be if the West were compelled to build hospitals for all the people she killed, and provide gardens for all the people she had deported.

French colonialism was no better than fascism, and he raged against the imbecility of the colonial powers. What had they given to the people they had conquered? The colonial offices pointed to the benefits they had conferred. But in the colonies of Morocco, Tunisia and Tripolitania the women were still veiled; Persia was not a colony, and there was scarcely a veil to be seen. In China and Japan the old feudal mandarinate no longer existed and therefore no longer oppressed the people, but the mandarins survived in the French colony of Annam. In independent Siam there were hospitals operated by Western doctors paid by the state. In Cambodia the people were too poor to enter the hospitals reserved for the rich and the middle classes. Compare Indochina with Siam, Morocco with Turkey, Beluchistan with Persia, and then ask yourself whether colonialism conferred benefits on the people.

Because he attacked French colonial policy he was detested by the Right, and because he rejected the party line he was regarded with increasing suspicion by the Left. He seemed not to care, and went on making speeches. Pale, intense, unsmiling, his dark hair occasionally falling over his eyes and blinding him, he continued to speak in a rasping voice about the two things he held to be most valuable—the authority of art and the dignity of man.

◄§ *The Queen of Sheba* §►

All through his childhood Malraux had dreamed of the mysterious East, and like many other children he developed a particular veneration for the Queen of Sheba. Since very little was known about her, the imagination could play around her at will. The Book of Kings is strangely reticent about the purpose of her journey to Solomon in Jerusalem. We are told only that she came with a great train, her camels laden with spices, gold and precious stones, and that "she communed with him of all that was in her heart." He received her in his palace, showed her all the rich appointments of his court, and overwhelmed her with his splendor. She emerges out of Arabia in a cloud of incense and jewels, and having occupied the attention of the reader for twelve verses, she vanishes forever from the pages of the Old Testament.

Inevitably legends accumulated around her. In the Koran, where she receives considerably more space than she receives in the Old Testament, Solomon receives her in his throne-room which is entirely paved with glass. The Queen, imagining that the room was deep in water, lifted up her skirts, thus enabling the King to see her legs. Some commentators suggested that Solomon wanted to see for himself whether the rumor that she was goat-footed was true; and other commentators have said she was indeed goat-footed, but as she walked toward the throne she touched some wood from Paradise and her legs were transformed into the most beautiful in the kingdom. In Persia and Abyssinia tales were told about her supernatural powers. According to the Persian philosopher Tabari, she was the daughter of the Emperor of China, a fact which would have commended itself to Malraux, who had a partiality for Chinese princesses, but there was a long-standing tradi-

tion that she was the Queen of the Sabaeans in southwest Arabia with
her capital at Ma'rib. When he wrote about the Queen of Sheba, Malraux described her arriving at the court of Solomon on an elephant
adorned with ostrich feathers, accompanied by a bodyguard of green-
robed horsemen on piebald horses and a retinue of dwarfs; and there
came with her across the desert a fleet of blue ships loaded with coffers
covered in dragon skins. Her clothes were decorated with gold and dia-
monds, and she limped a little, and a glory surrounded her.

Malraux's vision of her derived largely from a familiar source—
the extraordinary early work by Gustave Flaubert called *La Tentation
de saint Antoine,* where Saint Anthony is seen recoiling in horror in
the presence of the Queen. She is all beauty and radiance as she sits
among blue cushions on the howdah of an elephant, which kneels in
homage before the saint, thus permitting her to slide down the elephant's shoulder and advance toward him. In Flaubert's story she offers
herself and her kingdom to the saint, describes the immense treasure he
will receive if only he will abandon his mortifications, and promises
him eternal bliss in her arms. "We shall sleep together on swan's
down softer than clouds, we shall pour wines kept cold in the hollow
of fruit, we shall gaze on the sun through emeralds." But though she
summons celestial eagles to demonstrate her powers, he refuses to be
tempted; and after her pet monkey has lifted up her skirts, she
abandons him in derision and despair.

Flaubert put into his description of the Queen of Sheba all his resources of jeweled prose. Malraux was enchanted by the description,
and when he thought of the Queen of Sheba, he saw her through the
eyes of Flaubert, adding only some characteristic details of his own:
the dwarfs and the blue ships were his own invention. Above all, he
saw her as the temptress, the infinitely beguiling seductress armed with
the weapons of magic power and physical beauty. In her there was
represented all the romance of the East.

In the spring of 1934 he set out to discover her long-lost city. He
said later that the decision to find the city came to him one day in
Isfahan when he was listening to a storyteller recounting her adventures. In that setting, surrounded by brilliant blue and yellow mosques,
no one would have been particularly surprised if the Queen of Sheba

had suddenly appeared at the head of her caravan. On another day in Bushire on the Persian Gulf he heard a German adventurer describing the city of Ma'rib, hidden in the sands of the Yemen, with its seventy temples still standing. The German said he had caught a glimpse of them while wandering in disguise in the desert, but had hurried away when some unfriendly Arabs caught sight of him. There was no way of knowing whether he was speaking the truth, but Malraux was inclined to believe him. Thereafter he would let his imagination play around the seventy temples of Ma'rib and the marble tomb of the Queen of Sheba, which no doubt stood in the greatest and most luxurious of her temples.

In Paris he consulted Jean-Baptiste Charcot, the immensely learned doctor and explorer, one of the few Frenchmen who had explored Antarctica. The son of a more famous father, Dr. Charcot presided over the fortunes of the Geographical Society. From him Malraux learned that only three explorers had reached Ma'rib and returned alive. Two were Frenchmen, Théophile Arnaud and Joseph Halévy, and the third was the Austrian Eduard Glaser, who made four daring journeys into the Yemen during the eighties of the last century. Glaser and Halévy were Jews, and had no great difficulty in disguising themselves as Arabs. Arnaud was less fortunate. He came to Arabia as a druggist attached to an Egyptian regiment stationed at Jidda, the seaport of Mecca, and in 1841 he set himself up as a grocer. Two years later, accompanying a Turkish mission to Sana, he slipped out of the city without the authorization of the Imam and reached Ma'rib, where he made rubbings of forty-three inscriptions. For this success he was to pay dearly. Disguised as a merchant of candles and leading a hermaphroditic donkey by the halter, he made his way back to the coast, taking care to conceal the rubbings, for the Arabs, seeing any piece of paper with strange markings on it, were likely to assume that it was a chart showing the location of buried treasure. The hermaphroditic donkey proved to be his salvation, for as he journeyed from village to village he would exhibit it to the Beduins. In this way he reached Al Hudaydah on the seacoast of Yemen, where he once more set himself up as a grocer.

Arnaud was a man of great resourcefulness, proud of his accomplishment and determined that his discoveries should be published. But the glare of the desert sand had brought him close to blindness, and he was in failing health when he reached Al Hudaydah. He had also grown careless, and one day some hostile Arabs penetrated his disguise. He fled to Jidda by sea, and there took refuge with the French consul, who treated him well and sent the rubbings to Paris. The French consul very sensibly asked him to draw up a plan of Ma'rib, and since he was now too blind to make a drawing on paper, he was led down to the beach and with a stick he drew an outline of the city and the temple of the sun in the sand. The consul copied these sand drawings in his notebook, while the Arabs, fascinated by the appearance of a blind man scribbling on the sand, spoke of him kindly, thinking he was mad. Then the sea came in and washed the drawings away. "It was as though," Malraux commented in one of the newspaper articles he wrote about his search for the lost city, "everything that concerned Sheba, when recreated, summoned the elements that hurled it back to eternity."

The adventures of Arnaud were not yet over. He remained blind for nearly a year, and when he had recovered his sight he returned to Paris with his hermaphroditic donkey, which he presented to the Jardin des Plantes. The French government entrusted him with missions in Yemen, and he returned to Arabia in good spirits, determined to find Sabaean artifacts and present them to France. His explorations were successful, and in 1849 he came to Paris with his treasures. It was the year after the abortive revolution, and the government was no longer interested in the relics of ancient civilizations, especially those of the Sabaeans. Discouraged and in dire poverty, Arnaud ended his days in Algeria; the hermaphroditic donkey died of starvation in the Jardin des Plantes; and the collection of Sabaean antiquities vanished amid the litter of dusty bookshops along the Seine. All that was left of his explorations was contained in the papers printed in the *Journal Asiatique*. There was one sentence which Malraux found especially beguiling: "On leaving Ma'rib, I visited the ruins of ancient Saba, where there was nothing to be seen except mounds of earth. . . ."

Arnaud, of course, was not the sole authority on the lost city of Sheba, and in the library of the Geographical Society Malraux read the

works of Halévy and Glaser, as well as the records of the medieval
Persian geographers al-Hamdani and al-Himyari, and the Roman
geographer Strabo, who had described the ill-fated expedition of the
Roman general Aelius Gallus, who marched his troops across the
desert to Ma'rib and returned to the coast with nothing to show for
their endeavours except the knowledge that they had been in places
where no Romans had ever traveled before. According to Persian legends, all the Roman soldiers perished in the desert, and for centuries
the Arabs would come across their skeletons still encased in their
bronze armor, half-drowned in the desert sands, their skeletal fingers
holding up helmets filled with seashells.

It was a story which delighted Malraux, who might have invented
it for *The Kingdom of Farfelu.* Characteristically, for he enjoyed scenes
set in darkness or shadow, he imagined himself coming upon the dead
soldiers at sunset: "The dying sun offered the entire desert to the dead
legions, flinging the shadows of war to the very end of the smooth
sands: open hands above fallen helmets, fingers spread out and prolonged to infinity across the desert."

Malraux spent many days poring over the books in the library of
the Geographical Society. Arnaud, lost and forgotten, was disinterred,
to become the companion of his dreams. "I should like to have known
you, Arnaud," he wrote in 1934. "I would like to have seen your
zouave beard, your solemn air, your candles, your casual heroism, your
simple and charming genius for adventure. Perhaps, unwittingly, I
went to Sheba in search of your ghost. Or perhaps it was in search of
the ghost of your donkey, which I would also have liked, and no doubt
it died between the polar bear and the penguin, seeing neither of them,
stupefied by the Paradise assuredly promised to donkeys by Allah, but
unable to understand, absolutely unable to understand, why it was being kept a prisoner. . . ." More than thirty years later, when he came
to write *Antimémoires,* Malraux introduced this passage into his text,
making some slight alterations. He no longer addressed Arnaud with
the familiar *tu,* but in the third person, for they were now separated by
a long interval of time, and he added, with a deepening sympathy for
animals, the words: "or why they had ceased feeding it."

With Arnaud as his guide, he decided to make his way to Yemen and the lost city. He had picked up a smattering of Persian and spoke of going in the disguise of a Persian, if necessary alone. He was discussing his plans with some friends at vast length when he was interrupted by a young air force captain, Edward Corniglion-Molinier, who pronounced that it was perfectly ridiculous for a scholar or romantic adventurer to be killed in one of these dangerous explorations when there existed a safe and simple method of discovering lost cities—the airplane. Malraux was oddly quiet for the rest of the evening.

Corniglion-Molinier had other reasons for being dubious about Malraux's chances of surviving a journey in disguise through Yemen. He had no great faith in Malraux's knowledge of Persian. Malraux was not in fact a good, or even a passable, linguist, and the Yemenites would have no difficulty in discovering that he was a Frenchman.

Malraux was sufficiently impressed by Corniglion-Molinier to call him on the telephone the next day. It was a wonderful idea; what facilities were available? They met, pored over maps of Arabia, and discovered that all the maps were different, and therefore unreliable. Corniglion-Molinier calculated that it would be possible to fly from Djibuti to Ma'rib and back again without refueling. English and American airplanes were available, but where was the glory of flying in a foreign airplane? As it happened, Paul-Louis Weiller, the director of the Gnome airplane factory, was a personal friend, and as soon as Corniglion-Molinier broached the subject, Weiller made the offer of his own private airplane, which was beautifully upholstered, with central heating and all the latest devices. Technically it was a Gnome and Rhone K-7 300 CV model adapted to the needs of its owner. Further adaptations and modifications would be necessary before it could be flown across the desert, and these were undertaken by a smiling mechanic called Maillard, who later accompanied Malraux and Corniglion-Molinier to Djibuti. The luxurious furnishings were eviscerated; new wheels and extra gas tanks were added; and the luxury airplane was transformed into an ugly, stripped down workhorse with strange pipes protruding from the sides.

By the middle of February 1934 all tests had been completed successfully, and they were ready to leave. They flew to Orly and learned at the last moment that the original authorization to proceed to

Djibuti had been canceled because it was no longer the same airplane; there were so many modifications and alterations that in the eyes of the bureaucrats of the Ministry of Air it had become another airplane altogether. Pale and angry, Corniglion-Molinier went in search of a bureaucrat who would pronounce in good faith that the luxury craft and the workhorse were identical, and finally received permission to leave.

Money to cover the expenses of the flight was provided by *L'Intransigeant,* the Paris newspaper, and both Malraux and Corniglion-Molinier were expected to write long and detailed accounts of their explorations. Malraux was so sure he would find the lost city that he had already written some of the background material he would include in his articles.

They left Paris on February 23, 1934, and arrived in Djibuti on March 4 by way of Italy, Libya, Cairo, Assuan, Wadi Halfa, Khartum and Port Sudan. It was good flying weather. They were especially impressed by the Italian airmen and the facilities provided at the Italian air bases in Libya. They spent two or three days in Cairo, and had time to meet Hassan Anis Pasha, the Controller of Aviation in Egypt, who provided them with an excellent map. He was sympathetic to their dream of discovering the long-lost city, for he had once attempted to discover it himself, flying to Sana—he was the first airman ever to land an airplane on the sands of Sana—and then abandoning the project when the Imam Yahya absolutely forbade any further flights because there were rebellious tribes in the interior.

In Egypt Malraux gloried in the opportunity of visiting the Cairo Museum and the Sphinx, which was then still half-buried in the sand and thus resembled a sculptured mountain rather than a mysterious leonine beast of prey guarding the approaches to the pyramids. But there was little time for sightseeing, and on the morning of March 1 they flew south, each afternoon landing at a British air base where they were received, according to Corniglion-Molinier, "with polite indifference."

But if the British were cool, the French airmen at the military base in Djibuti could not have been more gracious or more enthusiastic. The flight was unofficial; the Air Ministry would have prevented it if the real purpose had become known; the French airmen gazed with wonder at the airplane and added their own subtle improvements, based on their unauthorized flights over southern Arabia, to the map provided by the amiable Hassan Anis Pasha. These airmen entered happily into the conspiracy, surrendering their own beds and bathrooms to the newcomers, who were entitled to enjoy at least two restful days and nights before flying to Arabia.

Arrangements were made to permit the airplane to come down at a small airfield in the north of French Somaliland, if there was not enough gasoline to enable them to return directly to Djibuti. Malraux still imagined that he might have to play the role of Arnaud, and accordingly they were supplied with long white Arab cloaks and some coloring matter to darken their faces. They were also well-equipped with rifles and revolvers.

On the night before they flew off, Corniglion-Molinier had the necessary but distasteful task of telling Maillard, the smiling mechanic, that his services would not be needed during the flight.

"We don't want to expose you to unnecessary danger," Corniglion-Molinier explained gently. "After all, we shall be flying over rebel territory, and if the engine fails . . ."

"In the first place, it will not fail if I am on the airplane," Maillard replied. "I'm the only one who really knows about the engine, and if anything goes wrong—if, for example, we have to land in the desert and do some necessary repairs before the Arabs catch up with us, and I have seen such things happen in Morocco—then I am more than ever essential to the success of your flight. You must understand that for your own sake it is necessary to take me with you."

Against these arguments Corniglion-Molinier had no recourse, and he reluctantly agreed to let the mechanic accompany them. Altogether there would be four men in the airplane, for they also took with them an Arab to act as their interpreter if they were forced down. Early in the morning of March 7 they flew off from the military airfield at Djibuti.

Malraux was not a journalist and he had no command of journalistic prose. In the dispatches he wrote for *L'Intransigeant* he described the flight as though he were writing a long richly textured essay on oriental aesthetics, his images and cadences deriving from Flaubert's *La Tentation de saint Antoine*. He wrote:

The airplane is waiting in the early dawn.

How often have I seen these airplanes crouched on the long fields on the edge of dawn in the Mohammedan odor of burnt grass, pepper and camels! Fields in southern Persia, steppes of central Asia—the Russian pilots passing their nights naked on swings to escape from the appalling heat—at the foot of the Himalayas, in the burned out gardens beneath the savage and scorching perfume of the withered lavender from the mountains. . . . Islam is all around us, as far as the depths of Africa, as far as the Pamirs; and I find myself thinking of the words uttered by the travelers at such an hour as they raise up the beasts of their caravans:

"This was a night of destiny. Blessed be this night until the coming of the dawn!"

But this was merely the trumpet blast announcing the beginning of his story, and soon enough he is describing how the airplane turned suddenly white as the night fell away, and Arabia lay somewhere below the clouds, for they had become cloud-hoppers by necessity: the city of Sana must have no advance warning of their coming. They flew toward the Bab-al-Mandab Straits and followed the coast of Yemen, which was scarcely visible through the reddish haze. Below them lay Mokha, one of the many cities Malraux had dreamed about in his childhood. He could remember looking up the city in the immense gray volumes of Bottin, which are found in post-offices and *bistros,* and he remembered reading the words: "Mokha: magnificent palace falling into ruins," and there came to him the smell of sawdust in the little *bistro,* and soon for some reason he found himself thinking of the Yezedis, a strange sect of devil-worshipers living in Mosul, and their prostitutes with heavy earrings sitting at enormous windows in the dying sun; and from these dreams he was awakened by the spectacle of the endless sand drifts below and the knowledge that they were flying at a speed of 160 kilometers an hour with the wind against them, and therefore it was unlikely that if they reached Ma'rib there would be enough gasoline left in the tanks to enable them to return to Djibuti.

Malraux had the illusion that he was crawling up the coast of

Arabia like a beetle. Through the reddish mist he could make out the shape of Al Hudaydah, the seaport from which Arnaud had once fled, taking with him his precious rubbings. He could see the white jetty and the mosque, and it looked civilized, reminding him of cities on the coast of Algeria, where he had spent a second honeymoon; but Al Hudaydah was forbidden territory, and they hid in the clouds before turning east toward Sana, that entirely improbable city described by Halévy and Glaser as though they could never quite bring themselves to believe that it existed. Sana lay in a well-watered valley nearly eight thousand feet above sea level, dominated by two immense, improbable peaks. Hassan Anis Pasha had warned them that they would not see these peaks until they were almost on top of them; and so it was. Sana came into view suddenly and unexpectedly, after they had lost their way, the peaks vanishing mysteriously from sight.

Though they flew low over Sana and photographed the great mosque, all this, they realized, was a waste of time. For them Sana was no more than a point on the map. They must find Ma'rib some sixty miles to the east, lost somewhere among the heavy folds of rock and the broken valleys. So they flew along the valley of Kharid, seeing villages where they expected none, and losing hope because there were no clear roads, because the earth below corresponded to scarcely anything on their maps, and because the gasoline was running out. They found Ma'rib, or what they thought was Ma'rib, but it was no more than a handful of columns and a few scattered stones and an oval-shaped temple wall. Arnaud, Halévy and Glaser had all reported that it was a barren place with a few columns standing. Corniglion-Molinier, seeing the place, flew low, and the Arab accompanying them became hopelessly confused, recognizing nothing. They had reached Ma'rib but it was not the legendary city with the seventy temples described by the German adventurer in Bushire.

Five hours had passed, and in another five hours they would have to be back in Djibuti or on some northern airfield in French Somaliland; there were only a few minutes left to search for a lost city in a tormented landscape half covered with brown mists and lit with a blue phosphorescence. They were coming to the edge of the great desert, the Rub' al Khali, which resembled an immense scaled scorpion glint-

ing and flaming in the sun, with here and there flashing whirlpools of
sand, and the earth was etched with strange lines like the veins of
leaves, a strange and desolate landscape from which nothing whatsoever could be expected except perhaps an occasional caravan bringing
spices to Sana.

It was then, quite suddenly, when they were coasting over the edge
of the desert and wondering how soon they would have to return that
they caught a glimpse of the white city, at first only a flash of white
rocks, and then the rocks assumed the shapes of palaces and towers
and great terraces near a dried-up river bed. There was also a horseshoe-
shaped containing wall. This was not just a rocky outcrop: everywhere
they looked they saw signs of intelligent planning and deliberate design. The buildings were so white that they seemed to be made of
marble. They counted the towers: there were at least twenty, some
square, others conical. Later, comparing this city with Sana, Corniglion-
Molinier concluded that it could have had a population of about two
hundred thousand people.

They descended as low as nine hundred feet in order to take
photographs, the airplane tiptilted at an angle of forty-five degrees.
They had still and movie cameras, and there was no time to do anything except take pictures and make wild guesses about the nature of
those sculptured buildings which so prodigiously conveyed a sense of
life, of a living city. Also, they were in grave danger of being shot
down, for some Beduins inside the walls of the city fired at them and
they saw the little spurts of red flame; but these joy-shots passed harm-
lessly. They circled the city three or four times to make sure they were
not looking at a mirage or creating it out of their own imaginations.
But it was real enough: high white bastions, processional roads, great
blocks of buildings like windowless skyscrapers, and here and there a
few red buildings which may have been erected in post-Islamic times,
and they thought they could make out some Beduin tents in the
shadows of the walls. "We were bewildered by this marvelous sight,"
Corniglion-Molinier said later, "and we forgot that our fuel was running out and that sooner or later we would probably be forced to land
in hostile territory." Malraux, too, was wondering what would happen
if they landed: sand dunes on one side of the city, volcanic rock on the

other. If they fell into the sand dunes, the airplane would simply capsize, and if they fell on the volcanic rock, it would be torn to shreds.

There were white buildings with only the walls standing, and there were other buildings which resembled immense warehouses, and these, Malraux thought, must have been the repository of the kingdom's wealth of spices in the days when the city was ruled by magician-queens and their astrologers. He was absolutely convinced that the city was the ancient capital of the Queen of Sheba and perhaps the relics of the Queen lay in the shadow of the airplane's wing.

Flying past the city, they came to a long valley which curved and glinted like a knife. Under the cliffs they could make out rows of tombs, some large and some small, and there seemed to be between fifteen hundred and two thousand of them. They were in orderly rows, and about forty of them were of great size. Malraux thought they were the tombs of the great men of the empire, another Valley of the Dead. Centuries passed, as one after another the lords of Saba were carried in pomp to their graves. But though they were able to photograph the valley, they had no time to examine it closely. A reddish mist or sand-cloud swept over it a few moments later. Malraux thought the red cloud resembled the shape of an eagle clawing at the tombs.

For Malraux the discovery of the tombs was almost as exciting as the discovery of the white city. Here was virgin land, yet to be conquered, promising further adventures. In his report on the discovery of the Valley of the Dead printed on the front page of *L'Intransigeant* on May 10, 1934, Malraux permitted himself the luxury of poetic prose as he described King Solomon in his endless old age standing guard over the tomb of his long-dead Queen:

> Many years had passed since Solomon fled from Jerusalem. Across the desert where the sands formed the shapes of petrified trees he had wandered, followed by the demons who were the slaves of the Seal, whose last letter can only be read by the dead. And in one of those valleys where the white rock lies low like a camel's skeleton, the King stands absolutely motionless on some barren ridge—this King who had written the greatest

of all poems of human despair. He stands there with his hands
folded under his chin, leaning on a long traveling staff, watching year after year as the demons raise up the palace of the
Queen of Sheba by the sweat of their brows. He no longer makes
the slightest movement, but his crooked forefinger still points
to the all-powerful Seal, and every evening his shadow stretches
to the utmost bounds of the desert. The demons of the sand,
perpetually at work, are full of envy for their brothers who
rage across the desert with the voices of whirlwinds.

An insect, coming in search of wood, saw the royal staff,
hesitated, grew more confident, and began to bite into it. A few
moments later the staff and the King crumbled into dust. The
Lord of Silence, in whose presence even the birds obeyed the
protocol, had wished to die standing, so that all the demons he
ruled over should be enslaved forever by the Queen. But now
they were set free. Abandoning the palace they had built for
ages during the silence of Solomon, with its Babylonian stairways opening haphazardly to the heavens, they hurried to the
city, now almost in ruins. The Queen had been dead for three
hundred years. Then they went in search of her tomb at the foot
of the mountains, and found it, together with the famous inscription:

> I have laid her enchanted heart among the roses, and on the
> balm tree I have hung a lock of her hair,
> And he who loves her presses to his heart this lock of hair,
> and breathing its scent, he is drunk with melancholy.

Then they fled away in terror, never to return, having found
the Queen with one leg longer than the other lying in her
crystal coffin, guarded by an immortal serpent, silent, motionless, strewn with mysterious stars.

The reader of *L'Intransigeant,* reading the small print on the front
page, may have wondered what all this had to do with a flight over a
desert. But for Malraux such questions did not arise. Every journey was
an occasion for legends; it was not enough that he should find her city,

but he must find her crystal coffin, her guardian serpents and the Seal of Solomon. As he recounted his adventures in Arabia and elsewhere, there was always the danger that the legends might take precedence over the simple things he had observed. Facts glowed in the light of legends, and legends glowed in the light of facts. In all his stories there are crystal coffins.

Corniglion-Molinier was considerably less interested in legends. What interested him as they flew back to French Somaliland was whether there was enough gasoline for the journey. According to the French airmen at Djibuti, the Arabs reserved excruciating tortures for white men who fell into their hands, and if the airplane was forced to land on the sea, they would be eaten by sharks. Neither prospect was inviting. By good luck they were able to land at the little town of Obock in French Somaliland, north of the Gulf of Tadjoura. There was a small airfield where they could fill up their tanks with gasoline. The district officer offered them drinks, presented them with a gazelle, and showed a proper solicitude. A few minutes later they were on their way to Djibuti, where they were royally greeted by the French airmen. A telegram was sent off to *L'Intransigeant:* HAVE DISCOVERED LEGENDARY CITY QUEEN OF SHEBA STOP TWENTY TOWERS OR TEMPLES STILL STANDING STOP ON NORTH BOUNDARY OF RUB' AL KHALI STOP HAVE TAKEN PHOTOGRAPHS FOR L'INTRANSIGEANT STOP GREETINGS CORNIGLION-MALRAUX.

This telegram caused a flurry of excitement in the capitals of Europe, where all the newspapers featured the news and commented upon it at considerable length, although there was very little hard fact to go on. Surmise, speculation, a little background information, brief accounts of the reign of the Queen of Sheba and her visit to the court of King Solomon filled two or three columns, and during the following days Arabists and archaeologists filled more columns with their views on whether Malraux had in fact discovered anything of importance. In America *The New York Times* and the *Herald Tribune* published long articles on the discovery with maps of Arabia, in which Ma'rib appeared as large as Mecca, and there were the inevitable reproductions of paintings of the Queen of Sheba. *The New York Times* interviewed Dr. Richard Gottheil, Professor of Semitic Languages at

Columbia University, who expressed guarded skepticism. He had definite opinions about the Queen of Sheba. "A nice story about Solomon and the Queen of Sheba," he commented, "but probably a mere myth. So far as we know, there never was such a Queen, and if there was no Queen the chances are there was no capital for her."

Dr. John K. Wright, librarian of the American Geographical Society, was more favorably impressed. "The report of the discovery of ruins in the Southern Desert of Arabia is intensely interesting to geographers and archaeologists," he said. "Judgment, of course, must be reserved regarding the alleged identification of the ruins seen with the Queen of Sheba's capital until more information is available, as to both the exact location and the character of the ruins." Most of the specialists who were consulted hedged their bets, and indeed they could hardly do otherwise. The only information came from the telegram, which in one respect was totally inaccurate. They had not reached the north boundary of the Rub' al Khali, and they had given no approximate indication of the location of their discovery.

Nevertheless the news was sufficiently provocative to produce innumerable articles and interviews. There was speculation that perhaps Malraux had discovered the long lost city of Ubar, "the Atlantis of the sands," of which Bertram Thomas heard rumors during his famous journey across the Rub' al Khali in 1930. He found some well-worn tracks in the desert, and the native guides said that anyone who followed them would eventually reach Ubar, once a great city, now fallen from its high estate because the people had been sinful in the face of Allah, who had thereupon transformed them into *nasnas*, half-monkeys, each having only one eye, one nostril, one ear, one leg and one arm. Concerning Ubar and its unfortunate inhabitants very little was known, and St. John Philby, the famous father of a more famous son, had carried on a heated correspondence with Bertram Thomas in the pages of the *Journal of the Royal Asiatic Society*, insisting that Ubar was merely Wabar under another name, and as for Wabar it was not a city but the mouth of a volcano. Bertram Thomas stuck to his story: he had seen the immense tracks carved on the plains—they were a hundred yards wide—and it was unlikely that Arab caravans in vast numbers would journey across an inhospitable desert merely for the pleasure of looking into the mouth of a volcano.

Arabists, like Arabs, tend to be hot-tempered people with very firm opinions, and sometimes the discussions on Malraux's discovery grew heated. Jules Barthoux, an eminent French archaeologist, announced that in July 1930 he had given Malraux the benefit of his knowledge of Arabian antiquities, but unfortunately Malraux had failed to put his knowledge to good use. Barthoux joined the ranks of those who believed he had discovered Ubar, which was therefore no discovery at all. William Albright, Professor of Semitic Languages at Johns Hopkins University, was certain that Ma'rib was the capital of the Queen of Sheba, and since many of the archaeologists who had visited Ma'rib returned with full reports, the claim to have discovered her capital could not be taken seriously. "Malraux is not known as an archaeologist," he declared firmly. It was not the first time professional archaeologists had dismissed him out of hand for his lack of professional status. Yet there was always the possibility that he might have stumbled upon something extraordinary, and Professor Albright concluded with the hope that further information would elucidate the problem.

Further information was exactly what Malraux was unable to offer until his articles were published in *L'Intransigeant*. In Djibuti he was busy developing the photographs; half would be developed there, the rest in Paris, for if there was an accident on the homeward journey the photographs left in Djibuti would still proclaim the discovery. He was being sensibly cautious, because he attached enormous importance to the newly discovered city.

Meanwhile there were ceremonial functions to be attended, the most important being an audience with Emperor Haile Selassie, who claimed to be descended from Solomon and the Queen of Sheba. His capital at Addis Ababa was three days' journey from Djibuti by rail, but only three hours by air. Although the Abyssinian government was exceedingly cautious about granting permits for airplanes to land at the capital, Malraux and Corniglion-Molinier concluded that the opportunity for visiting Addis Ababa and seeing the King of Kings was not to be missed. In ordinary circumstances it would have taken about three months to assemble all the documents needed for the journey; they therefore flew without any documents at all.

The airfield at Addis Ababa also served as a race track and polo field, and they landed in the midst of a polo game. No one bothered about their lack of documents; the French ambassador was cordial, and the Abyssinian minister of foreign affairs was impressed by Malraux's profound knowledge of Abyssinian history gained during his researches on the Queen of Sheba. At the audience given by Haile Selassie, the visitors bowed deeply and offered their apologies for not wearing the regulation top hats; it was explained that there was not room enough in their single-engined airplane for top hats. Haile Selassie's stern features broke into a smile. Malraux launched into a long lecture concerning the discovery of the great Sabaean city and the Valley of the Dead, where no doubt lay the tombs of the Emperor's ancestors, and once more from the throne there came a smile of gentle approval. The Emperor was not in the least surprised that the city had been discovered, he had always known of its existence, and he went on to congratulate them on their achievements. Then the Negro servants in brilliantly colored robes entered the throne room, bearing golden trays heaped with chocolate and cakes, and at the sight of the cakes a wolfhound began to leap and bark furiously, while the royal lions roared in their cages.

On March 13 they reached Cairo and gave their first brief interviews to reporters, and then flew to Benghazi. They were told the weather was likely to be bad over Tunisia, but they were not especially alarmed. There was no hint of a violent storm when they set off from Benghazi. The sky darkened, the clouds gathered, and when they peered out of the cockpit they saw snow-covered mountains where they had expected to see smooth plains and sand. They had been driven seventy miles off course, and were being tossed about like shuttlecocks over the Aurès mountains.

The next minutes were perhaps the most fearful that Malraux ever experienced. Quite suddenly the storm erupted into a hurricane; and from being tossed about like a shuttlecock, they were in mortal danger of being torn to pieces by the force of the hurricane. Hailstones poured into the cockpit, half blinding them. The compass needle began to revolve alarmingly, and they suddenly realized that they were in the eye of the hurricane, helplessly turning on their own axis, with an altimeter which was probably out of order and the battered cowling so shaken by the violence of the storm that it was a miracle it had not already been ripped away. If the cowling went, there would be very little left of the airplane. All the time Corniglion-Molinier was glued to the controls, and Malraux observed, not for the first time, the strange transformation of the human face at moments of intense danger: he looked like a child.

The airplane began to lose height rapidly, falling into a vast pit of darkness whose bottom was perhaps the jagged peaks of the Aurès mountains. Malraux was desperately frightened and at the same time exhilarated; at any moment the airplane might crash, and there was absolutely nothing he could do about it. They were descending into a blind kingdom, which was perhaps the Kingdom of Farfelu, at an angle of forty-five degrees, in an airplane that was about to fall apart. They had brought this upon themselves in their haste to reach Paris. When the altimeter plunged to twelve hundred feet Malraux felt that all hope was lost and prepared himself for death. Suddenly, three hundred feet below, they saw the black sharp-sided hills, a lake, the clouds overhead. Exhausted, crawling under the storm, brushing past the peaks of the hills, they came out into a level land of canals and rivers, quiet and peaceful in the evening light. A few minutes later they landed at the small airport of Bône on the eastern edge of Algeria.

When a man is snatched from death, he experiences in a brief space of time all those quick and vivid sensations which are associated with adolescence. Life flows back in little jets and spurts, colors glow with startling brilliance, familiar things acquire a strange significance. So now, driving into Bône, he was surprised by the sight of an immense red hand advertising a glover's shop. It occurred to him that the world was filled with hands, each hand having a life of its own, and the glover's shop and all the other shops were all new, because he had never expected to see them again; and so it was with everything else he saw.

Not many hours later he was back in Paris, working on his books and articles for *L'Intransigeant* and delivering speeches at left-wing rallies, as though there had been no interruption in his life, as though he had never flown over Arabia or fallen helpless through the eye of a storm.

ᴈ *Days of Wrath* ᴂ

Between May 3 and May 13, 1934, *L'Intransigeant* published Malraux's articles on the flight over the desert under the title "Discovery of the Mysterious Capital of the Queen of Sheba." The articles always began on the front page under banner headlines, and they were heavily illustrated with photographs taken during the flight or from photoagencies. Altogether there were ten articles, two of them being signed by Corniglion-Molinier. Set down among the front-page political upheavals and scandals, Malraux's articles with their jeweled prose had an oddly defiant appearance. The Queen of Sheba in all her magnificence was parading on the front page of a newspaper.

Malraux had no gift for journalism whatsoever, and there was in fact no special reason why he should write journalistically. The newspaper wanted his name and the sensational title, the photographs of the long-lost city, the breath of Arabia, the sense of mystery. These he provided in full measure. Only one of the photographs taken on the flight showed the entire city with its storied towers—tower after tower rising over the jagged plain. An architect and urbanist, André Hardy, drew plans of the city based on the photograph, tentatively identifying the royal palace, the storehouses and the Temple of the Sun. There was no doubt that a vast abandoned city had been seen by Malraux and Corniglion-Molinier somewhere in the region of Mar'ib, but there was considerable skepticism about whether this was the city of the Queen of Sheba. Gradually all interest in the discovery waned, and Malraux himself lost interest in it. To his friends Corniglion-Molinier said: "We saw something, but Heaven knows what it was."

Malraux had enjoyed the experience of flying over the desert, but what he remembered most about the journey was the terrifying descent over the Aurès mountains and the extraordinary feeling of relief when it was over. There was an escape from death and "a return to the earth," and a new knowledge of what people meant to him.

In the following months he wrote *Days of Wrath,* a novel about a Communist leader who is imprisoned by the Nazis. Although the novel fails as a work of art, it provides an absorbing light on Malraux's ideas at the time. He has reduced the stage machinery to the bare minimum: there is Kassner, the Communist leader, the prison, and "a return to the earth." Throughout the course of the novel Kassner occupies the forefront of the stage.

The author of a book on prison life has to contend with many great authors who have been prisoners and who have described their experiences with genius. Malraux had never been a prisoner, and the novel therefore lacks the authentic chill of prison life. To be a prisoner is a shattering experience, for everything about a prison is monstrous, illogical, deathly; and no one ever leaves a prison unchanged. In prison a man suffers a strange chemical change in the blood, and for the rest of his life his bone marrow is filled with terror and poison.

When Malraux set out to write the novel about Kassner, he knew imaginatively what prison was like; he had read widely in prison literature; he had thought himself day after day into the mind of a prisoner. Yet he was still far from knowing what happens to a man when the prison door closes behind him. The walls, the bars, the plank bed, the bucket, the scraping sound made by the jailor's footsteps, the faces of the Stormtroopers who preside over interrogations—all these were perfectly comprehensible to him in an intellectual way, and he could reproduce them imaginatively. Beyond this he could not go. Prison was one of those sacraments which had been denied to him.

Kassner is described as a tall, bony man with pointed ears, large eyes, chestnut-colored hair, with the look of a broken-down thoroughbred. He wears his hair long and he has fine hands. He was the son of a miner, a scholarship student in the university, the organizer of a proletarian theater, a prisoner in Russia who had gone over to the Communists and then entered the Red Army, a delegate to China and Mongolia, a former vice president of Red Aid, a revolutionary who had organized strikes in the Ruhr, a writer. The description suggests a compromise between Malraux and Gustav Regler, who had attempted to organize strikes in the Ruhr. Once more we are presented with the intellectual revolutionary within an inch of death.

When we first see Kassner, he has been pushed into a guard room and is listening to the interrogation of a Communist prisoner. It is an inconclusive interrogation, for the Communist refuses to answer many questions and evades others. Kassner feels himself intensely present, "at once riveted to the spot with his whole helplessness, and absent with his whole strength." His own interrogation is quickly over, for he no longer resembles the photograph of the famous, much-sought Kassner in the police files, and as the manager of a small factory in Czechoslovakia manufacturing variable pitch propellers he has a nearly perfect alibi. Would a propeller manufacturer be a Communist? Nevertheless the Nazis decide to keep him in jail until they have discovered who he is.

The preliminary scenes are sketched in roughly, almost impatiently. Malraux is chiefly interested in the behavior of the prisoner in his cell, which is dark and clammy, with inscriptions along the base of the wall, presumably written by prisoners without the strength to stand. One inscription reads: "I don't want . . ." The rest has been rubbed out. He stands there, very quiet, attempting to think logically, going over in his mind all the reasons which led him to join the intelligence service of the Communist Party. But these moments of logic are soon over, for he realizes that he must split his mind wide open in order to survive. "He must seek refuge in complete passivity, in the irresponsibility of sleep and madness; and yet keep watch with a mind sufficiently lucid to be able to defend himself, not to let himself be destroyed here irremediably; tear himself asunder so as to yield only what was unessential."

In his cell Kassner hears the cries of prisoners being beaten up in neighboring cells; these screams terrify him and set in motion the strange process by which he withdraws from the real world and takes refuge in dreams and hallucinations, for the screams become music and the music in turn creates images. Horsemen gallop, priests in jeweled robes ride out of nowhere and vanish just as swiftly. In this way Malraux succeeds in conveying the inner workings of a mind on the edge of sanity.

Meanwhile we continue to see Kassner in his cell, which resembles a dark carapace, stifling him, crushing him with its weight. The door is flung open. Two Stormtroopers enter, set a lighted lantern on the floor, and mechanically, in silence, they beat him up. The scene is described briefly, for the incident itself is brief, and the reader sees only the lantern on the floor, and strange shapes of violence flung up on the wall like spiders. Though one of the Stormtroopers gives Kassner a parting kick in the jaw, there is no impression of physical violence or of pain: the scene resembles one of those paintings by Caravaggio, with a single glowing lamp in the foreground and the distorted shapes of the tortured saints vanishing into the distance, while here and there, in no recognizable pattern, gleams of feverish light fall on them.

There is no feeling for physical brutality, and indeed throughout Malraux's novels descriptions of physical violence are very nearly absent: the violence takes place in the mind. We scarcely see the Stormtroopers, and Kassner himself is lost in the shadows. Mercifully he faints after receiving the kick in the jaw, and when he awakes he is in another cell, dreaming of his wife, summoning her into his presence, her face dark as a mulatto, with straggling hair, lips parted, blue eyes like those of a Siamese cat. He tells himself: "If I go round the cell ten times before the guard comes, she is alive." But the guard passes on his round before Kassner has completed his ten circles, and so, with a prisoner's instinct for preservation, he changes the rules of the game. Instead of counting to ten, he will count to a hundred.

Convinced that his wife is dead and that he is going insane, he deliberately encourages hallucinations. Like another Prometheus chained to the rock, he sees a vulture forming out of the darkness. Then the vulture disappears, the darkness turns to snow, and there is a dog barking at a flock of wild geese, and this changes abruptly to sunflowers mowed down during a battle with partisans—Malraux would use these sunflowers again, in a single close shot, in his film of *Man's Hope* four years later. The yellow petals stir in the wind, with blood dripping from them. But the sunflowers give way to the driven snow over the Mongolian plains, and this in turn to roses withering on their stems like dead butterflies, rain-drenched palm trees, Chinese merchants fleeing from the Red Lancers, the flooded Yangtze River with the corpses caught in the forks of dead trees. Most of the imagery was Chinese,

for Kassner finds himself reliving his experiences in the Red Army in
China and Mongolia. We remember that Malraux had described his
imaginary experiences in the Red Army in *Expedition to Isfahan,* and
these hallucinations, given to a man in the darkness of his cell, in the
hovering presence of the vulture swollen with the blood of darkness,
are perfectly comprehensible. We believe in Kassner's visions, as later
we will believe in his desperate and unavailing efforts to establish contact with his fellow prisoners. What is less credible is the figure of
Kassner the revolutionary, drowned in his own images.

As we follow Kassner through the various stages of his purgatory,
he appears to shed his physical body. We never learn when he eats,
how he eats, how he sleeps, whether he is standing or sitting or lying
on the floor. We never see the furniture of the cell. He lives in the
hollow of a rock, enclosed in total darkness. It is precisely this absence
of physical sensation which becomes oddly disturbing. He hears music,
drumming sounds, dogs barking, factory sirens, church bells, snatches
of song, but they all arise from within. Only the vulture, being formed
out of the darkness of the prison walls, comes from outside. Malraux
describes the return of the vulture as though it were a transfiguration
or a death:

> As the song finally subsided, the fervor of life and death now
> united was swallowed up in the world's limitless servitude: the
> stars would always follow the same course in that sky spangled
> with fatality, and those captive planets would forever turn in
> their captive immensity, like the prisoners in this prison, like
> himself in his cell. Then, upon three repeated notes like the
> peals of church bells, the first note bearing down upon all his
> wounds at once, the last shreds of the firmament receded to the
> depths of the world of anguish and little by little assumed the
> form of a vulture.
>
> With his eyelids tightly shut, a slight fever in his hands that
> were now clutching his chest, he waited. There was nothing—
> nothing but the enormous rock on every side and that other
> night, the dead night. He was pressed against the wall. "Like a
> centipede," he reflected, listening to all this music born of his

mind which now gradually was withdrawing, ebbing away with
the very sound of human happiness, leaving him stranded on
the shore.

When the novel was first published, Malraux was asked why passages like these should be included in a novel about the life of a Communist leader in a Nazi concentration camp. Was it conceivable that
Kassner would have reacted in precisely this way to his imprisonment?
Malraux answered: "The world of a work such as this, the world of
tragedy, is the ancient world still—man, the crowd, the elements,
woman, destiny. It reduces itself to two characters, the hero and his
sense of life." He might just as well have said, "the hero and his sense
of death." He might also have said that since all the great prison novels
had already been written, it was not his task to add one more. He was
concerned with imprisonment as a *visionary experience,* and this was,
of course, exactly what the dogmatic Communists found so perplexing.
They did not regard prison as a place where visions were permissible.

Without these visions recounted in great profusion, the novel would
be dead, for the story, as story, scarcely exists. The visions—for they
are more than hallucinations—give it life. They are described with
memorable force and conviction, and they are quite astonishingly
coherent. Shreds of memory, the color of many skies, all shining things,
the shapes of buildings and their associations go to form the visions,
and in addition he will sometimes remember scraps from the great Russian films of the early twenties like Dovchenko's *Earth* and Eisenstein's
The End of St. Petersburg.

At one moment he sees an iridescence spreading like oil over water,
which turns pink and is slashed with a network of black streaks.
Evidently it is a river or a sea, and he wonders where he has seen it
before, and then it occurs to him that once in a salmon-colored dawn
he had seen a river where the fish had been killed by the shells of the
Whites, and now he is gazing at the pink fish lying dead on the surface.
This vision of glinting fish gives way to the jewel-encrusted vestments
of priests like those he had seen in the antique shop where he was
arrested. The glittering vestments become winking icon lamps, and
these become the night lights he had seen on the Trans-Siberian rail-

road, which swell out to become the onion-shaped domes of St. Basil's Cathedral in Moscow. The cathedral fades into one of the great fortress-monasteries of Russia, which also have onion-shaped domes, and finally he sees himself again, a prisoner in his monk's cell. The vision has turned full circle, and once more he dreams of his wife in Prague and he has the illusion that he is hurrying after her, that she is close to him, that she is not dead.

Sometimes the effect of these visions is to pile unreality upon unreality. The extravagant processions and fiestas, like films projected on a screen, seem to be at two removes from reality. Priests in their heavy vestments continually appear:

> The priests who have come up over the brow of the hill continually advance, with their dalmatics and tiaras, under the crosses and banners, and a boundless unreality animates this marching treasure hoard, this goldsmith's folly let loose over the muddy fields, with all those white beards, and those trembling gleams of pearls and silver in the moonlight.

The priests advance, and behind them come the Whites. The Reds fall back and some are captured and hanged. Kassner remembers or half-remembers that he was present at the battle, and when the barrel of his machine gun became red hot, he cooled it by crushing grapes on it. Finally, while the snow is falling, the Reds recapture the town, hurl all the furniture into the street, and take part in a triumphal fiesta:

> The insurgents have dragged from the rich houses all the twisted furniture, a fantastic assortment of baroque Russian adaptations of Louis XV and Escargot; on the grand piano, with feet like cathedral gargoyles, there is an enormous spray of artificial white flowers. In the midst of all this a carnival of the bearded insurgents is in full swing: they have stripped the priests of their chasubles, and in the intervening few hours have tailored the brocade into Tales of Hoffmann costumes. They make their way between the gilt and silvered armchairs and pianos in the dim light in which snow now begins to fall, like lunatics who have suddenly taken over an Opera House.

The lunatics who have suddenly taken over an Opera House are familiar creatures; the Kingdom of Farfelu invades even the Nazi concentration camps. Kassner escapes from this kingdom by suddenly becoming conscious of his cell, of the footsteps of the guards and the knocking on the wall. At first the knocking is completely mysterious to him, for it does not correspond to the alphabet as he knows it. A is not one knock, B is not two knocks. He is almost terrified by what appears to be a wholly fortuitous series of knocks. Then it suddenly occurs to him that the prison alphabet is deliberately designed to mislead the guards. He wonders what would happen if F is one knock, G two knocks. He hears two knocks in quick succession, then twenty-six, then nine, then ten, then fourteen twice, then twenty-six. The numbers spell out *genosse,* which means "comrade," the word he has been searching for, the magic spell. He is overjoyed, because now at long last he has established contact with the world of men. In the same slow way he makes out the words *take courage* and then *one can* . . . The sentence is never completed, for the Stormtroopers rush into the man's cell and silence him. But at least for a few moments Kassner has enjoyed the knowledge of a strange comradeship, and he no longer takes refuge in visions.

He composes a speech, calmly, dispassionately, just such a speech as a veteran Communist might compose if he had been old enough to fight in the Civil War and seen the body of Lenin lying in state. He is still composing the speech when two Stormtroopers enter his cell. This, he tells himself, is the end. He will be tortured, and the thought occurs to him: "I shall become a man again just at the moment when I am being tortured." As he is marched away, his dominant hope is that he will be able to kill one of these two Stormtroopers before an hour is over.

Instead of being tortured, he is set free. From the guards he learns that someone else calling himself Kassner has given himself up. "I'd be surprised if the man was altogether alive," says one of the guards. It occurred to Kassner that this unknown comrade was probably already dead, having deliberately sacrificed himself for the cause. Kassner learns, too, that he has spent only nine days in jail. It seemed an eternity.

Kassner's victory is therefore not a tragic one. There has been no agonized wrestling with the forces of evil, no triumph over himself. He has escaped only because someone has been substituted in his place. But to have escaped at all from a Nazi prison is itself a triumph, and as he gradually realizes that he is free, there comes to him, as there comes to all men released from jail, a strange sense of renewal, as though he were being reborn. He returns to Czechoslovakia in one of his own company's two-seater airplanes. The experiences which Malraux had suffered over the Aurès mountains are given to Kassner flying over the Carpathians:

> They were caught from below, turned over like a sperm whale by a tidal wave. Still the same regular beating of the motor, but Kassner's stomach seemed to sink through the seat. Were they climbing or looping? He recovered his breath between two new whipcracks from the hail. He noticed with surprise that he was trembling; not his hand—he was still holding the cowling—only his left shoulder. He had barely begun to wonder if the plane was once more horizontal when the pilot pushed the joystick forward and shut off the motor.
>
> Kassner was familiar with the maneuver: let the plane drop, take advantage of the weight of the fall to pierce through the storm and attempt to straighten out the plane close to the ground. The altimeter registered 1850; but he knew that altimeters cannot be altogether relied on. Already 1600; the needle was swinging wildly, as the compass dial had done a moment ago. If the mist reached all the way down to the ground, or if the mountains were still beneath them, they would crash. It occurred to Kassner that only the proximity of death entitles one to be sufficiently close to a man to recognize the childlike look he had just seen, and this man too was about to die for him. But at least they would die together.

The fierce plunge through the dark was essential to Malraux's purpose, for in no other way, out of the experiences known to him, could he convey the sense of fatality, the knowledge of being born again. "The return to the earth," when at last they break through the clouds, is seen as a conquest. For them, for the rest of their lives, the earth will be bathed in a new and splendid light.

When Kassner leaves the airplane and enters Prague, he has the same sense of wild exhilaration that Malraux had known as he walked through Bône. "Behind some curtains, a woman was carefully ironing clothes, was working diligently; there were shirts, and linen, and hot irons in this strange place which is called the earth." He passes a glover's shop, and he is reminded that everything he sees is made by hands, and the whole earth is peopled with hands. Not finding his wife at home, he goes to a political meeting, knowing that she will be there; and losing himself in the crowd of people eagerly demonstrating for the release of the prisoners in Nazi jails, he recaptures "the passions and the truths which are given only to men gathered together."

From the platform a small, bald-headed speaker with a drooping mustache is calling on the workers to work for the release of their imprisoned comrades. The speech is an echo of Malraux's own speeches, notably one delivered in the Salle Wagram in Paris demanding the release of Ernst Thaelmann and Ludwig Renn, the pacifist novelist who had once been an officer in the German army. In his speech Malraux said:

> We are with him because he is noble and because he chose to be a Communist; because he was an officer and because he chose to write against war; because he is a writer and because, even though he had the possibility to escape, he chose to bear the singularly heavy burden of all he had said and all he had thought, and just a moment before judgment was passed on him he declared: "I belong to the Communist Party and I shall belong to it until my death. You are today the victors, and we are being tormented by you. This is to be expected. But you should know that at this time I assume full responsibility over my thoughts and on the day when I cease to say what I am now saying, then I will have ceased to be a man." . . .

This evening, in this hall where the sounds of automobiles

mingle with my words, in this atmosphere which resembles the
eve of a holiday, in this place where none of you can move
without encountering the elbows of a comrade, in this hall so
full of fraternal presences and of lights, may these poor words
reach beyond what I am trying to say when I say to Thaelmann,
to Renn, and to all our imprisoned brothers: "Comrades, we
are with you in your solitude and your darkness."

In this comradeship, in the shared community of men working for a
common purpose, he finds his peace. "No human speech goes so deep
as cruelty," he wrote in *Days of Wrath,* "but this comradeship could
cope with it, could go into the very bloodstream, to the forbidden places
of the heart where torture and death are lurking."

Yet he knew well that comradeship of this kind is rare, except perhaps between men and women. So the novel ends with the meeting
between Kassner and his wife and small son, which is described ten-
derly. To his wife Anna he can offer only his unavailing love. To his
son he can offer only the hope of a better world. While the boy is
sleeping, he places his hand on the side of the boy's face, feeling the
pressure of the cheek against his hand. At that moment he knows a
vast happiness, and at the same time he knows that he will continue to
work for the party and will inevitably return to Germany. He knows he
is doomed.

"It is not emotion that destroys a work of art," Malraux wrote in
an epilogue, "but the desire to demonstrate something." No doubt he
wrote these words to head off the accusation that he had written a
propaganda novel, yet the accusation is justified. Malraux was writing
as though he were a Communist, defending the Communist cause,
presenting Kassner, as he presented Ludwig Renn, as one of those
"who are noble and chose to be Communists." He depicts Kassner as
a tragic hero, forgetting that passive suffering is never the characteristic of the tragic hero. The same flaw appears in *The Stranger,* the
novel by Albert Camus, where Meursault suffers his fate as though it
were destined, as though it were beyond his power even to protest
against it. Both Camus and Malraux were fascinated by the world of

a man condemned to death: for such men there are no dark tunnels leading to life. They live in an enclosed world as silent and unresponsive as the grave.

Days of Wrath was written at the height of Malraux's involvement with communism, but already there are signs of strain. Too many questions remain unanswered; too often the issues are evaded. The false identity of Kassner seems to hint at doubts and perplexities, and there is no core to the book, no hardness. The mood changes continually, as though the author felt restless in the Communist straitjacket. Flawed, strained, yet strangely memorable, the book retains an urgent life of its own and will continue to hold a place among the documents of its time.

In the spring of 1936 Albert Camus, then twenty-one years old and unknown to fame, adapted the novel for a play. He had established a small theatrical group of students and workers; their theater was a wooden café built on piles in the port of Algiers. There was no need for elaborate sets, no one was paid, and admission was free. It was the first play he had ever written. While Kassner described his nightmarish visions in a cell, there came the sound of the sea slapping against the piles.

Devilish chicken on a spit.

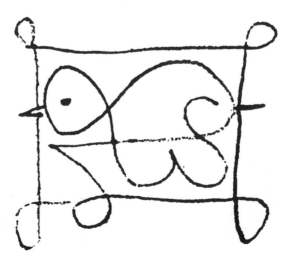

THE CIVIL WAR IN SPAIN

So they came in long columns from all countries, all who knew poverty well enough to die fighting it, and some had guns and those who had no guns used their hands, and one after another they came to lie down on the earth of Spain.

They spoke all languages, and there were even Chinese shoelace sellers among them.

And when altogether too many men had been killed, and when the last column of the poor began to march, then there appeared in the heavens a Star they had never seen before.

—MAN'S HOPE

Escadre España

In the summer of 1936 the war clouds were racing across Europe. From Rome and Berlin the dictators thundered, while in Paris and London the elected leaders of the democracies froze with fear. The war, which had become inevitable since the day Hitler seized power, was growing nearer and people could feel its hot breath on their faces.

On the night of July 17, 1936, the two hundred generals of the Spanish army received secret orders to rise against the government and to establish military rule over the entire peninsula during the next morning. The plot, organized by General José Sanjurjo, who proposed to assume dictatorial power, misfired, and General Sanjurjo himself was killed three days later when his airplane crashed into a wall shortly after its takeoff from an airfield in Portugal. The initiative then fell to General Francisco Franco. The conquest of Spain, which the generals hoped to accomplish in a night and a morning, was not accomplished until nearly a thousand days later.

The Spanish Civil War was the curtain raiser for World War II. The name by which the war is generally known is a misnomer, for Franco, aided by the airplanes and soldiers provided by Hitler and Mussolini, was fighting as much for the dictators as for himself. Overwhelming forces were placed at his disposal, while the Spanish Republic received only a bare minimum of help from the Soviet Union, and little more than sympathy from the democracies. From the beginning the dice were loaded in favor of Franco.

Five days after the revolt had broken out Malraux flew to Spain, accompanied by his wife. Under the dateline July 23 *The New York Times* wrote:

André Malraux, winner of the Goncourt literary prize, an aviator and president of the Committee against War and Fascism, left Paris by airplane today for Madrid. Accompanied by his wife, he declared his mission was to carry to the Spanish President and the Spanish Popular Front "a message of solidarity from all French men and women who are watching the Spanish struggle with emotion." He said he would also investigate and make a report for French opinion concerning what is happening in Spain.

The New York Times report was accurate. Malraux had not the least idea at the time that he would become the commander of a small international air force, and his sole purpose in coming to Spain was to prepare a report on the situation. The report was never written. Within a few days he was deeply immersed in the problems of buying airplanes wherever they could be found, hiring mercenaries to pilot them, and arranging with the Spanish Republican Government for equipment and supplies of gasoline. The first serious engagement by his hastily contrived air force took place less than a month after his arrival in Spain, within two weeks of establishing the Escadre España, the Spanish Squadron. There were no Spaniards in the squadron, which was given this name only to differentiate it from the Spanish Republican air force.

When the war began, the Spanish Republican air force consisted of some seventy antiquated Fokkers and Breguets. In addition there were about twelve airplanes belonging to the commercial line LAPE, and about twenty airplanes based on Spanish Morocco. All of these Spanish Moroccan planes were ordered back to the mainland by the Ministry of Air. They landed in Seville before it was known that Seville had been captured by General Queipo de Llano. The pilots were immediately shot and the airplanes fell into Franco's hands.

The situation was therefore desperate. The Republican airplanes were vastly outnumbered by the airplanes of Franco, but on the ground the opposing forces were more equally matched. Malraux's haste in building up the Escadre España was due to his fear that the war might be decided in the air.

The first engagement of the Escadre España took place on August 14

near Medellín, the birthplace of Hernán Cortés, the conqueror of
Mexico. It was learned that a column of Moors was advancing on
Medellín from Mérida, which had been captured by General Yagüe
four days before. At all costs the advance across Estremadura had to be
stopped, and heavy Republican forces were thrown into the battle.
They were thrown back, and the long motorized column advanced on
Medellín. According to reports received in Madrid, General Franco was
believed to be accompanying the column. In fact, he had established
his headquarters in Cáceres, in the palace of a friendly aristocrat, the
Conde de Montenegro, and he was a long way from the battle lines.

The Escadre España was ordered to attack the motorized column.
Six airplanes went up and flew directly southwest from Madrid in the
direction of Badajoz, where the Fascists had just massacred a thousand
disarmed Republican militiamen in the bullring. In *Man's Hope* Malraux, who took part in the flight, described the road leading to
Medellín:

> The road swerved round, the sun slipped to one side, and
> the red dots reappeared. They were too small to be cars, yet
> moving too mechanically to be men. It looked as if the roadway
> itself was in motion. Suddenly Darras understood. It was as if
> he had just acquired a gift of second sight—seeing things in his
> mind, not through his eyes. The road was a solid mass of trucks
> covered with drab tarpaulins, yellow with dust, and the red dots
> were the hoods, painted in red oxide; there had been no attempt
> at camouflage.

The six airplanes wheeled, dived, and bombed the trucks, bringing
the motorized column to a standstill. One truck had received a direct
hit, others were immobilized, still others were trying to make their way
down the embankment. The Moors escaped from the trucks and ran
madly across the fields, their white turbans making them resemble
"panicking ants carrying their eggs away."

Soon the airmen realized that the forward column had already entered Medellín, and they wheeled over the small town and bombed
the main square, which was crowded with trucks. The small town was

painted in pastel colors of salmon pink, pale blue, and pistachio green; suddenly there rose bursts of orange-colored flame. They were still bombing the main square when some Junkers came out of the sun and they were forced to flee.

This was the first official operation of the Escadre España, and they were very proud of it. For the rest of the year they were thrown into combat wherever they were needed. They dropped bombs on the Alcázar of Toledo, on the approaches to Madrid, and wherever they could find roads filled with trucks. Ignacio Hidalgo de Cisneros, the commander of the Spanish air force, complained bitterly when he heard that three airplanes crashed before they had seen a single battle. The Escadre España lost nearly all its machines, and there were few survivors. But having lost machines, they would buy others; and having lost airmen, they would find others.

Most of the airmen were mercenaries, who were paid fifty thousand francs a month. There were Germans, Americans, Italians, Frenchmen, White Russians, and at least one Algerian. Recruiting offices were set up; the incompetent were quickly weeded out. Malraux had his own staff around him: they were close friends, on whose loyalty he could depend. His chief lieutenant was Julien Segnaire, tall, hawklike, as devoted to literature as to flying. Later he would write the commentary for Malraux's superb edition of Vermeer's paintings.

About once a month Malraux would fly back to Paris for meetings with airplane manufacturers and officials of the Air Ministry, pleading for more planes. Pierre Cot was sympathetic; Léon Blum was overwhelmed with fear: only a small trickle of airplanes entered Spain. From his apartment in the Rue de Bac, Malraux was making long-distance calls all over Europe. He was the commanding officer of the Escadre España, but he was also its chief provisioning agent. He was lucky when he had four hours' sleep.

One day early in September André Gide called at the apartment. Malraux had just arrived from Spain and was soaking in a bath; three-year old Florence was tearing a dahlia to pieces to make a "salad"; Clara was brooding over a marriage which was broken and yet not broken. She had proclaimed complete sexual freedom in Spain and Malraux had thereupon announced that the marriage was over.

"Do you know what he said when he arrived?" she told Gide. "That since I had left him, he had been able to *act* much more."

Malraux was still soaking in the bath.

"Was there a scene?" Gide asked.

"Oh, no! He is right to detach himself from everything."

But of course he could not detach himself from everything. He had a wife, a child, an apartment, and at the same time he had perfect liberty, but this liberty was itself a servitude. He was enslaved by Spain. Gide wondered whether, since he was obviously in command of great operations, he would have time to talk. He need not have wondered. "He talks with that extraordinary volubility which often makes him so hard for me to follow," Gide noted in his journal for September 4, 1936. "His hope is to gather together the governmental forces; now he has the power to do so. His intention, as soon as he gets back, is to organize the attack on Oviedo."

On the following day Clara, Gide, and Malraux went to dinner at an excellent restaurant in the Place des Victoires. For two hours Gide listened to a staggering flow of theories, anecdotes, prophecies, technical explanations and political pronouncements. Most of it went over his head. He wrote in his diary: "As with Valéry, André Malraux's great strength lies in caring very little whether he winds, or tires, or 'drops by the wayside' whoever is listening." Nevertheless, with Gide as a benevolent auditor, Malraux was able to hammer out his own ideas.

Malraux fought for his squadron, protected it from the Spanish Republican government and from Communists, and was able to preserve its independence. He had no illusions about the danger of employing mercenaries, but there was no alternative. With a hard core of dedicated anti-fascists around him, he could be sure that no one would refuse to obey his orders. Segnaire, a reserve officer in the French air force, was firm and strong-willed: he took over the command during Malraux's occasional absences. Because the squadron owed its existence to Malraux, it was virtually a private air force with its own chain of command, its own resources, and its own political program, which was not the program of the Communists who were gradually extending their influence throughout Spain.

By nature solitary, Malraux found himself thrust among men, re-joicing in the "virile fraternity" which had been the theme of so many speeches. Since he also rejoiced in danger, he flew on the bombing raids and sometimes piloted the planes, though he had no pilot's license. Usually he served as a machine gunner. For the rest of his life he would remember those Spanish airfields marked out by the bluish flames from heaps of burning dried oranges as they flew off just before dawn, and then when the night mists cleared away he would find himself gazing through a pair of binoculars at enemy territory.

He never knew where he would be the next day, or whether he would be alive. One day early in December Louis Fischer saw a familiar face among the French delegates at the League of Nations in Geneva: it was Malraux advising Yvon Delbos, the French foreign minister. He was forever on the move, forever searching for airplanes and new ways to safeguard the Spanish Republic.

While Malraux in his headquarters at Albacete was struggling to keep his international air force alive, he was suddenly reminded that André Gide was capable of behaving with incredible thoughtlessness and stupidity. Toward the end of October, having completed the manu-script of his book *Retour de l'U.R.S.S.*, an account of his recent journey to the Soviet Union, Gide was beginning to have second thoughts about publishing it. The Soviet Union, alone among the great powers, was giving practical assistance to the hard-pressed Spanish Republic. In his book Gide attacked the Soviet Union with the bitterness of a lover who discovers that the beloved is suffering from syphilis. "I doubt if there is any other country today, including Hitler's Germany, where the mind is less free, more fettered, more terrorized, more enslaved," he wrote of Stalin's Russia, and in page after page he offered evidence for his summary judgment. He had many pleasant things to say about the Russian people, but none about the Communist Party.

The journalist Pierre Herbart, who had accompanied Gide through-out his journey to the Soviet Union, was appalled. He did not dispute the judgment, but thought the publication of the book should be post-poned at least until Gide had consulted someone in authority whose advice he could trust. Herbart suggested that Malraux should be the arbiter. Gide agreed, gave Herbart a copy of the manuscript, and promised or half-promised to abide by Malraux's decision. Herbart flew off to Spain, staying in Barcelona long enough to learn that the Communists and Anarchists were at each others' throats, and then making his way to Albacete where André Marty, the most ferocious of the French Communist leaders, was shooting volunteers in the International Brigade on the grounds that it was better to kill ten innocent men than permit one traitor to enter the ranks of the revolution. Malraux's international air force formed an autonomous unit, and remained unaffected by the turmoil caused by Marty.

As soon as he reached Albacete, Herbart sought out Malraux and gave him the manuscript. Malraux agreed to give his opinion and later in the day, meeting the young German novelist Gustav Regler, he suggested that they should read the manuscript together. Regler was a brilliant novelist, a Communist disenchanted with Communism as practiced in the Soviet Union. They sat down in a dark, gloomy, fly-spotted café, and began reading. Regler found himself in full agreement with Gide's views, but felt that the publication of the book should be postponed. He said nothing. The decision would have to be made by Malraux alone. Herbart, who was standing outside the café, was summoned.

"You've got yourself in a mess," Malraux said.

"Why?"

"Are you *absolutely* sure that Gide won't publish the book while you are here?"

Herbart was dumbfounded. It had never occurred to him that Gide could be totally irresponsible, although it was well known that he lacked any real political sense. The manuscript was already in proofs, and he usually liked to get his books published as soon as possible after writing them.

"Even if he doesn't publish it," Malraux continued, "the mere fact that you are found in possession of it . . ."

He did not complete the sentence. Herbart now realized that he was in grave danger from the hands of the Communist executioners. Scarcely knowing in which direction to turn, he decided to place himself under the protection of Mikhail Koltsov, the former editor-in-chief of *Pravda,* now press secretary at the Soviet Embassy in Madrid, with wide and undefined diplomatic powers. Koltsov had arranged for Gide's journey to the Soviet Union, and Herbart, who had worked in Moscow, knew him well and enjoyed his company, for he was an amusing *raconteur,* civilized, generous, unpredictable, and possessed a genuine admiration for French literature. If Herbart had been sensible, he would simply have burned the manuscript. Instead, he laid it on Koltsov's desk and in time it became known to the Soviet secret police, and Herbart was more than ever in danger. One night he was awakened in his hotel bedroom and cross-examined by a Soviet secret service official. On another day he was led out into the street by armed Soviet agents and would almost certainly have been executed if he had not caught sight of José Bergamin, the Catholic scholar and critic, who knew him and vouched for his impeccable revolutionary morality. Herbart returned to the Soviet Embassy to confront Koltsov, and while he was in no danger in the embassy, he was still in danger whenever he ventured outside. Koltsov made up a bed for him in his own office.

Publishing in France is a very simple matter compared to publishing in America. Since no hard covers have to be made, only a few days separate the corrected galleys from publication. The *Nouvelle Revue Française* had published the book while Herbart was in Madrid.

A week after arriving in Madrid, Herbart put in a long-distance call to Clara Malraux in Paris, for Koltsov had obligingly told him that one of the telephones on his desk was connected directly with the Kremlin, the other with Louis Aragon, the Communist novelist, whose decisions concerning French intervention in the Spanish Civil War were regarded by the Russians with high favor. Herbart reasoned that a direct line to Aragon was also a direct line to anyone in Paris. He also knew that he could not stay permanently in the Soviet Embassy, and only Malraux could save him.

By good fortune Clara Malraux had not gone out shopping, and she answered the telephone at once. Herbart asked her to get in touch with his wife, and was able to suggest his predicament in such a way that the censors would imagine he was talking about harmless things. Clara Malraux promptly telephoned her husband in Albacete, and that same afternoon Malraux arrived at the Soviet Embassy in Madrid.

"Herbart is wasting his time here," Malraux told Koltsov. "Send him to Barcelona. I'll find an airplane for him in Albacete."

Koltsov was in awe of Malraux and immediately wrote out a *laissez-passer* for Herbart, giving him instructions to report on the Anarchist situation in Barcelona. There were letters of introduction to Communist officials in Barcelona, and all these letters and the *laissez-passer* were embellished with rubber stamps bearing the official seal of the Soviet Embassy. As the bearer of important documents from the embassy, Herbart would be free from the attentions of the Soviet agents.

"I will see you soon," Koltsov said, and then added thoughtfully, "or rather, I won't be seeing you soon. I shall soon be recalled to the Soviet Union."

Koltsov was afraid he would be recalled to Moscow to answer charges that he had helped Gide, now an enemy of Communism. He was recalled briefly and was back again in Madrid early in the new year. In November 1937 he was summoned to Moscow to answer a long list of charges. He weathered the storm, returned to his sumptuous office in the *Pravda* building, and continued to act as editor-in-chief. At the beginning of 1939 he vanished from sight, and in 1942 he was shot at the orders of Stalin, who had come to believe that nearly all the Russians who went to Spain were traitors. Among those who went to Spain only Ilya Ehrenburg and a handful of others survived.

But all this was in the future. Herbart's unlucky journey to Spain ended satisfactorily. Leaving Madrid under the dual protection of Koltsov and Malraux, he arrived in Paris and immediately called on Louis Aragon. There was a stormy meeting. Herbart then drove to Gide's apartment and there was another stormy meeting.

"Through you I was very nearly shot!" Herbart exclaimed.

"What an absurd idea!" Gide replied mildly. "You do understand, don't you, that I did everything for the best, for after all you have come back safe and sound. Believe me, I thought about this matter very carefully."

As winter came down, Malraux's small international air force at Albacete was reduced to a bare skeleton. Only five or six airplanes survived, and these were relatively slow, with little fire power. Soviet airplanes were beginning to arrive in large numbers, and the Spanish Republican air force under the command of Hidalgo de Cisneros was at last in possession of a squadron of fighter planes. These were the

chatos, "the snub-nosed ones," which had been landed at the port of
Cartagena on November 2. Within a week they were uncrated, assembled, equipped, and thrown into the battle for Madrid.

The airfield at Albacete was abandoned, and a new airfield was established at Torrente, close to Valencia, where Malraux had to spend
a good deal of time talking with government officials. To Ilya Ehrenburg who met him in Valencia, he spoke hopefully of acquiring twelve
French bombers, but they never came; and whenever Ehrenburg began to talk about literature, Malraux changed the subject to the war
or remained silent. Toward the end of November Julien Segnaire on
behalf of the entire squadron secretly arranged with the Spanish Republic air force that henceforth the Escadre España should be known
as the Escadre André Malraux. Malraux was stunned, but it was too
late to raise any objections. What chiefly concerned him was whether
they would be able to secure enough replacements to survive the winter. There were never more than four or five airplanes standing in the
airfield.

Hidalgo de Cisneros had at one time thought of disbanding the
squadron: he was infuriated by the loss of so many planes in accidents.
The decision was postponed when he fell ill and left Spain to re-
cuperate in the Soviet Union. When he returned, the Escadre André
Malraux had ceased to exist.

Malraux fought to maintain his own air force because he was convinced that new airplanes would eventually arrive from France. Pierre
Cot and Leo Lagrange, both ministers in the French government, had
previously permitted a small number of obsolete army planes to join
the squadron and they made half-promises to send more. But the half-
promises were never fulfilled, and the French government even refused
to allow new American airplanes, bought by the Spanish Republic, to
leave France. Hidalgo de Cisneros saw them standing idle on the airfield at Toulouse, and wept.

Toward the end of the year, on December 27, there took place
one of the very last flights of the Escadre España. This was a bombing raid on Teruel, which had been the target of so many raids that
the airmen felt they knew the city and all the roads leading to it by
heart. The flight was unlucky from the beginning. The ungainly

Potez, in which Malraux was a machine gunner, crashed a few moments after takeoff. No one was seriously injured, but the plane was wrecked. The remaining airplanes flew over Teruel, dropped their bombs, and on the return flight were attacked by Heinkels. There could be no question of attacking the Heinkels, which had far more fire power, and they tried to escape into the clouds. One of the airplanes was shot down over the Sierra de Teruel, not far from the village of Mora de Rubielos. Of the seven members of the crew, one was killed, two were severely wounded, and four suffered lesser injuries. The dead man was Belaïdi, a powerfully built Algerian with handsome, square-cut features. He was one of the very few Algerians fighting for the Republic, and the airmen were stunned by his loss.

As soon as he heard that the airplane was down, Malraux organized a relief expedition. He drove to Linares, arranged for hospital facilities, and climbed up the steep jagged mountains on mule-back. He had been able to telephone one of the survivors. Mora de Rubielos was on the very edge of Republican-held territory, and he was particularly impressed by the staunchness and courage of the villagers who were so close to enemy territory, and therefore in such grave danger.

The journey of the dead Belaïdi and his wounded comrades down the mountainside with the villagers streaming up the mountain and bringing them offerings provided Malraux with one of the major themes of his novel *Man's Hope*. In this fraternity he saw the hope of the world. Seen against those stark and savage mountains, the thin columns seemed to be tracing a strange and hitherto unknown calligraphy; and there came to him memories of Dante's journeys and of Jacob's dreams. "And he dreamed, and behold a ladder set up on the earth, and the top of it reached to heaven: and behold the angels of God ascending and descending on it."

The ascending and descending peasants and airmen seemed to belong to another order of beings, larger than life and touched with divinity, outside time altogether. Some airmen hobbled down the mountain path, others came on stretchers, and at the head of the procession there was Belaïdi's rough-hewn coffin. Roped to his coffin was his shattered machine gun, like a badge of triumph, though it was also a badge of defeat. "Now Spain was that twisted machine gun on an Arab's coffin and birds numbed with cold crying in the ravines."

So the hours passed, while the solemn, primitive march continued under heavy clouds, and the peasants swept the loose stones from the paths of the stretcher-bearers. In *Man's Hope* Malraux speaks of seeing an apple tree outlined against the sky, with the windfalls forming a thick ring around it, almost lost in the grass. The apple tree was the only living thing among the rocks until the peasants came in sight; and this tree, with its ring of dead apples, was also an image of hope. It was a very small apple tree, infinitely pathetic in that harsh landscape, and the procession coming down the mountainside—for the peasants, having surged up the mountain, were now on their way down—was also infinitely pathetic in comparison with the dead mountains that enclosed and somehow protected them. All these people were companions of the living and the dead, and in the eyes of Malraux their companionship gave the earth its meaning:

> The path widened steadily as the valley approached Linares; the peasants were walking beside the stretchers now. The black-clothed women, scarves on their heads and baskets on their arms, were still bustling around the wounded, moving from one to another. The men were keeping pace with the stretchers, without ever getting in front of them, walking abreast of each other, holding themselves with the stiff erectness of those who have been carrying a weight on their shoulders. At each change-over, the new bearers abandoned their stiff walk as they took up the shafts with affectionate care, moving off again to the accompaniment of the grunts which tell of physical effort, as if anxious to mask the betrayal of their emotions which their solicitude denoted. Their attention concentrated on the stones which obstructed the path, thinking only of the necessity not to jolt the stretchers, they moved steadily forward, slowing up a little on the steeper slopes. And the steady rhythm of their tread over the long, pain-burdened journey seemed to fill the vast ravine, down which the last cries still came floating from

the birds above, with a solemn beat like a funeral drum. But it was not death that haunted the mountains at that moment; it was triumphant human will.

For Malraux it was almost a vision of what the world might be, if the sense of fraternity existed in men's hearts. The peasants and the airmen honored each other, and their meeting was a sacrament. He avoided, or attempted to avoid, all religious associations, but they remained insistently present. The journey down the mountain was a mystery and a passion play. In that frozen landscape there was another Easter.

Malraux's days as the commander of the Escadre España were coming to an end. There were only two or three battered airplanes left, and half his airmen had died in combat. He had flown on sixty-five missions, sometimes flying two a day, and he had been wounded twice. For a few more weeks he remained in Valencia, winding up the affairs of the squadron, and then he flew to Paris.

⋅ᦈ *Man's Hope* ᦈ⋅

During nearly all the months he spent in Spain directing the international air force, Malraux was at work on a long philosophical novel. When asked how he could possibly sit down to write a novel during a war in which he was busily engaged, he would answer, "It grows dark at night." He had no illusions about his chances of survival: he had perhaps one chance in a thousand of surviving the first six months of the war. Nevertheless, as though he had many years in front of him, he began writing an immensely complex and intricate novel with a vast cast of characters. The subject was the war in Spain, the characters were the people he knew, and the development of the novel depended upon the fortunes of the war.

Malraux's ideas about the novel as a literary form had undergone many changes since he wrote *Man's Fate,* a book that he regarded with affection and a lingering dissatisfaction. He had never known his characters well enough to make them completely convincing, and in some mysterious way the novel had become dominated by the old and venerable Frenchman Gisors, the former professor of sociology at the University of Peking, who wore the mask of a Chinese sage. His description of the fighting in Shanghai suffered from the fact that he had no direct experience of fighting in a Chinese civil war. As a novel it was lacking in that ultimate authority that he demanded from great literature, and it would be remembered chiefly for six or seven passages written with extraordinary passion and intensity. No one could possibly forget the scene where the terrorist Ch'en kills the man lying under the mosquito curtain, but there were many scenes that were scarcely more than improvisations on the theme of murder.

What Malraux wanted to do was to write a novel for the age he

lived in, uncompromisingly authentic and final, bringing the reader
into immediate contact with his chosen heroes. For a long time he had
realized that the clue to the mystery lay somewhere in the region of
reportage, that in our age the novelist must be something of a reporter, and that the people in the novel must be seen with the
clarity and depth that are the marks of the good reporter. His friend
Andrée Viollis had traveled through Indochina during the autumn
of 1932, studying the decaying French empire, talking with Indochinese intellectuals and revolutionaries, visiting hospitals, schools,
ministries and prisons. After long delays her book *S.O.S. Indochine*
was finally published in September 1935, with an introduction by
Malraux. What struck him particularly in the book was the immediacy of the experience. Andrée Viollis wrote in such a way that the
reader traveled with her, saw through her eyes, and was vividly aware
of the faces and colors of Indochina as she presented them. It was
reportage on the highest level, clearcut, brutal. "The real strength of
reportage lies in the fact that it necessarily refuses to be evasive," Malraux commented. "Reportage achieves its highest form when it permits the intelligence and sensibility to take possession of the real, as
they do in the novels of Tolstoy, and not in the creation of an imaginary universe, even though an imaginary universe will sometimes lead
to the possession of the real." In his eyes Andrée Viollis had written
a novel *à l'état brut*. There were scenes in her book which belonged
all the more to the novel because they were seen by a sensitive and
intelligent woman who thought she was merely a journalist.

One scene in the book particularly attracted Malraux's attention.
Two days after her arrival in Saigon Andrée Viollis was taken to see
a political prisoner in the vast central prison. The name of the prisoner
was Huy. He had been arrested for complicity in the murder of a
French police inspector, and although there was considerable doubt
whether he had shot the inspector, he was sentenced to death. He was
seventeen. According to the prison official he had been trained in
Borodin's school in Canton, a fact that was at least disputable, since
Borodin had left China when the boy was twelve years old. "You
will see, he is a monster," the official said, leading the visitor down
the dark, evil-smelling prison corridor. Huy stood in the death cell.

He did not look like a monster. On the contrary he looked like a hurt child, with swollen lips and the eyes of a hunted animal. His head was bent to one shoulder, as he glared through the bars. The official asked him some questions, but there was no reply. The boy had deliberately ripped his tongue with his teeth to prevent himself from speaking. Suddenly the official leaned forward and cuffed the boy's head, shouting, "Filthy creature!" Huy leaped back, uttering a raucous cry of hate and terror. During the following month he was taken to Hanoi and executed on the guillotine.

For Malraux, the confrontation between the prison official and the condemned boy was the stuff of fiction: it was drama in its sharpest, most agonizing form. The cuffed head, the sudden leap, the raucous cry—all this belonged to literature and to psychological truth. A novelist could not have invented such a scene, nor could a reporter. In two or three lines Andrée Viollis had created a scene which belonged to the highest art.

The cinema and the journalist had changed the shape of the novel. Henceforward the novel would be subject to the rhythms and the sharp contrasts of the film and the newspaper, where in the same column a political discussion may be followed by an account of a murder and a list of stock market prices. The form of the "new novel" was as fluid as the film and as assertive as a headline. The panning shot, the close-up, the zoom, the expanding screen and the expanding lens had entered literature and were being used with remarkable effect by American novelists. Malraux proposed to use every device known to cameramen and practiced in the cutting room. His novel would have the precision of a well-ordered film or of a brilliantly assembled machine.

But all these innovations were of secondary importance, for above all there was the necessity of conceiving scenes charged with human tension and emotion, possessing a life of their own, capable of moving the reader by their intensity, their vigor, and their visionary grandeur. Malraux showed no interest in socialist realism: it was not through any gift for realism that Tolstoy was able to show Prince Andrey Bolkonsky lying on the battlefield of Austerlitz and gazing at the clouds and the stars. There were scenes in *War and Peace* that took the breath away, because even after they were read, it seemed that they could never have been written. They escaped from literature and became vision.

Malraux had made a profound study of *War and Peace,* and its influence can be detected on many pages of *Man's Hope.* Like Tolstoy, he would employ comparatively short chapters, each containing a single episode or a succession of brief episodes. These short chapters would be woven together in such a way that every character would have the opportunity to affect the lives of all the other characters. Just as Tolstoy permitted himself the widest latitude in discussing the political and economic problems of the day, with long disquisitions on philosophy, religion, art, science, agriculture, military strategy and tactics, so Malraux would permit his characters to argue and dispute to their hearts' content, and because these arguments were largely concerned with the nature of man in war and his duty to his fellow-men, they would assume something of the role played by the Greek chorus. At all costs he was determined to write a philosophical novel: one which would acquire meaning and substance by being aimed at philosophical ends. The destiny of Europe, perhaps of the world, depended on the outcome of the war in Spain. Destiny, too, would become one of the characters in the novel, all the more present because she was never seen. She was the voice that could sometimes be heard above the roaring of the guns and the cries of the dying.

As the principal characters finally emerged, they all bore a curious resemblance to Malraux himself. They were projections of himself, of various facets of himself. This is not unusual among authors, for it is scarcely possible for an author to dissociate himself from the characters he has spun out of himself. In *War and Peace* both Prince Andrey and Pierre Bezhukhov are self-portraits of Tolstoy, even though one is a dashing officer and the other a slow-moving phi-losopher. In *Man's Hope* Malraux split himself among his three lead-ing characters: Magnin, the aviator, Hernandez, the army officer, and Manuel, the militant card-carrying Communist. In appearance Magnin, with his round glasses, his drooping blond-gray mustache and his pro-truding underlip, resembled a younger and more amiable Voltaire in a white flying suit. Hernandez, with his long melancholy face, his long hands and long body, resembled many of the portraits of Spanish kings and carried himself with an air of unselfconscious nobility. Manuel was thickset, heavy-jowled, with pale green eyes under bushy eyebrows, and he could be taken for a Mediterranean fisherman or perhaps a Roman emperor. He was an accomplished musician who earned his living as a sound engineer in the Madrid film studios.

These men dominate the novel, but they are themselves so dominated by the war that they never give the impression of asserting themselves as characters. They have come together by the accidents of war, live out their lives in the shadow of the war, and regard themselves as instruments of war. Heroic, they refuse to regard themselves as heroes, and there is a strange humility about all of them. They are dedicated intellectuals, accustomed to giving precise outlines to their thoughts.

A surprisingly large number of the minor characters are intellectuals connected with the arts. Lopez is a sculptor and a painter; Alvear, the father of one of the aviators, is a former professor of the history of art and the owner of a prestigious art gallery in Madrid selling El Grecos, Picassos and Spanish primitives; Scali is the author of monographs on Masaccio and Piero della Francesca as well as an aviator; Guernico is a Catholic writer; and even Captain House, the English aviator, who plays a small and almost insignificant role in the novel, is described as a man who enjoys reading Plato in the original Greek. Most of the characters are intellectuals and artists. These were the people Malraux knew best, and he was therefore able to write about them with authority, from inside. Women make scarcely any appearance in the novel, and there are no love affairs.

As Malraux gradually built up the characters of his protagonists, he sometimes gave them the traits of living persons. Manuel's physical appearance was based on Gustavo Durán, the pianist and composer, who became the commander of a division in the Republican army when he was still in his twenties. Superbly intelligent and quick-witted, Durán came to know Malraux well, and he was one of the few who were asked to read the manuscript of *Man's Hope* before publication. The physical appearance of Hernandez was probably suggested by Ignacio Hidalgo de Cisneros, the commander of the Spanish Republican air force, one of the very few members of the Spanish nobility who fought on the side of the Republic. He had the long face, the courtly manners, the quiet arrogance of the medieval courtiers from whom he was descended. But Malraux borrowed only the outward shapes: the fire that blazed in Manuel and Hernandez was his own.

Although Malraux set out to write a philosophical novel in which ideas would play at least as great a role as action, he was under no illusions about the difficulty of the task. Only by the extraordinary intensity of his ideas could he integrate long philosophical discussions with the violent action continually taking place. There was therefore a great danger that the action would drown the philosophical argument. In a well-ordered novel a precise balance might be achieved by introducing the argument at long intervals. Malraux was not writing a well-ordered novel, and he was in no mood to *construct* his arguments. They advanced with their own momentum, took command of the story, collided with the story, and possessed such a vivid and corruscating life of their own that they became acts. He had written, *"Vivre ses idées* [live one's ideas]." In *Man's Hope* he set at least twenty people living their ideas at full throttle, with the result that ideas and acts become almost interchangeable.

The novel begins in the railway terminus at Madrid, with the two Communists, Ramos and Manuel, telephoning up the line to discover which towns are holding out for the Republic and which for the Fascists. The replies are brief:

> "Is that Huesca?"
> "Who's speaking?"
> "The Workers' Committee, Madrid."
> "Not for long, you swine! *Arriba España!"* . . .
> "Hullo, Vallodolid! Who's speaking?"
> "The station delegate."
> "Oh! We'd heard the Fascists were in."
> "You heard wrong. All's well. What about you? Have the troops revolted?"
> "No."

So it goes on, the thrust and counterthrust of urgent information up and down the line. On that hot, early morning of July, the Apocalypse had begun. When we next see Manuel and Ramos they are driving at breakneck speed through the dark streets of Madrid in an automobile loaded with hand grenades which collides with an Anarchist truck loaded with dynamite. There will be many more collisions between the Communists and Anarchists in the course of the novel. As it happens, the dynamite does not explode and the hand grenades are safe. Manuel gets a bloody nose and his automobile is a wreck. Somewhere a radio blares: "The insurgent troops are marching on the center of Barcelona. The Government has the situation well in hand."

The scene shifts to Barcelona, and we meet the Anarchist known as the Negus because of his swarthy Abyssinian beard. A dockworker, he has succeeded in rifling the armories of two warships, and is busily doling our revolvers and ammunition to his fellow Anarchists. He was an experienced revolutionary, and once with a dozen friends he set fire to the trams on Tibidabo, the hill overlooking Barcelona, and sent them flaming down into the center of the city. When the Fascists march into Barcelona, they are confronted with men like the Negus and the dwarflike Puig, a printer, whose idea of making war on a column of troops is to charge them in an automobile with a submachine gun blazing through the windshield. The battle in Barcelona was soon over, for the *Guardia Civil* and the airmen came out for the Government, with the result that the Anarchists soon found themselves on speaking terms with the police they had despised and distrusted twenty-four hours before. Colonel Ximenes, chief of the *Guardia Civil,* known as "Old Quack-Quack," finds himself discussing religion with Puig, while the churches burn around them. Barcelona is in their hands, and they can afford the luxury of meditation until, at night, another column of Fascists appears. Then Puig, his head so heavily bandaged that he resembles an Arab in a turban, drives a truck against the enemy once too often. Barcelona had been won by the reckless courage of the Anarchists: would reckless courage be enough to win the war?

In Madrid the people stormed the Montaña barracks, killed the officers defending it, and seized the weapons in the armory. Malraux's description of the fighting in Barcelona is completely convincing, although he was not present and derived his knowledge by questioning participants. He is less convincing when he describes the storming of the Montaña barracks, for the action centers on the huge battering ram used for breaking down the doors; the battering ram dominates the scene, with the result that the reader has to invent the barracks and people it with imaginary Fascists, and the effect is oddly unreal. Only at the end, when we see the rescuers searching for the hostages captured by the Fascists does the lens come into sharp focus:

> In another room, rather dark, some soldiers lay on the ground, screaming: *"Salud! Hey! Salud!"* They did not move, for they had been tied hand and foot. These were the men the Fascists suspected of loyalty to the Republic or sympathy for the workers' movement. Out of sheer joy they were drumming with their heels on the ground, in spite of their bonds. Jaime and the militiamen untied them, embracing them in the Spanish fashion.
>
> "There are some more comrades down there," one of them said.
>
> Jaime and his companions ran down an inner staircase into an even darker room and hurled themselves on the comrades who lay there in chains, and kissed them. They had been shot the previous day.

This was Malraux's method—the preparations for combat, the evolution of any situation, would be seen through a diffuse lens, but the great heroic and tragic acts, and the acts of human fellowship, would be seen sharply, concretely, as though quite suddenly all the veils had been torn away. An intense light shines on heroes. He has no need to sketch in the details: in three lines we are made to see the dead lying in chains. There are no faces, no colors, no descriptions. We do not know how large the room was, or how many were the dead, yet we see them vividly. In much the same way Caravaggio will suddenly paint a brilliant splash of color on his somber canvases.

Throughout the novel we are aware that the lens is constantly

changing and that each scene is described in a different light, under
a different sky, the people standing at different distances from the
probing, all-seeing eye. Malraux manipulates time and space, sets
his characters exactly where he wants them in the landscape. He
resembles a painter continually arranging his models, checking the
lighting, standing back to observe a precise effect, while at the same
time, under the pressure of ideas and the explosive forces of history,
the story marches forward at breakneck pace. Whenever there is a
descriptive passage, one has the impression that there is only just
time enough to set the stage, and he is less interested in description
than in setting his characters free to do what they have to do.

Malraux's training in the arts had accustomed him to see drama
in paintings and sculptures; they were a part of life, almost the most
necessary part of life. This training he brought to the novel, with
the result that he often uses the vocabulary of a painter or a sculptor, and when he sets a scene there is often a real or imaginary painting in mind. A man launches a charge of dynamite "with the gesture
of a Discobolus." A certain color in the twilight sky will remind him
of an equestrian portrait, probably Titian's portrait of the Emperor
Charles V. Wolfhounds lying full length on the ground remind him
of similar wolfhounds seen on Greek bas reliefs. When he sees the
peasants streaming in full flight along the road, the scene instantly
composes into a *Flight into Egypt.*

Just as the characters tend to become painting or sculpture, so
the earth tends to become architecture. Every hill has its architectural
design; every field seen from an airplane seems to have been painted;
and like many painters Malraux likes to draw a line across the canvas to establish a plane of reference. Such a line is provided by the
embankment just outside Madrid, where two heroes are discussing the
fortunes of the war:

> Ramos and Manuel were walking along the embankment.
> The evening was like all those evenings when there was no
> cannonade. The twilight, resembling the background of an
> equestrian portrait, was bathed in the odor of pines and rock-
> plants, and the Sierra rolled in decorative foothills down to the

plain of Madrid, where night was falling as it falls on the sea. Strangely, the armored train crouching in its tunnel seemed to have been forgotten by a war which vanished when the vast sun went down.

We are not told where the tunnel is situated, and it scarcely matters. Somewhere in the scented twilight, lost among the shadows, all the more powerful because it is invisible, the armored train crouches like some mythological beast in its hiding place: the sea, and the vast sun, and the humble rock-plants are all implicated. Thus the lens opens wide to include not only the scene before him, but also the immense stretches of geological time and the eternal heavens. In the night pieces we are always remote from the earth we know: in the night worlds are conceived, and universes perish.

In all his writings up to *Man's Hope* Malraux had shown a strange partiality for night scenes. He seemed to be haunted by darkness and the long shadows of sunset. But in *Man's Hope*, though night scenes abound, there is the prevailing sense of daylight, of openness. For the first time we see the colors of the tawny and yellow earth, and there is the purest joy in being alive in the sun. In his last novel, *The Walnut Trees of Altenburg,* written five years later, the night comes down again.

Combined with the painter's instinct for the appropriate color and the novelist's feeling for character, there is also the reporter's sense of urgency, the sense of life cascading before him, brilliant and flashing, to be caught in an instant or lost forever. Large sections of the novel appear to have been written while the events he describes were still taking place, before they assumed the shape they would finally assume in history. When, for example, he describes the siege of the Alcázar at Toledo, where the Fascists were trapped in the vaults of the huge fortress dominating the city, Malraux writes as though the final destruction of the Fascists was a foregone conclusion. He describes Toledo—the narrow streets, the cafés, the museum, the Republican soldiers busily mining the fortress, shelling it, shooting at everyone who emerges from it, and bombing it from the air. He has evidently taken notes on the spot, and we are presented with a leisurely

account of the siege by a man who has come to know exactly what
was taking place. He has little need for invention. When he describes
an attack by flamethrowers, we know he had talked with men who
had taken part in the attack, and when he describes a bombing raid
on the Alcázar it is one in which he had himself taken part. All his
heroes, Manuel, Ximenes, the Negus, Hernandez, Magnin, and many
others, are present at Toledo. They argue vociferously, but their arguments are chiefly concerned with abstractions: fraternity, the apocalyptic vision, the virtues and vices of anarchism. At night the huge walls
of the Alcázar shine like ice in the searchlights, and by day the fortress
seems to crumble a little more with every shot that is fired. What is
absent is the sense of doom and fatality. The Alcázar never surrenders.
On September 27, 1936, General Yagüe's column broke through the
ring around Toledo and the Fascists won their most legendary victory,
while the Republicans fled in disorder or fell before the Fascist firing
squads.

Malraux's airplanes covered the retreat from Toledo. Every airplane
that could be patched together was thrown into the battle, but the
enemy had already acquired overwhelming superiority in numbers.
According to a credible estimate, the Republicans lost fifty-seven out
of sixty-five aircraft during the retreat. For two months they would
have almost no air protection at all.

As the story developed, the fall of the Alcázar was to be the crown-
ing achievement of the Republican forces. In fact the Alcázar did not
fall, and the mood of the story abruptly changes. Surprisingly, there
is no full-scale account of the retreat, and little is said about the
fighting in the air. The defeat is seen through the eyes of Hernandez,
the superbly intelligent captain of the forces attacking the Alcázar.
He fights through the streets of Toledo, and he is still fighting when
a rifle butt fells him. He is carried off to prison to await interrogation
by the enemy.

Into the portrait of Hernandez Malraux has poured all his own
knowledge of grace and dignity. Hernandez is the man who fights
without enjoyment, without hope, and without hate. He has no illusions about the war. "Men only die for something that does not exist,"
he says, haunted by death, haunted too by "something that does not

exist." Once captured, he feels no need to prolong the comedy. He will not defend himself, and when he is interrogated he will answer all questions quietly and patiently, realizing that the interrogation is meaningless. Led out to execution roped to another prisoner, he refuses to save himself when the prisoner cuts the rope with a razor blade and jumps into a gulley. For him, it is enough that he should die in the company of his fellow men, without bitterness.

The description of the march to the execution ground is among Malraux's greatest achievements. Like Perken's march across the compound in *The Royal Way,* it is written with an intensity which makes it almost unendurable, and it is all the more unendurable because it is told quietly, gravely, without the least artifice, as though by Hernandez himself:

> The column continued to march.
>
> Here the ground rose slightly, and ten Falangists with arms at rest were standing beside a trench. Hernandez could not see how deep the trench was. With the Falangists, their arms at rest, was an officer. On the right were the prisoners, and all together with the newcomers there must have been fifty of them. Their civilian clothes were the only dark stain in the brilliant morning light; the khaki uniforms of the Moors had the same color as Toledo.
>
> It had come, the moment that had so often haunted him, the moment when a man knows he will die without being able to defend himself.
>
> Seemingly, the prisoners were no more troubled by the thought of dying than the Falangists and the Moors were troubled by the thought of killing them. The tram conductor stood among them, and he did not differ from the rest. All looked a little dazed, like men who are overtired; no more than that. The firing squad was showing some signs of restlessness, though they had nothing to do except to fire their rifles which were already loaded.
>
> "Attention!"
>
> The command was uttered in peremptory tones: the ten

members of the firing squad stiffened to perform the comedy
of the honor of perfect obedience. Around Hernandez the fifty
prisoners were gazing into the distance, already beyond all
thoughts of comedy.

Three Fascists came to take three prisoners away. They were
led in front of the ditch, and then the Fascists withdrew.

"Aim!"

The prisoner on the left had a crewcut. All three were unusually tall, and they loomed above the men watching them,
silhouetted against the famous mountain range of the Tagus.
How small a thing is history confronted with the living flesh,
the still living flesh. . . .

The three men somersaulted backward. The squad fired, but
they were already in the trench. How can they hope to get
away? The prisoners laugh nervously.

They won't be getting away. The prisoners had seen the
leap first, but the squad had fired before that. Nerves.

Three more men were lined up. It was inconceivable that
fifty men can be tossed into the trench one after another. Something was bound to happen.

What happened, of course, was that the prisoners were all killed.
Hernandez, drained of emotion, watches quietly. He has no feeling
of terror, and he goes to his death with a kind of indifference. "Men
only die for something that does not exist."

With the death of Hernandez, the novelist returns to Madrid and
the long war fought on the edge of the city. Autumn gives way to
winter, while Madrid starves and bleeds. We see the fighters, but we
also see—at an infinite remove from them—the calm and contemplative Alvear, the owner of the prestigious art gallery, who has something of Hernandez in him. He knows that art perishes, but even as
it perishes it may serve a human purpose. He remembers with pleasure
that when the French invaded Saragossa, they tore town the paintings
of Murillo and made tents of them, and the Polish hussars in Napoleon's army knelt in their tents before the Virgin. Art serves its multi-
farious purposes, transfiguring the earth and the men who walk on it,

who suffer on it. "There is a terrible and profound hope in man," he says, thinking of the politicians who dash men's hopes to the ground.

The theme of *Man's Hope* is man's hope, though the English word fails to convey the precise connotation of *espoir,* which is more than hope: it is almost man's visionary portrait of himself as he might be, as he could be, if he could escape from his enemies, knowing full well that he hides many of his enemies in his own soul. Nearly all Malraux's heroes possess this visionary quality. They glow, burning themselves out for their visions, and they are therefore always a little larger than life, with the result that the Spanish Civil War sometimes seems to be a one-sided affair, with heroes on one side and pygmies on the other. For Malraux it could scarcely be otherwise. During the first year of the war a sense of exultation spread through Republican Spain. Later, when the Communists entrenched themselves and when the Fascist war machine went into high gear, the exultation vanished. Malraux fought in Spain when fighting was still possible; afterward it became a massacre.

Yet it is this visionary, exultant quality which gives the novel its extraordinary character. There is a vast sweep in this epic canvas, and Malraux seems to have realized from the very beginning that he was writing about legends which were taking place before his eyes. Sometimes the legends become explicit, as when Ximenes, the old police colonel, provokes Puig into telling the story of the Christ-child:

> "Christ came to Madrid, and to keep him quiet all the Kings of the earth began to kill the children of Madrid.
>
> "So Christ said to Himself there wasn't very much to be done with mankind. They're so disgusting that even if you bleed for them day and night through all eternity, you won't succeed in washing them clean.
>
> "The descendants of the Wise Men didn't attend His birth, since they had all become wanderers or government officials. And so it happened that for the first time on earth, from all countries, from countries nearby and others devil-knows-where, the people came. They came from the hot places and the frozen places, all who were brave or unhappy, and they came marching *with their guns.*

"And they knew in their hearts that Christ was living there among the poor and oppressed ones of the earth. And so they came in long columns from all countries, all who knew poverty well enough to die fighting it, and some had guns and those who had no guns used their hands, and one after another they came to lie down on the earth of Spain.

"They spoke all languages, and there were even Chinese shoelace sellers among them.

"And when altogether too many men had been killed, and when the last column of the poor began to march, then there appeared in the heavens a Star they had never seen before."

A large part—perhaps the most important part—of *Man's Hope* was about "a Star they had never seen before."

~§ *A Journey to America* ~§

When Malraux arrived in New York on the French liner *Paris* on February 24, 1937, he was a well-known and highly respected figure whose legendary exploits were regarded with something approaching awe. He was an authentic hero of the Spanish civil war, an intellectual whose works were already being discussed in colleges, an archaeologist and explorer who had traveled through remote regions of Asia. Such an unlikely combination of talents placed him among the ranks of folk heroes whose everyday conversations were expected to be fraught with significance and whose every action was expected to be a call for further action. In the eyes of young Americans he occupied a place close to Lindbergh among the very small group of men who have changed the destinies of nations.

Interviewers and reporters who came to meet him in his New York hotel found that he lived up to their expectations. The handsome, haggard, mobile face with the dark circles under the eyes suggested a man who was burning himself out in the flame of his ideas, and his sporadic gestures, the lightninglike play of the hands, and the way his whole body seemed to move according to the thrust of his mind, suggested that he was totally at the mercy of his intellect. He did not look like a hero; he looked like an intellectual. He did not simply speak; he made pronouncements that were charged with intellectual energy and at the same time he possessed the storyteller's gift of being able to evoke a scene in a few words, leaving the spectator to paint in the details. He had always told stories well, but the stories he told about Spain were colored with the excitement of a man who had lived them and was perfectly aware that the Spanish Civil War was great drama. Although he read English with comparative ease, he had no talent for speaking it, and most of these interviews were conducted with the aid of an interpreter. It was a measure of his remarkable gifts that the intellectual excitement survived the processes of translation.

He had come to America for several quite different reasons. Above all, he came as a propagandist for the cause of Republican Spain and to raise money to buy ambulances and medical supplies. He came, too, as the titular head of the Alliance of Anti-Fascist Intellectuals, hoping to broaden the scope of the Alliance by ensuring for it a solid American base. He wanted to see America, a country he knew largely through the works of William Faulkner. There was also a private reason. His marriage with Clara had broken up, and in his travels across America he was accompanied by Josette Clotis. A new life was opening up before him.

This new life was neither more nor less demanding than the life he had lived previously, for he still poured out his energies in the same prodigal manner, but sometimes there could be detected in him a new poetry, a new resilience. His days were now colored by the presence of a young woman possessing a grave beauty, who seemed to be unaware of her beauty, her talents, or the extraordinary effect she produced on everyone she met. There was something about her that suggested Scandinavia, but in fact her ancestors came from Catalonia and Greece, and at the same time she was wholly French and had spent all her childhood and youth in a remote town in the Auvergne. She was very pale, very slender, and she seemed not to walk so much as glide over the earth. She had long auburn hair, gray eyes, and high cheekbones. At eighteen she had written a novel called *Le Temps Vert* (*The Green Days*), filled with the melancholy of the provinces, but written in a style of great precision and deliberate simplicity, and later she had written articles for the *Nouvelle Revue Française*. She was a serious and gifted writer, who looked like a ballet dancer, and she was perfectly content to live with Malraux and to remain in his shadow. Since Clara refused to give her husband a divorce, they felt they had no alternative but to accept the fact, while regarding themselves as man and wife. She gave him two sons, Pierre-Gauthier and Vincent, and died in a senseless accident during the last months of World War II.

In New York Malraux spoke soberly about the chances of a Republican victory. He had no illusions about the strength of the forces under Franco's command, but more and more he was coming to believe that the war would be won, not on the battlefields, but in the hearts of the common people of Spain. The armies and the air forces would not decide the issue; the future belonged to the Spanish peasants. To a reporter of the New York *World Telegram* he said: "The important problem in Spain is the peasant problem, and Franco cannot cope with this problem after the next harvest. He has made promises to the peasants and to the landowners. He cannot keep faith with both. When the time comes for the harvest, the peasants will ask for land and implements, all the things he has promised. He will be unable to keep the promises. The peasants may not burn the crops, but they certainly will not continue to support Franco. The end will come."

Inevitably he was asked to talk about his experiences in building up the shattered Republican air force. He would talk about it as though it were the most natural thing in the world to build an air force. He spoke of the mercenaries who came flocking to Spain. "We had many freaks," he said. "The first freaks were the tragic kind—men who had not flown since the World War, but who claimed to be good aviators. Some were given good planes, but they broke them up immediately, killing themselves. We had an American who pestered the war offices for days trying to put across an idea he had for a trotting bomb. He said his bomb would trot into enemy territory and then explode."

Or else he would tell those brief, graphic and terrible stories, which everyone told in Spain, although they were still unfamiliar in the United States. "Once some tenants were searching the ruins of a bombarded house for their possessions," he said. "There was a line of them, similar to a line passing buckets at a fire. They passed shattered objects along the line until they reached their owners. A man picked up a baby and handed it along the line. It finally reached its mother. In the age-old gesture of motherhood she took the dead child and held it to her breast, and the head fell off."

There were many more stories and he told them well, with a savage bite in his voice. There was the story of the mountain of toys sent to the Spanish children from all over the world, heaped up in the center of the great bullring in Madrid. While the children were going to collect their toys, Junkers flew low over the city and bombarded it, but did not come near the bullring. When the children climbed out of their *refugios* to find their toys after the air raid, none touched the toy airplanes.

At rallies and dinners Malraux would make speeches which were continually interrupted by the interpreter, who sometimes attempted, not always successfully, to reproduce his gestures and cadences. For the speaker it was a gruelling experience, for the interruptions tended to make him feel like someone dictating to a slow-witted secretary: everything was dragged out, cut up into small pieces like baby food. Nevertheless he was understood, and sometimes the whole audience was raised to a pitch of excitement by his stories. The young literary critic Alfred Kazin recalled a speech delivered by Malraux in March 1937. "He spoke with such fire that his body itself seemed to be speaking the most glorious French," Kazin recalled. "Malraux was magnificently the writer as speaker, the writer as the conscience of intellectual and fraternal humanity, the writer as the master of men's souls." He spoke in stabbing sentences that drove the agony of Spain "like nails into our flesh."

On this evening Malraux told the story of the long descent of the dead and wounded airmen from the mountain. He painted in the background of barren slopes with no paths except mule tracks which the stretcher-bearers maneuvered with difficulty. The entire populace came out to salute and help the airmen, and the women and children cried when they saw the men wounded in the face. "When I raised my eyes, the file of peasants extended now from the heights of the mountain to its base; it was the grandest image of fraternity I have ever encountered."

But it was not enough to describe the images of fraternity: what was needed was active assistance from the American government, and this was not forthcoming. He could raise money, touch people's hearts, tell stories about the courage of the Spanish people better than any-one in his generation, but he was powerless to convert the government, which alone could provide the food, weapons, and airplanes needed to keep the Spanish Republic alive. No one in Washington granted him an interview, and there was even some talk of revoking his entry permit on the grounds that he was a dangerous revolutionary who threatened the safety of the United States. Most of the people who heard him were already converted to the cause, and the rest came to catch a glimpse of a famous literary figure who was also a man of action, a legendary hero. He did not disappoint them. The moment he was recognized on the platform there would come the wild, roaring, tumultuous applause, like the explosion of flames in a furnace, that is reserved only for people who have touched men's hearts, and when he began to speak there was a deathly silence, for every modulation of his voice, every gesture, every pause was being watched with close attention.

He gave three separate fund-raising speeches in Hollywood, talked to a group of writers at Princeton, attended a dinner given in his honor by *The Nation,* and granted endless interviews. His speeches often contained whole passages from *Man's Hope,* which he was still writing; it would not appear in France until the end of the year. There were other passages which demonstrated his command of rhetoric. Alfred Kazin speaks of those rhythmic passages which were so compelling that the audience swayed with them: *"We destroyed the airdrome of Seville, we did not bombard Seville. We destroyed the airdrome of Salamanca. I destroyed the airdrome of Avila at Olmedo, but I did not bombard Avila. For many months now the Fascists have been bombarding the streets of Madrid."* He cast a spell upon the audience by reciting a litany of cities, and sometimes in the middle of a sentence they rose to their feet and gave him a standing ovation.

Sometimes Communists planted in the audience asked leading questions about the Spanish Anarchists, having learned that he was in sympathy with them, or at least not opposed to them. Was it not true, he was asked, that the Anarchists were sabotaging the Republic? He replied coldly: "I will not say anything critical of any human being who fought and died in the defense of Madrid." The Communists were beginning to regard him as an enemy, for it was inconceivable to them that a man could simultaneously approve of Trotsky and Stalin. During the dinner given to him by *The Nation* he said:

"Trotsky is a great moral force in the world, but Stalin has lent dignity to mankind; and just as the Inquisition did not detract from the fundamental dignity of Christianity, so the Moscow trials did not detract from the fundamental dignity of communism."

Such statements were not calculated to please the Communists, nor did they please Trotsky, who now attacked Malraux as a crypto-Fascist. What particularly disturbed Trotsky was Malraux's attitude toward the purges, which were already terrible enough, although they had not yet reached the ghastly proportions they would reach later in the year. The true extent of the purges was not known until after Stalin's death. Malraux had long since come to the conclusion that nothing was to be gained by personal polemics, but when Trotsky denounced him in *The New York Times,* he replied angrily: "Mr Trotsky is so obsessed with whatever concerns his personal fate that if a man who has just come from seven months of active fighting in Spain makes the statement that help for Republican Spain comes before all else in importance—such a statement must needs hide something from Mr Trotsky."

One of Malraux's minor amusements during his visit to America was the reading of some of the articles written about him. Since very little was known about his early life, the journalists relied heavily on their imaginations. Thus an article in the New York *Evening Sun* described how "he teamed with Borodin and was one of seven men who virtually ran China for a year and a half." The article goes on to discuss his adventures in Persia, where "he flew and fought along a thousand mile battle front in the big rebellion of 1929." There was no big rebellion with a thousand mile battle front in Persia in 1929. Malraux had spent a few weeks in Persia that year, studying Islamic architecture and painting.

Another minor amusement was provided by a press conference at the Mayflower Hotel, where Edgard Varèse, the modernist composer, announced that he proposed to rewrite the lyric passages of *Days of Wrath* and set them to electronic music of his own composition. Malraux liked Varèse and raised no objection. At the press conference he began to say a few words in praise of his friend and was promptly silenced, while Varèse launched into a long dissertation on the beauty of electronic sound amplified by loudspeakers which would have the effect of "hitting the listener in the back of the neck." Varèse was one of the few people who ever succeeded in silencing Malraux.

American reporters had a field day, for he would talk about anything. Asked why he had risked his life in Spain when he could have lived a life of ease as one of France's most famous novelists, he answered: "Because I do not like myself." When a writer asked him why he regarded fighting as more important than writing, he answered: "Because death is a greater triumph." He could be very succinct, but he could tell stories at great length, as when he described the blind man walking through the streets of Madrid with his white cane held in front of him, while the militiamen on their way to the front lines stepped aside to give him right of way, humble before his blindness, swerving to avoid the circle of terror that surrounds a blind man walking down the middle of a street. The blind man is depicted as though he were a familiar presence, like destiny, haunting the ravaged city. Then:

> From the top of one of the big hotels, no doubt for the benefit of the police, a searchlight periodically swept the street. Suddenly, before me, in the vast flood of light, appeared two enormous hands, hands fifty feet long, that vanished into the night. The blind beggar was without a cane now, and protected himself with his groping hands; he was barely visible in the beam from the searchlight, but his outstretched hands, trembling like those of a god of the night, seemed to be seeking the living and the dead with a frightful maternal gesture.

The story about the blind beggar was told lovingly, in such detail that you could almost see the faces of the militiamen, and the beggar himself was three-dimensional, and his hands magnified by the searchlight were as large as houses. In his youth Malraux had dreamed of a landscape filled with giant hands like trees with their fingers stretching up to the skies, and he had never expected to see this landscape in war-torn Madrid.

These stories were told in the hope of bringing Spain physically present to the Americans who flocked to listen to him. It was a new kind of propaganda, but it suffered from a major defect—too few people heard it. In the end he came to realize that his mission was largely ineffective: he had spoken, and he had not been heard.

He returned to Paris, and once more in the summer he went off to Spain. This time it was to attend the second International Congress of Writers, which was being held in Madrid. Stephen Spender, the English poet, wanted to attend the Congress, but the Foreign Office had refused to grant him a visa. Malraux accordingly obliged him with a forged passport on a single sheet of paper, describing him as a Spanish citizen with the highly improbable name of Ramos Ramos. In Spanish "ramos" means "bouquet of flowers." At the frontier post it amused Malraux to explain that Ramos Ramos was a special kind of Spaniard, tall, blue-eyed, and fair-haired, speaking a dialect indistinguishable from English, and coming from the remote mountains of the north. From the Spanish frontier the delegates were driven in a fleet of cars to Barcelona, Valencia and Madrid.

During the journey Spender observed Malraux closely and argued with him about the nature of poetry. It appeared that Malraux had little faith in the future of poetry, which employed symbols like the forest, the lion, the crown, the cross, that had outlived their usefulness: only a new symbolic language closely linked with modern technology would save poetry from its inevitable doom. At the Congress he delivered a fighting speech. "He had the air of a battered youth, with face jutting pallidly over his intently crouching body as he looked at his audience," Spender reported. "The Congress was dominated by his nervous tic and sniff." Hemingway, who was then staying in Madrid, wondered how Malraux had gotten his tic. "It must have been at well over ten thousand feet," he commented.

Malraux dominated the Congress. Antonio Machado and José Bergamin led the Spanish delegation, and Ludwig Renn and Gustav Regler represented Germany. Regler had been severely wounded but was able to hobble onto the platform with the aid of a stick. With the French delegation came André Chamson, Julien Benda, Claude Aveline and Jean Cassou. Ilya Ehrenburg attended with a Russian delegation notable for its vehement attacks on André Gide. Sometimes people came up to Ehrenburg and asked him whether it was true that in the Soviet Union thousands of people were being shot in the cellars of the Lyubianka Prison, and he could only turn his head away and remain silent.

Malraux delivered a curiously lackluster speech. He simply told stories about his speaking tour in America. Once, when he was speaking in Montreal and asking for contributions to the Spanish Republic, an old workman had given him a watch dated 1860. Malraux asked the workman why he had chosen to make this gift. "Because it is the most precious thing I possess," the workman answered. He also told the familiar story about the bombs that failed to explode. When the bombs were opened, they always contained a message of solidarity from German workmen.

It was a strange conference: so purposeless, so frivolous. The words "democracy" and "freedom" were repeated endlessly, but they seemed to be dissolving into the same dust and ashes that filled the air of Madrid after an air raid. The Spanish Republic honored *los intelectuales* with banquets and parades. The President and the Prime Minister received the distinguished visitors, the best available automobiles were placed at their disposal, and all of them were given expensive gifts. They were the few who still kept faith with the Spanish Republic, and therefore deserved to be honored. But these writers and intellectuals knew that nothing they said would change the course of events.

The time for making speeches was over.

⋖ *Sierra de Teruel* ⋗

In the early weeks of 1938 Malraux formed the idea of making a
film about the Spanish Civil War. It would not be a direct adaptation
of *Man's Hope,* which had been published in France during the previous December, because the novel was too vast and too episodic to
be contained within a single film. At first he appears to have wanted
to remove himself as far as possible from the themes of the novel
and to concentrate on the peasants, with only a few brief interludes
about the Spanish Republic air force. As for the final shape the film
would take, he expected that it would reveal itself in Spain in the
presence of a people who were still fighting valiantly. In the early
months of 1938 the Republic was still powerful.

Although he had never made a film, he could scarcely remember
a time when he had not dreamed of making one. In the early twenties he was especially interested in the German expressionist films
and at one time hoped to import them into France. *The Cabinet of
Dr. Caligari* impressed him with the revelation that the film could
encompass all of madness, and go beyond madness into a rarefied
world where the intelligence seemed to splinter and turn against
itself. He had discussed filmmaking with Eisenstein, who had hoped
to make a film of *Man's Fate.* He was an eager and voracious student
of films, which he would analyze as relentlessly as he analyzed paintings and sculptures. There was nothing at all surprising in the fact
that he made a film in Spain: what was surprising was that he had
not made a film before.

With the help of his friend Edward Corniglion-Molinier, who offered to finance the film, he set about recruiting a staff and wrote a
provisional scenario. Louis Page, one of the best cameramen in France,

was engaged, and Boris Peskine and Max Aub, who spoke Spanish, were the cutters. Darius Milhaud promised to compose the music and Denis Marion served as Malraux's chief assistant. *Thème, dialogue et mise en scène*—story, dialogue and staging—were all by Malraux, who continually rewrote the dialogue, added new episodes, abandoned others, and was so deeply involved in the film that he seemed to be everywhere at once. When the film was completed and the credits were listed, Denis Marion's name was added to Malraux's as one of the authors of the scenario, but Marion subsequently denied responsibility for any of it. The credit, he felt, should go entirely to Malraux.

By June most of the preliminary arrangements had been completed. Headquarters for developing and printing rushes was set up in Toulouse, while the staff settled down in Barcelona. It was not the best time for visiting Barcelona, for the Ebro offensive was being prepared and all available manpower was being thrown into the coming battle. By this time Malraux seems to have decided that the peasants and the Escadre España should have equal importance in the film, and that it should end with the episode of the peasant who offers to show the pilots a hidden airfield behind the enemy lines, although he had never been in an airplane and had the greatest difficulty recognizing the place. The last scene of all should be the episode of the crashed airplane on the Sierra de Teruel and the long descent from the mountain. The film would be called *Sierra de Teruel,* not *Man's Hope.* For the rest, there would be continual modifications depending upon the availability of actors, studios, and sets.

Barcelona had three film studios with all the modern facilities. Make-up, lights and raw film were imported from France, but sunshades, trollies, cameras, filters and camera crews were already at hand in the studio. Since communication with Toulouse was irregular, Louis Page worked blindly, for many days passed before he was able to see the rushes. The sound equipment was defective, and most of the sound had to be scrapped and dubbed in later in France. Nevertheless, the appalling difficulties of making a film in wartime sometimes worked to their advantage. The electricity was always cut off during bombing raids, and there were days when Barcelona was bombed by five or six successive waves of Savoia-Marchettis based on Majorca. As a result of these delays there was sometimes a jagged edge to the film, but this was precisely what was needed.

Interior shots were made in the studio, where a mock-up of the interior of a bomber had been constructed out of plywood, but for greater realism Louis Page sometimes took shots inside a real bomber, installing his cameras with incredible ingenuity in the cockpit. The last surviving Potez in Republican hands was used for taking shots in the air. Scenes taken at a local airfield were liable to be interrupted by bombing raids on the airfield. When the bombers had vanished, the filmmakers would resume where they left off.

A year later, when the film was completed, Malraux wrote a long essay called *Outline for a Psychology of the Cinema.* Characteristically he wrote nothing about his own efforts as a film director. What chiefly interested him was the role played in the evolution of pictorial art by the cinema, the last, and perhaps the most fruitful, development of the Western concept of picture-making. He wrote:

> In the pictorial world there was scarcely anything else but symbolic representations of people and things, more or less subtly reproduced, until Christianity came. Buddhism has scenes, but no drama; pre-Columbian America had dramatic portraits, but no scenes. The weakening of Christianity did nothing to diminish the Western sense of drama; on the contrary it reinforced the drama, reinforced it in an even more profound sense, of which the following is merely a semblance: that consciousness of the Other, that need for relief and volume, the fanatic need for the *Object,* which is essential to the West and linked to the Western conquest of the world in a political sense. Europe substitutes relief for unity of tone, history for chronicles, drama for tragedy, novel for recitation, psychology for wisdom, action for contemplation, man for the gods.

So far the argument is a familiar one, for it was expressed at some length in *The Temptation of the West,* where the calm and sensuous East is contrasted with the agitated, sensual West. Now, going one step further, he compares the oriental theater and the theater of the ancient Greeks, where the actors mime and dance and speak through masks, with the film, "where the speech is apparently stenographed and where amid the rustling of the darkness we see a face whose fleeting expression fills a screen five yards wide."

Yet that face seen in close-up lends itself to quite extraordinary imaginative treatment. By cutting, by superimposing, by zooming back and forth, the director can change its significance at will and force it intó whatever mold he chooses. He is the emperor of images, for by selecting images according to his own whims or desires, he dominates the screen. The cinema has its own conventions: it cannot capture historical events as they occur. The trial of Robespierre, one of the most dramatic events in history, was recorded stenographically. We know what everyone said, but the report is only a pale rendering of what happened. Sometimes those reported words seem as confused and aimless as ordinary conversations. If cameras had been present, aimed at Robespierre, they also would produce only a pale stenographic record. In life there are chaotic confusions, hours and days when significance appears to have vanished from our lives, and if we sat down to record exactly what happened, we would think we were out of our minds. So, too, with the stenographic report on the trial of Robespierre: all is confusion, tumult, sudden silences. Robespierre is speaking, but suddenly no one is listening to him, they are all roaring abuse at him, and the voice of the greatest orator of the time is snuffed out. On radio we would hear Robespierre's voice dying away, and this would be enough. In the cinema it would be necessary to search for a symbol to recreate the atmosphere of total disenchantment. Malraux suggests that at this point the camera should abandon Robespierre altogether and turn toward one of the guards boxing the ears of some boys who have succeeded in entering the courtroom. As he talks about the trial of Robespierre, there is more than a suspicion that Malraux had once dreamed of making a film of the French Revolution.

Above all, in Malraux's eyes, the great film is always the recital of a myth. In Persia he had seen a film that consisted of an endless series of Charlie Chaplin shorts, thus forming a mythical life of Charlie the Clown. The film was shown in the open air, and he had the most pleasant memories of a walled enclosure and the black cats perching on the walls gazed at the film as intently as the spectators. Because the shorts were cunningly spliced together, the spectators witnessed the unfolding of an entire mythology. What was René Clair's *Le Million* but the myth of Cinderella brought up to date? The great Russian films *Potemkin* and *The Mother* belonged to mythology, and so did *The Cabinet of Dr. Caligari, The Blue Angel* and *I Was a Fugitive from a Chain Gang.* They were all films he admired, and all were myths. "The myth begins in Fantomas and ends in Christ."

Malraux's essay on the psychology of cinema, though written in 1939, was not published until 1946, when it appeared in an edition of twelve hundred copies, beautifully printed in bold italics. There were fifty pages of text, and the pages were deliberately left unnumbered. It was a book for bibliophiles, testifying to Malraux's pleasure in fine printing, and is now almost impossible to procure.

The theory of filmmaking would come later. Meanwhile he was working in Barcelona with the film crew, making occasional short journeys to Toulouse and Paris to see the rushes, and returning with vast quantities of tinned food and cigarettes, nearly unobtainable in Barcelona, which he would give away with prodigal openhandedness. He was having trouble with the Spanish actors, who were brought up in the tradition of the Spanish stage and tended to overact: he was continually having to tell them to underplay their parts. He was in good spirits in spite of the continual bombardments, though it was noticed that he chain-smoked alarmingly and the facial tics seemed to become more violent as the year went on. At the end of the year, when the mood of enchantment had passed and the war was becoming a rout, he would say: "The Civil War was once a bride, now it is a wife."

In the crowd scenes he had very little difficulty directing the actors, who played parts that were familiar to them. With the principal roles he was confronted with continual difficulties. The Spanish actors came from the comic stage; they were being asked to play a tragedy. The character of Magnin from *Man's Hope* became Muñoz, a Spanish air force captain, and the famous actor known as Mejuto had to be watched closely, for though he looked the part of an air force captain, his gestures betrayed him. Finally it became necessary to choreograph even his slightest gestures, to prevent him at all costs from using his hands, and to ensure that he never smiled. The peasant was played by José Lado, also a comic actor. In the scene where the peasant accompanies the airmen on a bombing mission to search for a hidden airfield, José Lado played his role perfectly. Fear, bewilderment, hesitation, anguish, joy were all registered on a face of extraordinary sensitivity. At first he looked like a small terrified rat with the mud of the gutters still clinging to him, but when the hidden airfield was found at last, he looked like a conqueror. All the scenes showing the peasant in the airplane were filmed in the studio in Barcelona.

The overture was jagged and violent. We see a village commune, ammunition being doled out, the peasants making their way along a deserted street, someone firing on them from behind a window screen, and then the Fifth Columnist is shot, and we see him lurching grotesquely against the screen. The pounding of artillery can be heard from far away; an enormous black butterfly suddenly falls within its glass case. The elders of the village come together in conference and debate the prospects of the village confronted with the Fifth Column and Franco's advancing forces. An automobile charges against a machine gun and explodes. Immediately after the shot of the dead driver, there is a brief shot of sunflowers waving in the wind; and again, after a traitor is shot, we see the sky dark with birds. These symbols play a memorable part in the film, though they are employed rarely. The Spanish air force captain decides that his bombers must leave the airfield at night for the attack on Teruel. Every available automobile in the commune must be rounded up, so that their headlights can illuminate the airstrip; and as the captain drives wearily from place to place, asking everyone who possesses an automobile to bring it to the airfield, and then returns to prepare his airmen for the flight, he has the appearance of a man who is so alone, so powerful, and so dedicated that when the ungainly bombers finally roar down the runway in the light of fifty headlights, it is as though he had himself lifted them into the air, catapulting them by the sheer force of his will. The night drive of the exhausted captain is one of the most brilliantly conceived passages in the film. Malraux deliberately prolonged it, as later he would deliberately prolong the passage in which the dead and wounded airmen are brought down the mountainside.

But it was in the small and unobtrusive details that Malraux showed his mastery. The dwarf who comes at the end of a long line of guerrillas must occasionally make a little skip to keep up with them. The place where the traitor is shot is a horrible little garden terrace overlooking the village roofs; and the glinting roofs are at odds with the pathetic little garden. When we see the village elders sitting in conference, we realize later that they have been deliberately arranged in a pattern derived from Rembrandt, and they speak with all the authority of burgomasters. Malraux's camera lingers lovingly on the old faces, wrinkled like old apples, and he will linger just as lovingly on the shapes of airplanes.

Through the summer and autumn of 1938 the work went on in fits and starts, with so many difficulties that Malraux sometimes wondered whether it would ever be completed. There was a time when the bombers came every day, hoping to reduce Barcelona to a shambles of lost hopes, to paralysis. Yet the film, when it was finally completed, gives the impression of a whole, all the parts properly interlocking, every gesture given its full weight, as though it had been made in a country at peace far from the battle lines.

One day in August 1938 Malraux met the veteran American novelist Theodore Dreiser. The meeting took place in the *grande salle* of the Hotel Majestic on the Paseo de Gracia at a time when the city's electric generators were no longer working and the filming was temporarily suspended. Malraux was oppressed by the difficulties of filmmaking, which were even greater than he had expected, but he was in good spirits when he attended the farewell dinner for Dreiser, who had been given an interview by the Prime Minister and had been shown all the sights, and was leaving on the following day for France. In a few days he would be in America, where, as he said, "he would tell the American people the truth about this damned war."

Among the guests who attended the dinner were Ernst Toller, the German poet who had once very briefly occupied the post of revolutionary dictator of Bavaria, the veteran correspondent Louis Fischer, and Herbert Matthews, the scholarly and cautious correspondent of *The New York Times*. Boleslavskaya, the correspondent of *Pravda*, was also present. Malraux had met her in Russia, where she had often acted as his interpreter. Malraux arrived a few minutes late—there had been some trouble finding an automobile for him—and since the guests had a high regard for him, everyone stood up when he appeared. Dreiser growled that he did not know who "this Mister Malraux" was, but he was assured that the party was being honored by his presence. Malraux was accompanied by Josette Clotis, whose long silken hair was continually falling over her eyes.

The guests sat around a large black circular table lit by candles stuck in bottles. There was little food—pale soup, bread cobs, squid and corn husks that pretended to be coffee—but there was a plentiful supply of Spanish wine of an excellent vintage. Dreiser, already a little drunk before the party began, became increasingly drunk as the party went on. His voice quavering with passion, he announced that the war was all the fault of the Catholics and Masons, who were together plotting a terrible war which would drown Europe in blood, and what was most terrible about this war was that it was inevitable, that nothing anyone could do would stop it, and he hoped to God that America would have the good sense to keep out of it. His dewlaps shaking, his eyes gleaming in the light of the flickering candles, he said: "I tell you there is going to be a war more terrible than any war that has ever been visited on man. There's no hope for Europe. The whole continent is riddled with the disease of war. I may not live to see it, but by God I know it is coming!" The Pope and the Grand Orient were responsible. Wasn't Franco a Catholic, and weren't the Masons everywhere?

Malraux could understand English when it was spoken slowly and distinctly, but Dreiser's low, growling, rasping voice was beyond his comprehension. So, from time to time, he would fling a question at Boleslavskaya and she would provide a running commentary. Finally, when he could stand it no longer, Malraux raised a long minatory finger, and for once speaking slowly and distinctly, as though he hoped that Dreiser would understand him, he explained that a war was perhaps inevitable, but its inevitability was in no way due to the causes advanced by Dreiser. If the war was inevitable, it was because people had abandoned the hope of directing their own affairs and saw war as the only possible way of removing the dictators from power; and in this they were wrong, for the war would only reinforce the power of the dictators, leaving the people in a worse plight than ever. Boleslavskaya would translate all this into English, while Dreiser kept shaking his head, more confused than ever. "What is the feller saying?" he asked, and Boleslavskaya patiently repeated Malraux's argument. "He's a Frenchman and a Catholic," Dreiser said. "I wouldn't expect him to think otherwise."

As the argument continued, Toller looked increasingly uneasy and Herbert Matthews, who listened with appalled politeness, occasionally interrupted with a suggestion that they should change the subject. Malraux's face was convulsed every four or five seconds with spasmodic twitching, and this seemed to infuriate Dreiser, who shouted: "You're guilty as hell, like all the rest of them!" Later he subsided, toyed with a bread cob, apologized meekly, gazed benevolently round the table, offered to buy drinks for everyone, and began to talk about his interview with the Prime Minister. Nothing more was said about the Catholics and the Masons.

During Dreiser's tirade Josette Clotis had clung to Malraux as though to protect him from an enemy. She was very beautiful and very pale, and wore a long clinging gown. Dreiser was immensely attracted by her, and imagining that she could speak English and that her affection for Malraux was mere playacting, he began to make advances to her, insisting that she sit beside him and becoming grotesquely ill-tempered when she refused. Soon the waiters came and stuck new candles in the wine bottles, and a few moments later Dreiser announced that he was off to bed. He rose, threw his arms round Malraux in a bear hug, thumped him on the back, and then very ponderously, very slowly, he climbed the marble stairs to his bedroom.

The filming continued through the summer and autumn. From time to time small portions of the streets of Barcelona would be cordoned off, reflectors would be set up, and Louis Page would get behind the camera and shoot a scene, which was rarely included in the finished film. The film, after editing, would show scarcely any signs that a film crew had ever been to Barcelona. This was not due to deliberate design so much as to the chaotic state of affairs in Barcelona and to the fact that the scenario was infinitely variable, since there were innumerable episodes in *Man's Hope* and any or all of them would provide material for the film. Malraux insisted from the beginning that the film should not be regarded as an adaptation of the book, and in the end only one episode was taken directly from it. But this episode was one of the longest and most powerful in the book, and remained the longest and most powerful in the film. This was the sequence showing the raid on Teruel followed by the crash in the mountains and the long mournful procession of peasants bearing the dead and wounded down the mountainside. This processional march was filmed in the autumn of 1938 in the wild mountains of the Sierra de Montserrat, thirty miles from Barcelona and not far from the ancient monastery of Montserrat where, according to tradition, a statue of the Virgin, carved by St. Luke, was found in a nearby grotto.

The site was well chosen, for there are no more rugged and strangely shaped mountains in all of Spain. Malraux was attempting to do something that was virtually impossible: to give legendary shape to human comradeship. The tortuous descent, the grief of the peasants, the stark mountains, and the strange patterns they formed were to be incorporated in a single image of mingled grief and hope. No priests would bless the dead, no doctors would bandage the wounded. As the peasants came down the mountainside, the procession would take on the form of a Pietà, a sacrament of unbounded love and a triumph. So he had written in *Man's Hope*: "All that long line of black-clothed peasants, the women with their hair hidden beneath the scarves they had worn from time immemorial, seemed to have more of the character of an austere triumphal progress than of a relief party bringing home wounded men."

Originally, when Belaïdi's airplane crashed in the Sierra de Teruel, perhaps a hundred peasants took part in the procession down the mountain. In the film a thousand peasants were taken by army trucks to the Sierra de Montserrat. Their descent was carefully orchestrated, gathering strength, the camera seeing only a handful at first, then a score, then a hundred, until by the time they are approaching Valdelinares the stream has become a swollen torrent.

In the original film this scene was prolonged almost beyond reason, for Malraux was determined that the descent should be made memorable even at the cost of repetition. So much footage was taken that it was possible to extend it for a full ten minutes. Close shots of the peasants alternated with long shots of the barren mountains. At intervals there were shots of the rough-hewn coffin swaying on the back of a mule, of the wounded on their stretchers, and of Muñoz watching them, hovering over them, gaunt with sorrow. There are moments, watching these last scenes, when the whole world seems to be descending the mountain in a triumphal procession, the dead and the living in an eternal communion.

Nothing in the film had prepared the spectator for this slow movement. Up to the crash in the Sierra de Teruel the pace was fast, for the Republicans on the ground were busily fighting the enemy or holding councils about how to fight the enemy, while the airmen were busy on the airfield or in the air. There had been mounting excitement when the peasant failed to recognize his own village where the enemy airplanes were concealed among trees: the Republican plane was forced to fly low, at the level of the treetops, before he could recognize the hiding place. All this had been done with a beautiful sense of form and energy, swiftly and directly. Then abruptly, after the crash, all movement comes to an end. There is only silence, until out of this silence there flows the procession.

While the film was being made, the war was coming to its inevitable end. The battle of the Ebro was won by the Republicans shortly after Malraux's return to Spain, but thereafter there were only defeats. Malraux stayed on. He saw the remnants of the International Brigade marching through the streets of Barcelona on November 15, after they had been withdrawn from the front lines, and he commented sadly: "The whole revolution is going home." A few days earlier he had attended a party given by Boleslavskaya. All the famous war correspondents were there: Hemingway, Vincent Sheean, Georges Soria, some twenty others. There was dancing and singing, while the Italian airplanes flew over Barcelona and the searchlights raced across the moonlit sky. They sang the songs of the Spanish war and the songs of the concentration camps, and at midnight a tall Madrileño, who was Boleslavskaya's bodyguard and chauffeur, suddenly stepped forward and suggested that they should all stand in silence for a few seconds and think of those who died in defense of Madrid.

The war was over, but the fighting went on. In January, when Franco's army was approaching Barcelona, Malraux left Spain with the uncompleted film. About two thirds of the film had been made, and the rest would be made in France, with the result that some of the earliest scenes in the finished film were among the last to be shot. There are villages in southern France near the Pyrenees which look like Spanish villages, and there was a church at Villefranche-de-Rouergue that looked like a Spanish church. Through the spring and summer he worked on the film, and it was ready for showing just before World War II broke out. The government banned the film, but two weeks before the war started there was a private showing at the Rex Cinema in Paris. There were about twenty spectators, including Ilya Ehrenburg, Louis Aragon, Edward Corniglion-Molinier, and Marcel Brandin, who had been Malraux's friend from his schooldays. Brandin asked Malraux why he had been invited among these distinguished specialists, and was told, "Well, you represent the French people." It was a strange premiere for a masterpiece.

During the war years the film vanished from sight. The German occupation troops found and destroyed a cannister of film bearing the label *Sierra de Teruel*. By good fortune the film was in another cannister bearing a more innocuous title. It had survived the war and Malraux's worst fears, for he had scarcely hoped to see it again. It was shown for the second time in Paris in the spring of 1945, under the title of *Espoir*. Corniglion-Molinier, who had financed the film, sold it to a distributor who promptly cut off over three hundred feet of the descent from the mountain. Even so, it won the prestigious *prix Louis-Delluc* given to the most artistic film of the year. Malraux was especially pleased with the award, for he had a great affection for the film which was lost and found again.

Two years later the film reached America, where it enjoyed only a moderate success. In 1947 the Spanish Civil War seemed as remote as the Middle Ages, and the Americans were perplexed by the theme of the descent from the mountain, which seemed inordinately long even after it had been cropped short. A few discerning critics recognized the value of the film. James Agee, the wisest and most clear-sighted of film critics, spoke of it almost with bated breath. Of the sequence showing the peasant searching for the hidden airplanes he wrote: "I need say of it only that it is so powerful in emotion and meaning, and so beautifully done, that as pure accomplishment it excels every other excellence in the film, and stands with the few great classical passages which have been achieved, in films, through the perfect identification of melodramatic suspense with meanings which are normally far above the proper purpose of melodrama." Of the great passage of the descent from the mountain, he wrote that it "falls possibly short of its full imaginable magnificence, considered syllable by syllable; but in its mass it is poetry even greater. Homer might know it, I think, for the one work of our time which was wholly sympathetic to him."

Malraux beside a bombing plane in
Spain. (GAETAN PICON, *Malraux par
Lui-Même*, LES ÉDITIONS DU SEUIL)

(ANDRÉ MALRAUX)

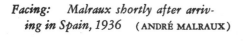

*Facing: Malraux shortly after arriv-
ing in Spain, 1936* (ANDRÉ MALRAUX)

(ANDRÉ MALRAUX)

(ANDRÉ MALRAUX)

Malraux resting after a bombing raid on Teruel. (GAETAN PICON, *Malraux par Lui-Même*, LES ÉDITIONS DU SEUIL.)

Malraux beside his airplane.   (ANDRÉ MALRAUX)

The plane after it crashed.   (GAETAN PICON, *Malraux par Lui-Même*, LES ÉDITIONS DU SEUIL)

Malraux at film conference in Barcelona.   (ANDRÉ MALRAUX)

Malraux and Max Aub (right).   (ANDRÉ MALRAUX)

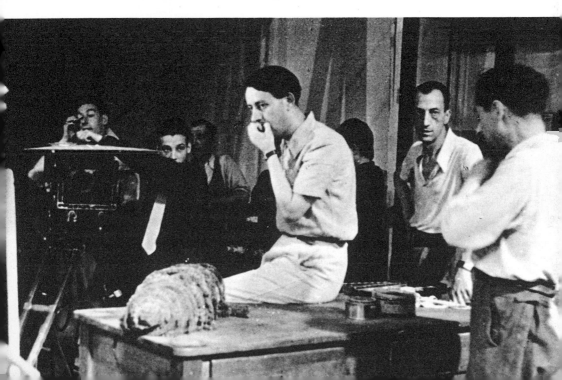

Muñoz addresses a dead airman. (CINEMATHÈQUE FRANCAISE AND ANDRÉ MALRAUX)

The automobile is about to explode under machine-gun fire. (CINEMATHÈQUE FRANCAISE AND ANDRÉ MALRAUX)

The peasant interrogated by the town committee. (CINEMATHÈQUE FRANCAISE AND ANDRÉ MALRAUX)

The automobiles light up the airfield. (CINEMATHÈQUE FRANCAISE AND ANDRÉ MALRAUX)

The peasant cannot recognize his own village. (CINEMATHÈQUE FRANCAISE AND ANDRÉ MALRAUX)

The moment when he recognizes it. (CINEMATHÈQUE FRANCAISE AND ANDRÉ MALRAUX)

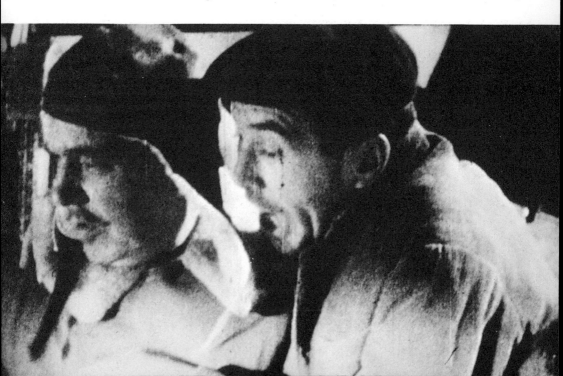

The Procession down the mountain.   (CINEMATHÈQUE FRANCAISE AND ANDRÉ MALRAUX)

Malraux during his speaking tour of the United States, 1938.   (ANDRÉ MALRAUX)

(ANDRÉ MALRAUX)

Malraux during fighting near Strasbourg, 1944.   (GAETAN PICON, *Malraux par Lui-Même*,
LES ÉDITIONS DU SEUIL)

Josette Clotis   (ANDRÉ MALRAUX)

HE WAR

If a shell comes, I shall again fling myself to the ground; I shall duck my head under the fire of the bullets; if I fall into another trap, I shall experience the same convulsive dementia and the same madman's calm.

But this morning I am not afraid of death.

—THE WALNUT TREES OF ALTENBURG

⊸§ *Prisoner of War* ᴂ⊷

When the German armies invaded Poland in September 1939, Malraux was staying in a hotel in Quercy, a region in southwestern France famous for its Romanesque churches. All morning the maidservants were listening to the radio, and his first knowledge of the war came from those old women with tears streaming down their cheeks. In the afternoon he was at Beaulieu-sur-Dordogne, where the call-up notices could be seen on the church, one of the finest of Romanesque churches with its huge Christ standing with outstretched arms in the tympanum, the shadow of the Cross looming behind the Last Judgment, and there seemed to be some strange significance in this Christ standing in judgment over the sins of men in September 1939.

We remember where we were at the exact moment when we become aware of the full impact of a war. So Malraux remembered Beaulieu-sur-Dordogne with a peculiar feeling of nostalgia, remembering the church as it appeared during the tropical downpour in the afternoon, seeing the statue of the Virgin and Child in front of the church drenched in the rain. It was the time of the wine harvest, and for centuries it had been the habit of the local cultivators to place a bunch of grapes in the hands of the Child; and now the raindrops fell from the grapes, and he watched them falling, as though in some mysterious way the cleansing rain had a message for him. There was Christ with His arms thrown out to embrace the world, and the rain falling from the grapes, and a war coming. Like everyone else he knew that life would never be the same again.

He was making his way to Paris, and by the time he reached Moulins the loudspeaker on the main square was announcing the first battles. Evening was falling, and there were some two or three thousand draftees wandering about awkwardly in their new uniforms, silent and somber, while bitter women from the farms brought their requisitioned farm horses into the town. Moulins is a small town, close to the peasantry, and the people were all knit together now, as they would have been before an oncoming flood.

When he reached Paris he knew exactly what he wanted to do. Because it would be a war of tanks, he wanted to join a tank corps. Simone de Beauvoir, industriously writing her war diary, noted early the following month that "Malraux appears to want to enlist in the tank corps, but has been rejected because of his nervous tics." Since her books were sometimes published by Gallimard, who also published Malraux, she had excellent sources of information. On the other hand, she was a little afraid of Malraux and inclined to find fault with him because he seemed in her eyes to threaten the position of Jean-Paul Sartre, her lover. The diary entry reflects her ambiguous attitude. Only half of the sentence was true, for he was not rejected. He spent the next nine months under training in the reserve, and saw no action until May 1940, when he was in a column of tanks advancing across the plains of Flanders against German positions. The Germans had broken through Holland and Belgium, and soon they would be driving the British into the sea at Dunkerque.

In his semi-autobiographical novel *The Walnut Trees of Altenburg* Malraux described the strange sensation of being cooped up in a tank at night, with the enemy only a few miles away. There were three others in the tank: Bonneau, Pradé and Léonard, all of them from the working class, hating authority, almost mindless, ill at ease in each other's company. Bonneau dreamed of the murders he claimed to have committed, Pradé dreamed of his eleven-year-old son, and Léonard dreamed of the evening at the Casino de Paris, where he was employed as a fireman, when he was invited into the dressing room of the star performer and happily seduced. Pradé drove the tank, the others were mechanics and gunners.

There have been few completely credible accounts of tank warfare in literature; the grinding roar of a tank in action cannot be reproduced in words. Malraux stops short of describing an engagement. Instead, he conveys the sense of mounting horror and excitement, the

dread and the exaltation of the advance under the enemy guns, while
the tank rattles and groans and lurches forward like a huge beetle into
the uncomprehending night, leaving in the young wheat a furrow
glistening white in the moonlight. Shells explode nearby; outside there
are ghostly orchards shrouded in mist; inside the tank there is darkness, the clatter of machinery, the hammering of the treads, the grinding of gears, an unearthly uproar of metal. Malraux in the turret held
strings which led to Pradé: in this way he could communicate direction to the driver, whose only view of the world was through a periscope. Their lives depended on a piece of string.

News had come over the radio that one of the tanks had already
fallen into a tank trap, and they were in mortal fear of the same fate.
Once they were in a trap, the German artillery could destroy them at
leisure, and they lived in continual expectation of being blown up by
shells or falling into cunningly constructed tank traps. Suddenly there
was a lurch, the entire tank quivered on the edge of a pit, and Malraux
found himself pulling on the strings to indicate that they should pull
back. The string broke. Bonneau was screaming. Somewhere in the
dark fields there could be seen the dim shapes of the other tanks moving up to the front line. Then the tank fell slowly into the trap:

> It was leaning forward with a vengeance now, its tail in the
> air like a Japanese fish, drew back, plunged the rear end into the
> wall of the pit, vibrating along its whole length, like an ax
> quivering in a tree. Then it slipped and sank. Was it blood or
> sweat flowing along my nose? We had fallen lopsided. Bon-
> neau was screaming as he tried to open the side door; it opened,
> and then he closed it again. The door must have been almost
> underneath the tank. One tread was turning in empty air. Pradé
> lurched the tank forward on the other, and then it dropped
> back in an upright position as though crashing into a second
> trap. My helmet rang against the turret, and I thought my head
> was swelling and swelling, while it buried itself between my
> shoulders like a screw, waiting for a shell to fall.

In darkness, for the lights had gone out, and only too well aware
that their position was known to the Germans, they waited for the

inevitable shell as a trapped animal waits for the moment when it will be released from pain. Fear nourished them, and sometimes panic ran through them like a current of electricity. To be inside a pit, knowing that they were hopelessly trapped, was to be enclosed within the heart of fear. "There came a terror," wrote Malraux, "that shattered my madman's calm: death was giving us warning." Death, indeed, had already taken up its residence inside the armored walls of the tank: only the periscope mirror, reflecting the streaming stars, seemed to be in league with life.

At last they crawled out of the tank and clung to the damp clay of the pit, which smelled of mushrooms, while the shells whistled overhead and there were sudden patches of red in the sky. To their horror they saw that the French tanks were retreating, or at least they seemed to be retreating. But their orders were to advance at all costs, and soon they clambered back into the tank, somehow righted it and set it in motion until, with a sound of shuddering metal, it somehow heaved itself slowly out of the trap and rolled on to a village abandoned by the peasants. There were a few other French tanks in the village, and they were all poorly camouflaged. Here they slept in the hay, and when the morning came they could scarcely believe they were still alive.

Malraux had experienced a similar return to life six years before when his airplane plummeted down over the Aurès mountains, and afterward he was driven into Bône to see a city which had become miraculously transformed, so that everything appeared larger than life and strangely beautiful. He was fascinated by the processes of resurrection. Just to see some chickens pecking in the dawn light was to be aware of an illumination; the flight of pigeons, swerving and turning white in the sun, filled him with wonder. This small abandoned village in Flanders, with its kennels and rabbit hutches and wash hanging on the line, was exquisitely perfect in the purity of the morning air, and the war seemed far away.

For him it was like entering a new country for the first time. It was a magical country, and he would not have been surprised if all the farm animals had begun to speak. He wrote about that morning:

> Like one who encounters India for the first time, I hear, beneath this picturesque profusion, a vast murmur of centuries

that reached almost as far back as the darkness of last night: those barns brimming with grain and straw, with their beams hidden by husks, full of harrows, yokes, shafts, wooden carts, and everywhere grain, wood, straw and leather (all the metallic objects have been requisitioned), all surrounded by the extinguished fires of refugees and soldiers: the barns of the Gothic age. Our tanks at the end of the street were being filled with water, monsters kneeling at biblical wells. . . . O life, so old!

And so obstinate! In every farmyard wood had been gathered for the winter. Our soldiers when they woke up used it to light their first fires. Everywhere there were vegetable plots, all well arranged. There was nothing here which did not bear man's imprint. The clothes pins danced in the wind like swallows, and sometimes the clothes hanging there were not yet dry: slender stockings, fancy gloves, the blue uniforms of farmers and workmen; and in the midst of this forsaken village, in the midst of disaster, there were serviettes with initials.

We and those on the other side are no longer good for anything except our mechanical instruments, our courage and our cowardice; but the old race of men whom we have chased away and who have left here only their implements, their linen and their serviettes with initials, seems to me to have come through thousands of years, out of the darkness encountered last night— slowly, avariciously loaded with all the flotsam which they abandoned only a little while ago, the wheelbarrows and the harrows, the biblical carts, the kennels and rabbit hutches, the empty furnaces.

Out of that peaceful desolation there could be constructed a new and perfectly valid theory of human history. Once more he thought of Pascal's complaint about the human condition, all men waiting patiently for the moment when they will have their throats cut. Two old peasants, a man and a woman, were sunning themselves on a bench; the man's clothes were covered with cobwebs, for he had been hiding in the cellar, and the woman wore a thin gray plait stretched tight. Pradé went up to them and said: "Well, grandpa, are you enjoying the sun?" The woman answered: "What else can we do? You, you are

young; when you are old, everything becomes worn out." And that,
too, was history.

The memory of that morning remained, and Malraux wrote about
it at length almost as though this was the culminating morning of the
war. He thought of his father, a tank officer in the First World War,
and death was very close to him; at the same time he was abundantly
aware that he had been reborn from the depths of the earth, like a
seed flowering out of the clayish loam of the tank trap. Of this rebirth
he wrote in the concluding passage of an early version of *The Walnut
Trees of Altenburg:*

> I know now the meaning of the ancient myths of men
> snatched from the kingdom of the dead. Scarcely do I remem-
> ber the terror; what I bear within me is the discovery of a sim-
> ple and holy secret. I have seen the earth with divine eyes. I
> find myself back upon it as if it had suddenly been given to me,
> I discover it although I bear it within me. Thus, perhaps, God
> looked upon the first man.
>
> If a shell comes, I shall again fling myself to the ground; I
> shall duck my head under the fire of bullets; if I fall into an-
> other trap, I shall experience the same convulsive dementia and
> the same madman's calm.
>
> But this morning I am not afraid of death.

In those days death was never far away, for the German *blitzkrieg*
was raging across Flanders and once more the villages were going up
in flames. May was atrocious, but June was worse. For a while the
French held up the German advance, with General Weygand massing
his troops in a solid line across their path, but the Germans broke
through. Malraux was wounded on June 14 and captured four days
later. Like thousands of others he was thrown into an internment camp.

The camp was at Sens, seventy miles southeast of Paris, a cathedral
city in the Middle Ages, now little more than an overgrown village in
the backwaters. Here was the first of the Gothic cathedrals, and there
was some irony in the fact that Malraux should be imprisoned in its
shadow. The haggard faces of the prisoners reminded him of Gothic

statues; the Middle Ages had returned; and life was reduced to the level of barbaric simplicity. The months passed, while his leg wounds healed slowly, and he grew accustomed to living in the medieval past, where all men were bearded and slept on straw.

They were days of appalling privation and almost intolerable isolation. The Germans permitted no communication with the outside world. Sometimes a girl would come up to the barbed wire, moving slowly until a guard passed out of sight, and she would throw some bread to the prisoners, who fought for it silently like wild beasts; and afterward there would be specks of blood on the barbed wire. A man would be lucky if he got more than a few crumbs.

The prisoners lived on rumors, and the more wildly improbable the rumor, the more satisfying it was. Letters could be sent out, but they were not ordinary letters. You were given a printed card, and you could scratch out any phrases which proved to be inapplicable. *I am a prisoner, I am well, I am being well treated, I am wounded, Yours Affectionately.* These, too, were crumbs. At the bottom of the card there were the instructions: *Give no address, Do not seal.* Not many of these letters reached their destination, and sometimes the wind would blow thousands of them across the camp from some waste-dump where the Germans had deposited them.

Malraux went on writing on scraps of paper, knowing that he could scarcely hope to keep his writings. One day in November, wearing shoes too small for him, dressed like a carpenter and carrying planks on his shoulder, he escaped. He must have looked very strange, for some lampblack in his pocket stained his hands and later his face. When he reached the Free Zone he saw himself in a mirror: he had the face of a Negro minstrel.

Gradually he made his way to the south of France, finally settling in the small town of Roquebrune in the hills above Nice. By good fortune he was able to lease a large villa belonging to an officer of the Bengal Lancers who had filled it with the relics of his Indian campaigns. Indian swords hung over the fireplace, tiger skins hung on the walls, and he half expected to find a turbanned Indian servant. Instead there was Luigi, the officer's butler, who wore white gloves and spent an impressive number of hours each day polishing the silver.

He had never lived in a villa so exotic as this, or so luxuriously furnished. Although there was very little to eat, the butler saw to it that the food was served immaculately; and every meal was given the decoration appropriate to a feast. Luigi was one of those men who treat the disasters of war with a studied indifference. When Malraux was out of cigarettes—and this happened often—Luigi would make his way across the Italian frontier and return with a fresh supply.

Roquebrune is not an especially interesting town. The seventeenth-century Church of St. Margaret was not likely to attract Malraux's attention; there was considerably more pleasure to be derived from the massive ruins of the castle built by Count Lascaris de Ventimiglia in the fourteenth century. Once, long ago, the town had been stormed by the Turks, but otherwise it had little recorded history. There were a few small hotels. Monte Carlo was only four miles away.

Here Malraux set down to write two books. One was an extended study of T. E. Lawrence, "the uncrowned king of Arabia," who had fascinated him ever sence he read *The Seven Pillars of Wisdom*. The work was to be an appraisal of the intellectual hero driven by his demons into the world of action, an extended commentary on Lawrence's ideas and actions. The second was to be a novel called *The Struggle with the Angel,* largely autobiographical, introducing his father and grandfather under various disguises, and continuing the long debate with himself which had begun with *Paper Moons* and continued through his novels.

Neither the study of T. E. Lawrence nor the novel were ever completed, and large sections were lost to the Gestapo. Nevertheless the uncompleted novel was published and a long chapter of the study on Lawrence appeared in a literary magazine after the war.

Inevitably, Malraux found himself drawing parallels between himself and Lawrence. They had both engaged in exotic adventures; they had fought battles and won victories, and at the end there was only the taste of ashes in the mouth. Even in smaller matters there were profound similarities. They shared a common love of airplanes, tanks, fine printing, color engraving, and everything that goes into the making of well-produced books. They were passionate archaeologists, and they shared a common interest in medieval chronicles, eighteenth-century music, and Gothic cathedrals. They had both dreamed of hustling into shape a new Asia, as though it had been given to them to command the giant forces stirring in an awakened continent. Lawrence in Arabia and Malraux in Spain had each singlehandedly diverted, if only for a short while, the current of history. Both were intensely religious, though they stood outside the Church. They were natural anarchists, proud and imperious in manner, their outward calm concealing the demons within.

There were also profound differences. Though there was little to choose between them in courage and resource, there was a profound difference of character and style. One can imagine Lawrence flying over the southern reaches of Arabia in search of the lost city of the Queen of Sheba, but it is beyond every effort of the imagination to see him addressing political rallies. Like a medieval monk, Lawrence treasured his solitude, and was far more solitary than Malraux would ever be. He was also more self-absorbed, more implacably determined to wrest the secrets from his soul, and therefore more tortured. On occasion Malraux could compromise: in Indochina he retreated from the battle, knowing that defeat was inevitable. Lawrence was exhilarated by defeat and plunged on recklessly in search of still more terrifying encounters, a still more ominous enemy. He never retreated. He would go to the very end, knowing that the only worthwhile encounters are those with the Absolute.

Although Malraux was not at ease in the English language, and although many of the subtleties and much of the music of *The Seven Pillars of Wisdom* escaped him, he understood Lawrence better than most of the critics who have written about him. He understood why the writing of the book was as arduous and exhausting as raising the Arab revolt. "The subject of the book which he believed himself to be writing had become the struggle of a being mercilessly scourged by the contempt he felt for certain aspects of himself, by a fatality experienced with excruciating humiliation as a permanent weakness of his will—against the frantic resolution of this same being to kill his demon by dint of conquest and lucidity. '*I wrote my will across the sky in stars. . . .*'"

Malraux was of course employing his own vocabulary to interpret a man who used a wholly different vocabulary. His own preoccupations with the Absurd and the Farfelu were introduced into the argument: he saw Lawrence, after leading his armies in triumph to Damascus, confronted with the absurdity of his own life and the discovery that all his acts, even the most noble and daring, were irremediably flawed because the British Government had made him the spokesman of promises to the Arabs that it never intended to keep. A stranger among the Arabs, an outcast among the British, detesting himself, he could turn nowhere for support, not even to the comforts of confession. *The Seven Pillars of Wisdom* was not a confession; it was an act of penance. This act of penance was performed in the knowledge that penance, like everything else in the world, is absurd. "Man is absurd," wrote Malraux. "He is master neither of time, nor of anguish, nor of Evil; the world is absurd because it is inseparable from Evil, and Evil is the sin of the world."

According to Malraux, Lawrence accomplished this penitential act by a prolonged, lucid and fearful examination of himself in terms of the Absolute. Lawrence wrestled with the angel, and the more he wrestled, the more he was forced to yield to the angel and to become his own enemy. Out of this struggle came the flawed masterpiece, the huge book written by a man so driven that he sometimes worked on it for thirty hours at a stretch, and even when he had printed it himself and embellished it with a gallery of superbly reproduced portraits by Augustus John, Eric Kennington, and many others, he was still not content with it, knowing that absurdity lay at the heart of it.

Again and again in the book Lawrence disguised his own role. His most courageous exploit—a long journey behind the enemy lines, which took him almost to the walls of Damascus—was not even mentioned in the book. His task was to tell his story in the light of his own truth. Thus he became his own judge, his own executioner. There could be no appeal to a higher authority, for he was not prepared to admit the existence of a higher authority.

In his summing up Malraux pronounced Lawrence to be "one of the most religious intelligences of his time":

> Lawrence, one of the most religious intelligences of his time,
> if one means by religious someone who knows the anguish of

being a man in the very depths of his soul; Lawrence, who had
received a religious education in England, who had attended
Jesuit schools in France, whose brother and mother were mis-
sionaries, who called *The Brothers Karamazov* the fifth gospel,
and yet there is not to be found in the nine hundred crowded
pages of his letters (nor in his books) more than fifty lines on
Christianity. There was within him, beneath his pride, if not
humility, at least a violent and sporadic tendency to humiliate
himself, sometimes by discipline and sometimes by veneration;
the horror of respectability; the disgust for property, for money,
a disinterestedness which itself took the form of a charity of the
heart; a profound consciousness of his guilt with its attendant
angels and minor demons; of Evil and of the nothingness of
nearly all that men cling to; the need of the Absolute, the instinctive bias toward asceticism. He seemed to be one of those
above all others, whom Jesus, stretched eternally on the Cross,
snatches away from the ultimate solitude. And there was in him
an anti-Christian of the first order; it was only from himself that
he expected forgiveness. He sought no appeasement. Instead he
sought victory, a peace gained by conquest.

Lawrence would probably not have recognized himself in this portrait, and it is extremely unlikely that he ever thought of himself as
anti-Christian. He would have agreed that he had a profound consciousness of guilt, but he would have wondered whether he was quite
so disinterested as Malraux believed, for it was precisely his lack of
disinterestedness in the war which precipitated his feelings of guilt. He
was far from being a knight errant; he had murdered and plundered
and taken part in a ferocious massacre of Turks when they were already
in full flight. He was not innocent: therefore he was guilty: therefore
he was damned. But the damnation of the tragic hero is never final.
"The Absolute," wrote Malraux, "is the supreme court of appeal for the
tragic man, the only efficacious one, because it alone can burn away—
even though the whole man burn with it—the deepest feelings of de-
pendence, the remorse of being oneself."
Malraux had much more to say about Lawrence, but the essence of

it was in that final paragraph where he conjured up the spectacle of the tragic hero wrestling with the angel, being defeated by the angel, and receiving the angelic benediction. The theme would be repeated in the novel he was writing, and in the last words of *The Voices of Silence* he would speak of the artists who alone know "the force and honor of being a man."

Visitors to Roquebrune were surprised to see him so much at ease. The defeat of France left him curiously untroubled, for there was simply nothing he could do. There was nothing to be gained by organizing a revolt against the Germans: the battle would be fought with tanks and airplanes on vast fronts spanning the entire continent. Jean-Paul Sartre, visiting Roquebrune in the late summer of 1941, having bicycled all the way from Paris, was astonished to find Malraux living like a young English lord in exquisite luxury. Josette Clotis was with him. Everything about the magnificent house suggested that there had never been a war, and indeed that war was unthinkable. Only a few weeks before the German armies had plunged into the heart of Russia.

Sartre had organized a small clandestine movement called "Socialism and Liberty." It was not a revolutionary movement, for it consisted of no more than about twenty people interminably debating the philosophical aspects of the war, whether they should engage in terrorism, and what platform the party should present to the people after the war was won. They decided against acts of terrorism, and no platform was ever prepared. While Sartre was outlining his ideas, Malraux listened politely in unaccustomed silence. Then he gave his own opinion. He said that for the time being action of any sort was quite useless; nothing would be gained, and too many Frenchmen would be killed. The war would be won by Russian tanks and American airplanes. Sartre, accustomed to more simple fare, remembered that they lunched on Chicken Maryland exquisitely prepared and served.

Other visitors came. Emmanuel D'Astier, diplomat and politician, aristocrat by birth and temperament although his sympathies were nearly always with the left—he had married the sister of a Soviet commissar—came with a similar invitation. He wanted Malraux to join his own clandestine movement, which was considerably more dangerous than Sartre's. Malraux had no intention of joining anyone else's movement, and Emmanuel D'Astier went away with the feeling that in due course Malraux would have his own revolutionary organization.

André Gide came and listened to Malraux reading from *The Struggle with the Angel,* and found himself quarreling with Malraux's strange syntax, his ambiguities and forced locutions. In Gide's eyes, Malraux wrote magnificently, but it was not French. It was a new language labeled "For the use of Malraux alone." Gide had enjoyed a classical education, with the result that he was very careful about grammar. Malraux, one of the few French writers of eminence without a classical education, was inclined to ride roughshod over elementary rules of grammar and syntax and had no feeling for the logical structure of a sentence. Reading the novel again some years later, Gide discovered that Malraux had paid no attention to his strictures; in revising the book, he had committed additional solecisms. Shaking his head, Gide observed in the tones of an elderly schoolmaster: "The excessive use of abstract terms is often prejudicial to the narration of action. One must not try simultaneously to make the reader visualize and make him understand."

Malraux could have answered: "Why not?" Wasn't this precisely what he was attempting to do, and very often succeeded in doing? Gide insisted on a classical clarity, the straight line, the nerve ends tied up tidily in little knots. Malraux, always an untidy writer, wanted to make the reader see, hear, know, feel, battle, rage. He was supremely indifferent to the rules of the game, and it could scarcely be otherwise, for he had grown up with Lautréamont, Max Jacob, Apollinaire, and the romantics. He wanted the reader to drown in the story, plunging him fathoms deep: he was closer to Dostoevsky than to Tolstoy. When Gide discussed exact grammatical constructions, he was speaking a language which Malraux had never understood.

Meanwhile Malraux continued to work on his novel, revising and polishing it. Occasionally he polished too well, as can be seen from some fragments translated by Haakon Chevalier into English, which show variations from the edition finally published in Switzerland. Malraux evidently omitted some rhetorical passages because he felt that they were too personal or too rhetorical; in fact, they were well suited to his theme and the work would have gained by retaining them.

So the days passed in writing and dreaming, while the war went on. Soon enough he would move away from the world of dreams into the world of action. But the novel written at Roquebrune would record an important stage in his progress. Though quite short, it covered a vast range of experience and intellectual effort. Just as it can be said with assurance that his *Vermeer* is the most beautiful book he ever edited, and that *Man's Hope* is his finest novel, so it can be said that this wartime novel contains his most mature reflections on life and is the book by which he will be remembered in generations to come.

⊸ The Walnut Trees of Altenburg ⊱

When the novel first appeared in Switzerland, it bore the title *The Struggle with the Angel*. Later, by a strange metamorphosis, it became *The Walnut Trees of Altenburg,* the name by which it is known to the comparatively few people who have read it. *The Struggle with the Angel* was a good title, for the theme was man's unending quarrel with divinity, Jacob wrestling with angelic forces. Divinity is revealed through works of art, but also through man's inalienable courage, his determination to wrest the fire from heaven. When the title was changed, there was no intention to suggest an abrupt change of focus, for, as we shall see, the walnut trees were as much symbols of a divine purpose as the apple tree in the concluding pages of *Man's Hope.*

The Struggle with the Angel was first published in Lausanne in 1943, and subsequently appeared in an *édition de luxe* of Malraux's complete works published by Skira in Geneva in 1945. Two years later it appeared in a collection of his novels published in Paris by the Bibliothèque de la Pléiade, and under the title of *The Walnut Trees of Altenburg* it came out in a limited edition published by Gallimard, who also publish the Bibliothèque de la Pléiade, in 1949. At the end of the book there was the ominous announcement, printed in capital letters: "This work will not be republished." Nor has it ever been republished. From time to time Malraux has said that he intends to rewrite the work, but in an introductory note to the 1949 edition he wrote that the Gestapo having destroyed a considerable part of the novel, it was unlikely that he would ever complete it.

All this is puzzling, because the novel is among his greatest achievements. The form of the work is a triptych, with the two outside panels describing wars and prison camps, while the central panel records a few days in the life of an Alsatian family called Berger and the wide-ranging discussions that take place in the house of old Dietrich Berger on the eve of the First World War. The hero of the novel is Vincent Berger, the narrator's father, a man who once dreamed of uniting Turkey with the Turkish tribes of central Asia. Throughout the book there are autobiographical overtones: Vincent Berger is evidently based on Malraux himself. In the opening scene he narrates his experiences in the prison camp and in the final scene he narrates his experiences in the days shortly before his capture. In these scenes there is very little fiction. For some reason Malraux chooses to have his prisoners in an internment camp at Chartres instead of at Sens, where he was himself interned. The account of the tank trap which comes at the end of the book is almost entirely autobiographical. But the meat of the book is a fictional evocation of scenes that take place in 1914 and 1915, on the eve of World War I and in the midst of battle. In this way the two wars confront each other. The effect is to produce an astonishing sense of balance, a pervading rhythm which flows backward and forward between the two wars. We are simultaneously in the present and in the past.

It is quite possible that Malraux hit upon this form by accident. The account of the camp appears to have been written while he was in the camp: it is charged with the atmosphere of a time and a place. The account of the tank trap may have been written about the same time, for it conveys the excitement of direct experience described while memory was still fresh, the wounds still aching. And while the central portion is fiction, it is nevertheless related to those other parts by the very nature of the two wars and by the continuing argument on the nature of man. It would appear that when the fictional account of the Bergers was completed, it seemed to lack a frame, and thereupon Malraux supplied the two autobiographical fragments at the beginning and at the end. They fit perfectly.

Like Goethe's *Dichtung und Wahrheit*, the work belongs to that category of books that are neither novels nor autobiographies nor essays, but are all of these. The mood is meditative and elegiac, the ancient Gothic past of Altenburg, a small town near Sainte Odile on the Alsatian borders of France, acting as a backcloth to the two wars.

Here, in Dietrich Berger's library, wise men deliberate on the miseries and splendors of man. Here Dietrich Berger dies by his own hand, and Vincent Berger, a German officer in the First World War, goes out from here to take part in a German gas attack on the Eastern Front. Here, too, Walter Berger asks the question that dominates the entire novel: "Does there exist any data on which we can base the concept of Man?"

As we might expect, the problem remains unsolved, for man is too variable, too complex, and altogether too destructive to fit neatly into any philosophical system. Nevertheless, the problem finds its solution on the edge of human understanding, in those regions of the spirit where the contemplative mind almost becomes the thing it contemplates. Quite suddenly Vincent Berger goes out into the fields for a breath of air. In the library they have been discussing the nature of art, and there has been some heavy discussion about two Gothic sculptures of saints and a rather pretentious ship's figurehead of Atlas, all carved out of walnut wood. These arguments still echo in his mind as he ponders the place of man in the universe, desperately seeking after certainties. Then he sees the trees:

> The sun was setting, kindling the red apples of the apple trees. Vain thoughts of orchards eternally reborn, which the same anguish always kindles like the same sun! Thoughts of long ago, thoughts of Asia, thoughts of this rainy and sunny summer day, so accidental, so unprecedented—like the white race of men seen in an evening of Marseilles, like the race of men outside the window of a dead man's room, the overwhelming and commonplace mystery of life in the restless light of dawn.
>
> He had reached the big trees: the fir trees already thick with night's darkness except for a single translucent droplet at the end of each needle; the lime trees rustling with sparrows; and the most beautiful were the two walnut trees. He thought of the statues in the library.
>
> The feeling of plenitude in the immemorial trees came from their bulk, and the bursting into dark leaves of this wood, which

was so heavy and so old that it seemed to be digging down into the earth and not wrenching itself away from the earth, compelled one to think simultaneously about its will power and about an endless metamorphosis. Between them the hills rolled down to the Rhine; they framed Strasbourg cathedral far off in the smiling twilight, as so many other trees framed other cathedrals in the meadows of the West. And that spire rising like the prayer of the maimed, and all the human patience and labor transformed into waves of vines descending to the river, were no more than the evening backdrop to the immemorial upsurge of the living wood, the two sturdy, gnarled trunks dragging the strength from the earth to display it in their branches. The setting sun cast their shadows across to the other side of the valley, like two broad furrows. My father was thinking of the two saints and of Atlas. Instead of supporting the weight of the world, the tortured wood of these walnut trees flourished with life everlasting in their polished leaves under the sky and in their nuts that were almost ripe, in all their venerable bulk, above the wide ring of young shoots and the dead nuts of winter. "Civilization or the animal, like statues or logs. . . ." Between the statues and the logs were the trees, and their design which was as mysterious as that of life itself. And the Atlas, and St. Mark's face consumed with Gothic fervor, were lost within it like culture, like the human intellect, like everything my father had just been listening to—all buried in the shadow of that indulgent statue which the powers of the earth had carved out for themselves, and which the sun at the level of the hills spread over the suffering of humanity to the far horizon.

When Malraux wrote in this way he was attempting to describe something close to a theophany. A god, a divinity, something far beyond normal human experience, had appeared in the vision of the two walnut trees in the setting sun, strong and everlasting. The intellectual conversations in the library fade away until they are no more than echoes; the trees remain, and beyond the trees are the mysterious powers of the earth, unnamed and unknown, fulfilling their destiny.

What Vincent Berger has seen in the walnut trees is perhaps not

very different from the ancient tree-worshipers' visions. There can be
no logical or intellectual explanation of their power or of their majesty. They exist, and it is enough that they are there; and beyond this
it is impossible to explore. These walnut trees evidently descend from
the apple tree seen in the Sierra de Teruel, and they proclaim the
eternity of man, and they do so by proclaiming the eternity of nature.

To the question: "Does there exist any data on which we can base
the concept of Man?" there comes the unexpected answer: "Yes, the
walnut trees of Altenburg."

This is not so strange as it may sound, for there is a sense in which
the trees are an extension of man. They have become visionary trees,
images of power and beauty, never to be forgotten by those who have
set eyes on them. It is precisely those images which give meaning to
man's journey on earth. "In this prison we draw images from ourselves
that are powerful enough to negate our nothingness," says Walter
Berger. The virtue of the walnut trees is that they negate man's nothingness.

In the course of the novel other images emerge, but these trees are
the most powerful and the most memorable. They are introduced
subtly. Möllberg, the ethnologist, with his habit of carving little
farfelu animals—squirrels with fins, birds of prey with simian bodies,
cat-faced penguins—has been dilating at some length on the walnut
wood that decorates the library, and while he is talking some workmen
can be heard dumping a load of logs that will ultimately be delivered
to the flames. Vincent Berger remembers the medieval woodsmen pil-
ing up logs in much the same way, and hints at an endless continuity.
Möllberg, with his brittle learning, laughs at the idea. He sees no continuity anywhere. "Those two Gothic statues and that ship's prow are
carved out of the same wood," he declares. "But beneath their forms
there is no ultimate walnut tree: there are only logs." Someone objects
that "logs" is merely a metaphor. Möllberg will not be placated by
metaphors. He has drunk his fill of life during his wanderings across
Africa, and his final conclusion, based on profound ethnological experience, is that man is best studied by observing the behavior of ants.
It is to escape Möllberg that Vincent walks across the fields in search
of his vision of the walnut trees.

It must be admitted that the argument is loaded in favor of Vincent.

Möllberg is something of a caricature; he is given two dimensions while Vincent is seen in the round. If the Baron de Clappique from *Man's Fate* were a little more meditative, and if he had traveled across Africa and written learned treatises on his studies, he would approximate to Möllberg. There is something in him of Frobenius, the German ethnologist who proclaimed the analogy between the development of civilization and that of plants; but there is also something of the young Malraux. He proclaims the law and pronounces his verdict, regarding himself as the greatest of all authorities on Africa and therefore a man of stature, the representative of German science at its best. This has not prevented him from indulging in spectacular ironies, as when he describes how he lost the manuscript of his book *Civilization as Conquest and as Destiny*. "The pages fell among the lower branches of a variety of trees between the Sahara and Zanzibar," he announces. "The conqueror bears the spoils of the vanquished." The conqueror is Africa. For Clappique the conqueror was China.

So with the other characters, the amorous Hermann Muller, the idealistic Edmé Thirard, and the altogether too courteous Count Rabaud: there hovers over them the faint odor of disingenuous caricature. They are ventriloquist's dummies, repeating arguments that Malraux had once entertained and since abandoned, or imitating the language of the celebrated conferences at Pontigny where the most learned men of France met to discuss life and destiny with a firework display of brilliance. As in all good stories, the best lines are reserved for the heroes, and we are never left in doubt who the heroes are. They are the members of the Berger family, or rather the male members of the family, for no women are ever permitted to appear. As soon as Vincent or Walter Berger begin to speak, the caricatures take to their heels.

The method serves its purpose, for the Bergers have important things to say and they resemble the heroes of Corneille's tragedies in that they like to occupy the center of the stage and to speak at great length. Also, they alone are permitted to have visions. Vincent, indeed, is credited with shamanistic powers, derived perhaps from his long residence among the Turkish tribes of central Asia. One day the narrator meets a Russian friend who has known Vincent.

"Do you know what a shaman is?" [the Russian asks.]

"A Siberian sorcerer?"

"Something more. Lenin was a great man, but not a shaman. Trotsky, though less great, is a shaman. Pushkin, Robespierre, Goethe? No shamans among them. But Dostoevsky, Mirabeau, Hölderlin, Poe—they were great shamans. There are also little shamans—Heine. Napoleon wasn't a true shaman; he believed too much in things. You find some shaman in geniuses and also, naturally, in idiots. Among us Russians you find more shamans than elsewhere. Well, the strength and the weakness of Vincent Berger lies in the fact that he is a little bit shaman."

Vincent, then, is a shaman in our own time, one of those men who can summon the birds and the beasts, disguise himself in the clothing of tigers or wolves, and communicate with spirits; or rather, since all these things are highly improbable in western Europe, he is a man endowed with strange and terrible powers, capable of entering into the heart of things, possessing a mysterious understanding of the forces that move the earth and the stars.

We come to know Vincent well, for Malraux has expended considerable care in describing him, and especially his adventures within the Young Turk movement, led by Enver Pasha. Vincent, a professor at the University of Constantinople, becomes the adviser of the Young Turks. He converts these argumentative students into a close-knit revolutionary organization capable of overthrowing the Sultan of Turkey; he accompanies Enver across the deserts of Cyrenaica during the war with Italy, supplies the Turkish guerrillas with weapons, and dreams of a Turkish empire stretching from Adrianople to northwest China, himself the prime mover and creator-behind-the-scenes of an empire greater than the Sultan had ever possessed. Why? "Because he possessed an urgent desire to escape from Europe, and also there was the summons of history, his fanatic wish to leave a scar on the earth, the fascination of a plan for which he was in no small part responsible, friendship and the comradeship of war."

These dreams pursued him even after the defeat of Turkey by the Italians and the Balkan war. He was searching for a country, and he would say: "If a man could choose his own country, it would be the one with the greatest clouds." By this he meant the greatest storms, those that sweep everything before them. He was not a humble man, for humility is not the mark of a shaman, and he rejoiced in his own legend.

There followed years of wandering in central Asia, for the time of action, he believed, had given way to the time for reflection, the quiet preparation for a new wave of conquest. Suffering from dysentery, he traveled across the Hindu Kush and wandered through Afghanistan. He was deeply sunburned, wore a thin, pointed beard which gave him a resemblance to a Persian prince, and, but for his blue eyes, passed for a native. One day in the bazaar at Ghazni a madman hurled himself at him. At that moment Vincent realized that the vast Turkish empire of his dreams would never come into being. At Port Said he met Enver, to whom he described his disillusionment, the hopelessness of the venture that had once seemed almost within sight. He then returned to France after six years absence. Five days after he reached Altenburg, his father committed suicide, leaving a strange note: "It is my formal desire that there will be no religious rites at my burial." What was strange was that the dying man in his last agony had vigorously crossed out the word "no."

No doubt the portrait of Vincent, the revolutionary shaman dreaming of bringing a new civilization to birth, derived partly from Malraux's own wanderings over central Asia and from his reading of T. E. Lawrence, and perhaps too from a sense of failure in Indochina. He was projecting himself across the whole of Asia, seeing himself vastly magnified, his failure all the greater because the dreams were so heavy with conquest. Vincent's dreams evaporated, the lightning struck and reduced him to ashes. He lived on, but he was no longer a shaman.

For Malraux the concept of the shaman, a certain kind of genius who has the power to tear aside the veils of the universe, was closely related to his concept of the artist. The greater the artist, the more he was in touch with the ultimate mysteries and the more lucidly he was able to depict them in painting, sculpture and poetry. In one of the finest passages of the novel Walter Berger describes how he was summoned to Turin to bring Friedrich Nietzsche back to Switzerland.

Nietzsche was quite mad, and it was necessary for his own safety that
he should be accompanied by friends. Overbeck, a dentist called
Miescher, and Walter Berger accordingly traveled with him in a third-
class carriage, and in the same carriage there was an old peasant woman
carrying a hen in a wickerwork basket. From time to time the hen
would peer out of the basket and the peasant woman would push it
back in again. Here Walter Berger describes what happened when the
train was going through the St. Gotthard tunnel:

> "The train entered the Gotthard tunnel, which had just been
> completed. In those days the journey through the tunnel took
> thirty-five minutes—thirty-five—and there was no light in the
> carriages, or at least there was none in third-class carriages. The
> rocking of the train in the dark, the smell of soot, the feeling
> that the journey would never come to an end. In spite of the
> clattering of the train, I could hear the hen pecking at the
> wickerwork basket, and I waited apprehensively. What would
> we do if Nietzsche suddenly grew violent in all this darkness?
>
> "And quite suddenly—you know, of course, that many of
> Friedrich's works remain unpublished—a voice rose in the dark,
> above the grinding roar of the wheels. Friedrich was chanting
> with perfect articulation, although when talking he always
> stammered—he was chanting a poem unknown to us, and it
> was his last poem *Venice*. I don't care very much for Friedrich's
> music. It is mediocre. But this chanting—by God, it was sub-
> lime.
>
> "He had finished long before we came to the end of the
> tunnel. When we emerged from the darkness, everything was
> as it was before. Exactly as it was before. The same wretched
> carriage, the same peasant woman, the same hen, the same
> workmen, the same dentist. As for us, we were stupefied. The
> mystery I was talking about—I never felt it so strongly. It was
> all so . . . fortuitous. And Friedrich was much more disturb-
> ing than a corpse. It was life—quite simply, it was life. An
> extraordinary thing had happened: the chant was as strong as
> life. I had just discovered something. Something important.

In the prison of which Pascal speaks, men have succeeded in
drawing from themselves an answer which, so to say, imbues
those who are worthy of it with immortality. And in that carriage . . .

"Yes, in that carriage, and sometimes afterward—I merely
say sometimes—the infinitudes of the starry sky have seemed to
me to be as far outshone by man as our pitiable destinies are
outshone by the starry sky."

This story about Nietzsche belongs to mythology. Nevertheless it was
a true story, for Nietzsche comes alive—that Nietzsche who concealed
his delicate, almost feminine features with a horrendous mustache.
Walter Berger claimed to have known him well, and letters in the
philosopher's handwriting were enclosed in glass cases in Berger's
library. Malraux, by inventing the story, was paying tribute to a man
who had deeply influenced him, not so much by his theories of
cosmology as by his theories of aesthetics. Nietzsche was to be counted
among the great shamans of the time. The title of Malraux's novel concealed a further tribute to Nietzsche, whose father had been the private
tutor of the four princesses of Saxe-Altenburg, living with them at the
castle of Altenburg.

There are moments when Walter speaks with the authentic voice of
Malraux. When he says, for example, that "the greatest mystery is not
that we have been hurled at random between the profusion of matter
and of the stars, but that in this prison we draw images from ourselves
that are powerful enough to negate our nothingness," then he is speaking in myths, the same myths on which Malraux has based his theories
of art. Yet, in that context, following immediately upon the story of
Nietzsche, the myth acquires relevance in our own time; for not only
the philosopher was singing in the dark tunnel. Those who sing in defiance of the stars are the true shamans, and those who are silent are
doomed.

A shaggy man whose beard somehow gives him the appearance of a
cat's paw wound in wool continues the argument on another level, for
he announces that the three great novels written for the reconquest of
the world were all by men who had been crushed by the world. The

three novels were *Don Quixote, The Idiot* and *Robinson Crusoe.* "One was written by Cervantes, a former slave, another by Dostoevsky, a former convict, and the third by Daniel Defoe, who was condemned to the pillory." They wrote about shipwreck, folly of grandeur, insanity; they were solitary men attempting to wrestle with the angel, inventing heroes who wanted desperately to return to the bosom of humanity. They, too, were singing in the tunnel.

But this was commentary: the work of the novelist is to suggest those images which are so powerful that they illuminate the human condition, and Malraux was well aware that this was demanded of him. The conference at Altenburg in June 1914 is followed by Vincent's experiences on the Eastern Front a year later during a gas attack so terrible that the German soldiers went out to rescue the Russians who had been gassed. The background is sketched in at some length. We are introduced to the sinister Professor Hoffmann, the scientist in charge of chemical warfare, who relishes this new weapon of destruction that will bring total victory to Germany. The gas, which smells of bitter almonds, acts almost instantaneously; it turns the cornea blue and the iris black; and no one who has ever breathed the gas ever recovers from it. Vincent Berger is horrified by Hoffman, and while the attack is being prepared he wanders along the trenches, listening to the disconnected, totally inconsequential conversations of the German soldiers waiting patiently for the moment for the attack to begin: the gas attack, and then their own advance. It is the Day of Judgment fraught with apocalyptic visions, and they talk about their wives, deal out cards, read silently or tell stories to one another as though it was a day like all the other days.

In a yellow cloud the gas pours over the valley, blotting out the world. A favorable wind carries it away from the German lines into the trenches of the Russians, while high overhead the birds fly in the pale blue summer sky. Suddenly, in the awful silence, a riderless horse dashes into the yellow cloud, neighing plaintively, and even when it has vanished into the cloud the German soldiers can hear the hoofbeats of the horse, which sometimes emerges briefly to taunt them with its beauty and irrelevance. The Russians pound the German lines with their heavy artillery; and red flames erupt through the cloud.

All this is related cleanly, as though by someone present. Then, when the full horror of the gas attack becomes apparent, there occurs an abrupt change of style. The lens becomes blurred: shapes of terror and disaster move across the landscape dissolving in the poison gas: and once more we are in the world of *Expedition to Isfahan,* a world of miraculous devastation. Out of this world, like Brocken specters, there emerge the German soldiers carrying the dying Russians on their backs because they cannot tolerate the sight of the death inflicted by the poison gas. The Russians are naked, for they have torn at their clothes, their lips are blue, their eyes are like lead pellets, and those who have still some life left in them are choking to death.

Vincent rides across the valley on horseback, aware that something terrible has happened, but unaware of the full extent of the devastation. The earth, too, has been poisoned. The trees are dead or dying, and the most living thing in sight is a long-dead tree. Like the German soldiers, he realizes that something worse than death is taking place, and against the evil let loose upon the world there is only one antidote: the sense of common humanity with the dying Russians. At all costs those who are still alive must be rescued and carried into the safety of the German lines. He loses his horse, stumbles blindly through a copse, watches stupefied while a naked Russian hops beside him like a bloated frog, and finally he finds a Russian who seems to be alive and carries him back to the German lines. Vincent has absorbed so much gas in his lungs that he falls unconscious, and we are left in little doubt that he dies a few minutes later.

Like the description of Nietzsche singing in the tunnel, this story is a myth; nothing remotely resembling it ever happened. Nevertheless, the myth has imaginative force and coherence. In terror and despair, writing with great power, Malraux sees the world given over to ultimate corruption, the poison gas playing the same role as the scorpions in *Expedition to Isfahan.*

The Walnut Trees of Altenburg is a flawed work only in the sense that *King Lear* is a flawed play. It is a tragedy in four acts, all the scenes taking place on a blasted heath; and though the scene changes from Chartres to Altenburg, to the Vistula and some abandoned corner of Flanders, they are all places of devastation and horror. There remains only the vision of the walnut trees and the knowledge that men can still save themselves by their pity for one another. *Man's Hope* was written when it was still possible to believe that there was something to hope for. A more appropriate title for *The Walnut Trees of Altenburg* might have been *Man's Despair.*

Yet even in the midst of despair there were seeds of hope. Once, in the library at Altenburg, old Walter Berger, still shuddering from the shock of his brother's suicide, had delivered himself of his own definition of man. "Man," he declared, "is what he conceals—a miserable little heap of secrets." It was not a definition which commended itself to Vincent, who replied: "No, man is what he makes."

Soon after finishing *The Walnut Trees of Altenburg,* Malraux left Roquebrune in the Free Zone and made his way secretly to German-occupied Toulouse. His intention was to make war against the Germans.

~§ *The Resistance Fighters* §~

By the spring of 1943 there were small pockets of resistance fighters scattered all over France. They were to be found especially in the mountains and in the wooded areas of the southwest. Most of them were ill-armed and ill-equipped, and very few of them were led by professional soldiers. They lived off the land, and sometimes raided food stores in the villages and attacked German convoys, and while they regarded themselves as the future saviors of France, the majority of the French peasants regarded them as bandits. They came to be known as *maquisards,* or collectively the *maquis,* which means "scrub land."

A certain Captain Kervenoael, one of the few professional soldiers to join the *maquis,* reported in the spring of 1943 that the total armaments in the possession of the resistance fighters in the Montagne Noire were sixty muskets, two rusty submachine guns, two grenades, forty-five revolvers and four rifles. There were several hundred men under his command, and he sometimes wondered what would happen to them if they were confronted with a well-armed German regiment.

The *maquisards* belonged to different political affiliations and fought for different ends: they were never brought under the control of a central directorate. If they had one single belief, it was that the Germans must be taught that they were not in complete command of the country. The political philosophy of the resistance fighters, though endlessly debated in the clandestine journals of the time, was never carefully worked out. Emmanuel D'Astier dreamed of bringing into being a single great revolutionary organization which would include Communists, Socialists, Catholics and trade union members, but the movement he led was never more than a small, rather haphazard

317

group of men loyal to himself. It was called *"Libération."* Other movements were called *"Franc-Tireur," "Temoignage Chrétien,"* and *"Combat."* By the end of 1943 there could be discerned two main groups: the Communists (*Franc-Tireurs-Partisans-Français*) and those who owed allegiance to General Charles de Gaulle (*Forces Françaises de l'Intérieur*). In theory the Communist group was incorporated in the FFI, but in practice they retained their independence and did very much as they pleased. They regarded themselves as the advance guards for the coming Communist political takeover.

In the spring of 1943 Malraux was in command of a small group of resistance fighters in the Corrèze. At first there were no more than a handful of men, but the numbers increased rapidly as the year advanced. Including the Communist groups there were said to be three thousand men under arms in December in the Corrèze, at a time when there were scarcely more than ten thousand armed *maquisards* in the whole of France. Malraux took the name of Berger, thus identifying himself with the family he had described in *The Walnut Trees of Altenburg.* As a pseudonym the name was remarkably ineffective, for although everyone called him Berger, everyone knew he was Malraux. He enjoyed giving new names to things, and so it came about that his resistance fighters came to be known as the *Corps franc de la Libération* (CFL), or the Free Corps of the Liberation. A more accurate description would have been Malraux's Sharpshooters.

Around him Malraux had gathered some of his close companions from the Escadre España, some Spaniards, a good many students from Alsace-Lorraine, and a stiffening of the local malcontents. Raymond Maréchal, who had been a machine gunner during the ill-fated bombing mission to Teruel at the end of 1936, was his second-in-command. He was one of those who walked away from the airplane that crashed near Mora de Rubielos, but his luck ran out in the Corrèze, where he was killed during a skirmish with the Germans. He was a reserve officer in the French air force, and was one of the few trained men in the Corrèze *maquis.*

For a while Malraux's command post was a château near the small village of Limeuil on the edge of the valley of the Dordogne. He lived quite openly in the château, with only a small bodyguard, and he traveled up and down the roads of the Corrèze as though there were no Germans within a hundred miles. Anyone who wanted to find him had only to ask one of the boys in Limeuil: "Where is the command post?" and he would receive the answer: "In the château." But if he was absurdly brave, he was not foolhardy, and he took the precaution of changing his headquarters from time to time. At various times many of the châteaux in the area became temporary command posts, and there were many days when he lay hiding in the woods.

One of the things that especially delighted him about this region was the prehistoric cave at Les Eyzies, where the first painting of a reindeer had been found eighty years before. The whole area was honeycombed with caves, which were used to store the ammunition of the resistance fighters. The most impressive of all the painted caves had been found at Lascaux by two boys in 1940, but it was not yet widely known; and Malraux wrote later of his excitement when he was making his way deep into the cave and saw the great painted bulls and bison high up on the walls, while below, on a shelf of rock, two machine guns stood guard on their tripods among containers of ammunition. No one had told him about those galaxies of long-horned bulls and bison caught in the loops of their own entrails, and he saw them for the first time by the light of his own flashlight. "It was like a flight of heraldic emblems," he wrote, and he was struck by the strange congruity of the savage beasts and the savage machine guns. The beauty of those caves haunted him, and it was always strange to come out of them at night, seeing the earth dark under the streaming stars, the Vézère River winding below, and here and there the small trees white with frost.

Originally Malraux had been sent out as a kind of inspector general of guerrilla forces. He had not expected to keep his post for long, for he had written a letter to General de Gaulle through an English friend in Marseilles, offering his services to the Free French in London. The letter was never delivered, because the woman to whom it was entrusted was arrested and she very sensibly swallowed it in the prison van taking her to jail. Malraux believed that De Gaulle would be able to find some use for him, and he was puzzled by the general's silence.

When he ceased being an inspector general of guerrilla forces and settled down in the Corrèze, there was never any question why he chose that rather desolate region of France for his operations. It was simply that the Corrèze was traditionally militant, and vied with Vercors in the Savoie in being the most hostile to the Germans. The Communist Party had made great inroads among the farmers, and there were whole districts under Communist domination. He had chosen a region where the resistance fighters were known to be ruthless and dedicated. Blowing up railroad lines was one of their chief pleasures.

Malraux's arrival was a signal for considerable rejoicing. He was known for his novels and for his legendary exploits in Spain. He seemed to be a man who had spent his whole life training to be a guerrilla chieftain. One of the resistance fighters who knew him well described the impact he made on the men around him:

> He made an indelible impression on us because he had a decisive mind and his strength of character was combined with great courtesy, an extraordinary facility of speech and a truly magnificent clarity. He was one of those personalities who stand out at first glance and whose luminous contours are never afterward forgotten.
>
> Physically, he was rather tall, lean, nervous, and suffered from a slight facial tic. Through his outward appearance there shone the inner fire that blazed in him. He might perhaps give the impression of being emotional, but however important the work he was doing he never allowed himself to be encumbered with superfluous details. No one had a clearer judgment, a greater sense of what was necessary, and a greater ability to make himself heard.
>
> He was lacking in personal ambition, but sometimes I would ask myself whether there was not a certain dilettantism in his way of handling men and things. Men of his class and writers of his importance have the habit of splitting themselves up into

two people, and so it happened that he became both the author and the actor in his own drama, behaving as though he and his men were characters in a play, and to his delighted amusement he was at once the inspired creator and the most detached spectator.

He had no illusions about the men surrounding him, and he employed them according to their value without the least regard to their rank or social position. This is how real leaders work.

The man who wrote this came from the working class and was bitterly opposed to the official Resistance leadership represented by Martial, the *nom de guerre* of De Gaulle's envoy. Malraux was able to arrange a settlement between them.

No one was left in any doubt that Malraux was in complete command in his own district; and when, as sometimes happened, there were quarrels among the leaders in the neighboring regions over territorial limits, he was usually called in to be the judge. These rivalries were constant, and perhaps unavoidable, but they poisoned the air. Usually he was on the side of the free corps against the official delegates of the Free French, who were anxious to prevent the Communists from becoming too powerful, but he absolutely refused to take up any political position. The war had to be won: afterward the political parties could fly at each other's throats.

The first serious blow against the Germans came on January 7, 1944, when his group blew up the arsenal at Tulle, putting it out of action so effectively that it never produced any more weapons. The explosives arrived by parachute drop from England. From about this time he was in continual touch with the secret British organization known as Special Operations Executive (SOE), which operated from London, working independently of the Free French. The SOE, which was directly under the British War Ministry, was responsible for some of the most daring acts of sabotage performed during the war. They had secret agents all over France. They did not always inform the French about what they were doing, and there was sometimes ill-feeling between De Gaulle and the SOE. Malraux was so closely allied

with the work of the SOE that he usually had a British officer with him
at his headquarters, which therefore became known as "allied headquarters."

It was a winter of tragedy and frustration, with the Germans still
riding high. If there had been some central accounting agency record-
ing the victories and defeats of the *maquis,* the figures would have
recorded few victories and innumerable defeats. A few powerhouses
were destroyed, some locomotives and rolling stock were rendered useless, and many factories were attacked with the result that their output
was reduced. They freed many men who were being sent in convoys to
Germany. But on balance, these were small successes. The *maquis* was
waiting for D-Day.

Meanwhile the best young Frenchmen continued to be killed. In
Corrèze German patrols sometimes fell upon groups of *maquisards* and
massacred them. Later, in the small graveyards, the women would wait
silently for the coffins, their heads unbowed. In these Communist villages the women had learned not to grieve and they uttered no
prayers.

So the long winter passed, and when spring came the *maquis* in the
Corrèze was stronger than ever, and better trained. They had their
bazookas and machine guns in the prehistoric caves, and they had
worked out a nearly perfect system of communication. At night they
were in radio contact with London, and by day they vanished into the
landscape. Then there would come a signal, and a small group of them
would make their way to the deserted hills to watch the manna falling
from heaven, the parachutes opening, the airplane disappearing in the
darkness a few moments later. At these moments they knew beyond
any doubt that the days of the German occupation of France were
numbered.

While Malraux commanded his growing army of resistance fighters
in the Corrèze, his two half-brothers, Roland and Claude, were also
fighting in the resistance movement. All their lives they had lived in
his shadow, worshiping him as only younger brothers worship older
brothers. In their eyes he could do no wrong. All they could ever hope
to do was to emulate him in courage and daring.

In 1944 Roland Malraux was thirty-one years old, tall, well built, almost preposterously handsome, with deep blue eyes and the manner of a young Viking prince. He had spent eighteen months in the Soviet Union and a year in Germany, and spoke English, German and Russian fluently. Women adored him, and for many years he kept a mistress who called herself Princess Galitsin. In 1943 his years of philandering came to an end with his marriage to Marie-Madeleine Lioux, the daughter of a textile manufacturer in Toulouse. She was a woman of grave beauty, a talented musician, who had studied at the Conservatoire de Paris and later with the formidable Nadia Boulanger. She was one of those calm and very gentle women who draw their strength from music and cast a spell on everyone around them. From this marriage there was born Roland's only son, Alain.

Like many wartime marriages, this one was very brief. Roland made his way to the Corrèze, contacted his brother, worked with him for a while, and then became the chief assistant of one of the many secret agents dropped by SOE into France. This was Harry Peulevé, a man of almost incredible skill and daring. He was parachuted into France in 1942 from such a low height that he broke his leg and was forced to hobble to Spain, where he was immediately interned in a concentration camp. He escaped, made his way back to France, and by October 1943 was in command of his own group of *maquisards* in the Dordogne. He was operating a secret radio from a house near Brive in March 1944. Everything was going well; parachute drops of weapons and equipment were arriving in increasing quantities, and the network was rapidly extending its influence.

A suspicious peasant living nearby observed the comings and goings of strangers to the house, and decided they were black marketeers. He denounced them to the police, who broke into the house on March 21 and found Harry Peulevé and Roland Malraux operating their secret radio. They were taken to Paris and thrown into Fresnes prison. Peulevé succeeded in escaping—this was the only known escape from Fresnes during the German occupation—but he was quickly recaptured. They were sent to a concentration camp in Germany. During the last days of the war Roland Malraux was released to the Swedish Red

Cross. He was on the ship *Cap-Arcona* when it was torpedoed off the
coast of Sweden. The rescue ship sank five days before the war came
to an end. There were a few survivors, but Roland Malraux was not
among them.

Claude Malraux, the younger brother, was only twenty-two in 1944.
According to Clara Malraux, who knew him well, he was one of those
"who pass without the slightest pause from the idea to the act." She
remembered one occasion when he was strolling through the Tuileries,
drew out a revolver, and fired several shots at a gardener's hut for no
better reason than that it amused him. He was then about twelve years
old. Obviously, he was destined for the army, and just as obviously he
would enter a regiment of Spahis serving in North Africa, because
their costumes are colorful and because North Africa offered more adventures than France. He was twenty years younger than André, but
he was determined to be equally famous.

Just as Roland worked as the second-in-command of a conspiratorial
group, so too did Claude. His chief was Philippe Liewer, a thirty-two
year old French journalist whose code name was "Clement." Claude's
code name was "Cicero." They worked in the neighborhood of Le
Havre, and their principal aim was to sink ships in the harbor and to
make life as intolerable as possible for the Germans who now commanded the port. This was desperately dangerous work without the excitement which comes from fighting the enemy in the open. Their task
was to destroy docks, ships, electric substations, transformers. During
the previous October they succeeded in destroying an electric substation
just outside Rouen, and they had sunk at least one ship in the harbor
at Le Havre. There were about 350 men in the group. At a very early
age Claude Malraux was learning to take command.

Suddenly in early March the police caught up with them, captured
their secret stores of weapons and ammunition, and destroyed the entire organization. From Rouen news of the arrests reached Brive, where
Roland Malraux and Harry Peulevé heard it. On their secret transmitter, known as *Mackintosh Red,* they sent the news that reached them
from northern France to the SOE headquarters in London. The de-
coded message with all its errors of transmission has survived. The
message reads:

TOR 1028   12TH MARCH 1944
BLUFF CHECK OMITTED   TRUE CHECK OMITTED

73 SEVEN THREE STOP
    FOLLOWING NEWS FROM ROUEN STOP XLAUDE-
MALRAUX DISAPPEARED BELGIVED ARRESTED BY
GESTAPO STOP RADIO OPERATOR PIERRE ARRESTES
STOP IF CLETENT STILL WITH YOU DO NOT SEND
HEM STOP DOFTOR ARRESTES STOP EIGHTEEN
TONS ARMS REMOVED BS POLIFE STOP BELEIVE
THIS DUE ARRESTATION OF A SEFTION FHEIF WHO
GAVE ASRESSES ADIEU

This was one of the last messages sent to London by *Mackintosh
Red.* Eleven days later the secret transmitter was captured. In a single
month both brothers became prisoners of the Gestapo and André Malraux never saw them again.

Long ago he had become accustomed to disasters: he had studied the
map of grief and knew every detail of it by heart. His father had committed suicide, his mother had died in 1933, he had sent many of his
friends to their deaths in Spain and in the Corrèze. Death was his
familiar companion, and he expected it daily.

June 6, 1944, was D-Day, when the Allies landed on the coast of
Normandy. On that day the SS Panzer Division *Das Reich* was still
stationed in the neighborhood of Toulouse, and it was not until the
following day that it received orders to join the embattled Germans in
the north. The task of the resistance fighters was to prevent the division
from reaching Normandy by cutting the railroads and constantly harassing it when it traveled along the main highways. Part of the division
marched through the Corrèze, and Malraux's free corps was in the
thick of the fighting.

As the Panzer Division marched northward, Malraux kept London
informed of its progress. Bulletins went out hour by hour, and in this
way he was able to inform them that the division had divided into two
main groups after reaching Brive: the lightly armed units making for

Limoges by way of Tulle and Oradour, while the heavy armor made
for Périgueux. North of Périgueux the railroad was in a comparatively
good state of repair, but there was only a single line. The exact time
when the trains would reach Libourne, Angoulême and Poitiers was
known, and thanks to the secret radio at Malraux's headquarters the
RAF was able to bombard the trains loaded with tanks at all these sta-
tions. An eyewitness report describes how the railroad lines were blown
up, the roads were cut, and huge rocks fell on the roadways just before
the tanks came into view. At Périgueux the surviving tanks formed a
ring around the city, for fear of an imminent attack by the Free French
forces, and at Brive part of the division surrendered to the French, who
thus came into possession of an immense quantity of weapons and
ammunition, later to be used by Malraux's Brigade Alsace-Lorraine.
The remnants of the SS Panzer Division *Das Reich* reached Normandy
seventeen days after D-Day. A man could have walked with ease from
Toulouse to Cherbourg in that time.

The *Das Reich* division did not cover itself with glory. At the small
village of Oradour-sur-Vayres, some twenty-five miles west of Limoges, a German company commander was killed by snipers. In retalia-
tion the Germans decided to punish the village, and on the following
day some SS troops were sent out to exact vengeance. They arrived
at Oradour-sur-Glane, another village fifteen miles from Oradour-
sur-Vayres, ordered the entire population into the village square, sent
the women and children into the church, shot down the men, and then
set the church on fire, while armed SS troops formed a ring around the
church to prevent anyone from escaping. The massacre at Oradour
took place on June 10, three days after the division had received its
marching orders. Some seven hundred women, children and men died
at Oradour on that summer day. The resistance fighters remembered
the massacre, and the fury of their attacks on the Panzer Division
owed much to their memories.

While Malraux remained in the Corrèze a rumor spread around
Paris that he was dead. The newspaper *Combat,* edited by Camus, denied the rumor in a front-page article on September 9, saying that he
was alive somewhere in the region of Limoges, after being wounded
and taken prisoner by the Germans. According to the newspaper, he

had slipped into Paris a few weeks before the liberation, and a friend, saying goodbye to him on the Pont Royal, heard him say: "*Il ne peut rien m'arriver. Je sortirai de là.* [Nothing can happen to me. I will come out of it]."

He was—and knew himself to be—indestructible. He was one of the very few.

❧ *Ambush* ❧

One day, toward the end of July, Malraux was driving along the road to Gramat after attending a conference between the Francs Tireurs and some British officers attached to SOE who were responsible for the parachute drops, when there occurred the event he had half expected for so long. It was a beautiful clear day, the warm sun striking hard against the earth, and the pennant with the Cross of Lorraine was flapping in the wind. With him was his bodyguard and a British officer, and the chauffeur was driving at high speed. They had been driving for three hours, and Malraux was dozing in the heat. No Germans were known to be in the vicinity of Gramat, and he thought it was as safe a journey as any he had undertaken.

Suddenly there was a burst of machine-gun fire, the back window of the car exploded, and the car, caught in the crossfire of two machine guns, toppled into a ditch. The chauffeur had a bullet through his head; in his last moment his foot had pressed down on the brake. The bodyguard was dead, slumped over his weapons. The British officer succeeded in climbing out of the car, and was immediately shot down. Malraux had a glimpse of him holding his blood-red hands to his stomach.* The firing continued, seeming strangely inappropriate in the quiet countryside. Malraux had escaped from the car unhurt, and he was invisible to one of the machine gunners because the car was in the way, but the other machine gun opened up on him, and he was

---

* The British officer was Captain George Hiller, who was left for dead. He was found some hours later by the *maquis,* who summoned a doctor from Cahors to operate on him. He recovered and later took part in other operations on French soil.

wounded in the right leg. Another wound in the left leg, and he became unconscious.

When he woke up a few minutes later, his legs had been roughly
bandaged by two German soldiers and he was lying on a stretcher.
Since he was in full uniform, there was no question of shooting him out
of hand. Instead, he would be given over to the intelligence officers of
the Wehrmacht, who had singularly drastic ways of extracting information from their captives. The two German soldiers accompanied
by a noncommissioned officer carried him along the road to Gramat,
which seemed endlessly far away, though it was only a few miles from
the place where the car had fallen into a ditch. During the journey to
Gramat Malraux could reflect that his three companions were perhaps
lucky in being dead, for he could expect no kindness from his captors.

In Gramat he saw the tanks lined up in the street. A section of the
Das Reich division had rolled into the town only a few hours before,
and the whole district was in the hands of the enemy. There were German soldiers everywhere: no possibility of escape. He was taken to a
barn, where he was interrogated by a German officer who claimed to
be an army chaplain. An unctuous man who incongruously resembled
Buster Keaton, he kept saying: "Such a pity for your family," pronounc-
ing the word *dommage* (pity) in the German way: *tommage.* Then
the officer left, and Malraux, still lying on the stretcher, his wounds
bleeding profusely, found himself quietly contemplating the fact of his
approaching death. No bones had been broken, and he would not die
of his wounds. He thought he would die under torture or before a
firing squad, and he was exquisitely curious. A few minutes later he
was ordered to leave the barn. He could still walk, though painfully
and with great difficulty. In the yard outside the barn soldiers were
lined up to form a firing squad. He was ordered to stand with his face
against a wall, arms flung upward. He did this, and then thought better of it, swinging round to confront the soldiers whose rifles were
trained on him. Suddenly there was the order: "Present arms!" It was
the traditional salute to a condemned prisoner, and was followed by
the order: "Aim!" Once more the firing squad was aiming at him.
Finally there came the command: "At ease!" The charade played by an

amused noncommissioned officer came to an end and the soldiers wandered away to amuse themselves with other games.

Unlike Dostoevsky, who had been acutely aware of the infinite value of every passing moment while he faced a firing squad, Malraux had absolutely no awareness that his life was in danger, no feeling that death was imminent. All the circumstances pointed to instant death, and there was not the least doubt that the noncommissioned officer was capable of cold-blooded murder. In his novels Malraux had invented many executions, living them as he wrote them, playing the roles of the executioners and of the condemned men until he knew them intimately. He was a connoisseur of sudden death: long before he faced the firing squad he had explored the landscape of death, the geography of executions. Step by step, heartbeat by heartbeat, he had followed the men who were to be executed by the Fascists on a hill outside Toledo; he had seen them through the eyes of Hernandez, the proud Spanish Republican officer who disdained to escape from the long line of prisoners marching to their certain death. No one had ever described a mass execution so relentlessly, with such fierce and despairing logic. But in the farmyard at Gramat it was precisely this logic that was lacking. Germans do not shoot a French officer until they have extracted all the information he can give them. Appropriate rituals were performed in the farmyard, but many other rituals had been omitted: inquisition, torture, sentence. Officers condemn officers, and a German noncommissioned officer, however brutal, rarely assumes responsibilities above his rank. All this was known to Malraux from long experience of fighting Germans. In a strange mood of resignation and perplexity, thinking of the three dead men on the roadside, he walked back into the barn.

There followed days so fantastic, so filled with the naked comedy of *farfelu,* that afterward he could scarcely believe that he had lived through them. He was taken into a cellar, and knowing well the German habit of torturing their victims in cellars, he expected the worst. Nothing happened. Like the Seven Deadly Sins wandering blindly through the enchanted forest, his German guards seemed to blunder from one place to another. They left the cellar and took him to another farm house, locked him in a shed, and then moved back again to the center of the small town, taking him to the Hotel de France, which he knew well enough because the *maquis* had its post-box there. There, in a small room, began the first serious interrogation. The officer resembled a red-headed sparrow, while the soldier who acted as secretary, taking the interrogation down in shorthand, resembled a haricot bean.

There were to be many more interrogations during the following days, and all of them were oddly farcical, comic and menacing by turns. The questions were the obvious questions, the answers were logical and exact, and therefore all the more unintelligible to the German officers, who could not understand anything so simple as a novelist in command of an army of French *maquisards*. Malraux had only to tell them the truth to put them in a quandary: the truth was not credible. He admitted to being Lieutenant Colonel André Malraux, *alias* Colonel Berger, who had lectured on art at the universities of Marburg, Leipzig and Berlin, and whose novel *The Conquerors* had won a certain acclaim in Germany. He claimed to be the military commander of the region, taking orders from De Gaulle, in possession of a hundred German prisoners of war. When asked the location of his command posts, he reeled off a list of abandoned châteaux and clearings in the woods, knowing that they were no longer being used, and when asked the names of the leaders of the *maquis* groups he supplied them, knowing that they had no names, only pseudonyms, which were known to the Gestapo and the Milice, the French police force that worked for the enemy. A dossier was being compiled, the same questions were being asked interminably. Still lying on a stretcher, he saw his interrogators from below and was more aware of their legs than of their faces. He had a floor-eye view of the world, and it amused him to note how people walking across the floor stepped in the blood dripping from his wounds and left bloody trails across the room.

The German interrogators scarcely knew what to do with him, but their uncertainty was part of a larger uncertainty: they scarcely knew what they were doing in this corner of southwestern France. The Allied landing in Normandy had taken place seven weeks before, and they were likely to be completely cut off from their homeland. Meanwhile they were determined to exact retribution from a rebellious people. The Germans at Gramat received orders to send him to the south in an armored car, and through the small barred window he saw the smoke rising from burning villages.

It was country he knew well: the country of the Romanesque churches and simple pieties. The armored car drove through Figeac, where his friend Roger Martin du Gard had lived, and Villefranche-de-Rouergue, where he had filmed a brief scene incorporated in his film of the Spanish Civil War. Here they halted for the night, and Malraux was put up in the old Carthusian convent with an armed guard stationed at the door. He asked the Mother Superior to lend him the Gospel according to St. John, not that he was a Christian, for he had never held any faith, but because, knowing that he might soon be killed, he felt an obscure need to read about the origins of a religion which had covered the earth with so many admirable churches and brought into being so many paintings and sculptures. He thought of death, and the scorpions of Isfahan, and wondered why his chauffeur had been killed with bullets in the head, while he survived with bullets in his leg. St. John seemed very distant that night, but the music of Christianity was alive in the small room. It occurred to him that his life was one of those human adventures which Shakespeare justifies by calling them dreams, though they are not dreams; and beyond Shakespeare there was Christ, the love that is stronger than death and stronger than justice. But it was not love so much as fraternity that he had been seeking, and he found it in the Mother Superior with her mysterious smile of benediction.

They drove south—always south. They passed through Albi, Castres, and Revel, where he was put up in a deserted villa and allowed to wander in the garden. On the following day he was taken to the headquarters of the local garrison forces, another château set in a park, with a lot of automobiles in the driveway. He had been blindfolded when he entered the car, and when the blindfold was removed and he saw the automobiles, he feared the worst. There would be one last interrogation, a brief court martial, and he would be shot. But once inside the château he heard music coming from the ballroom.

German officers were dancing with their women, those "gray mice," the female auxiliaries. It was the supreme irony: instead of a court martial, there was a dance.

Taken to a large room, the french windows overlooking a park and a quiet summer lake, he was confronted with a German general sitting behind a Louis XV desk. The general looked like a caricature of all German generals: dark glasses, a face like a skull, the Iron Cross with oak leaves. The general wanted to know what the *maquisards* hoped to accomplish, and Malraux explained that their very existence was a guarantee of the survival of France. Whether victors, vanquished, killed, or tortured, they were France, and would endure; and Germany would endure; and they would fight again, the two countries that were destined to be adversaries, because they could not be torn from the map of Europe. The general had nothing but disdain for Russia, England, and America. "The brutes of the East, and the salesmen of cars and canned food who have never known how to wage war, and England led by that Shakespearean drunkard!" It was as good an introduction to a German general's mentality as one could hope for, but the long-drawn argument answered none of the questions uppermost in Malraux's mind. He wanted to know what they were going to do with him, and what it was like to die. He was taken back to the villa at Revel with its carnation beds in the small garden. Revel is famous for its peppermint liqueurs. It did not seem to be a proper place to die in.

The next day the strange journey continued. Once more there was the armored car, the guards, the sense of impending doom. Instead of continuing south, the armored car swung east to Toulouse, where he had spent many days while making the Spanish film. Here his prison was a bourgeois living room overlooking one of the main squares; he could see the couples strolling outside. If the armored car signified that he was an important prisoner, what was the significance of his new prison? They offered him ham and eggs and a bottle of Bordeaux, and later took him to a luxury hotel, an ominous and unexpected change of residence, but on the following day he was thrust in St. Michel Prison. It was as though the Germans wanted to demonstrate to him all the various kinds of real estate in their possession. He might have guessed that prison was waiting for him at the end of the road.

Like all French prisons, St. Michel resembles a fortress built at a time when architects had forgotten how to build fortresses. Dark, ugly, and sinister in peacetime, it was no darker or uglier in wartime—but it was far more sinister. The prison had become a way station for convoys to be sent to Germany, a torture chamber, an execution ground. The bath torture was the one most commonly employed; the savage beatings provided the Gestapo officers with their daily exercise. The men for the convoys were selected at random. It was Kafka's world, the world of the concentration camps. No one knew from day to day who would be taken out, shot, beaten, tortured or transported to Germany. Malraux spent more than three weeks in the prison.

He was not placed in a cell but in a room with about a dozen prisoners; the barred windows were blocked up with boxes, and only a frail vertical light entered the room. The grapevine brought continual news, much of it dubious: Malraux was able to bring them the news that Caen and Saint-Lô had been taken by the Allies. This news was nearly a week old, yet it came as a surprise to the prisoners, whose sources of information were to be found largely in their imaginations. They lived in squalor, almost in apathy, waiting for their sentences. Every evening at six o'clock there would be footsteps in the corridor, the door would be unlocked, and a name or several names would be pronounced. Interrogation, torture, trial? They were marched off with their hands handcuffed behind their backs.

The day came when Malraux's name was pronounced. He was marched off and taken to a kind of guardhouse transformed into bedlam, where people were being beaten into pulp and a soldier was hammering sheet iron to drown the cries of the tortured. It was a scene straight out of Goya. In the midst of this inferno of noise and blood and naked bodies, a blond, curly-headed German officer sat behind a desk examining a dossier. Shouting above the din, the officer interrogated him. Had he spent eighteen months in the Soviet Union and a year in Germany? Was he thirty-three years of age? Was he the son of Fernand Malraux, deceased? Suddenly Malraux realized that the officer was talking about someone else. He was forty-two, and in the past ten years he had spent less than three months in the Soviet Union. The dossier was not his, but his brother's, for it was Roland, the son of Fernand Malraux by his second wife, who had spent eighteen months in the Soviet Union and a year in Germany. The curly-headed officer with the small tight features was confronted with the military intelligence report obtained at Gramat and another report obtained from Gestapo headquarters in Paris, and no amount of juggling could make the reports agree.

"We'll have to start all over again from the beginning," the officer said in despair, dismissing him.

Malraux was escorted back to his room in the prison, where he shared the good news with the other prisoners.

"Match postponed," he said. "They had the wrong dossier."

There was no further duel between them, because on the following day the Germans began to evacuate Toulouse. If the right dossier had arrived, Malraux would almost certainly have had the unenviable distinction of being the last prisoner shot by the Germans in Toulouse. He owed his life to an administrative error.

All through the night of August 18, 1944, the Germans blew up the buildings they had occupied in Toulouse, destroyed papers, set fires, and began their long disorderly march out of the city. When the firemen arrived to put out the fires, German engineers stood by with axes and cut the hoses, poured gasoline on the flames, and prevented anyone from going near the burning buildings. They were the splendid Firemen of Massacre, who enjoyed flames for their own sake. All through the following day, while the fires sank down, Toulouse was covered with a blanket of charred paper.

In the St. Michel prison, no one knew what was happening. The prisoners heard the explosions and thought they were an air raid. Suddenly the prison doors were opened, and everyone was ordered to go below, "with your belongings." In the past that meant being sent to Germany, but no one knew what it meant now. Five hundred prisoners were herded into an enormous room, each with his small bundle. Against the theory that they would be taken to Germany was the fact that the railroad lines had been blown up by the *maquisards,* and it was inconceivable that so many men would be taken by truck across the whole length of France. Some thought they would be massacred, for it does not take many machine guns to massacre five hundred men. Finally, they were all ordered back to their cells. The prison was on the evacuation route, and they heard the grinding noise of the tanks and trucks moving past. Later they heard something they never expected to hear: women were in the prison courtyard singing the *Marseillaise.* They had been standing outside the prison, watching the Germans, and when the last of them had left they rushed in and took the prison by storm. It was like something out of the French Revolution or Alexander Dumas' novel *Georges.* Everyone was shouting. People were running up and down the corridor shouting: "Come out! Come out!" But the cells were locked, no one could find the keys, and suddenly there came the booming of an immense wooden gong, signifying to all the prisoners that the time had come to break down the doors with whatever was available.

In Malraux's room there was a heavy table, dating probably from the Second Empire. Using the table as a battering ram, the prisoners forced the door and ran out into the corridor. Because he alone among the prisoners was still wearing a uniform, or because the prison grapevine had come to know him well during the three weeks of his imprisonment, there were cries of *"Malraux au commandement!"* He climbed up on a packing case, called for doctors, posted sentries, sent a search party out for ammunition—they found sixty German hand grenades—and placed the prison in a state of preparedness in case the Germans should return. The packing case in the courtyard had become a command post.

From the prison towers the sentries kept watch, under orders to whistle at the first sign of any Germans. The whistle came: nine German tanks were rumbling up the road. The tanks could easily break down the prison gates and mow down the prisoners with their guns. Guards were posted at the gates to hurl hand grenades at the tanks the moment they broke through, but there was no need. The tanks, the last stragglers of a large army, vanished down the road.

In Toulouse the resistance was over and the offensive had begun.

The Independent Brigade Alsace-Lorraine

Among the most dedicated and determined of the resistance fighters were the young men from Alsace-Lorraine. Most of them spoke German, and they were therefore especially useful in the *maquis,* where their knowledge of the German mentality could be put to good use. They cross-examined prisoners, and on occasion they could pass themselves off as German soldiers, infiltrate the enemy ranks and act as saboteurs. There were five or six hundred of them in and around Toulouse, while thousands more were scattered all over France.

When Malraux left the prison of St. Michel and returned to the Corrèze, he learned that the German garrison at Tulle had surrendered to his successor, that his radio connection with London was still operating, and that the young resistance fighters from Alsace-Lorraine were hoping to form an independent brigade of their own to take part in the reconquest of their own land. The chief spokesmen for the independent brigade were Bernard Metz, a young doctor from Strasbourg, and Father Pierre Bockel, later to become one of the three chaplains of the Brigade Alsace-Lorraine. They were absolutely determined to have their own brigade, and Malraux, who had watched the men from Alsace-Lorraine in his own group, and was sometimes alarmed by their ferocity, did everything he could to help them. Men from Alsace-Lorraine had been in the forefront of the fighting against the Panzer Division *Das Reich,* cutting up the enemy all the way from Toulouse to Périgueux and beyond, and if they wanted an independent brigade, there were good psychological reasons why they should be permitted to have it. There was another reason why he sympathized with these young men. He had come to regard himself as a kind of

339

honorary citizen of Alsace-Lorraine by virtue of *The Walnut Trees of Altenburg.*

But it was one thing to want such a brigade and another to bring it into existence. The Free French headquarters in London were supremely indifferent, and a radio message to General Koenig, the commander of the *Forces Françaises de l'Intérieur,* remained unanswered. It therefore became necessary to have recourse to certain subterfuges. These included a forged radio message from General Koenig and a certain amount of deliberate arm-twisting. Malraux, Metz and Jacquot, who was Malraux's second-in-command, descended on Toulouse, sought out General Bertin, the recently appointed commander of all the Free French forces in the southern zone, and received permission to form the brigade. It was decided that a regular army officer of impeccable Alsatian lineage should be placed in command. This officer was then in London, and orders were given that he should be parachuted into southwestern France. Instead he was parachuted into the Vosges mountains, where his mistress was operating a secret radio. Suddenly it occurred to Metz that there was no particular advantage in having an Alsatian commander. He had long admired Malraux, whose novel *Man's Hope* he knew by heart. It had been his first introduction to revolutionary warfare and he regarded the novel with something of the same reverence with which a priest regards his Bible. He had not read *The Walnut Trees of Altenburg,* and it was only much later that he came to realize that Malraux had been conducting a love affair with Alsace-Lorraine for some time. There was another matter that weighed heavily with him. He detested the parochialism of Alsace-Lorraine and thought the time had come for a change. When it became clear that the original officer selected for the task was not going to be parachuted into southwestern France, he asked Malraux to become the commander. The appointment was sanctioned by the authorities in Toulouse, and thus there came into being the Independent Brigade Alsace-Lorraine.

Although this was the name by which they liked to be known, the claim to independence was dubious. The brigade was firmly attached to the French Army, and had no more independence than any other brigade. What it had was a certain style, an informality in keeping with its colonel, and a ferocious determination to rid Alsace-Lorraine of its German conquerors. It was sometimes known as "The Gangster Brigade of Colonel Malraux," and in more affectionate tones "The Very Christian Brigade of Colonel Malraux." Although Malraux still maintained the *nom de guerre* of Berger, nearly all the official documents give his real name.

André Chamson, the novelist and short story writer, was at this time active in the resistance around Toulouse, with his own followers, most of them from Alsace-Lorraine. He was one of those men who perform many roles simultaneously, for he was also inspector general of the museums of France and one of his most important assignments had been to hide the great treasures of the Louvre in the châteaux of the Lot, the Dordogne and the Corrèze, where the Germans would be unable to find them. Earlier in the war he had served briefly on the staff of General Jean de Lattre de Tassigny, and when France fell the general suggested that Chamson should accompany him to Africa. Chamson, however, preferred to stay in France, and arrangements were made that if ever he was in great danger General de Lattre de Tassigny would attempt to rescue him. They were on close terms; Chamson's work for the museums was important; and although he was often in danger, there was never any occasion when he felt that the coded message would have to be sent.

When General de Lattre de Tassigny landed at the head of the French First Army near Toulon on August 15, together with a vast Allied force which began to march up the valley of the Rhône, Chamson remembered that he had a claim on the general and he knew exactly what he wanted—enough trucks to carry his men across France so that they could join the French First Army. He met the general in Aix-en-Provence, drove forty borrowed trucks to Montauban, and filled them with his men. A short while later he met Malraux, who said: "We are going the same way, why don't we go together?"

Chamson agreed. He had four hundred men in his trucks, and there was Malraux's larger army. Somehow they all got into the trucks and roared across France, fighting off several companies of guerrillas who attempted to waylay them and use the trucks for their own purposes. For the next six months Malraux and Chamson were very nearly inseparable, taking their meals together, poring over maps together, and sleeping in the same farmhouses. With his high forehead and heavy triangular jaw, Chamson looked like a skilled mechanic; he had one of the keenest brains in France; and the two men were perfectly at ease in each other's company. They reached the French First Army between Mâcon and Autun. The Brigade Alsace-Lorraine was swollen with still more men from Alsace and Lorraine flocking from all the corners of France.

"So here is Chamson, who swiped forty trucks from me," General de Lattre de Tassigny commented at Autun. "He promised to bring me a battalion, and I hope he hasn't brought me forty good-for-nothings."

"General, I have brought you 2,400 men."

"Good. You're in command?"

"No, a Colonel Berger."

"There is no Colonel Berger in the French Army."

"Yes, but there is a Colonel André Malraux in French literature."

In these polite terms General de Lattre de Tassigny learned of the existence of the Brigade Alsace-Lorraine, which was to serve under him for the rest of the campaign. He also learned that in spite of its name the brigade was being led by three men who had not an ounce of Alsace or Lorraine blood among them. They were Malraux from Flanders, Jacquot from the Vosges and Chamson from the south of France. Only Jacquot was a professional soldier.

There were three batallions to the brigade, and they were predictably named after the three most important cities in Alsace-Lorraine: Metz, Strasbourg, and Mulhouse. Only the Strasbourg battalion had come from the southwest. The Metz battalion came from Aquitaine and the Mulhouse battalion was made up of men who had been fighting in the *maquis* around Belfort.

While the Strasbourg battalion was on the way to the front line, Father Pierre Bockel caught up with them. He was to become their chaplain and one of Malraux's closest friends, but their first encounter was curiously strained. In the first place Malraux did not look like a regular officer, though he wore the regulation uniform with the proper elegance, permitting himself only one luxury—instead of the regulation cap he insisted on wearing a black beret. He looked very young, very tired, and the facial tics were very pronounced. He spoke coldly, dryly, without fire. Father Bockel was shocked. He had expected to see the legendary Malraux, the man on the barricades, but instead there was a cold intellectual who chose his words carefully and appeared totally uninterested in his visitor. Father Bockel ruefully remembered the words of André Gide: "In the presence of Malraux one does not feel very intelligent."

A few days later he encountered Malraux again near the headquarters of General de Lattre de Tassigny at Besançon. As they walked together along the Rue du Lycée, Father Bockel saw an altogether different Malraux. This time there was the man of the barricades, and the glowing fire. He was speaking about his affection for the men of Alsace-Lorraine, all young, all refugees determined to reconquer their homeland. What he admired in them most was their absolute determination, their ferocity. He was talking largely in religious terms, and indeed his attitude to his men was deeply religious. He spoke of "what is eternal in man" and "a man's will to subordinate himself to something that is greater than himself." He spoke of himself as "an accomplice in a heroic adventure," and he liked to use the word "complicity," which suggested a kind of medieval compact with the forces of righteousness against the forces of evil. Father Bockel suspected that Malraux regarded his present position as the logical consequence of the years he had spent in clandestine activity. Now everything was in the open and it was no longer necessary to live in fear of Germans. Now they could be fought openly, and eventually thrown back beyond their own borders.

They went out to dinner in a small restaurant in Besançon. Jacquot and Chamson were present, and at first there was polite banter and the normal pleasantries of the dinner table. Malraux was *très grand seigneur*, very much at his ease. He laughed and joked, and told stories about the ruthlessness of his men. He enjoyed their "savagery" and delighted in the picturesque details of their exploits. Chamson, a brilliant story writer with a profound knowledge of the arts, told stories as well as he wrote them, and if Jacquot was a little pontifical he was a good foil for the others. Father Bockel was beginning to regard his dinner companions as a little larger than life, and their conversation reminded him of "a salon, a circus, and an arena." Then, while the dinner was still in progress, there began the inevitable monologue by Malraux who had caught a half-finished sentence by one of his companions in midair and proceeded to toss it up to the skies. Father Bockel was not yet accustomed to those breathtaking monologues, although he knew André Gide's opinion of them. Fantasy, logic, passion and erudition kept the balloon bouncing on the wall of heaven, as Malraux examined one by one all the extraordinary consequences of the half-finished sentence. The words took wings, life flowed into his improvisations, and suddenly the argument would take off in another direction entirely. History, with its heavy tread, marched alongside the argument, and the Future opened out its welcoming arms. The Abstract became concrete, almost it came running into the room. For Malraux, it was merely a simple exploration among ideas, while for Father Bockel, who remembered the cold impassive intellectual of a few days earlier, it was a revelation, for he recognized the human warmth and the desperate uncertainty that lay behind so many affirmations. When the dinner came to an end, Father Bockel felt that he knew Malraux as well as he knew any man.

This dinner took place about the middle of September. A few days later the Brigade Alsace-Lorraine marched up to the front lines.

There had been a time when Malraux had hoped that the brigade would go through a period of training. In the *maquis* they had fought with revolvers and hunting rifles; now they had bazookas and machine guns and were supported by tanks and heavy artillery. It was a new kind of fighting and they were not accustomed to it. But there was no time for training them, and they had to learn while fighting.

On September 26, five weeks after his release from the St. Michel prison in Toulouse, Malraux was at his headquarters in Froideconche when he received orders to send a company of his men into action on the following day. Few of his men wore uniforms. Some of them wore only shirts, shorts and sandals, and they were without helmets. During the afternoon and evening of the following day the brigade received its baptism of fire. The enemy was solidly entrenched in the wooded heights, the brigade was in the marshy lowlands, and everyone knew that the enemy would not be dislodged easily. Mist covered the hills, and a freezing rain fell. The company went into action and fought against a heavily fortified post of young German officers from the officers' training school at Colmar. Five Frenchmen were killed and six were wounded. When the bodies were recovered, they were seen to be wearing shorts, and instead of helmets they wore blue *képis*. On the morning of the next day the mist cleared, and for the first time they saw the shape of the hills facing them under the lowering skies.

For nearly two weeks the brigade attacked the hills known as Bois-le-Prince. When helmets arrived at last, a man from Lorraine, Captain Peltre, went up the line to distribute them and was killed, together with four machine gunners. Jacquot was wounded three times in five days, and became known in consequence as "the sieve." The young Germans on the heights were well supplied with mortars; the brigade was well supplied with machine guns. The French fought from their waterlogged dugouts clearly visible among the pools and lakes, while the enemy was well concealed in the woods. Sometimes, when the heavy artillery was brought up, the whole hill seemed to burst into flame, but afterward the Germans were still there.

Sometimes Malraux would gather some of his men around him to explain the purpose of the attack on the hill and outline the battle positions. Once, after an unusually brutal engagement, he said: "Gentlemen, I salute our dead of yesterday, and I salute those among you who will die tomorrow." Father Bockel, who was present, wondered whether any other officer in the French army would dare to address his men in this way.

At the height of the battle, when the hills shook with explosions and the air was full of the whistling of shells, a lean dark silhouette would sometimes appear in the forward positions. It was a familiar silhouette, for even those who had never before set eyes on him recognized him by the black beret and the cigarette dangling from the corner of his lips. He had come to make his own appraisal of the situation; he would give orders; then, in silence, he would gaze in the direction of the enemy as though daring them to shoot him. There was something almost suicidal in these appearances in the front lines, for he refused to take cover, and they wondered whether he was not tempting death too hard. They remembered, too, that when he gazed in the direction of the enemy, there was not the slightest expression of hate, and he seemed to be searching for something.

On October 7 the last outposts on the crest of the hill were taken by storm with the help of some Moroccan troops, and they reached the Moselle. The cost was heavy. "The forests," as General de Lattre de Tassigny wrote in one of his reports, "eat up the infantry," and during the entire engagement they had been fighting over forested hills. Three days later the brigade was withdrawn from the front lines and went into camp at Remiremont. At the beginning of November a new camp was set up in the Haute-Saône, and there they rested, while General Leclerc and the Americans slashed their way through the outer defenses of Strasbourg, and then in a series of quick maneuvers captured the city before the Germans were aware that it was in danger. The city fell on November 23, and there was a hurried parade to honor the occasion. For the French this was a victory above all other victories, to be remembered with gratitude during the long months of battle in front of them.

About this time Malraux suffered the worst blow he had ever suffered. Josette Clotis, the mother of his two young sons, Pierre-Gauthier and Vincent, both born during the war, was killed in a railroad accident. She had gone to the railroad station to put her mother on the train, but they were late and there was only just time to settle her mother in the seat when she had to jump hurriedly off the train. She slipped on the icy platform and fell under the wheels. She was still alive when they carried her to the hospital at Brive, but died a few hours later.

Her death was not announced until a few days later. On December 2, 1944, *The New York Times* had a short paragraph announcing the death of Madame André Malraux while her husband was fighting in the Vosges mountains.

A grief never dies. It has a strange life of its own, throws out many branches, and many bitter fruits. He would speak of "this old earth gorged with the dead," and there was scarcely a moment of his life when he was not aware of death's presence. He had looked so often in its face that he thought he knew it well, but he scarcely knew it at all. This time it wore an unfamiliar face: it was a little patch of ice on a distant station platform.

Some days later, crossing the main square of Altkirch, a small town near the Swiss frontier, he encountered a friend whose sons were fighting in the Brigade Alsace-Lorraine. They were all well, and he told his friend where to find them. Then, remembering that he had not replied to this man's letter of condolence, he said: "I am sorry. I wanted to write to you. Please forgive me. One should never allow oneself to be weighed down by these painful occasions, at least in public . . ." Then he walked away with a quick stride, knowing that more grief lay in store for him.

On November 21 the Brigade Alsace-Lorraine began its long march toward the Doubs River, which marks the Swiss frontier. General de Lattre de Tassigny had decided upon a massive feint. Orders, directives and maps were drawn up, showing that the army under his command was about to make a direct assault across the Vosges when in fact he intended to attack in the southern sector and thus turn the German flank. Arrangements were made to make sure that German spies in France and Switzerland knew about these false plans, and on the Vosges front a large number of troops were ordered to go through the motions of preparing for an attack which would never be delivered. The Brigade Alsace-Lorraine was one of the units thrown into the southern sector.

The aim was to advance on Dannemarie and thus open the road to Belfort. The Germans had fortified Ballersdorf, and they were well supplied with tanks and antitank weapons. Every house in Ballersdorf had been transformed into a blockhouse, and the SS troops had taken the precaution of using the inhabitants as shields, hiding with them in the cellars. It was bitterly cold, the rain fell, ice formed on the roads. Sometimes it was necessary for the companies to make their way along forest pathways, where ambushes awaited them. There was scarcely a farm left standing. It took seven days to reach Dannemarie, which was only seven miles to the west on the road to Belfort. The Germans fought every inch of the way.

The drive from Altkirch to Dannemarie was one of the most heart-breaking Malraux ever made. The earth seemed dead under its blanket of ice, and everywhere he looked he saw farms and hamlets in flames. André Chamson was with him. "When you come from the peasantry, as I do," Chamson said, "then you look at a burning village with despair." The flames of the burning farms were mirrored in the ice, and the black smoke waved under the broken skies. "These villages and hamlets," Malraux wrote later, "were nothing more than the names of flames. They were all on fire, and there was that intermittent blaze which derives from ancient times: the ultimate calamity." The earth was transformed into fire and ice.

There was no time to take the wounded to a hospital: they slept in the stables beside the warm beasts, those few stables that were not yet in flames, and Malraux would find himself wondering about those who were not wounded but would soon die and spend their first night of death in these barren fields where the flames roared. At such moments he would find consolation in the knowledge that the primordial flames were coeval with the primordial comradeship of men. "And this comradeship comes from the most ancient times, as far back as the first smile of the first child, as profound and invincible as the calamity that now shook the earth. The crackling of these flames thousands of years old, this eternity of disaster, does not drown the eternity of our silent comradeship."

No general history of World War II records the battle for Danne-marie, a village of about a thousand inhabitants. For Malraux and the men who fought with him it was one of the most terrible and re-warding of the war. The final battle for the village was fought on November 27, beginning at dawn when Malraux called for volunteers to accompany the tanks. The village was ringed round with German tanks and the Germans had an armored train. The roads were slippery with ice, the wind howled, three French tanks were blown up by mines on the outskirts of the village, and there were times when it seemed that all the available artillery of Germany and France was pounding a small area around a village factory. One by one the German tanks were immobilized or forced to retreat; the armored train was put out of action. At nightfall the Brigade Alsace-Lorraine and a column of Foreign Legionnaires forced their way into Dannemarie from three directions, while the remaining German tanks withdrew to shell the village they had defended for a week. In the light of burning farmhouses Malraux, so recently a prisoner of the Germans, passed in review the long columns of German prisoners, frozen and miserable in their first night of captivity.

The battle for Dannemarie and the engagement at Ballersdorf were commemorated in a general order promulgated by the commanding general of the Fifth Armored Division of the French First Army:

GENERAL ORDER NO. 25
OFFICERS, NON-COMMISSIONED
OFFICERS, AND SOLDIERS
OF THE BRIGADE ALSACE-LORRAINE

From November 24 to 28, 1944, under the leadership of Colonel Malraux, you have taken part in the battles fought by the Fifth Armored Division for the liberation of our soil.

Everywhere you have been involved in our operations.

At Ballersdorf and Dannemarie, where the enemy dug in with fierce tenacity, your share in the final success was of immense importance.

Your losses have been heavy, men of Alsace-Lorraine, and you have bathed the earth of Alsace, your native home, so dear to all Frenchmen, in your blood.

I salute your dead and bow down before your wounded. Your sacrifice has not been in vain, for soon all of Alsace will be liberated.

You leave us now for other battlefields. It is my hope that the luck of battles will bring us together again. You will always be welcomed among us with joy and with the spirit of fraternity born of these last days from victories won and ordeals suffered together.

General DE VERNEJOUL

This ornate testimony to the valor of the brigade was written on November 29. A few days later the brigade was ordered to Strasbourg, and Malraux set up his headquarters in the Maison Rouge, the best hotel in the city, only to find it completely deserted, with no waiters and no management, while his troops occupied the approaches to the city's outskirts. No one had entered the cathedral, which had been closed because of bomb damage; he therefore ordered it opened, and was the first Frenchman to walk up the vast nave since its liberation. He was also the first Frenchman to set eyes on the great paintings of Grünewald which were the glory of the Unterlinden Museum in Colmar. They had been hidden in a nearby mineshaft. Strasbourg Cathedral, Grünewald, the caves of Lascaux, these were gifts given to him by a war, which had taken so much away.

On December 16 Field Marshal Karl Rudolf Gerd von Rundstedt, the commander in chief of German forces on the Western Front, launched a startling offensive in the Ardennes forest, and within a few days his armies carved a sixty-mile gap in the Allied lines. Ten days later General Eisenhower ordered a counter offensive; the Germans were pushed back. Eisenhower's strategy involved the abandonment of Strasbourg to the enemy in order to shorten the front, a decision which General de Gaulle regarded with something less than enthusiasm. "The French government," he wrote to Eisenhower, "cannot permit Strasbourg to fall into the hands of the enemy without doing everything possible to defend it." To General de Lattre de Tassigny he wrote on the same day: "It is obvious that the French Army will never agree to abandon Strasbourg." Eisenhower fumed, but the will of De Gaulle prevailed. The Brigade Alsace-Lorraine was thrown into the defense of Strasbourg.

The brigade was not, of course, alone in defending Strasbourg, for important units of the French First Army also took part. But it was given particularly difficult sectors to defend, and when General von Maur ordered the attack on Strasbourg on January 7, his order of the day left no doubt that the Germans were absolutely determined to take the city at whatever the cost in lives and treasure. Once more the swastika must fly over Strasbourg, for the Führer had demanded it. On that day the Germans reached Erstein, twenty miles to the south of Strasbourg, and it was clear that they planned to mount a massive attack from the north, south, and east. The villages around Strasbourg were in flames, and once more, as at Dannemarie, the brigade fought over ice and snow in bitter winds. Patrols went out, and sometimes they were ill-equipped, ill-fed, their clothes frozen to them, and their weapons also frozen. If the Germans had come upon them, they would have had to fight with their bare fists or with knives.

One patrol was sent out across the river which forms one of the branches of the Rhine. This river, known as the Old Rhine, was covered with ice, yet the ice was not strong enough to support a man. Two volunteers broke the thin covering of ice and swam across, and then, completely naked, tried to make contact with their comrades on the other side, and then vanished, to appear some hours later at the farmhouse where Jacquot had set up his headquarters. Their feet were frostbitten and they were more dead than alive, but they still carried their weapons. At one time Malraux thought of making a film around the Brigade Alsace-Lorraine, and one of the most important scenes would show these frozen men making their way across the river, naked and alone.

Strasbourg was saved because the French wore out the German advance, and when at last the Germans were ready to pounce upon the city it was too late, for the Allies were already advancing into the Fatherland.

Toward the end of January Malraux attended the Congress of the National Liberation Movement, which was held in Paris. The Congress represented all the various factions which took part in the Resistance and was very largely dominated by the Communists. Malraux, as a member of the executive committee, was determined to use whatever influence he possessed to prevent a Communist takeover. There were many reasons for his disillusion with the Communists, and not the least of them was the knowledge that many of the delegates to the Congress who professed to belong to other parties were secret members of the party. Nor had he been happy with the behavior of the leaders of the Francs-Tireurs in the Corrèze, for they professed to be fighting for France when in fact they were fighting for Russia. Quite deliberately, using the stratagems they had used so successfully in the past, the Communists were preparing to seize power. He implored the Congress to set aside any hope of introducing soviets into France; the socialism of Russia was tainted with too many crimes, and it would be far better if France turned to the socialism of England. Someone taunted him with a famous phrase from *Man's Hope*: "A man who is active and a pessimist at the same time is or will be a fascist unless he has a fidelity behind him." He answered: "I have a fidelity behind me, and this fidelity is dynamite." His fidelity was France.

He enraged the Communists at the Congress still more by insisting that France owed a debt of gratitude to the British parachute operations. "We must not forget," he added, "that the Allies did help us; that we were armed by them; that without them we would have had nothing. In this respect France can be grateful, but Resistance owes no debt." The Communists were enraged because the British had deliberately refused to drop parachutes in the territory of the Communist *maquis*. Malraux was happy to give honor where it was due. He was accused of being a reactionary and it was generally assumed that he was working closely with De Gaulle, an assumption based on the well known story that there had been a meeting between him and De Gaulle in the snow-covered fields of Alsace. General de Gaulle is supposed to have said, in the words of Napoleon speaking about Goethe, "*Enfin, voilà un homme* [here is a man]!" In fact no such incident took place, nor was it likely that De Gaulle would ever have uttered these words. The general had reviewed the Brigade Alsace-Lorraine shortly after the battle for Bois-le-Prince, but at that precise moment the brigade commander was elsewhere, and De Gaulle was received by Jacquot and Chamson. Malraux's first meeting with De Gaulle took place in the summer of 1945.

After the Congress, at which the Communists were roundly defeated, Malraux returned to the front through the snow-covered fields of Champagne. He was now more than ever determined to take some part in what he called "the new resistance": this time it was against the Communists. As he drove closer to the front, the air seemed to become purer and sweeter, for here the treacheries of the Communists could be momentarily forgotten: in the front line there was only one enemy and he could be recognized by his uniform.

Early in February Malraux was present at the battle of Colmar and the capture of the hill of Sainte Odile, the patron saint of Alsace, with its vast sprawling convent perched on the summit. This pocket in Alsace, long a great obstacle to the French, was now cleared, and the First Army continued its march into Germany, not always with the approval of General Eisenhower, who seems to have regarded the French troops as less reliable than his own, and who would have been happier if they limited themselves to small mopping up operations in the Black Forest. Instead, obeying the orders of General de Gaulle and without very much concern for the orders of General Eisenhower, the French First Army under General de Lattre de Tassigny swept into Stuttgart, thereby giving the French a claim to be one of the occupying forces. On April 20, 1945, Stuttgart flew the French flag, and a few days later there was a review in the main square, and Malraux received his fourth citation to his Croix de Guerre. The first had been given to him for his harassing action against the Panzer Division *Das Reich* on the eve of the invasion, the second for his conduct in German captivity, and the third for the action at Dannemarie. Other medals would come later, including the Distinguished Service Order from King George VI.

When Malraux stood amid the rubble at Stuttgart, the war had only a few more days to run. The Germans, who had spilled out like a black viscous fluid over all of Europe from the Pyrenees to the Caucasus, were now at last contained within their own frontiers, but already the new wars were beginning.

The guardian of the piglets.

THE WORKS OF ART

Let the God of the Old Testament on the Resurrection Day summon up on one hand the multitude of the dead and on the other draw up from the ruins the silent company of statues. And then the true aspect of the Christian of the Middle Ages, the Christ-made man, will be found not in the company of those who worshipped in the nave, but incarnate in the statues.

—REFLECTIONS ON OUR AGE

⋙ The Shaking of the Dice ⋘

The wars were over, and Malraux could now return to his unfinished work. He was forty-four years old, the veteran of many wars, with many wounds to show for it, and he had practiced so many trades that he could no longer remember them all. For a long time he had known the trade he would follow when the wars were over. He would write about art, and at the same time he would throw his weight into the inevitable struggle against the Communists, who were threatening to take over France.

In those days the country was in a state of semiparalysis, with the writ of the government scarcely extending beyond the boundaries of a few major cities. He had encountered many Communists during the resistance and he had come to learn their methods of operation: they were Communists first, Frenchmen second. They concealed their weapons, and were determined to use them against whatever government was installed in France. The war had given Malraux an intense devotion to France, and he was determined that it should be ruled by Frenchmen, not from Moscow.

Since he already possessed an assured place in French literature, it was unlikely that he would suffer any grave financial difficulties. He would make a living from writing and editing at the publishing house of Gallimard. His expenses were fairly heavy, for he had two young sons to support and he had rented the greater part of a large and capacious house at Boulogne-sur-Seine in the suburbs of Paris. He had expensive tastes, and he could be wildly generous with his money. Meeting Manes Sperber shortly after the war, and seeing him in great poverty, he opened his purse and gave him all the money in it. "I can always get some more," he said. "For you, it may not be so easy."

Though he lived among books and ideas, and was wholly immersed in them, he was still feared. There were French writers and politicians who regarded him with a wary eye, remembering his reputation as a man of action. France, on the verge of civil war, seemed to be crying out for a younger leader than General de Gaulle, and there were some who quite seriously regarded Malraux as a potential dictator or at the very least the leader of a new political party of the extreme right. Malraux had a simple answer to these critics. "When a man has written what I have written," he said, "he does not become a fascist."

During the war, when there were quarrels between the FFI and the Communist-led partisans, Malraux had sometimes acted as mediator, showing no disposition to take up a political position. It was the same during the fighting in the Vosges, when he was observed to brush aside all political arguments, saying that he attached no importance to politics so long as Germany remained undefeated. Now it was a question of the survival of France against the Communists.

One evening in the summer of 1945 the telephone rang in the house at Boulogne-sur-Seine. It was an officer attached to General de Gaulle's staff, and he asked if he could come and speak to Malraux on a matter of some urgency. The officer arrived in a military automobile about two hours later, and the message was brief. "General de Gaulle wants to know, in the name of France, whether you will help him." Malraux, who always tended to regard himself as useful, was not overly surprised. He had not been expecting such a singular message, but in the circumstances he was pleased with it.

He went to see General de Gaulle in his office at the Ministry of War. Exactly what the general wanted from him was not stated, but Malraux knew exactly what he wanted from the general. He wanted above all a new kind of revolutionary leader capable of bringing about a new social order in France, and when De Gaulle introduced the name of Clemenceau, Malraux reminded him that Winston Churchill regarded Clemenceau as a man who seemed to have stepped straight out of the French Revolution. As they talked, the ghosts of the French Revolution announced their presence; soon it was the turn of Mirabeau, "this individualist who was ready to betray the

Revolution for the sake of the Queen's eyes and the King's small change." Malraux was inclined to regard him as a great adventurer, and indeed he had a romantic passion for the French Revolution, its generals and its victims. Hoche and Saint-Just were mentioned, and went down to defeat. General de Gaulle said: "Make no mistake. France no longer wants the Revolution. The time is past."

So, perhaps, it was, but it would have been interesting to know at exactly what moment he regarded the time as being past, for revolution was still a likely possibility during that long summer when the Communists were storing up arms. It occurred to Malraux that De Gaulle said "The time is past" in the tone of a mystic abjuring the flesh. Gradually it was becoming clear that the general had not invited him to an audience to discuss the Revolution.

What, then, had he been invited for? From Malraux's account of the meeting in his memoirs, it appears that De Gaulle was especially interested in Malraux's ideas about publicity and propaganda, and he had been called in for exactly the same reason that a business executive would call in a public relations man. There had been long discussions between Malraux and Gaston Palewski, the general's *chef du cabinet*. Malraux had spoken about the need for audiovisual aids in education— it would be much better, for example, to show a film of the Garonne than to subject pupils to a dry lesson on the Garonne, and why not show talking films in the schools with the expert professors taking the place of the bumbling schoolteachers? Why not reproduce great paintings and distribute them all over France, so that the pupils could develop good taste? In a technological age, endowed with films, radio, photoengraving, and phonograph records, students were still being taught in a manner which had not notably changed since the middle ages. And then, too, Malraux had pointed out the extraordinary effectiveness of films and radio in projecting political images, and he had insisted on the need for public opinion polls to enable a government to know whether it was really reaching out to the public. De Gaulle was especially impressed by these last ideas, and he had summoned Malraux chiefly in order to discover whether he would be useful as a technical adviser.

It was a long meeting, and for most of the time De Gaulle remained

silent. In a few clipped words, he would suggest a subject for one of
Malraux's interminable monologues, and then there would be a raised
forefinger or another brief interjection to set the monologue rolling in
another direction. De Gaulle remained impassive, showing no signs of
agreement or disagreement as Malraux discussed the British parliamentary system, the decline of liberalism, the uses of writers at times
of revolutionary upheaval, and the curious fate of all Popular Fronts,
with anecdotes to illustrate each argument. He was not being cross-
examined, for De Gaulle was too well bred to employ any lawyer's
tricks. He listened, was bemused, and kept his own counsel.

When the meeting was over, Malraux reflected on those long silences, his remoteness and strangeness. It was as though De Gaulle
scarcely existed except as a political figure, as though the man was
totally absorbed in his political destiny. He wore a uniform, and it was
unthinkable that he would ever wear civilian clothes. There was in
him something of the priest, who offers his conventional benedictions
with never a hint of his own mysterious acquaintance with God, and
there was also something of the dedicated revolutionary who, like
Trotsky, was perhaps resigned to inevitable defeat. Malraux had seen
the legend, but he had not yet seen the man.

A few days later he was invited to join De Gaulle's staff as a technical adviser, and soon work began on plans for the modernization of
education (which were never carried very far) and on public opinion
polls (which would not be employed efficiently for twenty years).
Nevertheless he was now in a closer position to observe the mechanics
of power and the mechanism of De Gaulle's mind. His title was
attaché culturel to the cabinet of De Gaulle. Predictably, when De
Gaulle formed his second government in November, Malraux was
appointed Minister of Information. He was in office for slightly less
than two months, for De Gaulle's government fell on January 20,
1946, and both De Gaulle and Malraux then disappeared into political
obscurity.

As Minister of Information Malraux showed no particular distinction, his chief task being to prepare the official communiqués following ministerial meetings. What interested him was not information but
education, especially education in the arts. And while he was uncon-

vincing as Minister of Information, he was far more convincing as *attaché culturel* with a program designed to employ modern technological advances in all schools and colleges and in the Maisons de la Culture which he hoped to establish throughout France. On the day when De Gaulle's cabinet was defeated, there appeared the first fruit of his labors as *attaché culturel*. This was a magnificent reproduction in full color of Renoir's painting called *Moulin de la Galette,* with its nineteenth-century couples waltzing in lantern light. It was intended that about a dozen masterpieces by French painters would be published and distributed to the schools. This would form the first series, and would be followed by many more. In fact, only one painting was published, and after the fall of the government the entire project was abandoned.

Yet during those sixty days Malraux had been laying the foundations for the ministry of culture which would come into existence thirteen years later. The general plan for the *Maisons de la Culture* was drawn up and refined. Experiments in the use of films, posters, traveling exhibitions and lantern slides were being carried out with a small group of devoted assistants. He seems to have guessed that the government would fall, for he worked feverishly. An American who visited him in his unheated office near the Étoile found him in a mood of intense excitement. He was talking about his art projects. "The strength of his feelings was nearly unbearable," the American reported. "You'd think he'd explode. His eyes were bleak, sad, and intense, and he didn't look at you much when he talked. It was as if he were mostly talking to himself, though he'd flash glances at you occasionally, in detached observation. He was really hypnotic when he talked. You'd come about a piece of business that never got finished, or really even started, and you felt richly rewarded by his telling you about something else that was absolutely no use to you." Abruptly, with the fall of the government, Malraux abandoned the public projection of art for the private understanding of it, and he returned to his books.

Since the end of the war he had been attempting to come to terms with Europe, which had been crushed by the Germans and was now slowly returning to life. The Nazis had left no traces on the civilizations of the people they had conquered; it was as though a hurricane had passed over the land, destroying millions of people, but the survivors were able to resume their lives as though nothing had happened. The Nazis had advanced no new ideas; they had not produced any art, any architecture, any films, any new understanding of the process by which living communities are formed and permitted to grow. In the United States, however, there had been massive changes which deeply influenced the Western world. American automobiles, skyscrapers, films, city planning, and a host of inventions, and an entire American mythology, were invading Europe. Whether this was good or bad was irrelevant: that it was happening was indisputable. Just as Napoleon had brought about the rise of British power, so Hitler had hastened the rise of American power, and a new Atlantic civilization was being forged.

Malraux outlined this argument in an article published in the Swiss monthly *Labyrinthe* in April 1945. In the following year, in a lecture given at the opening session of UNESCO at the Sorbonne, he repeated the argument with some important reservations concerning the fate of man in an age given over to torture and mass murder. It was an electrifying speech, covering a vast range of ideas, and should be quoted at some length because it represents certain fundamental concepts which he had hammered out during the war years and which were to remain virtually unchanged during the ensuing years. He said:

> The problem facing us today is that of knowing whether or not, on this old continent of Europe, Man is dead.
>
> The main reasons why this problem has arisen and confronts us now are obvious.
>
> To begin with, the nineteenth century nursed vast hopes, founded on science, on peace, on the quest of human dignity.
>
> A hundred years ago it was assumed that the great hopes the men of those days bore in their hearts would lead inevitably to a series of discoveries that would serve man's welfare, a series of ideas to serve the cause of peace, and a new range of feelings that would promote man's dignity.
>
> As for the furtherance of peace—well, it would be idle to press that point.

As for science, we have our answer in Bikini.

As for human dignity. . . .

The problem of Evil was by no means ruled out in the nineteenth century. But when it makes its reappearance amongst us today, it is no longer merely through the antics of those dark and tragic puppets manipulated by the psychoanalysts. It is the huge and somber figure of the Dostoevskian archangel that once again appears in our midst, and again we hear him say: "I refuse my mission if the torture of an innocent child, by a brute, is to be the ransom of the world."

Above all we see, above the phantom towns and ruined cities of our continent, there hovers today a yet more terrible presence; for Europe, bloodstained and ravaged though she be, is not more ravaged, not more bloodstained than the face of Man she had hoped to bring into the world. . . .

The strength of the West lies in its acceptance of the unknown. True, there is a humanism possible to European man, but we must tell ourselves quite frankly that it is a tragic humanism. We are confronted by an unknown world, we face it consciously, and this will to face it consciously is ours alone. For—let us make no mistake about this—the will to discovery and awareness, regarded as fundamental values, is peculiarly and exclusively European. You will have seen these two activities of the will at work, day in, day out, in the scientific field. If we wish to define a form of intellectual activity today, we begin by making clear its starting point and the nature of its investigations. Columbus knew better where he started from than where he was going. And we can base a truly humane attitude only on the tragic because man does not know where he is going; and on humanism because he knows where he sets out from, and whereon his will is set. . . .

Are we dying? I spoke just now of the Battle of Britain. None of us has forgotten his impression when Churchill said that never since Thermopylae had so small a number of men saved the freedom of the world. Well, even if the British Empire were in its death throes—which, to my thinking, it is *not*—we can but wish for all the Empires that have fought beside us a death so admirable.

But our Continent today is not a field of death. We are, rather, at a crucial phase, when Europe in her will to fulfill herself must remember that all great heirs ignore or squander the assets they inherit; the only legacy they can truly make their own is that of intelligence and strength. The heir of happy Christendom was Pascal. The European heritage is tragic humanism.

From the great days of Greece onward, it has taken its stand against what men called the gods. Not such gods as Venus or Apollo, but the true gods, the lords of destiny. Greek tragedy misleads us; it rises like a burning shadow from the vast sandy wastes of Egypt, from man's abasement by the gods of Babylon. It is a challenge to man's destiny; and before that challenge destiny retreats and man comes into his own.

Let the God of the Old Testament on the Resurrection Day summon up on one hand the multitude of the dead, and on the other draw up from the ruins the silent company of statues. And then the true aspect of the Christian of the Middle Ages, the Christ-made man, will be found not in the company of those who worshipped in the nave, but incarnate in the statues.

Like the speech delivered at the same conference by Pierre Bertaux, the great authority on Hölderlin, who called for a total revolution in education and a total response to the needs of the young, Malraux's speech was designed to state the case for an intellectual revolution. He was talking passionately and coherently about matters which were urgently in need of solution, unlike most of the speakers, who merely contributed learned essays. So Dr. Joseph Needham celebrated the founding of UNESCO with a dissertation on Chinese science, the Abbé Breuil discussed the prehistoric caves of Lascaux, and Louis Massignon read a paper on the influence of Arab civilization on French culture. They were admirable lectures, but they could have been delivered at any university at any time. Malraux was saying things that demanded to be said in that second winter following the war.

The speech incensed Louis Aragon, the novelist who was also the official representative of the French Communist Party. A thin, wiry, tight-lipped man, he assailed Malraux for having commended Churchill and the British Empire while forgetting to commend Stalin and the Red Army which alone, in Aragon's view, had saved Europe from tyranny. He objected to Malraux's question whether or not European man was dead. Had not the fate of Europe been decided at Stalingrad? European man survived only because hundreds of thousands of Red Army soldiers had sacrificed their lives. He was also incensed because Malraux had spoken about the Resurrection Day. "Malraux has stated the problem more accurately than he realizes," Aragon said, "for he has created two opposing camps: the lifeless statues and the people of flesh and blood." As Aragon continued to attack Malraux and many other French writers for underestimating the benevolence of Stalin, he was interrupted by cries from the audience. For the first and last time during the UNESCO conference the speaker and the audience engaged in a shouting match.

In the eyes of the Communists Malraux was someone worth fighting. He was the renegade who had abandoned the Left for service under De Gaulle, and therefore no words were too harsh for him. Roger Garaudy, a Communist member of the French National Assembly, came out with a book called *Literature of the Graveyard,* a vehement attack on Jean-Paul Sartre, François Mauriac, Arthur Koestler and Malraux, who received the lion's share of vituperation. Sartre was a false prophet, Mauriac was a prisoner of his class, Koestler was a man who had deliberately misunderstood Bukharin's statements during his trial for high treason and had then incorporated them in *Darkness at Noon.* But these were all small crimes compared to the perfidy of Malraux, "the man with the knife between his teeth." A chapter was called "The Death Mask of André Malraux." In the eyes of Garaudy, Malraux was a man totally indifferent to the fate of his fellow men; he resembled one of the Greek gods who descends to earth only long enough to attend blood-sacrifices and to ensure that the warriors are intoxicated with the smell of blood, and then returns to the comfort of heaven. In the empyrean, remote from all human preoccupations, he amuses himself by spinning a web of metaphysical questions and performing elaborate gestures, like those performed by magicians. Indeed, there was much of the magician in him, and he belonged among those heretics who are welcomed by the Church because they are useful in a decadent society. In any other age they would be burned at the stake.

Garaudy found no redeeming features in Malraux except that he was "quite obviously a great writer." His novels, his essays, his ideas were consigned to the flames: for was he not the archenemy? "Malraux is the medium for a dying class and a dying social system, because he furnishes a psychological transposition and a metaphysical justification of their disorder and agony," he wrote, contrasting Malraux, the embalmer, with the followers of Stalin busily pouring new life into mankind.

Malraux was well aware how bitterly he was hated by the Communists. He was convinced that the Communists were preparing to seize power, and he was determined to prevent them. He was one of the founding members of a new political party called the *Rassemblement du Peuple Français,* the Rally of the French People, which had two fundamental aims—to bring De Gaulle to power and to prevent a Communist takeover. The party, founded on April 17, 1947, failed to bring De Gaulle to power, and had scarcely any real influence on French political life during its brief and unhappy existence. Nevertheless it provided a forum for De Gaulle and kept him in the public eye, so that when he eventually came to power eleven years later he was well known to the electorate, knew exactly what he wanted to do, and possessed a considerable experience of political strategy.

The Communists spoke of De Gaulle as another Hitler with Malraux assuming the role of Goebbels, but it would have been more accurate to describe De Gaulle as another Cromwell with Malraux playing the role of Milton. His contribution to the *Rassemblement du Peuple Français* was poetry and excitement, literary elegance, a sense of drama. Sometimes the drama became melodrama. In a speech delivered at the Vélodrome d'Hiver on February 17, 1948, Malraux prophesied that before the end of the month the Communists would rise in France and all the resources of the Soviet government would be thrown into the fray. A civil war of incalculable proportions was only a few days away. There was not the least doubt that the Communists were plotting an uprising, but there was some doubt whether the plot had advanced very far.

François Mauriac was one of the spectators at the Vélodrome d'Hiver on that bitterly cold day. As usual, he was fascinated by Malraux's performance, but he wondered whether it was anything more than a performance by "a gambler forever shaking the dice in his feverish hands." He did not doubt the sincerity of the speaker, but he was disturbed by the apocalyptic tone. "All those acts of sabotage, those simultaneous derailments of trains which he predicted, were being savored in advance, and he would pause to contemplate them with visible enjoyment and with the excitement of a gambler who observes that the game is boring and he is waiting only for the moment when he will throw everything he possesses into the ring, for he feels he is alive only in those moments when it is given to him to play double or nothing with his destiny."

In fact, Malraux had good cause for alarm: and so had France. Stalin was in an adventurous mood, reaching out across Europe toward new triumphs while simultaneously stamping out resistance in the countries he had conquered. The great show trials in eastern Europe demonstrated that he was capable of every kind of infamy; the great purges had begun again; and the dice were loaded in favor of a gambler far more audacious than Malraux. François Mauriac had forgotten that Stalin existed.

Malraux returned to the attack less than three weeks later with another speech delivered at the Salle Pleyel on March 5. He spoke of the tyranny that threatened to settle on Europe like a dead hand, and reminded his listeners that Michelangelo had engraved on the pedestal of the sculpture of *Night* the words: "If it be to open thine eyes upon tyranny, mayest thou never awaken." There was no doubt that Soviet Russia was determined to expand at the expense of Europe, and there was no doubt that European culture would be destroyed if she succeeded. "The Soviet structure despises Europe's past, detests her present, and accepts from her only a future in which exactly nothing remains of what she once was," he declared, and went on to contrast totalitarian Russia with the Atlantic community where European values were still respected. What was at stake was European civilization, the entire history of Europe: if Stalin ruled over France, as he ruled over East Germany, then all her history would be canceled out.

In this speech Malraux spoke as a cultural historian, briefly tracing the development of the European mind from its beginnings in ancient Egypt, through the long, slow, painful emergence of free inquiry and the continuing dialogue of the arts. Europe was Chartres, Michelangelo, Shakespeare, Rembrandt, and it was beyond belief that a great cultural tradition could be allowed to perish. Stalin was an archenemy of the arts. He had no use for the artist unless he served the state, with the result that the Soviet sculptors and painters were compelled to create vast images of Stalin, and if they attempted to sculpt and paint out of their own needs they were punished. Liberty could be guaranteed only by a strong state at the service of all its citizens, and it remained to be seen whether the voice of France would be heard in this hour of danger. In his peroration he said: "There are countries like Great Britain—and this may well redound to their honor—which are the mightier for being the lonelier. France was never greater than when she spoke for all men, and that is why her silence is heard so poignantly today."

Malraux reprinted the speech later as an afterword to a new edition of *The Conquerors.* This, he felt, was a reasoned answer to the aimless violence of Garin, who had never considered that culture was worth saving.

He made many more speeches during the year, but the theme was always the same. Not France only, but all of Europe was in danger from Soviet Russia, which was neither European nor Asiatic, and therefore had no real roots in the East or the West. The same theme returns in a strange dialogue he conducted with James Burnham, an American political commentator who saw a United States of Europe as the only alternative to a Communist empire stretching from the Pacific to the Atlantic. Malraux would lead the subject around to the Atlantic culture. Like an astronomer prophesying the appearance of a new star, he said the first faint glimmerings of the new culture would probably become visible around 1950.

All this was in keeping with the cultural historian, not with the political figure, who seemed destined to play the role of Cassandra. The *Rassemblement du Peuple Français* survived for another five years, its chief purpose being to remind the French people of the existence of De Gaulle, a remote and visionary hero who had taken up his position in the wings of the theater while waiting to be summoned to occupy the center of the stage. The party finally dissolved in 1953 when the death of Stalin made it less likely that the Russians would take Europe by storm. With no political duties to perform, Malraux had more time for his books. He had married again, for Clara had at last consented to give him a divorce. His wife was Marie-Madeleine Lioux, the widow of his half-brother Roland, and the marriage ceremony was performed in the town hall of Riquewihr, a small wine village near Colmar, on March 13, 1948, a week after the famous speech in the Salle Pleyel.

His family now consisted of his wife and sons: his two sons by Josette Clotis, and his adopted son, Alain, born of the marriage of Roland and his wife. In the fifties, living quietly in the large apartment at Boulogne-sur-Seine, he settled down to domesticity. He played duets on the piano with his wife, amused his children with stories from the world of *farfelu,* collected Hopi Indian dolls, and continued to write his books. One day the general atmosphere of calm was broken when one of the boys accidentally knocked over the beautiful Gandhara statue he had brought back from Afghanistan, but it was quickly repaired. He had come at last to the fate reserved for all revolutionaries, if they survive. He was leading a conventional married life.

◈ Vermeer and Goya ◈

From the beginning of his association with the *Nouvelle Revue Française* Malraux had played with the idea of bringing out sumptuous editions in full color of his favorite painters. Bosch, Leonardo da Vinci, Vermeer, Braque, Ensor, and many others would be included, and this long gallery of painters would be presented with only the briefest of introductions, for the paintings would speak for themselves. The problems of color photography as reproduced on a white page fascinated him, and he was never happier than when sitting on the floor, surrounded by photographs, choosing them, drawing them together, permitting them to reflect and illustrate one another, arranging them so that they would show themselves to their best advantage. At such moments he seemed to be totally immersed in the photographs, lost among them, no longer in the intelligible world.

Of the books he planned only three saw the light of day. One, the least successful, was devoted to Leonardo da Vinci. Paul Valéry's famous essay, *An Introduction to the Method of Leonardo da Vinci,* served as the preface, and Malraux combed Western literature in search of the necessary commentaries. Goethe, Chateaubriand, Hegel, Ruskin, Delacroix, Oscar Wilde and a dozen others were pressed into service as commentators on the individual paintings or on aspects of Leonardo's life and thought, while Malraux added his own brief comments. All the paintings known to be by Leonardo, all the works of the School of Verrocchio in which Leonardo's hand can be discerned and all the paintings made with the help of his pupils would be reproduced. The edition would be so sumptuous that the reader would half expect to find an authentic drawing by Leonardo included in each volume. When it finally appeared, the book had only one failing: the color plates were catastrophically inadequate. A strange bluish-gray cloud seemed to have settled on all the reproductions of the paintings, and the artist who demands the most careful and cautious treatment by the photoengravers was ill-served. Although the book is now a collector's item and fetches high prices, it was very nearly a total disaster.

In the same series known as "La Galerie de la Pléiade," Malraux produced a companion volume on Vermeer. This time the results exceeded all expectations. Never before had Vermeer been presented so brilliantly, with exactly the right kind of text and exactly the right reproductions. All of Vermeer's paintings were especially rephotographed for the occasion. The introduction consisted of three passages from Proust printed in heroic type, followed in more conventional type by a short essay by Malraux on "An Artist Forever Unknown." But was he unknown? Had he not revealed himself more abundantly than most artists, painting his own portrait and those of his wife and daughters into so many of his canvases? By printing the portraits in the same size, four on a page, Malraux was able to show the family likenesses: Vermeer himself, growing older, gradually losing his own expression of unguarded youthfulness, but finding it again in his youngest daughter, while his wife Catherine pours milk or weighs gold or sits by her spinet, growing heavier with time but remaining in some strange way unchanged and imperturbable, as though time could do no more to her than make her monumental.

Malraux showed how the known chronology of the paintings fitted in with the growth of Vermeer's family: how the abrupt changes of scale fitted in with the artist's change of residence; how the self-portraits, like those of Rembrandt, show, when they are studied, an extraordinary development of self-knowledge, as though through all these years he had been attempting to discover himself, to catch himself on the wing, and he did not do this in the usual way by slow accretions of knowledge, but instead by continually returning to his own past, recapturing positions already taken, moving between the past and the present in a strange spiral, so that sometimes when he was advancing most rapidly he seemed to be falling back.

He was the painter who dedicated his art to his family and to the landscape he saw from his window, never moving more than a few yards from himself. When he abandoned his family and his window, his genius abandoned him, for his commissioned paintings were always unworthy of him. His world was small and self-contained, and it was as though nothing existed for him outside the colors of the streets and the faces of his wife and daughters. He was a man who lived behind his fortress walls, apparently uninterested in the affairs of the world, content with a few familiar things, as Cézanne was content with his apples and his mountain. Within that fortress Vermeer kept a quiet vigil, and when he died at the age of forty-three he had invented a whole world.

The essay was remarkable for the fact that it stated a thesis, hitherto unknown, which suddenly seemed to be obvious. No one had previously suggested that *The Geographer, The Astronomer,* and the other portraits of men were one and the same person, and that there were excellent reasons for believing that they were all portraits of Vermeer. The famous painting showing the artist from behind had suggested to generations of art critics that Vermeer delighted in concealing his features and deliberately conspired to create a mystery about himself. Malraux pointed out that there was no mystery, only the mystery of great art. Far from concealing himself, the artist took pains to reveal himself. He painted himself as a soldier, a roisterer, a geographer, an astronomer, but he was none of these. He was a man of quiet faith, who believed above all in the beauty of his wife and daughters, and this was enough, for he wanted nothing else.

In Malraux's eyes Vermeer was to be counted among the guardian angels of Western civilization. Other painters excited him more, but none inspired greater reverence. Vermeer was the touchstone. His clear colors, clear air, immaculate calm, his sense of order dispassionately displayed—but how much passion was concealed in the apparent calm!—all these spoke of an absolute mastery. In an obscure street in Delft a painter who had been forgotten after his death had reached the pinnacle of perfection.

So Malraux made this book, lavishing upon it all his knowledge of good bookmaking, choosing the type and the paper, writing a *catalogue raisonné,* describing each painting, and going in search of the brief commentaries by Claudel, Renoir, Huizinga, and a few others, that seemed to be necessary. He was a lover of fine books and responsible for the design of many handsome ones, but this was the most handsome of all. Never again would he produce a book so admirable in its presentation.

At the opposite pole to Vermeer stood Goya, who never protected himself within a fortress but went out into the world of people and ghosts, a man as hungry for experience as Vermeer was immune to it. Vermeer was Apollonian, Goya was Dionysiac, and between them, like springing arches, they enclosed a vast area of European art. Malraux's essay on Goya was a more substantial work than his introduction to Vermeer's paintings, which had been largely concerned with a single idea. The essay on Goya proliferated with ideas. It was as though Goya's vast restlessness had been communicated to the critic, who found himself in such total sympathy with the subject that it was as if he were able to burrow underneath Goya's skin and skull, looking out on the world through Goya's eyes.

Malraux's sympathy for Goya was not new, but it had been quickened by his experiences during the Spanish Civil War. So often what he saw in Spain seemed to be a Goya drawing come to life. Spain, the World War, and the horrors of the Nazi concentration camps had only confirmed for him the truth of Goya's vision of man haunted by demons and at the mercy of the phantoms who were the projections of his own anxieties and fears. Here was an artist who understood the modern world long before it came into existence, but had understood it only in his later years when deafness and sorrow drove him to the edge of madness. In his drawings Absurdity is king. There is nothing comic in his royal progress. He draws with a pitiless passion, impatiently dismissing the ordinary, everyday world of the senses: there is only horror. "Bosch introduced men into his infernal world, Goya on the other hand introduced the infernal into the human world."

Men choking in their own blood, men being garroted, men being drawn asunder or hanging like dead fruit from trees, the lame, the halt, the blind, monsters, sorcerers, demons, specters, incubi, people with asses' heads and the legs of cockerels, strange ghosts and stranger demons haunt those pages, and there is never any relief from horror. He must go on and on until he has exhausted the resources of terror.

On the walls of the Quinta del Sordo, the House of the Deaf Man, on
the banks of the Manzanares River just outside Madrid, Goya painted
his most fearful nightmares. Saturn devours his son, the witches brood
over the witches' Sabbath, two men sinking in quicksand are beating
each other to death with cudgels, and over the horizon a giant dog
glares at the immense emptiness of the universe. Terror stalks through
the house where Goya lived alone except for his shrewish housekeeper
and her beautiful daughter, who was perhaps Goya's daughter. In the
Caprichos, the *Disasters of War* and the *Disparates* Goya drew images
of earthly terror, but on the walls of his house he painted terror in all
its metaphysical majesty, so that the paintings are almost too fearful to
be looked at. Malraux set out to discover the roads by which Goya
reached his own incredible dining room.

The essay, which he called *Saturn* after the stupendous figure of
the giant devouring his son, was published in 1950. Some preliminary
conclusions appeared in the introduction to a handsomely illustrated
collection of drawings called *Drawings of Goya in the Prado Museum,*
published by Skira in the spring of 1947. In this brief essay Malraux
described the historic setting and sketched out the circumstances that
brought Goya to see the world in the light of the dark stars. The
Renaissance conception of man as a being higher than the angels had
never taken root in Spain. "To the 'Christ, man made perfect' of
Nicholas of Cusa, all the profound voices of Spain replied that man's
only worth lay in what he owed to Christ." For Goya, too, man was
corrupt and evil, irremediably cast out from the regions of divine
grace. In addition Goya was deaf and ill, apparently with some syphi-
litic complaint, and he appears to have regarded his infirmities as a
consequence of his sins. Then, too, as court painter, he had the opportunity to see a debauched court in all its ineffable absurdity, which
Malraux describes with evident enjoyment:

> Goya was the first great stage manager of the Absurd. Cer-
> tainly the court and the city where he lived lent themselves to
> it. The Queen pilfered the powder destined for the army fighting
> against Portugal, thus avoiding the necessity of seeing the state
> treasury squandered when it could be legally appropriated for

staging comedies and operas. According to the legend, the late King had attempted to violate his wife's corpse amid the burning tapers and the praying monks. In the squares actors performed the *auto sacramental* of the Annunciation: St. Michael removes his black cape in the presence of the Virgin, revealing a leg-of-mutton ruff and little violet-colored wings; she offers him chocolate, but he refuses on the grounds that God the Father has promised him a *paella* for dinner; and when the Holy Ghost enters, all three personages celebrate their unanimity by performing a most immodest fandango before the stupefied ambassadors. The devil, like the Virgin, is at all the crossroads.

Because the devil was only too evidently present in Spain, Goya pays him the inevitable tribute of believing in him, studying his works, and coming to the inevitable conclusions. The heart of the mystery is a man hanging on a branch with his arms and legs cut off for no reason except that it has occurred to someone to cut them off, and this "someone" is not the devil. Man conspires to his own destruction, and Goya watches in terror but also with a kind of affection and a strange laughter. Malraux had heard that laughter. It was the laughter of men condemned to death, and belonged very much more to our century than to Goya's, for very many more people have been condemned to death in our day than in his. Goya is our contemporary.

As always Malraux interprets the artist in terms of *experience*. What interests him is not the experience of the man but of the age, and Goya was not simply Goya: he was the age speaking. Except in the easel portraits he was not painting a representation of his times; he was painting its ghosts, its obsessions, its accusing shapes. Hence on the walls of the House of the Deaf Man he painted a crowded gallery of self-portraits. He was himself Saturn, but he was also the son who is being devoured. He was the peasant battering another peasant to death, though subsiding into quicksand, and he was all the witches at their Sabbath. Ultimately it was perhaps a form of self-defense, for in a room hung with mirrors a man can be sure of seeing himself and can prepare himself for any encounter with intruders.

One looks in vain for any hint of compassion in his drawings or in the desperate paintings in the House of the Deaf Man. The man who is being butchered does not appeal for mercy, since he knows that mercy is unobtainable. As Malraux depicts him, Goya is almost content that it should be so, for he asks no mercy. Those shapes that tormented him, baffled him, and seemed always about to destroy him were his familiars: he was in league with ghosts. They were ghosts of all kinds, and Malraux was delighted to discover that on rare occasions Goya depicted the same goblins who appear in *Paper Moons* and *The Diary of a Fireman of Massacre*. "These are of another kind," Goya wrote. "They are gay, amusing, quick to render service, perhaps a little greedy and inclined to play pranks; for the rest, they are good little people." But the good little people were heavily outnumbered by the bad, and it was only on the very rarest occasions that Goya paid any attention to them.

Malraux pointed out that Goya did not go out and draw what he saw in the streets. Neither in the paintings in the House of the Deaf Man nor in the *Caprichos* nor in the *Disasters of War* was he studying from life. He drew men dying of torture, but there is no evidence that he ever watched a man dying of torture. He drew two-headed women, birds with the heads of dogs, and men with the heads of asses: these he had seen with his own eyes in the depths of his soul. Daumier, who was very close to Goya in spirit, once exclaimed: "You know very well I cannot draw from life." So it was with Goya, whose paintings came miraculously from life, but whose drawings came from his soul.

"He discovered his genius the day he dared to stop pleasing," Malraux wrote. "His solitude breaks the dialogue with his whole epoch." But had he ever wanted to please anyone but himself? Was the dialogue ever really broken? From time to time Malraux will interrupt his argument with an epigram, usually trenchant and often involving widely separate painters who are suddenly forced into a confrontation. "Underlying a Poussin nude, there is contemplation; underlying a Rembrandt, the everlasting; an eighteenth-century French nude suggests only complicity in rape." Such statements are intended to catch the reader up short, and they succeed in doing exactly what they set out to do. Later, the reader returns to the marked passage and wonders

whether it is true, for the Poussin nudes in the *Bacchanalian Revels* in
the National Gallery in London suggest nothing so much as rubber
dolls engaged in horseplay, Rembrandt's nudes sometimes convey the
weight and splendor of the flesh, and Boucher's nudes, reclining am-
biguously among cushions, invite the spectator to go to bed with them
and are not amenable to rape. Malraux's comments on the nude resemble his rare excursions into eroticism in his novels. The nude is not
a subject that profoundly interests him.

What did interest him, almost to the exclusion of everything else,
was the violent drama of destiny: man confronted with death, with
evil, with his demons, with suffering and absurdity and all their trap-
pings. This is a landscape he knew well; all his life he had wandered
through those dark woods, listening to the witches' spells. He knew
what it is like to die, and he had looked closely enough at hell to feel
its heat on his face. All that is savage and untameable in Goya made
an instant appeal to him, and when he spoke of the paintings of the
House of the Deaf Man he was at ease, but he was baffled the moment
he turned his attention to the court paintings, as though it were beyond
him to understand that Goya could take delight in a corrupt court
coruscating with jewels and fine brocades. When he spoke of Goya's
addiction to the darkness in the soul, he had wise and profoundly
original things to say. Even the physical darkness, the black spaces on
the engravings, are, for the first time, given their proper meaning.

> His patches of dark color often seem to represent darkness,
> but their function is more like that of the golden backgrounds
> of the Middle Ages; they take the scene out of reality and, as
> with the Byzantine scene, place it at once in a universe that does
> not belong to man. This black is devil's gold; it marks out the
> fantastic as strictly as the golden background had marked out
> the sacred. It is very rare in the preparatory designs, even when
> they are in ink, but nearly always it interposes itself to give the
> engraving its disturbing emphasis and to remove the scene into
> the supernatural.

This is well said, and needed to be said. All the elements of Malraux's particular expertise were brought to a focus in a single idea. The

farfelu, the Byzantine experience and the engraver's art are all brought into happy juxtaposition and made to reveal something of importance about Goya: we are a few more inches deeper into his mind. And when he says: "Christian art was an answer; Goya's art is a question," he is on the same firm ground, discovering at last the dividing line which separates Goya from the tradition that brought him into being. But when Malraux insists that Goya is against Christianity, he is on more debatable ground. Sometimes Christianity throws its darkest shadow at times of greatest faith; and the altarpiece of Grünewald is not less Christian for being conceived in terror and beauty. Like Grünewald, Goya drew strength from his dark visions and majestic apparitions, and he had more pity for men than Malraux was willing to grant him.

"Goya was not groping toward God, but toward a power older and beyond salvation, the everlasting Saturn." But this is to give more weight to a single painting than it can bear. His drawings are curses uttered with terrible force, dirges, laments, imprecations against the surrounding horror. He has not cut himself off from men, or from the Church, or from painting; he has not surrendered to madness. Malraux sees him as a man crushed under the strain of living in the world, rejecting the cruelty and absurdity of the world, and determined to appeal to the gods who came into existence centuries before the birth of Christ, as though they, and they alone, could somehow purge the world of illusions. Malraux sees Saturn enthroned, and God cast down.

In this way and in many other ways Malraux is inclined to force the argument. His Goya becomes destiny, a being fraught with meta-physical significance, and he forgets the poetry present in Goya's most terrifying paintings and engravings. Then suddenly he turns about face, abandons all his metaphysical speculations, appeals to Shakespeare, and presents a new Goya—the poet of the darkest hour of the night. In a long passage, one of the most memorable he ever wrote, he sets Goya amid all the other heroes, real or imaginary, who suffered in Gethsemane:

> Another artist of genius, perhaps separated from Christ by the same subterranean voice, had also called upon a people of madmen, sleepwalkers, and witches for the unconquerable ascent that before this time had always been a Christian ascent

—the Shakespeare of Macbeth and Hamlet. The mist that trans-
forms the figures wandering on the heath of *Lear* is quite different from the murky light in which the outstretched arms of
the pathetic little man of the *Third of May* call upon the
Spanish people; but both, when they make their appeal to the
powers of darkness, are bent on equaling or surpassing the element of the everlasting which is inherent in classical tragedy
and Italian painting. Shakespeare uses character, Goya figures;
but since painting began, what painter but Goya would have
been able to realize the depth of the endless corridors around
the imagined spot of blood that all the perfumes of Arabia
would never wash away?

"In such a night as this, when the sweet wind did gently kiss
and they did make no noise. . . ." Ah, song of love! In such a
night, Macbeth, you heard "Thou shalt be king," and in such
a night the forest marched on Dunsinane. In such a night Saul
went to the witch of Endor's cave, Helen saw the first dead of
Troy return, and Alexander crucified the philosopher who had
brought him wisdom; Rome, Persepolis, Alexandria and Babylon went up in flames, the heiress of Tamerlane gave to the fish
in her turquoise pool all the pearls of Samarkand, and the be-
leaguered companions of Cortés heard the Spanish prisoners
shriek when their hearts were torn out to the beating of gongs;
in such a night Cervantes learned that he was a slave.

In this passage Malraux seems to break loose from art criticism altogether. The images of splendor rise and fall, his private obsessions
are given free play, the music comes in a flood, and yet the total effect
is one of extraordinary exhilaration such as comes to one who has long
been wrestling with an angel and at last holds him in his power. He
has found Goya at last among the legendary heroes of the long-distant
past.

Malraux's essays on art are nearly always episodic, personal, fluid.
His aim is to convey the excitement and the flow of art, not to pronounce judgment. He is superbly uninterested in the commentaries of
art critics and all the academic paraphernalia. He cheerfully contradicts

himself, so that at one place in his essay on Goya we find him saying: "Goya also was a prophet, but he did not know precisely of what," and in another place he says categorically: "Goya was not a prophet but a painter." As in his conversation he turns suddenly from one subject to another, and we are given no reasons for the abrupt transitions. Yet the method is astonishingly successful, for the excitement is continually being conveyed, and we are never left in doubt about his intentions.

In Siberia a shaman would hold up a bundle consisting of bones, feathers and strips of blood-clotted cloth and say: "This is what the god is saying." In a trance he enters into communion with the dead, saying things that seem to come from the experience of bones, feathers and blood. Before a work of art Malraux does not so much throw himself into a trance as throw himself into the work, becoming it, understanding it from inside; and what he says seems to come from the experience of the artist at work, his struggle with the demon and with destiny. By an imaginative leap he attempts to come into the presence of the artist and to listen to the voices of silence.

⤳ The Voices of Silence ⤶

At some very early stage in his life Malraux began meditating on a lengthy study of the psychology of art. It would be a vast work, or a collection of works, knitting together all his theories and accumulated insights into many cultures. It would be a work of generous physical proportions, well printed and magnificently illustrated with all the resources of the modern photoengraver, with the illustrations as an integral part of the text. From time to time he compiled notes for the work, and some of these were lost during the war. When he traveled, he was always visiting museums and collecting catalogues and photographs of works of art. If the catalogues and photographs were lost, no great harm was done, for he had an extraordinarily precise visual memory and could remember the exact details of paintings and sculptures. On the other hand he had very little memory for faces and he was apt to forget entire episodes in his own life, as though they had vanished into oblivion.

This study of art would not be a systematic treatise: there was no question of erecting a formal system of aesthetics or of attempting a philosophical inquiry into the nature of art. He would give himself the utmost freedom to develop his ideas, writing about whatever interested him and leaving to others the task of adding the scholarly footnotes. Ideas he had discussed in *The Temptation of the West* and *The Royal Way* would be elaborated; the strange transmutations of works of art would be examined; and the photographs would be so cunningly arranged that they would provide a kind of parallel argument. The essential themes were the artist in relation to his destiny and the destiny of his fellow men, and the primacy of art in a world which had lost its religious values.

The first fruits of the three-volume work appeared in 1947 with the publication of *The Imaginary Museum* by Skira in Geneva. It was a large book, admirably printed and bound, according to the current French bibliophilic custom, in cheap boards. There were twenty color plates and sixty-six black and white photographs, all of them reproduced with a quality rarely found even in the most expensive art books. Much of the space was taken up by the photographs, and of the 156 pages only about half bore full pages of letterpress. Except for the cheap boards, it was a book of considerable magnificence. A second edition was published two years later, and subsequently the greater part of the text was included in *The Voices of Silence.*

The Imaginary Museum opens with the now familiar statement that the museum is relatively unknown outside western Europe, where it has existed for less than two centuries. A museum is a collection of works of art out of context. Museums answered a need, but what need? And what happened to the statues and paintings on their journey from their original homes? A Gothic statue was an integral part of the church, a religious object and not merely a piece of sculpture. What happened when a Gothic statue was stood up against the wall of a museum beside twenty other statues of different periods? What had been lost? What had been gained?

These questions were not new, but Malraux demanded new answers, and sometimes he would color his questions with irony. Museums, even the greatest museums, suffered from curious limitations. The Metropolitan Museum of Art in New York, with its prestigious resources, would never be able to exhibit the Royal Portal at Chartres, and Napoleon, with all his armies, was never able to transport the Sistine Chapel to Paris. In all his life, Baudelaire, a wise and learned critic of art, never set eyes on a single work by Michelangelo, Masaccio, Piero della Francesca, Grünewald, or El Greco, for none of their works had ever reached France. Baudelaire knew very little about them. The names of El Greco and Grünewald would have meant nothing to him, and if he had heard of Michelangelo, it was only because many Frenchmen had visited the Sistine Chapel and some of them had written down their impressions or published books in which the tumultuous designs were rendered by frigid line drawings. And what Baudelaire did not know was known today by every fifteen-year-old schoolboy taking a course in the history of art.

The change had come about through the art of printing. The printer, in alliance with the photographer, reproduced paintings and sculptures in color with such accuracy that they could be regarded as authoritative substitutes for the original works, and these photographs were owned by millions. The arts of remote ages had become the common possession of all men.

Malraux did not use the phrase "the museum without walls." This was the invention of his translator. His "imaginary museum" was a museum vastly larger than any existing museums, for it included the entire corpus of the world's art, and at the same time, as though even an imaginary museum could be divided into separate rooms, it invited attention to the individual artist. A student of Rubens did not have to travel all over Europe to see his paintings. He could study them through photographs, acquiring without too much difficulty a more or less complete anthology of Rubens' works. Out of these anthologies there emerged an understanding of the artist's sudden changes of direction, the influences he accepted and those he rejected, the moments when he achieved supreme mastery of his own vision. The photographs could be shuffled, compared, set in opposition. With the totality of an artist's work lying in front of him in a single room, the critic was in the position of God on the Day of Judgment. He had all the evidence before him, and he could render a just verdict.

Nevertheless, the "imaginary museum" suffered from certain ineradicable defects. Because a photograph is not merely a mechanical reproduction, but depends upon the eye of the photographer, every photograph of a work of art is betrayed by the invisible presence of the photographer. Inevitably he distorts. He uses lighting to emphasize a detail he likes, but it may not have been a detail which the artist wanted to emphasize. Statues lose their volume, paintings lose their texture, a small detail can be magnified to the size of a page and a towering monument can be reduced to the size of a postage stamp. The reproductions of works of art are *transformations,* and the history of art, as taught in the schools, suffers from the misuses of photography. The dangers of the "imaginary museum" are only too evident; so are its triumphs. For the first time man has become heir to all the world's art. For the first time it is possible to trace the mysterious forces, like solar winds, which play upon the artists.

For the greater part of the work and throughout the two subsequent volumes, Malraux examines the arts with a kind of grave detachment, as though he were gazing at them from another planet. He sees the artist wrestling with destiny. The artist is the conqueror, or rather he is the man who goes forth to conquer. Words of conquest and strategy pepper the pages—*conflit, conquérir, imposer, arracher, acharnement, annexer, acquérir* are continually employed to suggest the violence of the encounter between the artist and destiny.

Throughout, Malraux speaks in grave generalities. He is not in the least interested in dates and attributions and aesthetic information; nor is he deeply interested in any single work of art. For him Romanesque and Gothic are supreme works of art, and when he speaks about them, it is as though he were involved in a passionate encounter with their destinies. He is continually attempting to say what paintings and sculptures would say if they could speak. He is Jacob wrestling with the angel, and sometimes in the heat of battle he will permit himself to say things that a fifteen-year-old boy would regard as ludicrous, and at other times he will say wise and simple things that had never been said before.

The method is a dangerous one, for it offers hostages to fortune. Having once established that all the world's art is a field to be explored, and that the same or very similar general laws pertain to all the generations of art, he scarcely knows where to begin, and runs backward and forward across those immense flower gardens, too dazzled by their beauty to pause for any length of time. He is always abandoning an argument to pursue another, as though the world of art were so full of arguments that all of them must be enjoyed. The transitions are sometimes hair-raising, and as he hurtles from one idea to another the reader sometimes has the impression that he is riding on a roller coaster and is in imminent danger of being hurled out of the car while riding hundreds of feet above the earth.

The method is a strictly personal one, and the book sometimes reads like disjointed notes from a philosopher's diary, with excerpts from all his previous works. Part of his *Sketch for a Psychology of the Cinema* is incorporated boldly in *The Imaginary Museum,* and here and there one recognizes portions of essays written earlier. Yet these disjointed notes have a cumulative effect. We are in the presence of a mind passionately engrossed in art: he is not simply talking about art, but is speaking as though his whole life depended on it.

With *The Creation of Art,* the second volume of the series, which appeared in 1948, Malraux virtually abandons the "imaginary museum" for a long discursive essay on the theme of the artist's vision of the Eternal. Divinity shapes the features of the gods, but man shapes the features of the Eternal. So we find that in the portraits of the gods, man and divinity are seen in uneasy alliance, and sometimes man predominates, sometimes divinity. Some of the best pages describe the changing faces of Buddha and Christ over the centuries:

> Christianity was dominated by the dramatic image of an execution, Buddhism by the serene image of a meditation. Hence, throughout the centuries of the great periods of Buddhism, the gradual lowering of the eyelids, the calligraphy becoming increasingly strained, seeming "to close" the face of Buddha upon his silent meditations. Meanwhile the folds of his garment become more closely fitted to his body, and the body itself becomes increasingly an abstraction. Throughout the Buddhist South, the body of the Buddha in meditation becomes naked. But whereas the Greek nudes of the late period (and even those of the sixth century before Christ unlike their predecessors in Egypt) always suggested movement, the naked Buddha is not merely motionless, he is released from all movement.

Just as Buddha changes his features, becoming more attenuated and ethereal the further he travels from India, so Christ changes his features and his royal emblems as soon as he escapes from the domination of Byzantium:

> The cathedrals came into being at the same time as French royalty: the Christ-King crowning the Virgin takes his place beside the Crucified. The Virgin, whose consoling shadow

lengthens unceasingly over Europe, ushers women into possession of the Western world sorrow by sorrow, according to their
calling, into that congregation to which every saint brings his
meed of charity. Nearly all the Cathedrals of the time were
dedicated to her; the theme of her coronation became ever more
prominent; and the Christ who crowns her is less and less the
Lord, more and more the King.

On the brows of the Son of God, who came to die on the
cross of the doomed, the kingly crown (for in the Middle Ages
there is nothing abstract about the crown) replaces the crown of
thorns. The victory of this image of the new Christendom is all
the more assured since for many sculptors it is soon to become
incarnate, and for those of Rheims it is already incarnate: the
mightiest monarch of Europe is St. Louis. Here is no longer the
Christ of Moissac, the romanesque Pantocrator. Instead, for
the first time, Christian man finds himself in harmony with the
world. The crowned head which sculptors are now carving on
cathedral porches, that face where power and justice are for the
first time united, is such a face as they would ascribe to the
King of France in their dreams.

From such passages Malraux's method becomes clear, for these
meditations on works of art always begin with a single work and
then flow out beyond it, like the ripples when a stone is flung into a
pool. Very often the meditations appear to arise from photographs,
not from the original object. In *The Creation of Art* he reproduces
a brilliant closeup of the Rheim's Christ, then reproduces the same
photograph many times enlarged, but without the crown, thus emphasizing the tragic grandeur of the face, so stern, so august, so
powerful that it might have been carved by Michelangelo.

The photographs are far more than a running commentary on the
text. Expertly selected, brilliantly engraved, they assert the primacy
of art by their sheer splendor. Most of them are sculptures, and the
best have a three-dimensional quality which makes them seem to
leap from the page. Later, when the same photographs were reproduced in *The Voices of Silence* on a reduced scale, they lost much

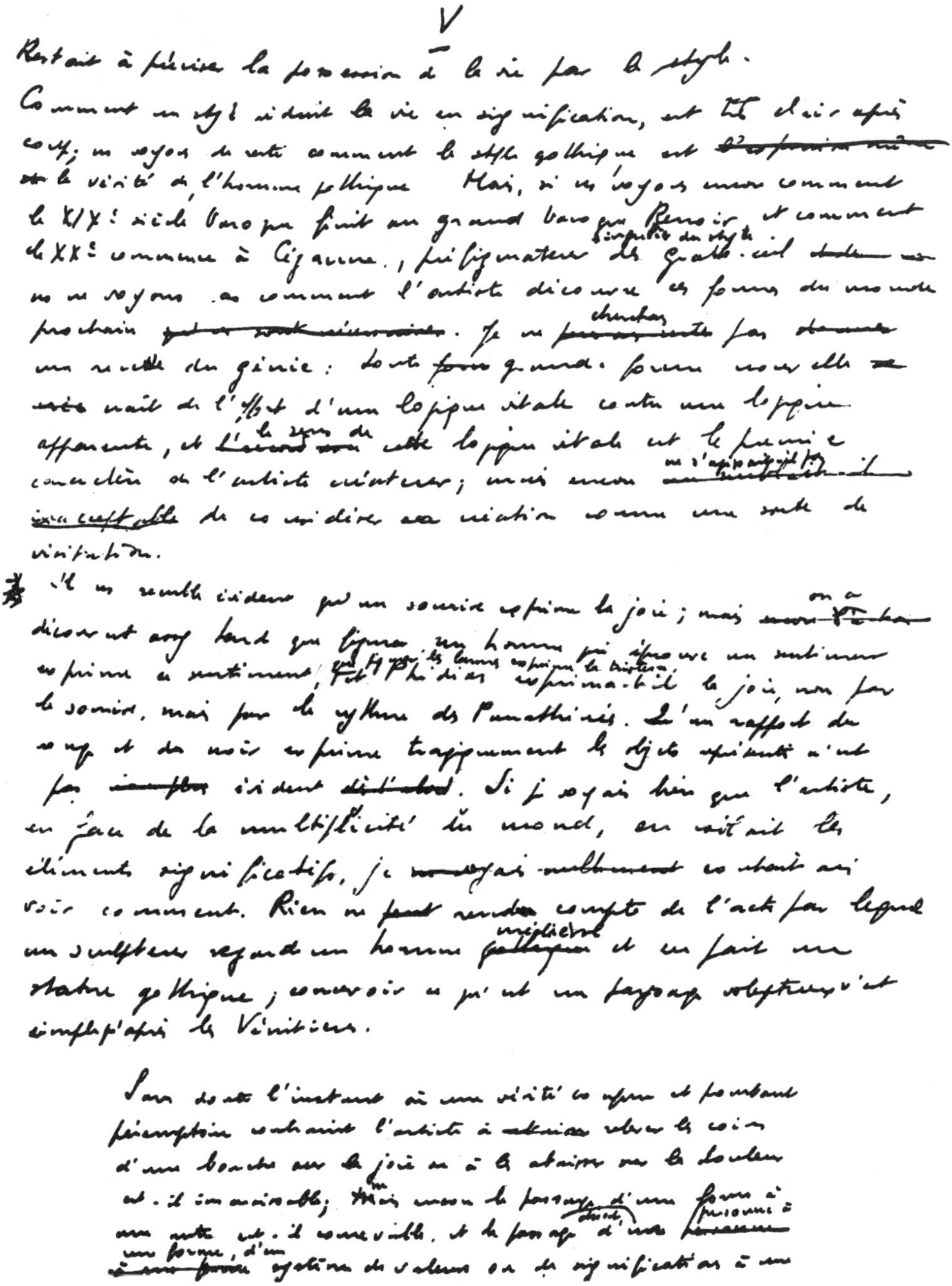

V

Restait à préciser la possession de la vie par le style.

Comment un style réduit la vie en signification, est très clair après coup; nous voyons de reste comment le style gothique est [illegible] la vérité de l'homme gothique. Mais, si nous voyons mieux comment le XIXe siècle baroque finit au grand baroque Renoir, et comment le XXe commence à Cézanne, [illegible] des gratte-ciel [illegible] nous ne voyons pas comment l'artiste découvre ces formes du monde prochain [illegible]. Je ne chercherai pas [illegible] une recette du génie: toute grande forme nouvelle naît de l'effet d'une logique vitale contre une logique apparente, et le sens de cette logique vitale est la première conscience de l'artiste créateur; mais encore ne s'apparaît-il pas [illegible] de considérer sa création comme une sorte de révélation.

Il me semble évident qu'un sourire exprime la joie; mais on a découvert assez tard que [illegible] un homme qui éprouve un sentiment exprime ce sentiment, [illegible] Phidias exprima-t-il la joie, non par le sourire, mais par le rythme des Panathénées. Qu'un rapport de rouge et de noir exprime tragiquement les objets représentés n'est pas [illegible] évident [illegible]. Si je savais bien que l'artiste, en face de la multiplicité du monde, en extrait les éléments significatifs, je ne savais nullement [illegible] voir comment. Rien ne peut rendre compte de l'acte par lequel un sculpteur regarde un homme [illegible] et en fait une statue gothique; [illegible] un paysage voluptueux n'est simple qu'après les Vénitiens.

Sans doute l'instant où une vérité se [illegible] et pourtant [illegible] l'artiste à [illegible] les coins d'une bouche avec la joie ou à les abaisser avec la douleur est-il inconcevable; mais [illegible] le passage d'une forme à une autre est-il concevable, et le passage d'une [illegible] à une forme, d'un système de valeurs ou de significations à un

Manuscript worksheet from The Psychology of Art.

of their essential beauty. Malraux seems at ease in the large clear pages of *The Psychology of Art;* in the smaller pages of *The Voices of Silence,* with its crowded text, the words seem to be constrained and crushed under the burden of the illustrations.

Many historians of art were offended by Malraux's intensely personal commentaries on art. He was accused of recklessly entering a field in which he had no competence. Georges Duthuit, an art historian of some competence, was so incensed by *The Voices of Silence* that he began to write a pamphlet against it, and in time the pamphlet was expanded into a book of over six hundred pages, which he called *The Unimaginable Museum.* He charged that Malraux had failed to read the proper authorities, and was especially at fault in his study of Gandhara art. The long, exhausting speech for the prosecution is among the curiosities of French literature, for Duthuit sometimes follows Malraux sentence by sentence, demonstrating that each word is reprehensible and every idea is horrible beyond measure; but of course he is not horrified so much as fascinated by Malraux's progress through the arts, and he demonstrates the extent of his fascination by a prolonged study of Malraux's ideas.

Malraux's contemporary, René Huyghe, the honorary curator-in-chief of the Louvre, covers much the same ground as Malraux in his book *Ideas and Images of World Art: Dialogue with the Visible.* He is interested in the specific artist and his relationship to his times, avoids generalities, and scarcely permits himself a thought on man and destiny. He sees art, even the most terrifying art, as though it were embraced in a delicate, shimmering, radiance. Malraux clings to the heights where the storms gather and the lightning strikes. Huyghe, a scholar who prefers to wear his scholarship lightly, clings to the foothills and the valleys. In this way they complement each other admirably.

In *The Currency of the Absolute,* the third volume of the series, amid discussion of Negro masks, the *douanier* Rousseau, Gallic coins, tombs from Fayyum, and various aspects of the art of Rembrandt, Vermeer and Caravaggio, Malraux discourses on the strange metamorphoses of works of art. At first a work of art belongs to the currency of the divine, then of poetry, then of the people and of nature. In our time, where the gods are absent, it enters the domain of the absolute. Thus it is constantly changing, acquiring new meanings, accustoming itself to new spectators, and offering always new sensations to its worshipers. A chair painted by Von Gogh meant nothing to his contemporaries, but means something very clear to the people living today. In a hundred years time it will become another chair altogether.

Malraux continued this argument in a later work, *The Metamorphosis of the Gods,* published in 1957. He examines the question historically, beginning with the earliest works of art and ending with the Flemish masters, to whom he had long been devoted. The changing forms of the gods and their changing commerce with men are discussed in a far more orderly fashion than in his previous works. The voice is more somber, more mature; he had mastered his tendency to ignite fireworks at every opportunity. The work of art holds the stage, and Malraux no longer looms above it like a Brocken specter haranguing destiny.

As he works out his theory of the metamorphoses of art, Malraux introduces new elements into the equation. Time and eternity now make their appearance as active protagonists, as indeed they must, since he is discussing art in historical terms, and eternity is contained within a work of art. The procession passes before our eyes in logical order. Malraux's discovery of order gives precision to his judgments, but there is less poetry in *The Metamorphosis of the Gods* than in his other works; and sometimes there is a note of exhaustion.

While *The Currency of the Absolute* was being printed Malraux fell ill, and during the long months of convalescence he began to rearrange and elaborate his ideas, shaping the three long essays into the single volume that eventually became *The Voices of Silence.* Something of the enforced quietness and of the subtle excitement of convalescence enters into the work; the tone deepens; the urgent voice sometimes grows less urgent, because it is more assured. While the gods were suffering their metamorphosis, Malraux was suffering his. He was himself entering into the Gothic world of decay and resurrection.

Recovered from his illness, he went on his travels. In 1952 he traveled to Greece, Egypt, Persia and the Middle East, his favorite hunting ground, which he had not seen for twenty years. In the following years he traveled twice to the United States to give speeches at Columbia University and the Metropolitan Museum of Art. The speeches were remembered excerpts from his own books, but delivered with great verve. He was back in harness again, ready for whatever adventures awaited him. For a long time he had lived the inactive life of a scholar, and he was thirsting for action.

During 1957 the troubles in Algeria were rapidly approaching a crisis. The French *colons* had taken up arms against the Algerian rebels and on both sides atrocities were being committed on an unprecedented scale. Algeria was becoming a nightmare of burned villages, well-equipped torture chambers, and automobiles speeding through the streets and spraying machine-gun fire on crowds of innocent shoppers. The torture chambers belonged to the French Army, and they were operated openly by men in full uniform. They tortured the Algerians who fell into their hands and they sometimes tortured Frenchmen who sided with the rebels. They tortured women as well as men, and they tortured children. General Massu, one of the French generals, was credited with the statement: "We employ torture regularly, whenever it is needed. I, too, have submitted to torture to see what it is like. A strong man can survive it."

Among those who were tortured was Henri Alleg, a French Communist working for the rebels. When he was finally released, he wrote a restrained account of his experiences, which was published by Les Éditions de Minuit and immediately banned by the French government "as tending to bring disrepute upon the French Army." In spite of the official ban, some sixty thousand copies were sold in a few weeks. Henri Alleg's book was called *The Question,* and the essential question to be answered was whether the French Army in Algiers was to be permitted to employ torture as a weapon against its enemies. Another question was whether they had acted with the authority of the French government. A third question was whether the government had the right to ban a book which was so palpably truthful that the French Army never troubled to dispute the author's account of his sufferings. Alleg was a very sick man, and many years would pass before he would be able to resume work. Should a man be compensated for his sufferings under torture? Was there any way in which the government could be brought to judgment?

Four men, André Malraux, Roger Martin du Gard, François Mauriac, and Jean-Paul Sartre, decided to appeal to René Coty, the President of the Republic. They were men of different political opinions and persuasions. Sartre cordially disliked Malraux and Mauriac was always critical of him, always fearing that he would emerge as the Saint-Just of the coming revolution. Nevertheless they were united in their opposition to torture. They wrote:

> The undersigned:—
>
> —Protest against the seizure of Henri Alleg's book, *The Question,* and against all the attacks against liberty of opinion and expression of ideas that recently preceded this seizure.
>
> —Ask that the facts reported by Henri Alleg be disclosed publicly and with complete impartiality.
>
> —Call on the Administration, in the name of the Declaration of the Rights of Man and of the Citizen, to condemn unequivocally the use of torture, which brings shame to the cause that it supposedly serves.
>
> —And call on all Frenchmen to join us in signing his "personal petition" and sending it to the League for the Rights of Man.
>
> ANDRÉ MALRAUX
> ROGER MARTIN DU GARD
> FRANÇOIS MAURIAC
> JEAN-PAUL SARTRE

The appeal, which was printed on the front page of the Communist newspaper *L'Humanité* on April 17, 1958, had almost no effect, and the tortures continued as before. Roger Martin du Gard had long ago lost his faith in the French government, and in all governments, and a few months later he died a bitterly disappointed man. In the last year of his life there was only one moment which gave him any particular pleasure. This moment occurred when he learned that Albert Camus had won the Nobel Prize for literature. He had himself won the prize exactly twenty years before. Camus himself said he would have given the prize to Malraux.

As Roger Martin du Gard lay dying, the Fourth Republic was in its death throes. An incompetent President, and an even more incompetent Prime Minister, supervised the burial rites, while De Gaulle kept silent watch from his retreat at Colombey-les-deux-Églises. In Algeria the Army confronted the government with its growing determination to wrest power and bring about a Committee of Public Safety, ruling by military decree, and if necessary they would take Paris by storm and submit France to the same regimen.

The country was on the verge of civil war, with the Communists preparing to install a Commune in Paris and the French officers in Algeria preparing to invade France exactly as Franco had invaded Spain. No one in the government knew how to deal with this threatening situation. Suddenly De Gaulle emerged long enough from his country retreat to announce that he was ready to assume the powers of the Republic. At these words the Fourth Republic crumbled like the walls of Jericho before the trumpets of Joshua. On June 1, 1958, De Gaulle swept into power, and there began the long, slow, tortuous task of bringing order and sanity to France and peace to Algeria.

Malraux became the Minister of Information in the new government. He was neither a particularly efficient nor particularly amenable Minister of Information, for he had his own theories on how the war in Algeria should be settled. A month later he became a minister of state without portfolio. On January 8, 1959, when De Gaulle became the President of France and Michel Debré became Prime Minister, Malraux was appointed minister of state in charge of cultural affairs. Then for the first time he was in a position of power.

Malraux in his office, 1945. (FRENCH EMBASSY PRESS AND INFORMATION DIVISION, NEW YORK)

*May 1962, at the White House. From left to right: French Ambassador Hervé Alphand,
Malraux, Mme. Malraux, Lyndon Johnson, Mrs. Kennedy, President Kennedy.*
(FRENCH EMBASSY PRESS AND INFORMATION DIVISION, NEW YORK)

*Malraux delivering funeral oration for Georges Braque in front of the
Colonnade of the Louvre.* (FRENCH EMBASSY PRESS AND
INFORMATION DIVISION, NEW YORK)

Facing: Georges Braque (FRENCH EMBASSY PRESS AND INFORMATION DIVISION, NEW YORK)

Peking, August 1965. From left to right: Liu Shao-chi, Mao Tse-tung,
Chen Yi, Interpreter, Malraux, French Ambassador Lucien Paye.
(ANDRÉ MALRAUX)

Nehru and Malraux, with Marcel Brandin above Malraux's left shoulder.
(PHOTO MICHEL ROY)

Malraux after receiving honorary doctorate at Oxford.
(ANDRÉ MALRAUX)

Facing: *Malraux and Le Corbusier* (ANDRÉ MALRAUX)

Bronze Medal by André Masson. (FRENCH EMBASSY PRESS AND
INFORMATION DIVISION, NEW YORK)

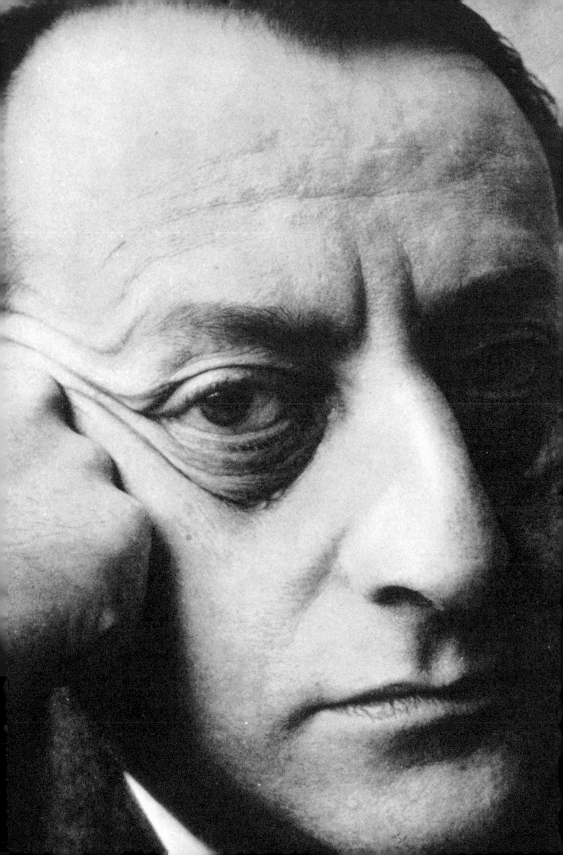

THE MINISTER

> One night Mallarmé was listening to the cats talking to one another on the roof. One inquisitive black cat said to another: "And what do you do?" And the other said: "At the moment I am pretending to be the cat of the Mallarmés."
>
> —ANTIMÉMOIRES

⊸ The Ceremony of Art ⊱

When in May 1958 General De Gaulle announced that he was ready to assume the powers of the Republic, Malraux was lecturing in Venice. He knew, as all Frenchmen knew, that the words were decisive, if only because no one else would have dared to utter them with any hope of being listened to. They were not the words of a man, but of a legend. Charles de Gaulle had been a shadow; now he was granite. Though the crowds marched in the street and proclaimed that the Fourth Republic must be defended at all costs, there were very few who had any illusions about his power. He had only to shake his finger and the Fourth Republic would go down to defeat.

Malraux hurried back to Paris and was soon closeted with De Gaulle in the suite which was always kept ready for the general in the Hotel Lapérouse. They knew each other well, but there was always a distance between them. De Gaulle rarely unbent. He had the Roman *gravitas* and the Roman fixity of purpose; the mask, which was ruthlessly maintained, concealed the turmoil which derived inevitably from his mixed ancestry, for there was Irish and German blood in him. Malraux watched him closely. He had aged considerably, there were deep lines on his face, and the mustache was gray. At sixty-seven he seemed as indestructible and uncompromising as ever, though uncertain about his aims. He had no plans for bringing the war in Algeria to an end, but seemed to believe that if France could be regenerated, the war in Algeria could somehow take care of itself. Malraux was particularly impressed by his essentially military cast of mind; he was far more the general than the politician.

It was a time of myths, of legends, of desperate stratagems. Since no one in Paris really knew what was happening in Algeria, where the

secret armies were being led by secret societies, and where the center
of power was continually shifting, General de Gaulle seemed to be
waiting for the moment when the emerging pattern would crystallize.
The days passed; the emerging pattern remained as elusive as ever.
Malraux, appointed Minister of Information, with very little knowledge
about what was happening in Algeria, convinced himself that a new
Moslem-French fraternity had come into existence. He believed that
Arabs were fraternizing with young French soldiers against the *pieds
noirs,* the French colonials with their vested interests in Algeria. "It is
clearly apparent," he announced, "that an extraordinarily popular and
powerful movement, with an historic sweep has come into existence."
The soldiers represented the new France, swept clean of political
dogmas, rejoicing in equality, fraternity, and liberty. "For the first time,"
he declared, "an Islamic revolution is not being fought against the
West, but in its name, for in Algeria they are crying, 'Long live
Algérie française!' "

Malraux's theory of a *pax franco-islamica* was not borne out by the
radio broadcasting from Algiers or by the press correspondents on the
spot. In his impatience with facts, he had invented an imaginary situation, seeing the France of the Crusades and of the French Revolution
meeting on the soil of North Africa, the Arabs caught up in the spirit
of revolutionary brotherhood, the despised *colons* retreating in confusion. He was Minister of Information from June 4 to July 7, and was
then replaced by Jacques Soustelle.

As minister without portfolio, Malraux was given a variety of ceremonial tasks, many of them pleasant because they involved extensive
travel. Shortly before the referendum on the new constitution, De
Gaulle sent him to the French possessions in the Caribbean, where
the people would soon vote on whether they would remain within the
French community. He flew to Guadaloupe and found himself for the
first time delivering a speech before a black audience, the brilliant
turbans of the women glowing in the light of a tropical evening. He
flew on to Martinique, where the ceremonial reading of a message from
General de Gaulle was followed by a strange, ecstatic, frenzied singing
of the *Marseillaise,* frightening in its unexpected intensity. But at
Cayenne, in French Guiana, the mood was far more terrifying. Malraux

spoke from a kind of bandstand set in a vast square, and in the darkness he was aware of a seething mass of people beyond the glare of the floodlights. It was a speech he had delivered many times, calling upon the people to remain within the French community and to grant De Gaulle the necessary powers to raise France to its proper height of grandeur. The people were strangely quiet; he was aware of movement in the darkness, but he had no idea what they were doing. Suddenly three banners began to rise. They were inscribed: DOWN WITH FASCISM, DOWN WITH DE GAULLE, DOWN WITH FRANCE. Some time later sticks with nails driven into them were showered onto the platform. Malraux continued speaking. There was polite applause from the people bathed in the light of the floodlamps, while screams could be heard from the darkness. He had the feeling that at any moment the crowd would surrender to an orgy of bloodshed, and he remembered the novel *Georges,* which he had read when he was very young: the massacres and the uprisings. In fact, there had been a half-hearted attempt to provoke a revolution, but the attempt failed, apparently because of a general unwillingness to shed blood. Anti-French tracts had been found printed on the government press, and there was a rumor that Communists had crossed the border from British Guiana. Later in the evening there was a reception, with all the dignitaries of the colony being presented to Malraux and his wife, and a few days later came an overwhelming vote in favor of De Gaulle, but Malraux was never to forget the strange night when the sticks with their protruding nails came winging out of the darkness.

Returning from the Caribbean, he was sent to India to confer with Nehru. He had known India under the British; now for the first time he saw India under Indian rule. Nehru was an old friend, for they had met in Paris at the time of the Spanish Civil War and discussed a subject that interested them profoundly: how had it come about that Buddhism, after centuries of dominance in India, had been extinguished in the country of its birth while remaining alive in the other countries of the Far East? Now they resumed their interrupted discussions, faintly amused by their changed circumstances. Malraux lectured Nehru on art; Nehru lectured Malraux on Gandhi and on the difficulties of creating a secular state in a deeply religious country. "Tomorrow," said

Nehru, "we shall learn from the newspapers what we have said to each other." But the newspapers were strangely silent about the meeting between the two former revolutionaries. And Malraux expressed astonishment at a revolution which had been carried out without any of the conventional revolutionary acts—"No coronation of Napoleon, no cruiser *Aurora* searching for the Winter Palace with the great fingers of its guns." The Indian revolution puzzled him. Many years later, when a student uprising broke out in Paris and threatened De Gaulle's government, Malraux said it lacked the proper legendary instruments necessary in a real revolution. He seemed to be looking for coronations and guns.

India fascinated him and Nehru's quick subtle mind delighted him with its ironies. Indeed, there were ironies everywhere in New Delhi. Two lines of Bengal Lancers, dressed in rainbow colors, saluted him as he made his way to official receptions. The British symbols of imperial rule remained, while in the darkness beyond the walls of the government buildings fakirs still smeared themselves with ashes and the recitation of the *Bhagavad-Gita* continued uninterruptedly. Malraux found himself wondering why Nehru had not adopted the tactics of Mao Tse-tung, crushing the landlords, the moneylenders and the caste system by force of arms.

When he returned to France, the long-awaited plan to institute a ministry of culture had already been approved by De Gaulle. On January 8, 1959, Malraux entered the cabinet of Michel Debré as *Ministre d'État chargé des Affaires Culturelles.* Almost no limit was placed on his powers, but very little money was granted to the new ministry, which was housed in the Rue de Valois on the site of a palace once occupied by Cardinal Richelieu. There he gathered around him a group of dedicated assistants determined to change the cultural face of France. Visitors were dazzled by mirrors, tapestries, gold and white paneling, an air of religious decorum induced by the presence of the frock-coated *huissiers,* and by a strange statue of a naked youth in black bronze; but the luxurious furnishings were misleading. Most of Malraux's hard-working assistants worked in small cubby holes.

The plans proliferated, but not all of them got beyond the drawing board. Above all, Malraux wanted to establish cultural centers all over

France. They would comprise theaters, exhibition halls, cinemas, libraries, reading rooms. In America something very similar was evolving in the public libraries, where exhibitions and cinema shows are often held, but the French were more inclined toward a private interest in the arts. Malraux fought for his *Maisons de la Culture* with the fury of an aroused pedagogue, but there was little response from the parliament and less from the treasury. He had plans for a French Biennale, for an inventory of French art treasures, for a national orchestra, for new theaters. There would be exhibitions of art on a scale hitherto unknown. Paris would be washed clean, while Versailles, Chambord and Fontainebleau would be restored to their ancient glory. A vigorous campaign to protect works of art in danger of destruction or disintegration would be introduced. Inevitably there were conflicts, for artists are notoriously quarrelsome. In the course of time there were quarrels with conductors, leading actors, cinema directors, the Cinemathèque Française, and nearly every cultural institution in France. Malraux had to judge every situation in the light of "the totality of French culture"; and sometimes it was necessary to pass judgment on men who were his close friends.

It was not the best time to organize a ministry of culture. The war in Algeria was still going on, with no end in sight. It was not so much a war as a series of senseless revolts and massacres, a perpetual bloodletting which drained the energies of the Arabs and the *colons* alike. De Gaulle made ineffective gestures to put an end to the war, but failed. It was the time of the plastic bombs, of mysterious arrests and disappearances, the police beating up everyone who protested against the continuance of the "dirty war." By April 1961 the pot was boiling over, as the generals in Algeria threatened to send an army of parachuters to Paris, and De Gaulle and Debré appealed to the French to be vigilant against the traitors descending from the skies. Debré urged the people to go by foot or by car to meet the insurgents and to argue them out of their absurd fantasies. Malraux, too, went to the microphone and appealed for a popular militia against the threatened insurrection, with the result that thousands of volunteers clamored for firearms. Nothing happened; the war went on.

In the following month Malraux suffered the most cruel blow of all.

His two sons, Pierre-Gauthier, who was twenty, and Vincent, who was eighteen, were killed in an automobile accident. They were both handsome, gifted, in love with life. Vincent, who was engaged to be married to a beautiful Russian girl, was showing remarkable talent as a writer. Those who were close to Malraux feared that he would lose the desire to live, and he was a broken man when De Gaulle hurried to his house to offer his condolences.

Father Bockel, the chaplain of the Brigade Alsace-Lorraine, hurried from Strasbourg to be by his side. "There must be a church service," he said quietly, and Malraux objected, saying that he had been an agnostic all his life, and did not feel he could change his beliefs because his sons had been killed. Nevertheless there was a solemn mass, and the boys were buried side by side in a small cemetery in Paris. Not far away lay the grave of their mother, who had died in Brive but whose remains had been transported to Paris.

A few days after the burial President Kennedy made his official visit to Paris. The youthful President, about to undertake a dangerous confrontation with Khrushchev in Vienna, had little time to see the sights of Paris. Malraux, white and haggard, accompanied Jacqueline Kennedy to the Louvre, Versailles and Malmaison. Sometimes, as he delivered his intense lectures on art, he would momentarily forget the weight of the tragedy, his interminable commerce with death.

Violence was in the air, and no one ever counted the number of victims slain or permanently injured in France and Algeria during the Algerian war. On February 6, 1962, somebody placed a plastic bomb on a windowsill of the house where he was living. It exploded and a four-year-old girl, Delphine Renard, was struck in the eye by a splinter of glass. The bomb had been placed on the windowsill of her nursery on the ground floor; the perpetrators had forgotten, or did not know, that Malraux and his family lived on the first and second floors. Delphine Renard lost the sight of her eye.

There had been attempts to kill Malraux before. Once, when he was working in his office in the building of the *Rassemblement du Peuple Français* on the Boulevard des Capucines, near the Opera, a bullet smashed through the shutter of a window, narrowly missing him. Since that time he had always kept a loaded revolver within easy reach.

In May 1962 he was invited to speak in New York on the occasion of the fifteenth anniversary of the French Institute. Death hovered over the speech—the deaths in Algeria, the death which is implicit in every surviving culture and all forms of art. Once more he attempted to define culture. "The culture of every one of us is the mysterious presence in our lives of what should belong to death." And then again, later in the same speech: "Culture is the highest form of rivalry known to humanity. It does not act upon our imaginations, as religious values do, by its exemplary nature; it orients our imaginations, orienting them 'toward the heights,' by compelling them to compete with the greatest human dreams." The artists wrestle with the angel, and the angel is the human heart. So, again and again, he would confront the nature of art, as though he could reach out and grasp the fiery core.

He was continually escaping from his office and making brief official journeys abroad—to Moscow, Athens, Brasilia, Senegal, Egypt. In 1963 he sent the *Mona Lisa* to America, and in the following year he sent the Venus de Milo to Japan. The same year saw the unveiling of Chagall's vast painting for the ceiling of the Paris Opera where the features of Malraux, disguised as Pelléas, the lover of Mélisande, were painted into the rainbow colors. That year, too, saw the beginning of the great inventory of French artistic treasures, which he had planned long ago. It would take thirty years to complete, and fill a hundred volumes, but it was on its way. The *Maisons de la Culture* were progressing slowly—too slowly for Malraux's taste. These cultural centers lay at the center of his hopes, and every year he pleaded more and more vehemently for more and more money for them, but since his ministry received less than a third of one per cent of the total budget, progress was inevitably slow. Nine centers were built. They were at Amiens, Bourges, Le Havre, Grenoble, Rennes, Rheims, Nevors, Paris, and Firminy, the last being a small mining town in the Loire. In every way possible he was asserting the primacy of art against the powers that fought relentlessly against art.

When the painter Georges Braque died at the age of eighty-one, Malraux, who had known him well, felt that the time had come for the state to pay its tribute to a great artist. It was not only that Braque was the founder of Cubism, and was therefore one of the great seminal influences on modern art, but there was also something extraordinarily heroic in the artist's adventures through unexplored regions of color. In a famous essay Apollinaire had pointed to Braque's heroic qualities, and it was proper that he should be given a hero's funeral. In 1885 the body of Victor Hugo lay in state beneath the Arc de Triomphe, and two million Frenchmen followed the simple hearse in the dawn light to his burial in the Pantheon. Braque had wanted to be buried in Normandy, and therefore there could be no funeral procession on the scale accorded to Victor Hugo. But at the very least there could be a spectacular ceremony in honor of the dead painter.

On September 3, 1963, in the evening, while the rain fell and the scudding clouds assumed the shapes of Braque's guitars, the simple coffin lay on a monumental catafalque covered with the tricolor in the Cour Carrée opposite the flamboyant Gothic tower of St. Germain l'Auxerrois, the church of the French kings. Guards from the state museums and soldiers carrying torches accompanied the coffin to the catafalque, while the musicians of the Garde Républicaine played Beethoven's *Funeral March*. The bells of the royal church were tolling for the dead painter. Malraux delivered the funeral oration, addressing himself across the cobblestones to the artist's widow, hidden in her black veils. He said:

> Never before has a modern country rendered such a homage to one of her dead painters. The history of painting, which finds authoritative achievement in the work of Braque, has been a long history of disdain, misery and despair. By his very death Braque seems to avenge the pathetic obsequies of Modigliani, the grim funeral of Van Gogh. And since all Frenchmen know that part of the honor of France is called Victor Hugo, it is well to tell them there is also a part of the honor of France which is called Braque—for the honor of a country is in what it gives to the world.
>
> His paintings are to be seen in all the great museums, and in Tokyo more than a hundred thousand Japanese came to his exhibition as though on a pilgrimage. In his studio, which knew no other passion than painting, glory entered and then stepped

Hommage
à Braque

Avant que G. B. ayen dans le plus _____ _____ fait
a choisi, j'apposti __ l'hommage solennel à la France.

[Vous avez reconnu, Madame, le message par le vrai
d'un tendre, venant en clochen par _____ partir pour les ro.
c'est le M. F. pour le M. d'un _____ donnant un pays, ne devie
__ a rendre 2 un de ces peintres mais un hommage de __

__ nature d'histoire à la peinture par Pinne de l'œuvre de Braque un
accomplissement impossible ___ a été un _____ ~~_____~~ histoire de dédans
l'chaos de _____ et de d-_____ Et je ne fu de mort, Braque _____
_____ la recherche des _____ disigne de Modigliana des _____
_____ de Van Gogh... Et puisque ──────────────→

De plus, en se révélant avec une puissance contagieuse, la liberté de la peinture. Braque et ses amis de 1910 nous révèlent aussi dans l'art les plus rebelle à l'illusion, depuis notre peinture romane jusqu'à un fond de siècles [...] Fidèlement ou rigoureusement pendu sur leurs table sans immédiat, ces peintures nous montraient pour nous tout le fond du monde...

Enfin, ces peintures exprimant la France à l'égalité celle de Corot, — mais plus mystérieusement, car Corot, lui, l'avait beaucoup représentée. Braque l'exprimera [...] avec une force de qualité si grande qu'il est aussi légitime... moment [...] leur en douter que l'ange de Reims dans sa cathédrale. Samedi, ses ors retrouveraient bientôt toute leur...

mais bien connue : alors que ceux à jamais ~~quand~~ quelques regards ces accords entendus de Debussy est mort. »

[Madame,] [Demain matin] Lili par l'un d'eux aux marins et aux ouvriers de Varengeville, qui admiraient Georges Braque, instinctivement, sans comprendre son art ... quand il était devant le palais des rois de la ~~...~~ premier peintre du monde, il y avait donc l'~~autre~~ la main plus pure une voix indistincte qui disait merci, et une main plus humble, une main usée de paysan, qui était la main de la France, et qui se lève une dernière fois dans la nuit pour caresser doucement ses cheveux blancs. »

aside, so as not to disturb a single color, or line, or article of furniture. Glory remained silent and motionless like those white birds that began to appear in his paintings in his old age. He had become one of the great painters of the century. . . .

Tomorrow morning, Madame, let it be known to the sailors and peasants of Varangeville, who knew Georges Braque without perhaps understanding his art: "Yesterday, when he was facing the palace of the kings and the first museum in the world, a dim voice was heard on a rainy night, a voice of gratitude; and a simple hand, the worn hand of a peasant woman, the hand of France, rose for the last time during the night and softly caressed his white hair."

As Malraux finished speaking, the moon came out, white and glittering, as though he had summoned it out of the sky to smile on the white birds and the white hair. Then he walked across the cobblestones and embraced the widow of Georges Braque and the ceremony was over.

Malraux's notes for the funeral oration, written on some slips of paper, have survived, and they show him writing with ease and with scarcely any corrections or erasures. He had evidently pondered the speech for a long time and then let it burst forth like a completed poem, with only such changes as were necessary for the sake of rhythm or the spirit of the occasion. So, originally, he wrote that the history of painting was "a long history of despair," and this was changed to "a long history of disdain, misery and despair." At the very end he had written of a dim voice coming out of the shadows, and this was changed to a dim voice "heard on a rainy night."

Official orations in France nearly always follow a fixed and predictable pattern, and there was need for someone to break the mold. Malraux had exactly the right qualifications for breaking it.

In the following year the ashes of Jean Moulin were solemnly entombed in the Pantheon. Moulin was an authentic hero of the Resistance, one of those men whose courage went far beyond ordinary courage. Sent by De Gaulle from London to take command of the Resistance forces, he parachuted into southern France, but was arrested by the Germans at Lyons a few weeks later. Tortured, beaten, clubbed into insensibility and then revived by cold water, he was to know all the subtleties of spiritual and physical pain, but gave nothing away. He had been a man of mystery who went by many aliases—Max, Rex, Regis—but that he was a man of mystery was the least mysterious thing about him. Earlier in the war, after being captured by the Germans, he broke a windowpane and slashed his own throat. The nuns of Chartres saved his life, and he was heard to say in a weak voice, "I will never again seek escape in death." He escaped to England, and De Gaulle was one of the many who realized that this rather self-effacing man with the husky voice would inevitably assume high position, if he survived. He died of his tortures while being taken on a train to a prison camp in Germany.

Moulin was the symbol of the Resistance, and the transfer of his ashes to the Pantheon therefore took on the aspects of a national rite. The ceremony took place during the night of December 19, 1964, with the ashes being solemnly transported from the Crypt of the Deportees in the shadow of Nôtre-Dame to another crypt in the Pantheon. They were placed in a child's coffin and borne on a tank, which rumbled up the Boulevard St. Michel with a guard of honor formed of thousands of former Resistance fighters. In the morning, with an icy wind blowing, Malraux pronounced the funeral oration. It was a very long oration, covering some eleven pages of text, and Malraux poured into it all his reverence for Moulin, whom he had never known, and for the Resistance fighters he knew well. He described the uncanny atmosphere of France during the German occupation:

> This was the time when in the countryside we strained our ears for the barking of dogs in the depth of the night; the time when the many-colored parachutes laden with arms and cigarettes dropped from the sky in the glow of the signal flares in the clearings and the chalky plains; the time of the cellars, and of the despairing cries of tortured men, who sounded like children.
>
> The great battle of the shadows had begun.
>
> And there was that day at Fort Montluc in Lyons when an agent of the Gestapo offered a pencil to Jean Moulin, because

he could no longer speak, and instead of writing he drew a caricature of his torturer. The terrible sequel has been described in simple words by his sister: "He had played his part, his Calvary began. Scoffed at, savagely beaten, his head bloody, he reached the limits of human suffering without betraying a single secret, he who knew them all."

Remember, too, that during those days when he could still speak and write, the destiny of the Resistance hung on the courage of this man. For, as his sister said, he knew everything.

Georges Bidault became his successor. Behold now the triumph of a silence so terribly rewarded; destiny swings. Commander of the Resistance, tortured in hideous cellars, look with your vanished eyes at all these women clothed in black who watch over our companions: they are in mourning for France, and for you! Look at the men of the *maquis* slipping among the dwarf oaks of Quercy, bearing a flag made of strips of muslin knotted together; the Gestapo will never find them, because it believes only in great trees. Look, too, at the prisoner who enters a luxury villa and wonders why he is being given a bathroom—he has not yet heard of the bath torture.

Poor tortured king of the shades, look at your shadowy people rising in the June night spangled with tortures!

So he went on, painting the tragedy and triumph of the Resistance in somber colors, seeing himself in the distance as one of the members of that strange shadow play, where all were brothers and sisters of the Order of the Night; and at the end he spoke of the broken, bloodstained face of Moulin, and said very simply: "On that day, this was the face of France."

As he spoke, he was attempting to do many things: to place Moulin in perspective, to recreate the visionary, apocalyptic years of the Resistance, to pronounce sentence on the weak and judgment on the strong. Inevitably the prose became tense and convoluted, and sometimes he seemed to lose himself in dreams of a France still tortured, as though he could never quite believe that the Resistance had come to an end.

In France especially there was need for someone who could speak poetically of the illustrious dead, and Malraux was the inevitable choice. When Le Corbusier died in the following year, Malraux once more delivered the funeral oration beside the catafalque, once more set up in the Cour Carrée opposite St. Germain l'Auxerrois. He had known Le Corbusier and admired him, and therefore took some pains to examine his real achievements, reminding his listeners that a man who was most famous for saying "A house is a machine for living," had also said "A house must be a jewel box." Like an old general reading out the honor roll of battles, Malraux recited Le Corbusier's conquests, and when it was all over he turned to the coffin and said quietly: *"Adieu, mon vieux maître et vieil ami, bonne nuit* [goodbye, my old master, old friend, good night]."

~§ A Journey to China §~

In the late spring of 1965 it became clear that Malraux, who had been ill during the winter, had not shaken off the various viruses that had been attacking him. He continued to attend the usual Wednesday meetings of the cabinet, looking very pale, distracted, and strangely unsure of himself. De Gaulle was solicitous and suggested that he should take a long rest, but Malraux insisted that he was quite well, though a little overworked. Finally the doctors announced firmly that they would not be responsible for his health unless he took a long sea voyage. He must stay as much as possible in the sun, conduct no business, see as few people as possible, and remain at least two months away from Paris. At the end of June, accompanied by one of the members of his staff, he sailed for the Far East on the steamer *Le Cambodge* belonging to the Messageries Maritimes.

At the time he had no very clear idea where he was going. There was no definite itinerary, although he hoped to spend a few days in Saigon, and perhaps to visit Tahiti, where Gauguin spent his last years. The ship's doctor had been informed of Malraux's condition, and it was expected that he would make the final decisions. Thirty-four years had passed since Malraux had visited the Far East. China had changed beyond recognition, peaceful Annam had become Vietnam, a country in a permanent state of civil war, Formosa, which housed most of the artistic treasures of the Peking Museum, was closed to him because General de Gaulle had cut off all relations with the government of Chiang Kai-shek. Most of his memories of the Far East were tragic ones. Paul Monin, his closest friend in Saigon, had died miserably in Canton many years ago. For Malraux in 1965 the Far East was a desert full of ghosts.

The ship made a leisurely progress, touching at Aden, where he

415

went ashore and visited the small museum which contained a few treasures from Ma'rib, the city that still fascinated him because it was the capital of the Queen of Sheba. The few reliefs in the museum were placed like books on a shelf so that only the spines could be seen, and he went away unrewarded except for the sight of huge Arabian butterflies impaled on corks. Then he was crossing the Indian Ocean again, skirting India and making for Singapore, the city which had been his first introduction to the Far East. Early one morning, outside Singapore, the impossible happened. An oil tanker collided with the ship, carving a hundred-foot gash in the ship's plates. Malraux woke up to see the tanker slowly pulling away, its bow crushed. There was the danger that the *Cambodge* would sink like a stone in sight of the island. Happily, with the help of frogmen, the plates were patched up and the ship was able to sail under its own steam to Singapore.

In the ordinary course of events the next port of call would have been Saigon. He would have liked to visit Saigon again, but was not distressed when a telegram arrived from the French ambassador saying that such a visit was not considered advisable. Although no itinerary had been worked out, there had been some talk of a journey to Japan and Malraux had discussed with De Gaulle the possibility of visiting Peking. He was fascinated by the character of Mao Tse-tung and had read virtually every book written on him. By this time his health had improved and he had no intention of wasting his time in Singapore. A telegram from De Gaulle approving the expedition to China came hard on the heels of the telegram from Saigon. He flew to Hong Kong, where he was pleased to discover that the city was still recognizable in spite of the galaxy of new skyscrapers; and from the windows of the French consulate general he found himself looking at the tiled roof of the old Jesuit mission where, long ago, he had bought the type he needed for his short-lived newspaper *L'Indochine Enchaînée*.

On July 19 he crossed over into Red China, spending two days in Canton before taking the plane to Peking. In Canton he visited the Museum of the Revolution, where he was startled to find that the general strike of 1925 and the Russian advisers who flocked to Canton during the rebellion had no place in the selective memory of the Chinese Communists. There were photographs of Chou En-lai when he was an obscure political officer in the Whampoa Military Academy, but there were none of Chiang Kai-shek, who commanded the academy, and there was only a very small photograph of General Galen, the chief military instructor, standing among fifty other officers. Borodin, of course, was absent, his very existence denied by official Chinese Communist histories. Malraux looked searchingly at the photographs as though he were trying to find Pierre Garin, the brilliant and tormented revolutionary who owed his existence to Malraux's imagination. The Canton of *The Conquerors* was also imaginary. Now, confronted with the real Canton a whole generation later, he was like someone who wanders into an unrecognizable past, which is his own and not his own. He was taken to see a performance of *The East is Red,* an opera in praise of Mao Tse-tung, and found it very nearly insufferable, though he admired the youthful voices and the long floating sleeves of the dancers. This was not the Canton he had expected to see.

The journey to Peking was shrouded in mystery. In Paris, Alain Peyrefitte, the Minister of Information, commented that the visit was purely private, while not without interest from a general point of view. Contacts would be established, and there would be reciprocal exchanges of information. It was to be understood that the visit had no connection with the situation in Southeast Asia, where, according to the Minister of Information, the present outlook was "not favorable for peaceful developments." He pointed out that Malraux had a personal interest in China and knew many of its leaders. Legend and rumor plagued the journey to Peking, and even in Washington there were diplomats who hoped that Malraux had some private *entrée* into Chinese Communist circles and would bring about peace in Vietnam. The French government wanted it known that this was a private visit that might reap public dividends. The Chinese government, being less reticent, announced that the visit was "official" and that he came as General de Gaulle's personal envoy.

As an official, Malraux was subject to the ordeals that officials must undergo. On July 22 he had a three-hour meeting with the Foreign Minister, Marshal Chen Yi, the veteran of many revolutionary battles. Malraux said later that there was a general *tour d'horizon,* and in his autobiography he drew a portrait of a genial, smooth-faced bureaucrat who smiled pleasantly, laughed piercingly, and continually recited ritualistic arguments that had little or no relation to anything happening in the world. "Externally, the Chinese government is pursuing a policy of peace," the Foreign Minister announced. "It wants a peaceful world in which the people choose their own political systems." Malraux had hoped for more intellectual fare, or at least for more cogent arguments. The Marshal had stereotyped views on everything. America was a paper tiger with vast armies deployed in Vietnam, Formosa, Korea, Thailand, and a hundred other places; it was doomed to failure in Vietnam, and probably in all the other places. The Chinese had no interest in dominating other countries. Was there a single Chinese soldier in Hawaii or Mexico or Canada? Do Chinese spy planes fly over the United States? The Vietnamese are fighting not only for Vietnam and China but for the whole world. So the long argument went on, while Malraux found himself disturbed by the contrast between the Foreign Minister who simply repeated convenient clichés and the soldier who had fought during the Long March and conquered entire provinces during 1949, the year of storm, when the Red armies exploded over the length and breadth of China.

Chen Yi, the son of a magistrate, served as an officer on the staff of a Szechuan warlord until he went over to the Communists. His roots were in the middle classes. Now he was one of the four or five men who wielded effective power in China, but it was impossible to tell what purposes ruled his mind, what he wanted, or what he despaired of having. The brilliant soldier had become a scratched phonograph record, and from time to time there would come his piercing laughter.

After this interview Malraux escaped for a few days to the northwest, for it became apparent that Chou En-lai would not be able to see him until the following week. He visited Loyang, Sian and Yenan, the former Communist capital, where Mao Tse-tung and his captains once lived in caves. From Loyang he made the fifteen mile journey to the Lungmen caves with their innumerable Buddhas carved during the Wei and T'ang dynasties—the Wei Buddhas smiling inwardly, lost in their meditations, while the T'ang Buddhas looked like kings dominating everything they surveyed with only a lingering smile about their lips. The great Buddha Vairocana, standing fifty feet high, seemed on that indifferent day and among the indifferent visitors to have lost the religious significance it had once possessed. Malraux was amused at the thought that it might have been carved at the orders of the Empress Wu, who combined a profoundly meditative spirit with a streak of savagery, for she liked to transfix her lovers with arrows to the palace walls. Under this superb Buddha the hens squawked and a radio blared. It was not a good day for visiting the Lungmen caves.

Sian, like Loyang, was once the capital of the empire, and he was happy in the museum. He enjoyed the carved stone animals leading to the tomb of T'ai Tsung and the famous bas reliefs of the emperor's favorite horses. Two of these reliefs were in America, and accordingly two lifesize photographs had been mounted bearing the inscription "Stolen by the Americans." In every house and cottage there seemed to be posters showing an intrepid and youthful Communist driving a spear into an enormous paper tiger.

In December 1936 Chiang Kai-shek had been summarily arrested in Sian and threatened with death by the "Young Marshal" Chang Hsueh-liang. Malraux visited the hotel where the Generalissimo had set up his headquarters, and talked with one of the soldiers who had been ordered to arrest him. The next day Chiang Kai-shek was found hiding in a cave in the nearby mountains and taken in triumph to the "Young Marshal's" headquarters, where a military court martial sat and deliberated what should be done with him. They were terrified by the prisoner in their power and were about to kill him when Chou En-lai flew in from Pao-an and saved his life, a fact which the Generalissimo failed to mention in his account of the adventure. It was a brilliant account, but left many other questions unanswered, and to this day no one knows exactly what happened in Sian or exactly why he was released.

On August 2 Malraux had an interview with Chou En-lai, who was born into a family of the mandarin class. Thin and swarthy, with glowing eyes beneath shaggy brows, he had a reputation for intellectual tightrope dancing. He was the Prime Minister of Red China, the only member of the Central Committee who was credited with any

understanding of the West. Malraux had a special interest in meeting
him, because it was widely believed, although erroneously, that he
was the model for one of the characters in *Man's Fate*.

Chou En-lai was affable, polite, remote. The interview lasted for
three hours, and was not made easier by the presence of an interpreter
who seemed to possess an active dislike for Malraux. Nevertheless, they
were able to discuss a wide range of subjects; unhappily, they were
the subjects that scarcely permitted any real discussion. Once again a
Chinese Communist had transformed himself into a phonograph record.
The United States would have to abandon all its overseas bases before
it would be allowed to negotiate with China. They must abandon the
naval base of Guantánamo, and all their outposts in the Congo, Laos,
Thailand and Japan. They must leave Korea and Formosa and dis-
mantle their rocket-launching sites in Pakistan and elsewhere. Only
when they had abandoned colonialism would they be allowed to the
conference table. With the gesture of an innocent man who calls upon
the whole world to witness his good faith and the bad faith of the
Americans, he threw up his hands in horror. "How can we negotiate
with people who do not respect agreements?"

This was not diplomacy; this was a ritualistic act. Malraux was not
unduly mystified, for he was a student of ritualistic acts. He wrote in
Antimémoires: "I observe that when a shamelessly realistic politician
appeals to virtue, he assumes the mask of his ancestors. Communists
disguise themselves as believers in Orthodoxy, the French disguise themselves as revolutionaries of the time of the French Revolution, the
Anglo-Saxons disguise themselves as Puritans."

Chou En-lai was playing the role of the Confucian in full possession
of virtue. Red China was virtuous; all other countries were evil. When
China aided the underdeveloped countries, then it was an act of pure
disinterestedness; when France poured aid into Algeria, it was only to
ensure her command of the Algerian oil deposits. Protected by virtue
and by her vast numbers, China would inevitably triumph and just as
inevitably America would go to her downfall. Yet "inevitably," too,
seemed to belong to ritual. It did not mean what it seemed to mean: it
was another gesture summoned out of the air, or out of the past.

The interview with Chou En-lai was as unsuccessful as the one with Chen Yi. The French embassy in Peking predictably announced that there had been "a very cordial meeting, permitting the exchange of views concerning the international situation." Malraux had indicated that he was not convinced that the Americans were paper tigers; Chou En-lai had spoken in favor of virtue.

Chen Yi and Chou En-lai were merely the *hors d'oeuvres*. On the following day the main course was served. By this time there had arrived in the French embassy a letter from General de Gaulle officially authorizing discussions with the Chinese leaders "on the great problems of interest to France and China, and, consequently, of interest to the world." The letter was characteristically flamboyant, but it was not quite the flamboyance that Mao Tse-tung understands. Armed with this letter addressed to the President of the People's Republic of China, Malraux, accompanied by the French ambassador, walked down the immense corridor leading to the presidential reception room. He offered the letter to the President, Liu Shao-chi, a small horse-faced man with prominent teeth, and a few moments later he was talking to Mao Tse-tung.

The man had been a legend for so long that scarcely anyone could see him with fresh eyes. He was a monument, an epoch. His name had become a hymn, his writings were regarded as inspired scriptures destined to be read in China for thousands of years to come, and his portrait hung on countless banners and on a million million walls. He was seventy-one years old, plump, heavy, with sagging dewlaps. A nurse hovered beside him, like a white butterfly permanently attached to a bronze statute. Although he was very old and very tired, he could sometimes suggest a certain faded youthfulness. He sat on a wickerwork chair with little white napkins on the armrests, and there were scroll paintings on the walls. The paintings and the chairs suggested an earlier, less convulsive age.

The immense August sun was pouring through the blinds, and there was something about the reception room that suggested a tropical railroad station. Mao Tse-tung sat with his back to the light, smiling faintly. Malraux was reminded of Buddha—the calm and serenity of the man, and even the famous wart on his chin resembled a Buddhist symbol. How strange that a man so calm should have such a reputation for violence!

Knowing that his visitor had just returned from Yenan, Mao Tse-tung asked him whether he had enjoyed seeing the city. Malraux had visited the cave where Mao Tse-tung had lived for ten years. "It was like the tombs in Egypt," he said, shifting the metaphor so that Buddha became Pharaoh. From talking about caves they went on to talk about the beginnings of the Chinese Communist movement. At what point had Mao Tse-tung come to the conclusion that the Communists would seize power? "I always knew it," Mao Tse-tung answered, and launched into a lengthy account of the Chinese Communist rise to power. He had known it was inevitable when he saw the trees stripped to their bark to a height of twelve feet just outside his native village. That was in 1927, during the great Hunan famine. And when Malraux said Gorky had once told him in Stalin's presence: "The peasants are the same everywhere," Mao Tse-tung demurred. "Stalin knew nothing about the peasants," he replied drily. What could Stalin know about the stripped and naked trees, and the naked peasants despoiled of all their possessions? Stalin had never fought a revolutionary war in China. At the end of World War II Stalin sent Mao Tse-tung a manual of partisan warfare as practiced in the Soviet Union. Mao Tse-tung read it, and then tossed it casually to Liu Shao-chi, saying: "Read this, if you want to know what we should have done—so that all of us would end up dead!" On the walls hung framed portraits of Marx, Engels, Lenin and Stalin.

As so often before, Mao Tse-tung spoke of the misery of the Chinese peasants under the Kuomintang and how the Chinese Communists had no difficulty convincing the peasants that the Kuomintang armies were their enemies. The tide had turned because the Kuomintang had always failed to understand the peasants, but it might not have turned if the Kuomintang had not attacked the Red armies at the end of the war. "What I am about to say may surprise you," Mao Tse-tung said. "We would not have attacked if we had not been forced to do so by the enemy offensive."

This was perhaps the most important single statement made during the long interview. The intentions of the Chinese Communists in 1946 have never been satisfactorily established. At the time Mao Tse-tung spoke of conquering China in one or perhaps two generations, for his armies were ill-equipped against the massive mechanized power of the Kuomintang armies, and Communist propaganda had not yet penetrated into the areas dominated by the Kuomintang. What Mao Tse-tung was saying was that if the Kuomintang had not attacked the Red army, there would have been no Communist victory, that China would have remained largely under the control of the Kuomintang, and that but for the help given to him by the Kuomintang he might have remained in his cave in Yenan. Chiang Kai-shek had never learned the advantages of doing nothing. According to Mao Tse-tung, his generals had lied to him and he lied to the Americans.

Mao Tse-tung was talking calmly, with no noticeable gestures except those that came from the slow lifting of a cigarette to his mouth. There were the inevitable long pauses, with the interpreter struggling for the right words. Nothing was being decided about Vietnam or about any other important issue, but there was a meeting of minds, a tentative approximation of ideas. Malraux was deeply moved by the presence of the hieratic leader, and Mao Tse-tung was far from being a phonograph record.

At the end Mao Tse-tung accompanied Malraux to the waiting automobile, walking one step at a time, so old, so courteous, and so slow that he seemed to be a legendary emperor risen from some ancient imperial grave. He was talking as he walked, and sometimes he found himself talking of the future, which was always distant. "We need another twenty or thirty years of effort to make China a powerful country," he said. He thought that in another fifty years the revolution would be accomplished. By that time all the existing customs and the entire fabric of Chinese culture would be changed, changed utterly, and at last there would come into existence a true proletarian and revolutionary society. He would not live to see it, but its coming was "inevitable."

Sometimes as Malraux records these conversations, we are aware of a slight shift of focus, a curious flickering. By a process only too familiar among writers, the voice of the author and the voice of the man he is talking to dissolve into a single voice, and we are never quite clear whether Malraux's own opinions may have not colored the speech of Mao Tse-tung. The interpreter would later transcribe her shorthand notes, there would be a general review of these notes, there would be corrections and interpolations, and in the end there would be the entire conversation in a French transcript bound up in a manila folder, as accurate as human intelligence could make it. But always something would be missing: an abrupt tone, a sidelong glance, a puzzled frown. Sometimes Mao Tse-tung sounds uncommonly like General de Gaulle in a Chinese gown.

Malraux was perfectly aware that his account of his meeting with Mao Tse-tung would be questioned, if only because they seemed to talk so effortlessly across impassable barriers of language. His reply was that the original shorthand notes and all the other documents connected with the interview were being preserved in the library of the French Foreign Office. The time would come when the original notes and his own version could be compared. Until that time, his account would be the only one.

Nevertheless, his portrait of Mao Tse-tung rings true, though the parts are greater than the whole. Malraux saw him as the "bronze emperor," but also as the still center at the heart of the whirlwind, a man in command of all destinies except his own. He had expected to see a man bearing subliminal traces of violence, but saw none; nor was there arrogance. Out of the East there had emerged a formidable champion for a new proletarian society which might never come into existence, but the conditions by which it might come into existence were being hammered into shape by the man who sat in a wicker chair with a nurse beside him. Alone among all the Chinese he had no need of a phonograph record.

The French Foreign Office announced that the meeting had been eminently successful, and the exchanges of views went even further than expected. Opposing positions had been clarified, and at least one general conclusion had been reached: "China needs time as she needs friends."

Later in the year the French government drew up a cultural agreement with China. There would be a greater exchange of students, films, dance companies, and books. There would be medical, scientific and technical missions, and special attention would be given to teaching the French language with audiovisual methods. The agreement, which was signed on October 1, brought the French and the Chinese a little closer together. Malraux had succeeded in blowing away some of the cold wind between the two countries.

Malraux could congratulate himself that his journey to the Far East in search of health had produced, however slightly, an improvement in Franco-Chinese relations. The journey also produced something more permanent. Out of his memories of this journey and of other journeys he began to write the first volume of *Antimémoires*.

◄§ *The Golden Honeycomb* §►

As Malraux grew older, the long lean face with the superb forehead and the jutting chin filled out, grew heavier, larger, so that he began to resemble one of those heavy-set sailors who can be seen shouldering their way through the streets of Dunkerque. He came to look more Flemish than French, and there was something in his expression which suggested a throwback to the Middle Ages, for you see those faces in medieval paintings and tapestries made in Antwerp or Bruges. His hair was still jet black, and his eyes glowed as feverishly as ever, and he spoke at the same breakneck speed as in his youth, but age was already claiming him for her own.

In many open and subtle ways the years were changing him. He had been in power so long that he could not imagine himself out of power, just as he could not imagine himself not absorbed in the arts. He spoke with astonishing authority when he was young, but the habits of power had only reinforced his belief in the authority of art. He knew exactly where he was going and what he wanted to do, but he knew that there was not time enough for more than a fraction of the things he wanted to accomplish. Many books would remain unwritten, many lands and cultures would remain unexplored, many programs for increasing the artistic heritage of France would inevitably come to grief. He was older now than his long-lived grandfather, and as he approached seventy—an age he never thought he would reach—he could reflect that he had spent most of his life as he had wanted to spend it, and for himself, the man alone divorced from his attachments, there could be few regrets.

But for the man who was deeply attached to his family there were only too many regrets. Sorrow and grief had dug their claws in him.

His father had killed himself, his mother had died when he was quite young, his two half-brothers were killed by the Germans, his sons had died in an automobile accident, and the woman he had loved most in the world had perished in a railroad accident. As a boy he had looked death in the face and imagined he would be one of those who would die young. As an old man, he saw that death had rejected him: he was one of those who survive. It is not easy to be a survivor, and he had no illusions about the causes of his own longevity, for he had survived by the purest chance. He could have died a thousand times over in the Spanish Civil War or when fighting in France. Death was his companion through most of his life.

Though old, he remained young. Neither age nor tragedy had affected his youthful courtesy, the grace of his presence, the intensity of his ideas. The mind had not lost its resilience, and the dark greenish-brown eyes remained keen and searching. Only the voice, once clear and penetrating, had become gravelly from too much smoking, so that it became more and more difficult to follow the elusive course of his arguments. But these arguments still proliferated; new plans were continually being formed; and he was continually confronting the impossible. Why not transport all the treasure from the tomb of King Tutankhamen to Paris? It was done, and some 1,250,000 people came to see the treasure and to be blinded by gold. Why not collect together all the surviving works by Vermeer? Why not a general retrospective show of Picasso? Why not bring together a comprehensive survey of Chinese art from the museums of Communist China? In this he failed, but it was not for want of trying. While he was minister, Paris saw one dazzling display of art after another. Nothing like this had ever been attempted before.

Whenever he drew up a balance sheet of his accomplishments as minister of culture, he would see much to his credit, but there was also a sense of failure. He had made Paris shine again, offered great exhibitions, exerted his influence increasingly on music, cinema and the theater, he had restored the châteaux of Versailles, Fontainebleau and Chambord, instituted a campaign for safeguarding works of art in danger, and preserved many archaeological sites which would otherwise have been lost to the builders. These were signal successes: but he had not succeeded in the one thing he wanted most. The *Maisons de la Culture* were very close to his heart, but he had not succeeded in bringing more than a handful into existence. He had hoped they would spring up like the cathedrals of the twelfth century, with everyone helping. Instead, he had had to fight for them. It had been a gruelling battle with little to show for it.

During the years when he was a minister, he had done little writing. Drama had always excited him, and he worked intermittently on a long play about Alexander the Great. Nothing came of it, and the play was abandoned to join the other unfinished papers in his desk. He began a revision of his early novel *The Royal Way*, but this too was abandoned. As a minister he was embroiled in continual arguments and endless negotiations: there was simply no time for concentrated literary work.

In the summer of 1965, when he was ordered by his doctor to take a sea voyage for his health, it never occurred to him that he was about to embark on an exhausting literary work. For nearly a quarter of a century the fountain had been dry; was it to be expected that it would suddenly spring up again? During his journey to the Far East, he began to write again. While the ship was coasting off the shores of Crete, he sketched out the general shape of the work which would not be completed for another year and a half.

He saw it as a long book, shaped like a symphony, the same themes of death and destiny continually recurring, the narrator observing himself at those moments of intensity which appeared to give validity to a life otherwise purposeless and bloody. He had no great liking for his own life, detested his childhood, never looked very deeply into the minds of his friends and companions, and was exceedingly suspicious of his own memory: he therefore lacked the equipment of the conventional autobiographer, who merrily reconstructs his life out of documents and remembered fragments of experience, imposing a pattern on them so that they form an ascending curve. For Malraux there was no ascending curve: there was only a series of explosions, illuminations, visitations. Sometimes, and always very briefly, the heavens rolled back and he saw what lay beyond them.

While the ship was steaming in the Eastern Mediterranean, he wrote his apologia for an autobiography which was not in a strict sense an autobiography at all, but something other, almost beyond definition, because it could not be spoken about except in images of love and death. Why, he asked, should he remember a man he had never found particularly interesting as a person, and who was never at ease in "the roadless roadhouse of life," and he answered:

> Because, having lived in the inconstant realm of the spirit and fiction which is the abode of artists, and then in the realm of combat and that of history, having known when I was twenty an Asia whose agony could still illuminate the meaning of the West, I encountered many times those humble or exalted moments when the fundamental mystery of life appears to each of us as it appears to nearly all women looking at a child's face and nearly all men looking at the faces of the dead. In all the forms of life's driving force, in all I have seen of man's struggle against humiliation, and even in thee, O Sweetness, such that one asks oneself what thou art doing on this earth, life, resembling the gods of vanished religions, appears to me at times like the libretto of an unknown music.

The theme of the book is therefore "those humble or exalted moments" which are touched in some strange way with divinity, those moments when the lightning strikes or the rain falls gently from a cloudless sky. Benediction and tragedy will have their place; beauty and *douceur* will be implicated. The person of the narrator will remain disguised, for he will have no history, no ancestors, no parents, and we shall be given only fleeting glimpses of a private life. What concerned him above all was the interplay of life with the forces of destiny and the men who incarnated destiny in his generation. "Art and death are all I hope to rediscover here," he wrote; and for him art and death were joined together.

He was giving himself a task which is almost beyond human accomplishment except by musicians and poets of genius. Essentially the narration would take the form of a fable, himself the fabulist and the fable's hero and all the remaining characters. Since he had long pon-

dered the fable of Jacob and the angel, he would describe them
wrestling together.

If he failed in carrying out his task, it was not so much because
he aimed too high as because words simply will not bear the weight of
revelation. What he wanted to say could scarcely be said. He was attempting to see himself and the world as though from another planet,
and at the same time he was attempting to trace the trajectories of
destiny and the position of the great suns of revelation. He could at
least hint at all these things by telling the story in terms of a fable,
thus giving it a dimension beyond the ordinary. Language would also
become one of the protagonists, for in the great passages, like the one
quoted above, he would employ the resources of music to hint at
mysteries.

In China there are storytellers who sit in the marketplace with
drums attached to their knees, rattles and clappers at their elbows, and
bells on their caps. They have a basket of musical instruments at their
side, and from time to time they will play on their flutes and violins,
and in addition they have the ventriloquist's power to throw their voices.
When they tell their stories, they can imitate whole armies, crowd
scenes, the sound of a palace burning, quarrelling peasants, the shrill
voices of young girls. In his own way Malraux would use all the instruments of language to convey his meditations. Like the storyteller he
would throw his voice, assume various disguises, become anyone he
pleased. There was no law to say that he must speak with one voice,
and so he spoke with many voices, even his own voices from the past,
for the book would contain many passages from his previous books,
now woven into the texture of the fable.

At its best, in the recital of his experiences as a guerrilla leader in
the Dordogne, and in his confrontations with Nehru, Mao Tse-tung and
De Gaulle, he was able to convey the sense of an immanent destiny,
the splendor of sudden revelation. He could describe the Lascaux caves,
where the ammunition of the resistance fighters was hidden, with a
haunting feeling for prehistoric magic, just as he describes the Hindu
and Buddhist caves at Ellora with an awareness of a heavenly majesty
which remained visible even in the darkest shadows. In the cave on the
island of Elephanta he had seen the glorious three-headed Siva, "whose

eyes are closed on the passing of time," and once more there had come
to him the sense of the presence of the gods expressed in a work of art
so perfect that it seemed impossible to believe that it was created with
human hands. India haunted him, for the people still seemed to live in
close communion with their gods. A good part of the central portion
in the book is concerned with India.

Malraux's chapters on India occupy over a hundred pages, and they
are written in a prose that is highly wrought, colored with feverish light,
and charged with music. They are therefore extremely difficult to
translate. The ideas reach to the edge of thought, and sometimes they
can only be expressed in legends and fables. One fable especially delighted him. Narada is meditating in a forest, his gaze fixed on a
shining leaf. Suddenly the leaf trembles: it is the sign that the god
Vishnu has appeared to him, offering him anything he desires. He
answers: "I desire only to know the secret of your *maya*." "You shall
know it," says Vishnu, "but first bring me some water."

Narada hurries off to do the god's bidding, and arrives at a hamlet
where he is welcomed so warmly that he settles down, marries, raises
children, and after the death of his father-in-law becomes the head
of the household. He has forgotten the god's command in his quiet
enjoyment of his family and the fruits of the earth. Many years pass,
and suddenly the village is visited by floods. He sees his livestock swept
away, his house vanishes under the water, and as he tries to carry his
wife and children to safety, they too are drowned and he is left clinging
to a rock, weeping for his lost children. Then he hears a voice in the
wind saying: "My child, where is the water? I have been waiting for
more than half an hour."

The fable, which is told in the sixth-century *Matsya Purana*, made
a deep impression on Malraux, who could reflect on many similarities
between himself and the luckless Narada. Wherever he turned in
India, he seemed to find answers to his questions in the shapes of
statues, in landscapes, in the sculptured faces of the people. He was
twenty when he first read the *Bhagavad-Gita* in translation, and that
strange triumphant poem uttered by a god in praise of himself had
impressed him so much that he decided to learn Sanskrit, and indeed
he once progressed a little way into that infinitely complicated lan-

guage. In his autobiography he quoted liberally from the *Bhagavad-Gita,* and he showed a special affection for some lines from Ananda Coomaraswamy's *The Dance of Siva*:

> Because Thou lovest the Burning-ground,
> I have made a Burning-ground of my heart—
> That Thou mayest dance Thy eternal dance.

For the Hindus all of life is comprehended in the dance of Siva, and from one temple to another Malraux found himself admiring the dancing god who continually assumed attitudes suggesting the release of divine energy. In this religion there was no Fall, no Redemption, no Last Judgment: there was only the dance. Sometimes the dance was merely hinted at: in the South Indian temple of Chindambaran he found only a circular dancing floor, and a priest saying: "Here Siva is dancing." In the center there was burning camphor, whose flame leaves no ash.

The rites, the myths and fables of the Hindus powerfully attracted him; and if his long conversations with Nehru were rarely rewarding, there was more to be gained by his conversations with his friend Raja Rao, the novelist, small and lithe, with an expression of great benignity, so that he resembled a medieval Buddhist monk. Raja Rao spoke French brilliantly, with a proper appreciation of all the nuances of the language, and he introduced Malraux to temples, wedding ceremonies and Sanskrit chants with the air of a magician opening the doors of treasure chambers.

The book Malraux began writing in the summer of 1965 had something in common with Keyserling's *Travel Diary of a Philosopher.* Musings, anecdotes, philosophical inquiries, encounters with people and places, reflections on the past and the future, all these were included, but where Keyserling had proceded in an orderly fashion, going from place to place and recounting his ideas and experiences in logical order, Malraux permitted himself the utmost license. He darts about as he pleases, opening with an extract from *The Walnut Trees of Altenburg,* dated 1913, then proceeding to his first visit to Egypt in 1930, which is followed by a visit to Mexico in 1950, and his brief return to Egypt in 1965. Interspersed between Mexico and Egypt there is an account of a visit to Senegal and a reception by the Queen of Casamance, a name which had haunted him in his childhood. In the third chapter he tells the story of his flight over south Arabia in a relatively straightforward manner, quoting extensively from his articles in *L'Intransigeant*. In the following chapter he visits Ceylon, travels across Afghanistan, and then describes his long interview with General de Gaulle in 1945. In this way, by free association, he is able to associate anything with anything. The effect is kaleidoscopic, and the reader feels he is being shunted backward and forward through time, and abruptly parachuted into different parts of the globe, without any coherent explanation. The wind bloweth where it listeth. The brilliance of these fragmentary reminiscences cannot conceal the author's self-indulgence.

In one section of the book, called *The Royal Way,* Malraux abandons his reminiscences altogether and devotes a hundred pages to a film scenario ostensibly written by the Baron de Clappique, the absurd impostor of *Man's Fate,* about David de Mayrena, the king of the Sedangs. The scenario is called *Le Règne du Malin,* which may be translated *The Kingdom of the Devil* or *The Kingdom of the Cunning One.* The *Malin* is clearly Malraux, and the scenario takes the form of a farce in which the author passes a farcical judgment on himself. Mayrena's repertoire of stories derives from Malraux's writings: once more we see the sacred fish of Timur swimming in ornate pools, once more the convoy moves through the insect-ridden forests of Cambodia, and once more there are the familiar discussions about death now made more terrible because death is no longer real but something seen in a film, remote and implausible. We are told that throughout the film Mayrena tells lies, "but not always, or at least not always absolute lies." As for his kingdom, we are told: "It will be difficult to film his kingdom, because it does not exist. It exists only in the imagination of Mayrena and the listeners' dreams." In this way the kingdom of Malin-Mayrena is reduced to zero. These hundred pages were intended as a *divertissement,* a comic interlude in an otherwise tragic adventure, but they are too chaotic to serve any intelligible purpose. In those pages the *farfelu* is reduced to its ultimate absurdity.

Yet Malraux's method had a serious purpose. Too often the orderly, well-constructed autobiography involves an unconscious pattern of distortion, concealment, and evasion. The cards are stacked in favor of certain attitudes; the biographer hides behind his mask. Malraux wanted to discover whether he could tell the truth about himself, about his many selves, without employing a mask. Colonel Berger would speak, and so would Vincent Berger, and so would the Baron de Clappique, for they were all aspects of himself. "I call this book *Antimémoires,*" he wrote in his introduction, "because it answers a question memoirs do not pose, and does not answer those that they do; and also because you will find here, often linked with tragedy, a recognizable gliding presence like a cat moving in the shadows: that of the *farfelu* whose name I unwittingly resurrected." This is one way of stating the problem, but there are many others. Sometimes he gives the impression that he is himself the cat gliding in the shadows.

According to Malraux, the trouble with memoirs is that they depend on the memory, which distorts at its own pleasure, and of all human faculties is the least reliable. Ultimately, he believes, there are two kinds of people: those who trust their memories and those who do not, those who regard memory as water pure and undefiled, and those who regard memory as a poisoned well. At the very best a man can tell his own story only fragmentarily. He can perhaps speak of a few things that moved him deeply: for the rest, he must lose himself in his own fictions. *Antimémoires* is an attempt to dissolve the fictions to find the residue of truth.

Although the book is a virtuoso performance of astonishing range and skill, it is not entirely convincing. The very unevenness of the text, written at various times and different places, predisposes one to the belief that he failed to create a work of art commensurate with his talents. The whole is less than the sum of the parts; too often the vision fades; and the man he had hoped to discover remains, except for rare moments, as elusive as ever.

The general plan was to produce a work in four volumes, of which at least two and possibly three would be published posthumously. It is known that the second volume is half completed, and that it deals with his adventures in Russia, Greece and North Africa. Of the remaining volumes nothing is known except that they contain a portrait of President Kennedy and will reveal the substance of many conversations with him.

As Gallimard had expected, *Antimémoires* was a resounding success, selling two hundred thousand copies in a few days. It was greeted as a historical rather than as a literary event, and the critics who found fault with it were reminded that historical events have a finality independent of criticism. There was the grave danger of its becoming a classic too soon. The French critics were inclined to wonder whether he had really thought out the problem implicit in the title, while British and American critics wondered why it was necessary to scramble so many eggs. The strange disorder of the book seemed to reflect an unsuspected disorder in the man; but the disorder was deliberately conceived to reflect the fragmentary nature of our times. Yet it remains to be determined whether a work of art can be constructed out of fragments.

The foreign rights for the book were sold for enormous sums. The American publisher paid $350,000 for the American rights. German, Italian, Dutch, Scandinavian and British publishers vied for the rights and seemed to be unimpressed by the fact that Malraux wrote a French so dense, so deliberately contrived, and so musical that the work was virtually untranslatable, calling for translators who were as skilled in the use of language as Malraux himself. The translations of all his works have signally failed to reproduce his cadences.

The sudden, extraordinary success had little effect on his daily life. Every morning an official limousine brought him from his residence in Versailles to the ministry on the Rue de Valois in Paris. For some time he had been released from the burden of attending official receptions in the evening, and he would spend a full day in the office before returning to his literary work in the evening. He was living two lives, but since both of them involved his most passionately held beliefs, there was no conflict. The administration of the ministry was largely in other hands: he was the generator of ideas, the creator of new energies. He needed little sleep and had never shown the slightest interest in taking exercise. He had, therefore, more time at his disposal than most men. Sometimes he would work so hard that even his formidable constitution would rebel, and sometimes he appeared in his office gray

and ghostlike with the glazed eyes of a sleepwalker, drained of all
energy. There were days when he looked so ill that people thought
he was taking drugs, but his drug was work. His brain refused to rest;
the stop signs had been removed long ago, and it was always speeding
relentlessly. It always surprised him that there were people in the
world who were not continually thinking.

Outwardly he lived in great luxury, occupying the small official palace
of the prime minister at Versailles, for Pompidou preferred his own
apartment in Paris. His office in the Rue de Valois was paneled in white
and gold, with soft carpets, a hundred electric lamps blazing in the
chandeliers, the frock-coated *huissiers* silently doing his bidding. A large
desk, telephones, five or six chairs comprised the *mise-en-scène*. The
walls were decorated with slender golden sphinxes in mutual contemplation. Hamlet in a gilded Elsinore! One expected to see the skull
lying on the desk, but there was none; nor were there any books, or
documents, or papers. It was as though he had built around himself
a space for contemplation with no adornments except the golden walls.

Alone in the golden honeycomb he superintended an empire which
stretched from the remote past to the present and the future: an empire which included only artists and their works. In this empire he was
sovereign, and he was perfectly aware of his power. Long ago, in his
earliest novel, he had spoken of a mysterious city which was cleansed
until it shone white, and now all the great buildings of Paris were
shining at his orders. In the obscure town of Sainte Colombe near
the ancient Gallic city of Vienne, the builders' excavating machines
clawed through Roman ruins; at his orders the machines were removed
and the archaeologists stepped in. Wherever he traveled in France he
would come upon churches restored at his orders, or crumbling châteaux
that were being shored up, or roads that were being diverted to protect
ancient monuments. What he called "the treasures of the ages, the
living past," were under his guardianship; the past belonged to him.
The emperor in the golden honeycomb was waving his wand and
summoning the past to live again.

Emperor or shaman? He did not know, and scarcely cared. Sometimes he thought he was living through a dream, and he liked to tell
a story once told by Mallarmé: "One night Mallarmé was listening to

the cats talking to one another on the roof. One inquisitive black cat said to another: 'And what do you do?' And the other said: 'At the moment I am pretending to be the cat of the Mallarmés.' " He, too, was pretending to be one of Mallarmé's cats, gliding mysteriously, at home in the dark.

Henri Bergson had said the universe was a machine for creating gods. For Malraux the universe was an instrument for creating great works of art, and the earth had been fashioned in order that the sculptors of Chartres and Ellora and Lungmen should spend their lives in the service of the silent goddess. All grief, all love, all life were redeemed by art, and to believe in anything else was the height of absurdity; and there the problems began, for absurdity, too, laid claim to the universe. Yet he was certain of one thing: at the heart of the mystery there was the artist, the violent adventurer, confronting destiny with the perfection of his art, creating images powerful enough to dispel the world's nothingness. Only the artist is sovereign: all the rest are slaves.

This had been his belief ever since he first studied art, and he has held fast to it throughout his life. "I have never known a time when I have not been studying art," he wrote once. Countries which had not produced masterpieces of art held no interest for him, and he could scarcely believe in their existence. But nearly all the art he knew belonged to the past. Ironically, he was born in an age "which never built a tomb or a temple worthy of it."

In the ministry he enjoyed his power to bring about a new awakening of the arts, and most of all he rejoiced in the *Maisons de la Culture,* which he regarded as his chief legacy to France. He had found the magic spell to bring them into existence, and it was much simpler than anyone had thought, for he had placed the responsibility for creating them on the people, not on the authorities. "There is not and will not be any *Maison de la Culture* based on the state or even on the municipality," he declared. "The *Maison de la Culture* is you. The only question is, do you want to build it?"

In 1969 the Ministry of Cultural Affairs celebrated its tenth birthday, and throughout all this time, except for brief periods of illness, he had been the driving force and the generator of ideas. The power of the ministry had grown from year to year, and its influence could be felt in the remotest regions of France. He had watched it progress from an idea until it had become a formidable instrument for coordinating all the forces of art: almost it had become too formidable, too secure. In the spring of that year General de Gaulle chose to appeal to the French people with a referendum designed to bring about some comparatively unimportant changes in the structure of the government; the appeal failed, and his government fell. Malraux resigned. He had accomplished what he set out to do, and he could return to his books, his contemplations and his memories. He was a free man, and one more fragment of his life was over.

In the end, it seemed to be a life made up of fragments. The lonely boy in Bondy, the schoolboy at the Lycée Turgot, the *chineur* in the Paris boulevards, the adventurer of Banteay Srei, the revolutionary journalist in Saigon, the champion of artistic freedom in Russia, the leader of the Spanish Republican air force, the Resistance fighter, the colonel of the Brigade Alsace-Lorraine, the novelist, the art historian, and the minister of culture—all these separate fragments finally fuse together in a single whole by the very intensity with which he played his many roles. If he was violent, it was because the age demanded it; and if he cherished art, it was sometimes because there was nothing left to cherish, or even to hold on to, except the work of art. He fought for the highest stakes—for whatever certainties exist. Shaman, emperor, tragic adventurer, he seemed in some strange way to be the incarnation of the hopes of an age.

Select Bibliography

Agee, James. *On Film.* New York: McDowell Obolensky, 1958.

Alleg, Henri. *The Question.* Translated by John Calder. New York: George Braziller, 1958.

Amoureux, Henri. *La Vie des Français sous l'Occupation.* Paris: Fayard, 1961.

Aron, Robert. *Histoire de la Libération de la France.* Paris: Fayard, 1959.

Barry, Joseph. *The People of Paris.* New York: Doubleday, 1966.

Baurit, Maurice. *Bondy et sa Forêt.* Paris: Imprimerie Générale du Centre, 1961.

Beauvoir, Simone de. *Force of Circumstance.* New York: G.P. Putnam's Sons, 1965.

———— *The Prime of Life.* New York: World Publishing Company, 1960.

Bergeret and Herman Grégoire. *Messages Personnels.* Bordeaux: Bière, 1945.

Berne-Joffroy, André. *Valéry.* Paris: Gallimard, 1960.

Bidault, Georges. *Resistance.* New York: Frederick A. Praeger, 1967.

Billy, André. *Max Jacob.* Paris: Pierre Seghers, 1945.

Blumenthal, Gerda. *André Malraux: The Conquest of Dread.* Baltimore: Johns Hopkins Press, 1960.

Boak, Denis. *André Malraux.* Oxford: Clarendon Press, 1968.

Boisdeffre, Pierre de. *Malraux.* Paris: Éditions Universitaires, 1960.

Brown, Edward J. *Russian Literature since the Revolution.* New York: Collier Books, 1963.

Carlut, Charles and Germaine Brée. *France de Nos Jours.* New York: The Macmillan Company, 1962.

Chaigne, Louis. *Paul Claudel, the Man and the Mystic.* New York: Appleton-Century-Crofts, 1964.

Chamson, André. *Devenir ce qu'on est.* Paris: Wesmael-Charlier, n.d.

441

Claudel, Paul. *Connaissance de l'Est.* Paris: Mercure de France, 1960.
—— *Tête d'or.* Paris: Mercure de France, 1959.
Clotis, Josette. *Le Temps Vert.* Paris: Gallimard, 1932.
Colodny, Robert G. *The Struggle for Madrid.* New York: Paine-Whitman Publishers, 1958.
Coomaraswamy, Ananda. *The Dance of Shiva.* New York: Noonday Press, 1957.

Delhomme, Jeanne. *Temps et Destin: Essai sur André Malraux.* Paris: Gallimard, 1955.
Deutscher, Isaac. *The Prophet Outcast.* New York: Vintage Books, 1963.
Doyon, René-Louis. *Memoire d'Homme.* Paris: La Connaissance, 1953.
Dumas, Alexandre. *Georges.* Paris: Grimaux et Cie, n.d.
Durtain, Luc. *Dieux blancs, hommes jaunes. Paris*: Flammarion, 1930.
Duthuit, Georges. *Le Musée Inimaginable.* Paris: Librairie José Corti, 1956.

Ehrenburg, Ilya. *Memoirs 1921–1941.* New York: Grosset and Dunlap, 1966.
—— *Vus par un écrivain d'URSS.* Paris: Gallimard, 1934.
Einstein, Carl. *Negerplastik.* Munich: Kurt Wolff Verlag, 1920.

Fitch, Brian T. *Les Deux Univers Romanesques d'André Malraux.* Paris: Archives des Lettres Modernes, 1964.
Flanner, Janet. *Men and Monuments.* New York: Harper, 1957.
—— *Paris Journal 1944–1965.* New York: Atheneum, 1965.
Foot, M.D.R. *SOE in France.* London: Her Majesty's Stationery Office, 1966.
Frobenius, Leo. *The Childhood of Man.* New York: Meridian Books, 1960.
Frohock, W.M. *André Malraux and the Tragic Imagination.* Stanford: Stanford University Press, 1952.

Gannon, Edward. *The Honor of Being a Man: The World of André Malraux.* Chicago: Loyola University Press, 1957.
Garaudy, Roger. *Literature of the Graveyard.* New York: International Publishers, 1948.
Gide, Andre. *Journals.* New York: Alfred A. Knopf, 1947–1951.
Glaize, Maurice. *Les Monuments du Groupe d'Angkor.* Paris: Adrien-Maisonneuve, 1963.
Gobineau, Comte de. *Les Religions et les Philosophies dans l'Asie Centrale.* Paris: G. Crès et Cie, 1923.

———— *Nouvelles Asiatiques.* Paris: Garnier Frères, 1965.
Goldman, Lucien. *Pour une Sociologie du Roman.* Paris: Gallimard, 1964.
Gorky, Maxim. *On Literature.* Moscow: Foreign Languages Publishing House, n.d.

Halda, Bernard. *Berenson et André Malraux.* Paris: Lettres Modernes, 1964.
Hartman, Geoffrey H. *Malraux.* New York: Hillary House, 1960.
Herbart, Pierre. *La Ligne de Force.* Paris: Gallimard, 1958.
Hodin, P.H. *The Dilemma of Being Modern.* London: Routledge and Kegan Paul, 1956.
Hoffmann, Joseph. *L'Humanisme de Malraux.* Paris: Librairie C. Klincksieck, 1963.

Jarry, Alfred. *Tout Ubu.* Paris: Librairie Générale Française, 1962.

Kahnweiler, D.-H. *Mes Galeries et Mes Peintres.* Paris: Gallimard, 1961.
Kazin, Alfred. *Starting out in the Thirties.* Boston: Atlantic Monthly Press, 1965.

Langlois, Walter G. *André Malraux: The Indochina Adventure.* New York: Frederick A. Praeger, 1965.
Launay, Jacques de. *De Gaulle and his France.* New York: Julian Press, 1968.
Lautréamont, Comte de. *Oeuvres Complètes.* Paris: José Corti, 1946.
Lawrence, T.E. *The Seven Pillars of Wisdom.* London: privately printed, 1926.
Lehmann, John. *The Whispering Gallery.* New York: Harcourt, Brace and Company, 1955.
Lewis, R.W.B., ed. *Malraux.* New Jersey: Prentice-Hall, 1964.

MALRAUX, ANDRÉ
  Editions in French in order of publication, all books being published in Paris unless otherwise stated.
  Lunes en Papier. Galerie Simon, 1921.
  La Tentation de l'Occident. Grasset, 1926.
  Les Conquérants. Grasset, 1928.
  Royaume Farfelu. Grasset, 1928.
  La Voie Royale. Grasset, 1930.
  Vie de Napoléon. Gallimard, 1930.
  Oeuvres Gothico-bouddhiques du Pamir. Gallimard, 1930.

La Condition Humaine. Gallimard, 1933.

Le Temps de Mépris. Gallimard, 1935

Pour Thaelmann (Malraux and others). Paris, Éditions Universelles, 1936.

L'Espoir. Gallimard, 1937.

La Lutte avec l'Ange. Geneva: Skira, 1945.

Oeuvres Complètes. Geneva: Skira, 1945.

Scènes Choisies. Gallimard, 1946.

Esquisse d'une Psychologie du Cinéma. Gallimard, 1946.

Goya: Dessins du Musée de Prado. Geneva: Skira, 1946.

Le Musée Imaginaire (La Psychologie de l'Art, Vol. I.). Geneva: Skira, 1947.

Romans (includes *Les Conquérants, La Condition Humaine,* and *L'Espoir*). Gallimard, 1947.

La Création Artistique (La Psychologie de l'Art, Vol. II). Geneva: Skira, 1949.

La Monnaie de l'Absolu (La Psychologie de l'Art, Vol. III). Geneva: Skira, 1950.

Saturne. Gallimard, 1950.

Les Voix de Silence. Gallimard, 1951.

Vermeer de Delft. Galerie de la Pleiade, 1952.

La Métamorphose des Dieux. Gallimard, 1957.

Le Musée Imaginaire de la Sculpture Mondiale: Vol. I, *La Statuaire,* Vol. II, *Des Bas-reliefs aux Grottes Sacrées,* Vol. III, *Le Monde Chrétien.* Gallimard, 1952–1954.

Antimémoires. Gallimard, 1967.

*

Editions in English in order of publication, all books being published in New York unless otherwise stated.

The Conquerors. Translated by Winifred Stephens Whale. Random House, 1929.

Man's Fate. Translated by Haakon M. Chevalier. Smith and Haas, 1934.

The Royal Way. Translated by Stuart Gilbert. Smith and Haas, 1935.

Day of Wrath. Translated by Haakon Chevalier. Random House, 1936.

Man's Hope, Translated by Stuart Gilbert and Alistair MacDonald. Random House, 1938.

The Psychology of Art. Translated by Stuart Gilbert. Three volumes. Pantheon, 1949–1950.

The Walnut Trees of Altenburg. Translated by A.W. Fielding. Limited edition. London: John Lehmann, 1952.

The Voices of Silence. Translated by Stuart Gilbert. Doubleday, 1953.

The Metamorphosis of the Gods. Translated by Stuart Gilbert. Doubleday, 1960.

Anti-Memoirs. Translated by Terence Kilmartin. Holt, Rinehart and Winston, 1968.

Malraux Clara. *Le Bruit de Nos Pas*. Vol. I: *Apprendre à Vivre*. Vol. II: *Nos Vingt Ans*. Vol. III: *Les Combats et les Jeux*. Paris: Grasset, 1963–1969.

———— *Par les Longs Chemins*. Paris: Librairie Stock, 1953.

Mauriac, Claude. *Malraux ou le Mal du Héros*. Paris: Grasset, 1946.

Mauriac, Francois. *Journal*. Paris: Grasset, 1937.

———— *Journal*. Paris: Flammarion, 1950.

———— *Le Nouveau Bloc-Notes 1958–1960*. Paris: Flammarion, 1961.

———— *Mémoires Politiques*. Paris: Grasset, 1967.

Maurras, Charles. *Mademoiselle Monk*. Paris: Stock, 1923.

Michel, Henri. *Histoire de la Résistance en France*. Paris: Presses Universitaires de France, 1965.

Mora, Constancia de la. *In Place of Splendor*. New York: Harcourt, Brace and Company, 1939.

Morand, Paul. *Papiers d'Identité*. Paris: Grasset, 1931.

Mounier, Emmanuel. *L'Espoir des Désespérés*. Paris: Éditions du Seuil, 1953.

O'Brien, Justin, ed. *From the N.R.F.* New York: Farrar, Straus and Cudahy, 1958.

———— *Portrait of André Gide*. New York: Alfred A. Knopf, 1953.

———— *The Journals of André Gide*. New York: Alfred A. Knopf, 1947–1951.

Picon, Gaëtan. *André Malraux*. Paris: Gallimard, 1945.

———— *Malraux par Lui-même*. Paris: Éditions du Seuil, 1966.

Pompidou, Georges, ed. *André Malraux: Pages Choisies*. Paris: Hachette, 1955.

Reflections of Our Age. Lectures delivered at the opening session of UNESCO at the Sorbonne University. London: Alan Wingate, 1948.

Regler, Gustav. *The Owl of Minerva*. New York: Farrar, Straus and Cudahy, 1960.
Righter, William. *The Rhetorical Hero: An Essay on the Aesthetics of André Malraux*. New York: Chilmark Press, 1964.
Rousseaux, André. *Littérature du Vingtième Siècle*. Paris. Albin Michel, 1953.

Sachs, Maurice. *The Decade of Illusion*. New York: Alfred A. Knopf, 1933.
———— *The Hunt*. New York: Stein and Day, 1965.
———— *Witches' Sabbath*. New York: Stein and Day, 1964.
Schalk, David L. *Roger Martin du Gard: The Novelist and History*. Ithaca: Cornell University Press, 1967.
Seton, Marie. *Sergei M. Eisenstein*. New York: A. A. Wyn, n.d.
Sheean, Vincent. *Not Peace but a Sword*. New York: Doubleday, Doran and Company, 1939.
Sitwell, Sacheverell. *The Red Chapels of Banteai Srei*. London: Weidenfeld and Nicholson, 1962.
Spender, Stephen. *World within World*. New York: Harcourt, Brace and Company, 1951.
Stéphane, Roger. *Portrait de l'aventurier*. Paris: Grasset, 1965.

Vandegans, André. *La Jeunesse Littéraire d'André Malraux*. Paris: Jean-Jacques Pauvert, 1964.

Werth, Alexander. *France 1940–1955*. London: Robert Hale, 1957.
White, Theodore H. *Fire in the Ashes*. New York: William Sloane Associates, 1953.
Wilson, Edmund. *The Shores of Light*. New York: Farrar, Straus and Young, 1952

In addition I have consulted the files of *Indochine, Indochine Enchaînée, L'Impartial* (Saigon), *L'Alsace Française, Commune, Action, Labyrinthe, Twice a Year, Esprit, Modern Language Notes, Bifur, Commerce, La Nouvelle Revue Française, World Review, L'Intransigeant,* and the morgue on Malraux at *The New York Times*.

Some Notes on Sources and Legends

Page 10   This was Alexandre Dumas's *Georges* . . . There is some
            mystery about the authorship of *Georges*. Eugène de
            Miracourt insisted that the real author was Félicien
            Mallefille, one of the members of Dumas's talented school
            of hack-writers, which included Gérard de Nerval. At
            least three separate styles can be discerned in the novel,
            and quite probably many people worked on it under the
            direction of Dumas. *Georges* was published in 1843,
            shortly before *The Three Musketeers* and *The Count of
            Monte Cristo*. I have discussed the plot and the characters
            at some length because they prefigure so much that
            happened to Malraux and define an exalted, haunted
            personality equally in love with life and death, with
            legend and with history.

Page 18   *"ce petit rapace herissé . . . magnifique."* François Mauriac,
            Mémoires Politiques, p.79.

Page 21   "When the ship arrived . . . cliffs." André Billy, *Max
            Jacob,* p.108.

Page 21   "Send me down . . . mouth." André Billy, *Max Jacob,*
            p.175.

Page 23   "And so we climbed down . . . Bach." Malraux, "À propos
            des illustrations de Galanis," in *Arts et métiers graphiques,*
            April 1, 1928, pp.230–231.

Page 26   "May the darkness . . . breast." Paul Claudel, *Tête d'or,*
            p.239.

Page 31   "Like a luminous sign . . . gone." Malraux, *Oeuvres
            complètes,* V, 159.

Page 32   "PRIDE: Gentlemen, I assume . . . Death." Idem, V, 167–8.
Page 34   "They are always saying: Death . . . gleaming." Idem,
            V, 181.

447

Page 44   "A book is nearly always . . . paints." *Action*, March–April, 1922, pp.19–20.

Page 45   "In going from intellectual anarchism . . . Crusades." Charles Maurras, *Mademoiselle Monk*, p.7.

Page 50   "A vast pool filled with . . . again." *Action*, July 1920, pp.13–14.

Page 51   "All the gold buttons . . . butterflies." *Signaux de France et de Belgique*, August, 1921, p.19.

Page 52   "Do you know . . . tired." *Accords*, October–November, p.43.

Page 53   "Then the devil lit . . . skeleton." *Action*, August 1921, pp.17–18.

Page 55   "I desire to record everything . . . sleeping." *900*, Summer 1927, pp.116–118.

Page 61   "For superior men . . . means." Georges Gabory, "Éloge de Landru," *Action*, February, 1920, p.68.

Page 62   "Around 1920 the word . . . him." Gaëtan Picon, *Malraux par Lui-même*, p.78.

Page 62   "Adventure begins with being . . . Féerie." Idem, p.80.
Page 63   "We were overwhelmed . . . world." Clara Malraux, *Memoirs*, p.220.

Page 66   "For me . . . existence." Malraux, *La Voie Royale*, p.50.
Page 67   "If he had looked . . . vulture." Clara Malraux, *Memoirs*, p.261.

Page 67   "I don't give a damn . . . wages." Idem, p.262.
Page 71   "It is the classic procedure . . . defense." *Indochine Enchaînée*, No.12, p.7.

Page 73   "Malraux is a tall, thin . . . Srei." *L'Impartial*, July 22, 1924, p.1.

Page 76   "A PLEA FOR ANDRÉ MALRAUX . . . them." Doyon, *Mémoire d'Homme*, p.81–84.

Page 79   "He arrived in the early afternoon . . . before." Clara Malraux, *Memoirs*, p.336.

Page 81   "FRENCH SLEUTH TRAILS . . . arrest." *The New York Times*, September 21, Part IX, p.6.

Page 83   "He has blonde hair . . . art." *L'Impartial*, September 1924, p.1.

Page 90   "What has happened . . . mankind." *Indochine*, No.2, p.1.

Page 92   "You are perfectly right . . . me." Idem, No.19, p.1.
Page 93   "Night came down . . . myself." Idem, No.42, back page.
Page 96   "Every power that is conscious . . . them." Idem, No.49, p.1.
Page 99   *"The scene is a large French . . . hair." Indochine Enchaînée,* No.1, p.6.
Page 101   "He was like a ghost . . . hospital." Paul Morand, *Papiers d'Identité,* p.172.
Page 103   "awaiting the day . . . custody." *Indochine Enchaînée,* No.1, p.1.
Page 104   "Our readers should not forget . . . century." Idem, No.1, p.7.
Page 106   "I well remember you . . . here." Andrée Viollis, *Indochine S.O.S.,* p. x – xi.
Page 108   "who wore the double mask . . . traitor." *Indochine Enchaînée,* No.1, p.11.
Page 108   "Yes, indeed, all these . . . them." Idem, No.3, p.2.
Page 110   "When the celebrations . . . Governor." Idem, No.5, pp.1–2.
Page 111   "The Annamites like to share . . . Malraux." Idem, No.7, p.9.
Page 112   "Nothing would please . . . friends." Idem, No.19, p.2.
Page 112   "Thereupon the Governor . . . stomach." Idem, No.19, p.2.
Page 112   "Perhaps you believe . . . by." Idem, No.11, p.1.
Page 113   "I would rather like to see . . . do." Idem, No.13, p.6.
Page 114   "We can have no confidence . . . France." Idem, No.16, p.2.
Page 115   "His shoulders squeezed together . . . death." Jean Prevost, *Les Caractères,* p.106.
Page 117   Our empire is a tapestry . . . sons." André Berne-Joffroy, *Valéry,* p.215-6.
Page 119   "All the enchantments . . . fingers." Malraux, *La Tentation de l'Occident,* p.18.
Page 121   "The intensity which ideas create . . . life." Idem, p.175-5.
Page 121   "The Europeans are weary . . . desire." Idem, p.139–40.
Page 122   "Europe, great cemetery . . . sea." Idem, p.217-8.

Page 123   "Man," says A.D. . . . him." Idem, p.93.
Page 123   "a perfect lucidity . . . precision." Idem, p.99.
Page 125   "A single human life . . . madness." Idem, p.68–9.
Page 125   "Our civilization was deprived . . . sciences." Malraux,
            Écrits: Les Cahiers Verts, p.145.
Page 126   "like the knights whose victories . . . shadows." Idem,
            p.146–7.
Page 126   "Youth would like to see . . . reality." Idem, p.151.
Page 132   "I do not love mankind . . . fight." Malraux, *Romans,*
            p.51.
Page 133   "We leave our revolvers . . . shots." Idem, p.122–3.
Page 135   "It is terribly easy . . . die." Idem, p.132.
Page 135   "What books," he asks . . . memoirs." Idem, p.42.
Page 135   "I have learned that though . . . life." Idem, p.143.
Page 135   "Borodin is not a man of genius . . . meant." *Bifur,* 31
            December 1929, pp.10–11.
Page 136   "We enter. A bare workshop . . . says." Malraux, *Romans,*
            p.135–6.
Page 137   "Shall we ever take . . . death." Idem, p.145.
Page 138   "The author's truly profound . . . Revolution." R.W.B.
            Lewis, *Malraux,* p.13.
Page 138   "a solid inoculation . . . mistakes." Idem, p.15.
Page 139   "If this novel has survived . . . lucidity." Idem, p.24.
Page 142   "As soon as we stepped ashore . . . origin." Malraux,
            Royaume Farfelu, pp.11–13.
Page 144   "You are an old man . . . substance." Idem, p.43.
Page 145   "Several hours passed . . . us." Idem, p.63–67.
Page 147   "We walked for a long time . . . fish." Idem, pp.77–81.
Page 154   "My view is that . . . theirs." Malraux, *La Voie Royale,*
            pp.49–51.
Page 156   "Stones, stones . . . them." Idem, p.98–9.
Page 157   Grabot, too, had dreamed of being a chieftain. . . . Grabot
            is a curious invention, never completely realized, perhaps
            because he owes too much to Conrad's "The Heart of
            Darkness." Kurtz, crawling on all fours to "unspeakable
            rites," while glorying in his power over the natives and
            leading raids against them, pillaging and destroying, is
            obviously the prototype of Grabot. Yet Malraux has
            added another dimension to Grabot by making him blind
            like Samson; and Gaza enters the forest of the Mois.

Page 159 "The spreading blood . . . possession." Malraux, *La Voie Royale*, p.194.

Page 159 "He gazed at her face . . . eyes." Idem, p.213–4.

Page 160 "There is . . . no death . . . die." Idem, p.248.

Page 162 "They kneel with their hands . . . world." Malraux, *Oeuvres Gothico-Bouddhiques*, p.6.

Page 169 "He remembered an afternoon . . . infinity." Malraux, *Romans*, p.230.

Page 171 "He remembered that he had to . . . thumb." Idem, p.354.

Page 172 "Absolutely, my dear girl . . . moreover." Idem, p.197.

Page 174 "Well, then, my dear little . . . voice." Idem, pp.198–9.

Page 176 "Can one know—really know . . . him." Idem, p.346.

Page 176 "Men are perhaps indifferent . . . God." Idem, p.349.

Page 177 "Very high up, the soft clouds . . . arms." Idem, p.431.

Page 185 "We live in a strange society . . . everything." François Mauriac, *Journal*, II, p.91.

Page 187 "Our literature is permeated . . . class." Edward J. Brown, *Russian Literature since the Revolution*, p.213.

Page 187 "We must make labour . . . art." Maxim Gorky, *On Literature*, p.254.

Page 188 "Perhaps," Malraux replied . . . burden." Gustav Regler, *The Owl of Minerva*, p.206–7.

Page 188 "In one of the factories . . . often." *Commune*, September–October 1934, p.71.

Page 191 "We are still far from . . . bourgeois." Gustav Regler, *The Owl of Minerva*, p.212.

Page 193 "If I were working here . . . books." Marie Seton, *Sergei M. Eisenstein*, p.491.

Page 193 "not to console the assassins . . . reigns." Malraux, *Antimémoires*, p.572.

Page 194 "Since you are on such good terms . . . fireplace." The story was told to me by Malraux.

Page 196 "Every work of art . . . man." *Commune*, July, 1935, pp.1265–6.

Page 198 "No civilization . . . men." *Commune*, December 1935, p.413.

Page 199 "Just at the moment . . . deported." *Commune*, December 1935, p.412–3.

Page 199 Because he attacked French colonial policy. . . . The legend that Malraux was a Communist died hard. In

Indochina the French colonial authorities were clearly under the impression that they had a dangerous revolutionary in their hands, and in the twenties a dangerous revolutionary could only mean a Communist. The accusation was revived in the thirties after Malraux's visit to Russia notwithstanding the fact that he was consistently attacking the lack of freedom in the Soviet Union even while on Russian soil. One day Marcel Brandin, idly rearranging the letters of MALRAUX, discovered to his surprise and delight that they could be read A LU MARX. The anagram, however, did not prove that Malraux had read Marx, and there is no trace in his works of any real understanding of Marxism.

Malraux possessed impeccable revolutionary credentials, but belonged to no party until he joined De Gaulle after World War II. In a letter written to Edmund Wilson, dated October 2, 1933, not long after the publication of *Man's Fate,* Malraux wrote: "I went to Asia at the age of twenty-three, entrusted with an archaeological mission. I then abandoned archaeology and organized the "Young Annam" movement, and later became commissar of the Kuomintang in Indochina and then in Canton." (Edmund Wilson, *The Shores of Light,* p.573.) A biographical notice on Malraux was printed in the *Europäische Revue* in 1928 as a forward to a translation of his novel *Les Conquérants.* The notice read: "Born in Paris. Sent by the French Colonial Ministry to make archaeological studies in Cambodia and Siam (1923). Leader of the "Young Annam" party (1924). Commissar of the Kuomintang for Cochinchina and later for all Indochina (1924–5). Vice-Commisar for Propaganda in the Nationalist Government in Canton at the time of Borodin (1925)."

The letter and the biographical notice raise many questions. Malraux's movements in 1925 are known, and at no time was he in Canton. The "Young Annam" movement, organized by Malraux and Monin, who had extensive connections with the Kuomintang, had only a very brief existence, scarcely existed as a political party, and left no visible trace on the revolutionary history of Annam. The names of the various commissars and vice-commissars in the Canton government are known, and all of them are Chinese. The inescapable conclusion is that Malraux was never a commissar in the Canton government. According to the legend, he was one of the "Committee of Seven" which ruled over Canton, but there was never a "Committee of Seven." Legend and fantasy have played over Malraux's revolutionary adventures in China, and nearly all the articles written about him mention the "Committee of Seven." When these adventures were supposed to have taken place, Malraux was either in Indochina or in France.

Page 204   . . . the papers printed in the *Journal Asiatique*. . . . Arnaud's manuscripts had a strange history. The *Journal Asiatique* announced their imminent publication in 1848, but they were not published until 1874. The manuscripts had passed into the hands of Prosper Mérimée, the novelist who was also inspector-general of French antiquities. He had received them from his cousin, Fresnel, who was the French consul-general at Jiddah. Mérimée, who was notoriously careless, lost the manuscripts. In 1870, during the siege of Paris, he fled to the south of France. Later, his house was burned down by the Communards. It was assumed that the manuscripts had perished in the blaze. One day in 1873 the editor of the *Journal Asiatique* was looking through a store-room attached to the office of the journal when he discovered the manuscripts and a covering note from Mérimée, who had found them shortly before fleeing Paris. In the January 1874 issue of the journal there appeared the long-lost article by Arnaud a quarter of a century after its publication was announced.

Page 205   "I should like . . . prisoner." *L'Intransigeant,* May 4, 1934, p.2.

Page 209   "The airplane is waiting . . . dawn." Idem, May 3, 1934, p.1.

Page 212   "Many years had passed . . . stars." Idem, May 10, 1934, p.1.

Page 223   "As the song . . . shore." Malraux, *Days of Wrath,* p.50–1.

Page 225   "The priests who have come up . . . moonlight." Idem, p.64.

Page 225   "The insurgents have dragged . . . House." Idem, p.69.

Page 227   "They were caught from below . . . together." Idem, p.129–130.

Page 228   "We are with him because . . . darkness." Malraux, *Pour Thaelmann,* p.17.

Page 235   "The road swerved . . . camouflage." Malraux, *Man's Hope,* p.98–9.

Page 237   "Do you know what he said . . . everything." André Gide, *Journals,* III, p.344.

Page 237   "He talks with that extraordinary . . . Oviedo." Idem, p.345.

Page 237   "As with Valéry . . . listening." Idem, p. 345.

Page 239   "You've got yourself . . . it." Pierre Herbart, *La Ligne de Force,* p. 151.

Page 240   "Herbart is wasting his time . . . Albacete." Idem, p.164.

Page 244   "The path widened steadily . . . will." *Man's Hope,* p.483–4.

Page 252   "Is that Huesca? . . . No." Idem, p.3–4.

Page 254   "In another room . . . day." Idem, p.41.

Page 255   "Ramos and Manuel were . . . down." Idem, p.89.

Page 257   "Men only die for something . . . exist." Idem, p.213.

Page 258   "The column continued . . . happen." Idem, p.255–6.

Page 260   "Christ came to Madrid . . . before." Idem, p.179–180.

Page 265   "The important problem . . . come." *World Telegram,* March 2, 1937.

Page 266   "He spoke with such fire . . . flesh." Alfred Kazin, *Starting out in the Thirties,* p.108.

Page 266   "When I raised my eyes . . . encountered." Idem, p.107.

Page 267   "*We destroyed . . . Madrid.*" Idem, p.108.

Page 268   "Trotsky is a great moral force . . . communism." Isaac Deutscher, *The Prophet Outcast,* p.370.

Page 268   "Mr. Trotsky is so obsessed . . . Trotsky." *The New York Times,* March 17, 1937.

Page 268   "he teamed up with Borodin . . . 1929." *Evening Sun,* February 24, 1937.

Page 268   The story about Edgard Varèse is given in *The New York Times,* March 4, 1937.

Page 270   "He had the air of . . . audience." Stephen Spender, *World within World,* p.217.

Page 271   "Because it is . . . possess." *Commune*, September 1937, p.41.

Page 275   "In the pictorial world . . . gods." Malraux, *Scènes Choisies*, p.325.

Page 277   "The myth begins . . . Christ." Idem, p.334.

Page 282   "All that long line . . . men." Malraux, *Man's Hope*, p.484.

Page 283   "The whole revolution . . . home." Vincent Sheean, *Not Peace but a Sword*, p.266.

Page 285   "I need say of it . . . him." James Agee, *Agee on Film*, p.241.

Page 291   "It was leaning forward . . . fall." Malraux, *La Lutte avec l'Ange (Oeuvres Complètes)*, p.184–5.

Page 292   "Like one who encounters . . . furnaces." Idem, p.193–4.

Page 293   "Well, grandpa, are you . . . out." Idem, p.195.

Page 294   "I know now the meaning . . . death." *Twice a Year*, 1946, p.41.

Page 297   "The subject of the book . . . stars." "The Demon of the Absolute", in *World Review*, October 1949, p.33.

Page 298   "Man is absurd . . . world." Idem, p.33.

Page 298   "Lawrence, one of the most religious . . . conquest." Idem, p.37.

Page 299   "The Absolute . . . oneself." Idem, p.37.

Page 300   Jean-Paul Sartre, visiting. . . . The meeting is described in Simone de Beauvoir, *The Prime of Life*, p.393.

Page 300   Emmanuel D'Astier, diplomat. . . . The meeting is described in *Événement*, September 1967, p.53.

Page 301   André Gide came. . . . Gide touches on this meeting in *Journals*, IV, p.243.

Page 305   "The sun was setting . . . horizon." *La Lutte avec l'Ange*, p.105–6.

Page 309   "Do you know what a shaman is . . . shaman." Idem, p.40.

Page 311   "The train entered the Gotthard tunnel . . . sky." Idem, p.70–1.

Page 312   "the greatest mystery . . . nothingness." Idem, p.72.

Page 320   "He made an indelible . . . work." Bergeret, *Messages Personnels*, p.175–6.

Page 325   "TOR 1028 . . . ADIEU." M.D.R. Foot, *SOE in France*, p.107.

Page 329   One day toward the end of July. . . . Captain George
            Hiller has confirmed the general accuracy of Malraux's ac-
            count of the ambush in *Antimémoires*. The inevitable
            legendary accounts appeared in the foreign press. An article
            by George Creel in *Collier's* magazine on December 23,
            1944, describes Malraux parachuting down in France.
            "Tragically enough, Malraux was shot down and taken
            prisoner. Not for nothing however had the author-soldier
            made a study of German mentality. Instead of pretending
            to be a simple private, unworthy of notice, he drew him-
            self up to his full height, tapped his chest impressively, and
            announced that he was a prize of supreme importance.
            "I am Malraux," he boomed, "field chieftain of the Army of
            Resistance. Take me to your superiors." The article goes
            on to describe how he was taken to Toulouse, and then
            sent to Paris under heavy guard. "The party arrived just
            as the allies were taking over the city, and the reception
            committee at the station was made up of Americans and
            Free French."

Page 342   "So here is Chamson . . . literature." Robert Aron, *His-
            toire de la Libération de la France,* II, p.87.

Page 342   While the Strasbourg battalion. . . . Father Bockel's remi-
            niscences of Malraux at the front are given in *Alsace
            Française,* October 1948, pp.26–7.

Page 347   Some days later. . . . The story about the letter of con-
            dolence is told by Jules-Albert Jaeger in *Alsace Française,*
            October 1948, p.5.

Page 348   "These villages and hamlets . . . calamity." Idem, p.3.

Page 349   "GENERAL ORDER NO. 25 . . . DE VERNEJOUL." Idem, p.31.

Page 352   "We must not forget . . . debt." M.D.R. Foot, *SOE in
            France,* pp.412–3.

Page 361   "The strength of his feelings . . . you." Janet Flanner, *Men
            and Monuments,* p.49–50.

Page 362   "The problem facing us today . . . statues." "Man and
            Artistic Culture" in *Reflections on Our Age,* pp.84–98.

Page 366   "Malraux is a medium . . . agony." Roger Garaudy, *Litera-
            ture of the Graveyard,* p.46.

Page 367   "All those acts of sabotage . . . destiny." François Mauriac,
            Mémoires Politiques, p.260.

Page 368   "There are countries . . . today." Malraux, *Romans,* p.178.

Page 375   On the walls of the Quinta del Sordo. . . . Among the apocryphal legends concerning Malraux is one recorded by Edmund Wilson in *The Bit Between My Teeth*. Mr. Wilson writes that he was told by Malraux that after being captured in Madrid, he was imprisoned in the Quinta del Sordo. "He was much struck, in this situation, by the nightmarish and savage murals that Goya had painted there." In fact, Malraux was never captured or imprisoned during the Spanish Civil War, and the murals in the Quinta del Sordo were transferred to canvas by Baron d'Erlanger in 1873 and sold to the Prado Museum.

Page 375   "Goya was the first great stage manager . . . crossroads." Malraux, *Dessins de Goya*, p. XIX.

Page 377   "They are gay, amusing . . . people." Malraux, *Saturn*, p.28.

Page 377   "You know very well . . . life." Idem, p.128.

Page 377   "Underlying a Poussin nude . . . rape." Idem, p.66.

Page 378   "His patches of dark color . . . supernatural." Idem, p.63.

Page 379   "Another artist of genius . . . slave." Idem, p.90–1.

Page 381   "Goya also was a prophet . . . what." Idem, p.63.

Page 381   "Goya was not a prophet . . . painter." Idem, p.158.

Page 387   "Christianity was dominated . . . movement." Malraux, *La Création Artistique*, p.41.

Page 387   "The cathedrals came into being . . . dreams." Idem, p.77.

Page 398   "It is clearly apparent . . . existence." Janet Flanner, *Paris Journal*, p.378.

Page 398   "For the first time . . . Française." Joseph Barry, *The People of Paris*, p.110.

Page 404   "Never before has a modern country . . . hair." Typescript from Ministry of Cultural Affairs.

Page 411   "This was the time when . . . tortures." Typescript from Ministry of Cultural Affairs.

Page 420   "I observe that . . . Puritans." Malraux, *Antimémoires*, p.515–6.

Page 430   "Because, having lived . . . music." Idem, p.10–11.

Page 433   "Because Thou lovest . . . dance." Ananda Coomaraswamy, *The Dance of Shiva*, p.73.

Page 434   "but not always . . . lies." Malraux, *Antimémoires*, p.449.

Page 434   "It will be difficult . . . dreams." Idem, p.441.

Page 435   "I call this book . . . resurrected." Idem, p.20.

Chronology

1901	November 3	Birth of Georges-André Malraux in Paris
1909	November 19	Death of Alphonse-Émile Malraux in Dunkerque
1915	Autumn	André Malraux enters École Turgot, which he leaves in the summer of 1917
1919		Malraux meets Mauriac and Doyon, and works on *Lunes en Papier*
1920		Malraux meets Galanis and Max Jacob
1921	April	*Lunes en Papier* published in a limited edition of a hundred copies
	June	Malraux meets Clara Goldschmidt, and later accompanies her to Florence and Venice
	October 28	Malraux marries Clara Goldschmidt in Paris
1922	Spring	Malraux publishes an article on André Gide in the magazine *Action*
	November 18	Death of Marcel Proust
1923	October 12	Malraux and his wife leave Marseilles for Indochina
	December 24	Malraux, Clara and Chevasson ordered to remain at Pnom Penh to await trial
1924	July 16–17	Malraux and Chevasson on trial. Malraux sentenced to three years' imprisonment, Chevasson to eighteen months'
	August 7	Clara Malraux, having been released in July by the authorities, reaches Marseilles
	August 9	Doyon publishes appeal on behalf of Malraux in *L'Éclair*
	September 6	*Les Nouvelles Littéraires* publishes an appeal on behalf of Malraux, signed by twenty-three well-known writers

1924	October 28	After new trial at Saigon, Malraux is given a suspended sentence of one year's imprisonment, Chevasson is given a suspended sentence of eight months' imprisonment
	November 1	Malraux and Chevasson sail for France
1925	January	Malraux and Clara return to Indochina
	June 17	Malraux and Monin published the first issue of *Indochine*
	August 14	*Indochine* suspends publication as a result of interference by the colonial government
	End of August	Malraux and Clara travel to Hongkong in search of type
	November 4	*Indochine Enchaînée* published for the first time
	December 26	Malraux writes his last editorial for *Indochine Enchaînée,* which survives for a few more issues
1926	January	Malraux returns to France
	July	*La Tentation de l'Occident* published
1928	March–July	*Les Conquérants* appears in the *Nouvelle Revue Française,* and is published in September
	Summer	Malraux and Clara visit Persia
	November	*Royaume Farfelu* published in a limited edition
1929	June 8	Malraux speaks at a public debate on *Les Conquérants* in Paris
	Summer	Malraux and Clara travel through Soviet Union to Persia
1930	Summer	Malraux and Clara again visit Afghanistan and Persia
	August 15– October 1	*La Voie Royale* appears in *La Revue de Paris*
	October	*La Voie Royale* published
	December 20	Fernand-Georges Malraux commits suicide
1931	Summer	Malraux and Clara make their last visit to Afghanistan and Persia, travel across India and China, and return to France via the United States
1932		Malraux writes *La Condition Humaine*

1933	March 28	Birth of Florence Malraux
	June	*La Condition Humaine,* which had appeared in the *Nouvelle Revue Française* between January and June, is published
1934	January	With André Gide goes to Berlin to appeal for the life of Dimitroff
	February	With Corniglion-Molinier begins flight from Paris to French Somaliland and the quest for the lost city of Sheba
	March 10	*L'Intransigeant* announces discovery of the lost city of Sheba
	May 3–13	*L'Intransigeant* publishes articles by Malraux and Corniglion-Molinier about their discoveries in Arabia
	August	Malraux attends Congress of Soviet writers in Moscow
1935	April	Malraux organizes the International Congress in Defence of Culture, to which Pasternak and Babel are invited. In the same year he publishes *Le Temps de Mépris*
1936	July 17	Spanish Civil War begins
	July 22	Malraux flies with Clara to Spain
1936	August–December	Malraux commands the Escadre España, takes part in 65 missions against the enemy and is twice wounded
	December 27	Last flight of the Escadre España
1937	February 24	Malraux arrives in New York on a speaking tour
	December	*L'Espoir* is published
1938	June	Begins shooting film called *Sierra de Teruel* in Barcelona
1939	January	Malraux leaves Spain and continues to work on film in south-western France
	August 23	Nazi-Soviet Pact
	September	Malraux mobilized in the French Army
1940	June 14	Malraux wounded and made prisoner four days later on the Yonne, and interned in camp at Sens
	November 3	Malraux escapes from camp and makes his way to Roquebrune near Monte Carlo

1941		Works on *Les Noyers d'Altenburg*. In the late summer receives visit from Jean-Paul Sartre.
1943	January 9	The novel begins to be serialized in *La Semaine Littéraire* in Geneva
	Autumn	Malraux commands maquis forces in the Corrèze under the name of Colonel Berger
1944	March	Malraux's half-brothers Roland and Claude arrested by the Gestapo
	June 10	Massacre at Oradour
	July 23	Malraux wounded and captured by Germans at Gramat
1944	August 20	Uprising in Toulouse. Malraux takes command of the St. Michel Prison
	August 25	Paris liberated
	September 27	First engagement of the Brigade Alsace-Lorraine under command of Malraux
	November 23	Strasbourg liberated by General Leclerc's Second Division
	November 24–28	Malraux commands French forces at battle of Dannemarie
	December 2	French radio announces accidental death of Madame Malraux (Josette Clotis)
	December 25	Malraux meets General Leclerc at Erstein
1945	January 26	Malraux speaks at Congress of M.L.N. in Paris
	July 20	Death of Paul Valéry
	Summer	Meets General de Gaulle for the first time, and becomes an adviser to the general
	November	Becomes Minister of Information in De Gaulle's government
1946	January 20	De Gaulle's government falls and Malraux retires to private life to work on his books. In this year he publishes *Esquisse d'une Psychologie du Cinéma* and *Scènes Choisies*, a selection of extracts from his novels, and revises *La Condition Humaine*
	November 6	At first UNESCO Conference at the Sorbonne Malraux delivers speech asking "whether or not, on this old continent of Europe, Man is dead?"

1947	April 7	*Rassemblement du Peuple Français,* the Gaullist political party, is founded in Strasbourg. *Le Musée Imaginaire,* the first of the three volumes comprising *La Psychologie de l'Art,* appears this year
1948	February 17	Malraux speaks at the Vélodrome d'Hiver, prophesying a Communist uprising
	March 5	In a speech at the Salle Pleyel he bitterly attacks the Soviet Union and calls for determined opposition to Stalin's attempt to dominate Europe
	March 13	After his divorce from Clara, he marries Marie-Madeleine Lioux, the widow of his half-brother Roland. *La Création Artistique,* the second volume of *La Psychologie de l'Art,* appears this year
1949		*Saturne,* a study of Goya, and *La Monnaie de l'Absolu,* appear this year. With this last book *La Psychologie de l'Art* is completed
1950	Spring	Malraux falls seriously ill
1951	February	Death of André Gide. Malraux revises the three volumes of *La Psychologie de l'Art,* which appears under the title *Les Voix de Silence* this year
1952		Malraux travels through Greece, Egypt, Persia and the Middle East
1953	January	Malraux visits New York
1954	May 7	Fall of Dienbienfu
1955		Malraux works on *La Métamorphose des Dieux,* a continuation and elaboration of his theories of art. *Le Musée Imaginaire de la Sculpture Mondiale* in three volumes of photographs with brief texts is completed this year. In this year he visits Egypt
1957	December	*La Métamorphose des Dieux* is published
1958	April 17	Signs protest against the banning of Alleg's *The Question,* an account of the torture Alleg suffered in Algeria from the French Army
	May	Malraux is lecturing in Venice when he is recalled to France by De Gaulle

	June 4–	Becomes briefly Minister of Information
	July 7	
	August 24	Malraux speaks in the Place de Rennes in honor of the Resistance heroes
1959	January 8	Becomes Minister of State charged with Cultural Affairs in the Debré cabinet
	May 28	Visits Athens
1960	January 4	Death of Albert Camus
1961	May 23	Death of his sons, Pierre-Gauthier and Vincent, in an automobile accident
1962	February 6	A plastic bomb explodes in his house, and a four-year-old girl Delphine Renard loses the sight of an eye
1963	January 9	Malraux officially loans the *Mona Lisa* to President Kennedy and attends reception at the National Gallery in Washington
	September 3	Delivers funeral speech beside the catafalque of Georges Braque
1964	August 4	*Venus de Milo* leaves Paris at Malraux's orders for exhibition in Japan
	September 23	Unveiling of Chagall painting on ceiling of the Paris Opera
	December 19	Malraux pays homage to Jean Moulin at the Pantheon
1965	Spring	Malraux falls ill, and in late June sets out on a long sea voyage to the Far East
	July 19	He enters Red China
	August 3	He meets Mao Tse-tung in Peking after visiting Yenan, and returns to France over the North Pole
1966		Works on *Antimémoires*
1967	September	Publication of *Antimémoires*
1968	May 3–30	Student and worker rebellion
1969		Malraux resigns from office with the fall of the De Gaulle government and works on a revised edition of *Les Voix de Silence*

❧ *Acknowledgements* ❧

I owe a great debt of gratitude to three students of Malraux's life and ideas. They are W. M. Frohock, whose *André Malraux and the Tragic Imagination* first led me to believe that it might be possible to draw a full length portrait of Malraux; Walter G. Langlois, whose *André Malraux: The Indochina Adventure* successfully disentangled for the first time the vast complexities of Malraux's activities in Indochina; and André Vandegans, whose *La Jeunesse Littéraire d'André Malraux* was the first serious and comprehensive study of the early writings, though I often differed from his conclusions.

I owe more than I can say to Marcel Brandin, the *chef de cabinet* in Malraux's ministry, who read the manuscript and commented upon it at length with remarkable kindness and patience. Professor Langlois, the *doyen* of Malraux students in the United States, also read the manuscript and gave me the benefit of his wide-ranging knowledge and permitted me to reproduce an original manuscript page of *Les Conquérants* from his private collection, and the flaming dragon drawn by Malraux, which appears in the *Malraux Miscellany* edited by him.

I owe very little to the Bibliothèque Nationale and the Fonds Doucet attached to the Bibliothèque Ste. Geneviève. They were traps baited with good meat, but the trap was usually sprung before I could taste the meat. To outwit the functionaries who rule over these libraries it became necessary to employ quite disproportionate amounts of mental energy. It is to be hoped that these functionaries will shortly be pensioned off.

While the French libraries were uniformly unhelpful, I received only kindness from the French people who had known Malraux, enjoyed talking about him, and endlessly theorized about his writings and his legend. Among those who were especially helpful were Paulette Thouvenin and Louis Chevasson, who knew Malraux in his teens, and Marcel Brandin, who was a fellow student at the École Turgot. Jean Alley, Albert Beuret, Jessie

Bouteille, Ernst van Leyden, Haakon Chevalier and Manes Sperber were helpful and informative. Mary Merson of the *Cinematheque Française* showed me that French institutions could be warm and enchanting places, and with her help it was possible to assemble the stills from the film *Espoir*, to see the film several times and to rejoice in the riches of that great collection of films. Henri Morisset and Paul Theveau kindly tracked down for me Malraux's school records. Dr. Bernard Metz lent me one of the few surviving copies of *L'Alsace Française*, October 1948, which is a prime source of the activities of the Brigade Alsace-Lorraine, and wrote to me at length about its complicated beginnings. Captain George Hiller and Miss Vera Atkins, both formerly of the S.O.E., helped me to understand the British connection with the French Resistance.

I owe a special debt to Clara Malraux, who on three occasions talked to me about Malraux with charm and clarity, and the three volumes of her memoirs were indispensable to an understanding of the period. Although it is often said that her memoirs exhibit a personal bias against her former husband, I could find little evidence of it. She wrote about him warmly and sympathetically with only the faintest trace of irony.

When the work was nearly completed, I had the good fortune to meet Florence Malraux in New York. She spoke about her father with penetrating insight, and she alone seemed to understand him in all his complexity. Like Jean Alley, she was one of the very few who saw him without benefit of any disguises.

My greatest debt was to André Malraux, whom I first met in Barcelona in 1938. He answered all questions generously and often went to great pains to secure some needed information. The photographs from his collection, which appear in this book, were found after a prolonged search, and are now published for the first time. I am indebted to him for permission to quote so extensively from his writings, but this was perhaps the least of his gifts, while the greatest was the gift of a copy of *Le Temps Vert* by Josette Clotis, which I had sought for vainly for a long time. In many different ways, sometimes silently, he offered his help, always with an uncommon and memorable courtesy.

Index

5b·11
85·11
OW